QUEEN OF THE SKIES

QUEEN OF THE SKIES
THE LOCKHEED CONSTELLATION

Claude G. Luisada

www.ivyhousebooks.com

PUBLISHED BY IVY HOUSE PUBLISHING GROUP
5122 Bur Oak Circle, Raleigh, NC 27612
United States of America
919-782-0281
www.ivyhousebooks.com

ISBN: 1-57197-417-2
Library of Congress Control Number: 2004101679

© 2005 Claude G. Luisada

All rights reserved, which includes the right to
reproduce this book or portions thereof in any form whatsoever
except as provided by the U.S. Copyright Law.

Printed in the United States of America

This book is dedicated to my father, Aldo A. Luisada, M.D., 1900–1987, physician, cardiologist, physiologist, teacher, researcher, author of 14 textbooks on the heart and 200 research papers, and a true idealist, who by his example unknowingly spurred me on to write this book.

My sincere and heartfelt thanks go to Steve Kimmell, industrial designer, artist, aviation enthusiast, and longtime loyal friend, who always believed I had it in me to write this book, and who was the artistic consultant for this project. Thanks also to Ted Spitzmiller, a co-worker in the Civil Air Patrol, who, after reading the manuscript, cajoled and pushed me to have this book published by his enthusiasm and support.

CONTENTS

Author's Note		ix
Prologue		xi
Introduction	*Modern Legend of the Skyways*	xv
Chapter 1	Whence It All Began	1
Chapter 2	The Birth of an Idea	13
Chapter 3	The First One	21
Chapter 4	World War II and the Constellation Enlists	45
Chapter 5	The Constellation Spreads Its Wings	61
Chapter 6	Horsepower, Give Me More Horsepower!	81
Chapter 7	The Constellation Stretch	95
Chapter 8	A New Member of the Family: The Warning Star	115
Chapter 9	The Constellation in Various Military Versions	153
Chapter 10	The Super G Constellation	167
Chapter 11	Byword of the Airlines	193
Chapter 12	The Last and Greatest: The L–1649A	223
Chapter 13	TWA and the Constellation	265
Chapter 14	Fading Glory	297
Chapter 15	Accidents, Incidents, and the Legend Grows	307
Chapter 16	Second String Star-SEA	321
Chapter 17	So Connies Don't Fly Anymore, Huh?	341
Epilogue	*How Did She Really Stack Up?*	367
Appendices		379
Bibliography		387
Acknowledgments		389
Index		391

AUTHOR'S NOTE

This book was written with certain reasons and goals in mind. I felt that the entire history of the Lockheed Constellation merited recounting as an integral and significant portion of the aerospace scene during the middle decades of the twentieth century. Many portions of the Constellation history have either never been told at all or never as a part of a single narrative. Thus, this book attempts to relate the total story in such a way that continuity is maintained throughout.

The many events that make up this piece of history happened because of various background circumstances. Throughout this book, this very context has been woven in so that readers may better understand why certain things came to pass. It was also felt that some of these circumstances would, in and of themselves, make interesting reading.

Last, I have attempted to verify the following thesis: That the Lockheed Constellation series of aircraft had a greater influence on the development of aviation in general, and commercial aviation in particular, than is generally recognized, and in fact more than other comparable aircraft built in larger numbers.

PROLOGUE

"Your attention please. This is the last call for Trans World Airlines, Flight 770, Polar Route service direct to London. Will any passengers holding tickets for Flight 770 please report to Gate G-7 immediately. This is the last call for Trans World Flight 770!"

It is August 1958, and the morning sun shines hot but smoggy on the busy ramp area at Los Angeles International Airport. At Gate G-7, the ramp agent seals the doorway. It's 10 A.M., and outside waiting patiently sits a TWA Lockheed L–1649A Jetstream Constellation. N7318C will shortly depart Los Angeles for London on a flight that only a few years before would have been considered impossible.

The trim plane sits high on its somewhat ungainly landing gear, the white fuselage paint glinting in the sun. The wing sweeps out, 150 feet of it, appearing almost oversized.

The boarding stairs have been removed and the passenger doors closed and sealed. It is engine start time, and a coveralled ramp attendant wheels a fire extinguisher over, ready to stand fire guard. He talks to the crew, visible in the cockpit, on his intercom, which, like an umbilical cord, can be seen extending down from the nose wheel well. Hands can be seen moving in the cockpit as switches are flicked. Number three propeller, on the inboard left engine, turns over slowly, the whine of the starter clearly audible.

The big Curtiss-Wright 3350 Turbo-Compound engine growls as combustion begins. A great gob of white smoke belches from the exhausts. The propeller begins to turn faster, then disappears into a shining blur, as number three catches. Unlike older aircraft engines, the Turbo-Compounds start slower and more gradually, almost like a turbo-prop. In short order, numbers four, two, and one are started, in that sequence, and now all four propellers are turning. The engines rumble quietly, yet with an undertone of power waiting to be unleashed.

Los Angeles Ground Control gives taxi clearance, and with a salute from the ramp attendant, TWA Flight 770 leaves the ramp. The 3350s make little noise, because not much power is needed to maintain safe taxiing speed. The plane rolls toward its assigned runway, bobbing on its struts, nose nodding up and down.

Holding short of the active runway, the crew methodically goes through the Before Take-Off Checklist. Engine noise increases substantially as the throttles are moved forward and propeller speed goes up to 1400 rpm for magneto and propeller control checks. The plane jerks against its landing gear, appearing eager to go.

All checks are completed, and Air Traffic Control's clearance has been received, copied, and read back for confirmation. Today, the flight will be routed via Salt Lake City; Billings, Montana; over the northern part of Lake Winnipeg in Manitoba; and then over the center of Hudson Bay to a tiny settlement some distance east of the bay. Here, at a field known as Frobisher Bay, lies a lonely and desolate airport used for refueling by many of the polar flights.

TWA 770 is notified that it is number one for take-off. Slowly, the big aircraft taxis into position at the head of the runway, take-off permission already given and acknowledged. Runway 27 right, 10,500 feet of white concrete, stretches before it, reflecting the sun. In the cockpit the first officer smoothly moves the throttles forward, and the plane starts to roll.

The noise from the four Turbo-Compounds grows louder and within a very few seconds reaches its peak. The bellow of the engines is unmistakable; a shout of power and authority.

TWA 770 accelerates slowly, the propellers tugging mightily at all 156,000 pounds, for today the aircraft is loaded to its full legal limit. Gradually, speed builds up, and inside the long, graceful fuselage the passengers can feel the aircraft jolting sideways against the landing gear.

Eighty knots comes and goes, and the captain has rudder control. On and on she rolls, roaring and accelerating. It will take over 135 knots and more than 7,000 feet of runway before the long, thin wing can sustain the entire weight of the aircraft and lift it into the air. Finally the first officer calls "V1" and then almost immediately afterward, "V2." The nose lifts and the Connie leaves the ground and climbs out at a flat angle.

A few seconds pass and then the gear starts to retract, and as the aircraft climbs out over the Pacific Ocean, the flaps slide slowly into the wings. A gradual right turn brings the Connie to a northeasterly heading. Ahead are some 2,500 miles to one of the loneliest airfields anywhere in the world—Frobisher Bay, Canada.

The noise fades, and TWA 770 grows smaller in the distance, that long wing somehow dominating the view of the entire aircraft. We have just witnessed the departure of an aircraft that is generally conceded to reflect the peak of reciprocating-engine airplanes. A new and different breed of aircraft is about to take to the skies and in short order overshadow all large propeller aircraft. But for the moment, the Connie L–1649A is queen of them all, the last example of a family of aircraft that first flew some fifteen years previously. A series of aircraft that through numerous design changes and improvements set the pace in commercial aircraft the world over. The famous queen of the skies, the Constellation.

O-1 A TWA L–1649A "Jetstream" Super Constellation, 1957. (Lockheed Martin)

O-2 An L–49/C–69 prototype Constellation during a test flight, July 1945. (Lockheed Martin)

Introduction

MODERN LEGEND OF THE SKYWAYS

To some, she was just an airplane. To others she was a huge, strange shape reminiscent in part of a fish and in part of a bird. But then that was entirely logical because she functioned in a kind of ocean—an ocean of fluid called air. An ocean we call the atmosphere.

She roamed the skies of this planet like some prehistoric monster, hurdling continents and oceans alike with equal disdain for their size. Mountains became hills, and her graceful wings shrugged off many storms. The roar of her powerful engines was heard over huge cities and desolate wastelands, and the shadow of her landing was cast over all parts of the planet. Children marveled at her, and men and women swore by her, and for over thirty years she operated in the Earth's skies with great distinction.

To her mother, the Lockheed Aircraft Corporation, she was known as the Model L–049 or any of the successive model numbers. To her father, Howard Hughes of Transcontinental Western Airlines (TWA), she was known as the Lockheed Constellation. To the U.S. Army Air Corps, the original user, she was the C–69. But to an untold number of pilots, crew members, maintenance personnel, as well as millions of passengers and aviation enthusiasts, she was known simply, affectionately, and with great respect as the Connie.

As with ships, aircraft are referred to as "she," and the Connie was all lady. In the over three decades of active life, the Connie established for herself a secure place in the lineup of all-time famous commercial aircraft, along with such as the

Ford Trimotor, the DC–3/C–47, the DC–6, the Vickers Viscount, the De Havilland Comet, and the Boeing 707 and 727.

The total number of Constellations produced was less than other well-known commercial aircraft, but for a number of reasons the Connie attracted more notice and is better remembered. It may have been because of her distinguishing shape, her long life, her honest flying characteristics, her passenger comfort and appeal, her low operating cost, or a combination of any or all of these. But whatever the reasons, the Connie has a history well worth examining.

On her maiden flight, she immediately attracted attention because of her virtually trouble-free operation. Sixteen months later, she was in the news again when she set a coast-to-coast speed record. Two years after that, she pioneered postwar transatlantic scheduled passenger service. During the same year, she also inaugurated nonstop coast-to-coast trans-America service for the first time.

Beginning in the late 1940s, Constellations began to be used on some very long-distance routes. For airlines to operate such routes, an aircraft was required that had long range on the one hand, and the reliability to fly a total of many hours with little or no maintenance during stopovers on the other. The Connies performed this function, and regular service on previously nonexistent routes now became a routine matter.

In the 1950s, an increase in the fuselage length of the Connies, coupled with more powerful engines, resulted in the famed Super Constellations. Able to carry more passengers over longer distances at higher speeds, the Super Constellations were responsible for dramatic changes on many long routes. Passengers were carried with considerably more comfort, and total flight times were reduced appreciably by abolishing previously necessary fuel stops.

Other sectors of aviation were also attracted to the Connie. The military used her as a personnel carrier, cargo mover, radar picket aircraft, and finally as a luxury aircraft for the president and other high government officials.

Cargo airlines took a leaf from the military and ordered the more advanced versions of the Super Connie as all-cargo aircraft. At that time, the air freight business was still in its relative infancy, and the introduction of the Super Connies did much to stimulate the growth of this field.

So it went, from year to year, throughout her career, Connie always seemed to operate in such a manner as to attract attention. Even when accidents or incidents occurred, there was something different about them, and a number of these accidents had wide-ranging results from which all of aviation benefited.

However, the Connie family of aircraft was more than famous or even highly visible in the news media. Connies in general were highly regarded by the people who bought them, flew them, and rode in them.

The airlines that purchased Connies found that seat-mile costs were generally as low or lower than comparable aircraft. Their reliability was good. The Connie was an excellent marketing tool for attracting passengers. Furthermore, the constant changes and improvements that flowed from Lockheed provided the air carriers with an opportunity to upgrade service periodically.

The military establishment was also a satisfied customer, even though the total number of aircraft procured was relatively small. The RC–121 early warning radar picket fleet, in particular, was an example of the taxpayers' money being well spent. First delivered in 1954, these aircraft were still operating in 1978, 24 years later!

Pilots and flight crews were strong supporters of the Connie. The aircraft was considered easy to fly for its size and especially docile during landings. The Connie also had the virtue of being able to fly through storms and turbulence with a minimum of excess motion. The cockpits were considered generally comfortable by the crews, with some versions of the Super Connies having crew rest compartments added for use on long nonstop flights.

Passengers were attracted by the Connie's reputation. Her highly distinctive shape and general appearance no doubt helped bring them aboard. But such items as the cabin comfort and low noise level contributed to the result of having many passengers ask for Connies for their air travel. There was also a generally intuitive awareness on the public's part that Connies had accumulated an enviable safety record over the years.

The Connie was an integral part of the growth and expansion of commercial aviation from 1946 until the advent of passenger jet liners in 1959. This 13-year period stands as a distinct phase of commercial aviation development, during which a quantum leap was made in terms of routes flown and passengers carried.

During this momentous period, the Connie exerted influence in a variety of significant ways. Constellations were involved in aerodynamic advances, power plant improvements, route pioneering and expansion, marketing innovations, maintenance standardization, operational and training developments, and even some noteworthy military applications.

In terms of the total number of Constellations built, the DC–6/DC–7 fleet was considerably larger. But it is this author's contention that the Connie exerted an influence on the field of aviation that was out of all proportion to the quantity built. This book will describe some of the changes and developments brought about by the Connie during her active life.

Thus, the story of the Constellations is not only an interesting subject for study but also an important one. It reflects much more than the events that related directly to the life of the Constellation. The story of the Connies must be looked at within the framework of aviation as a whole during that period and, furthermore, in the context of what was happening politically, economically, and socially during the roughly 20-year period when they were in widespread use.

Thus, this story is not merely for aviation enthusiasts, but also for those who wish to seriously study the history of aviation development in the two decades following World War II.

Chapter 1

WHENCE IT ALL BEGAN

Aircraft are the end result of a total design and production effort of aircraft manufacturers. The basic design of an airplane can generally be traced back to one individual or a handful at most. But almost every new aircraft embodies a general design philosophy that reflects the history of the manufacturer. Thus, the history and accomplishments of the Lockheed Aircraft Corporation had a direct bearing on the aircraft design that later came to be known as the Constellation.

The infancy of Lockheed dates back to the period 1910–1913, just prior to World War I. In early 1910 two brothers, Allan and Malcolm Loughead, decided they wanted to try their hand at building an airplane. The Lougheads lived in southern California, and their enthusism had been greatly increased by the efforts of two other California aviation pioneers, Glenn Curtiss and Glen Martin.

The two brothers managed to scrape up enough money, both their own and borrowed, to start building an aircraft of their own design in a garage. For three years they worked part-time on the project, which they called the Model G. Finally, in June 1913, they put the aircraft, a seaplane, into the water, and without any further ado they took off. The aircraft was a tremendous success as compared to other designs of the time!

For two years the Lougheads put aviation aside as they went prospecting for gold. But in 1915, they were back at it. First they made a name for themselves by using the Model G to fly passengers for sightseeing trips. Shortly thereafter, they decided that they wanted to build a much bigger seaplane, this one designated the F–1.

The Model G aircraft was bringing in some money by flying an aerial charter service. This income gave the brothers the impetus to go ahead with their new project. To build the F–1, which, as we shall see, was an extremely ambitious undertaking, they decided to form a corporation to manufacture aircraft. It was called originally the Loughead Aircraft Manufacturing Company. However, because the proper pronunciation of the name Loughead was Lockheed, the brothers quickly and legally changed the spelling of their last name.

The fledgling company was organized in the summer of 1916, and its first home was in the back of a garage. The Lockheed brothers' F–1 project was truly gigantic for that time. The initial design was of a seaplane with a wingspread of 74 feet, a gross weight of 7,300 pounds, powered by two 160-hp engines. Luckily for the new company and its directors, a young mechanic by the name of Jack Northrop became their associate. Largely self-taught, he brought to the company certain technical skills that the Lockheeds badly needed. So the F–1 took shape and in May 1918 flew for the first time. The plane flew very well and attracted a great deal of attention. It's interesting to note that the aircraft had triple rudders, which gave it a great deal of stability, a feature that twenty-five years later would be incorporated in the Constellation. Its young designer, Northrop, went on to great fame both with Douglas and later in his own company.

The F–1 managed to fly payloads of up to 12 passengers, which gained it a great deal of attention. The U.S. Navy became interested and tested the F–1 extensively, but unfortunately they never purchased it. The Lockheeds then decided to convert the F–1 from a seaplane configuration to a land plane. Known as the F1–A, it was badly damaged shortly after its redesign during an attempt to fly coast to coast.

Lockheed then landed a U.S. Navy contract for a scout seaplane. Fifty of these aircraft were to be built, but the armistice of 1918 put an untimely end to this project also.

Lockheed's next project was a peacetime sports plane known as the S–1. In the manufacture of the S–1, the Lockheed brothers employed a process of molding plywood that allowed them to form highly streamlined shapes. Although the single prototype was highly successful in its performance, the aircraft never sold, in part because of the war-surplus Curtiss JN–4 Jennies that flooded the general aviation market after World War I.

This final sales failure put an end to operations at the original Lockheed Aircraft Manufacturing Company, which closed its doors in 1921, ending the first chapter in the history of Lockheed. The two brothers went their separate ways after that, but Allan Lockheed retained his ambition of building better airplanes.

In December 1926, Allan and a businessman from Burbank, California, by the name of Fred S. Keeler formed the Lockheed Aircraft Company. Their first move was to rehire their former employee, Jack Northrop, who in the interim had been working for Douglas Aircraft as chief engineer. Working out of a factory in Hollywood, Lockheed and Northrop designed a high-wing monoplane that later came to be known as the Lockheed Vega.

The Vega is probably the aircraft that first made people generally conscious of the Lockheed name. This is true for two reasons. First, a total of 129 Vegas were built, which was a large quantity for a non-military aircraft in the late 1920s. Second, the Vega rapidly became famous when it was used repeatedly on flights that set records and thus made headlines.

The Vega was a sleek, high-wing, single-engine aircraft with an enclosed cockpit in the nose and a passenger compartment with eight windows just behind and below. It was powered by a Wright 225-hp radial engine, one of the first such applications. The wing was of single-span design, an innovation for those days, and the aircraft could carry an 1,800-pound payload at speeds over 145 mph. The Vegas were being constantly improved throughout their production run, resulting in better performances. The Vega was flown by innumerable famous pilots of that time, including Wiley Post, Ruth Nichols, Roscoe Turner, Amelia Earhart, and others, and altogether set 34 world records. Among these records are the following (courtesy of Lockheed):

- Time aloft: 36 hours, 56 minutes.
- 100-km closed course speed record: 174.897 mph.
- Altitude record (women): 28,743 feet.
- First women's nonstop transatlantic flight.
- Newfoundland-to-Ireland: 15 hours, 48 minutes
- First flight over North Pole.
- First flight over Antarctica.
- Fastest transatlantic crossing: Newfoundland to Berlin in 18 hours, 41 minutes.
- Around the world solo: 7 days, 18 hours, 49 minutes.

The Vega design in turn led rather quickly to a variation called the Air Express. Although this aircraft had the same basic fuselage, the wing was slightly raised above it and held in place by struts. The tail had a different shape, and the cockpit, now open, was moved back. More important, the big radial engine was now enclosed within a streamlined cowling developed by the National Advisory Committee of Aeronautics (NACA). This reduced the front drag substantially, and thus increased speed.

In July 1929, Lockheed was acquired by a group of other companies but retained its name and identity. Over the next three years, Lockheed continued to manufacture the Vega and the Air Express, although the entire company operated at a greatly reduced rate after the market crash of 1929.

During this time Lockheed introduced three more single-engine designs. Called the Sirius, Altair, and Orion, all had in common the basic Vega fuselage. But they differed in that they were low-wing monoplanes. The Orion also had another innovation: retractable landing gear. These three types of aircraft were, much like the Vega, used for a number of precedent-setting flights. Among the pilots who flew them were Charles Lindbergh and Jimmy Doolittle. Also of interest is the fact that Vegas, Air Expresses, and Orions were sold in small quantities to various commercial airlines, both domestic and foreign.

The Great Depression of the early 1930s finally caught up with Lockheed, and by April 1931 the company had to declare bankruptcy. Not only were there no orders for the company, but policies forced on Lockheed in the preceding years had reduced advance design work to nothing. Thus, Lockheed was still trying to sell aircraft that were only improvements on a 1927 design, the Vega. So the second chapter of Lockheed's corporate history came to an end. Little did anyone realize at that time that a far better future was near at hand.

With Lockheed in receivership and almost completely shut down, a value of a little over $40,000 was placed on the company by the courts. This happened in mid-1932, and in July of that year, a man by the name of Bob Gross purchased Lockheed for that amount.

Gross was a businessman who was already involved in the aviation business. He was a part-owner of the Stearman Airplane Company, helped form the Viking Flying Boat Company, and was also a part of the Varney Speed Lanes, a small airline he helped form together with Walter T. Varney. Gross, Varney, and Lloyd Stearman raised the money to purchase Lockheed.

Shortly after Gross reorganized Lockheed, he and the other corporate officers came to the conclusion that what the company needed to continue and flourish was a new aircraft design. This was precisely what was missing and was the point ignored by the previous stockholders who had controlled Lockheed.

As a first step, Gross hired a young aeronautical engineer, Hall Hibbard. A graduate of Massachusetts Institute of Technology, Hibbard teamed up with

Stearman in developing some new ideas. They came up with two versions of a new passenger transport: one single-engine, the other a twin-engine design.

After considerable discussion, Lockheed decided to go ahead with the twin-engine design. It was felt that a twin-engine configuration would not only allow for a larger payload but would also give passengers more confidence in the aircraft's safety. The new transport was known as the L–10 Electra. At the time the design was conceived, Boeing had already started work on their Model 247 twin-engine transport. Douglas, with their DC–1, was only a few months behind. Actually, the Boeing 247 first flew a full year before the L–10, and the DC–1, built at a very fast pace, first flew six months before the L–10.

The L–10, as initially designed and built, was an all-metal, twin-engine, low-wing monoplane. At a maximum gross take-off weight of 9,000 pounds, it carried eight passengers in single rows of four and a crew of two in the rounded cross-section fuselage. The wing was of single-span cantilever construction. The L–10, like its competitors, had stressed-skin construction using 24S light alloy metal. The aircraft also featured split flaps, variable pitch propellers, and a retractable landing gear. Its two Pratt and Whitney 450-hp engines gave it a cruising speed of 180 mph at only 50 percent power, and a top speed of over 200 mph. The big flaps allowed it to land at 65 to 70 mph, thus ensuring that the L–10 could safely operate from small airfields. Cost of the aircraft in 1934 was $50,000.

During the design phase, a scale model of the L–10 was built and sent to the University of Michigan for wind tunnel tests. A young aeronautical engineer informed Lockheed that their single rudder, as originally designed, did not provide for sufficient longitudinal control, especially if one engine was shut down.

The engineer's name was Clarence "Kelly" Johnson. In the next more than 40 years, he became Lockheed's guiding light in aircraft design and probably the foremost aircraft designer in this country during that period. He and Hall Hibbard would come to see their ideas reflected in all of the forthcoming Lockheed designs through the early 1970s. Johnson came to work at Lockheed shortly after his analysis of the L–10 design and as an initial assignment designed a twin-rudder tail that gave the L–10 the needed stability.

The L–10 was first flown in February 1934, and by August 1934, was in airline service with its first two customers, Northwest Airlines and Pan American Airlines. Before manufacture of this model ended, a total of 150 had been built, finally giving Lockheed the financial stability it so badly needed.

The L–10 and the successive models developed from it gave Lockheed a solid entry into the commercial aircraft market. True, the Lockheeds were smaller than either the Douglas or Boeing entries. Nevertheless, the lower purchase and operating costs, together with higher cruising speeds, made these twin-engine airliners very attractive to many airlines whose routes did not justify and could not economically support larger planes.

Two years after the introduction of the L–10, in mid-1936, Lockheed first flew their L–12A derivative. A smaller aircraft, carrying two fewer passengers, the L–12A boasted 20 mph more speed and proved popular with corporations and businesses, as well as feeder airlines and general aviation. A few L–10s and L–12As were even sold to the U.S. Army Air Corps. A total of 114 of the L–12s were built.

It is an interesting sidelight that in 1939 three of the L–12A models were used for an intelligence mission involving aerial photography. The aircraft were modified and flown by an Australian, Sidney Cotton. At the request of both French and British intelligence services, Cotton, starting in September 1938, made a number of aerial photo flights over Italian and German installations of naval and military interest. When one views Lockheed's later involvement in aerial reconnaissance with its U–2 and SR–71 aircraft, this particular mission becomes even more interesting. However, it should be made clear that Lockheed had nothing to do with the modifications carried out on these L–12s at that time.

In 1936 Lockheed began working on a larger version of the Electra. Identified as the L–14, it was not only considerably larger but also introduced a number of innovations. In the L–14, the wing was moved upward so that now it became a midwing, rather than a low-wing aircraft, and the wingspan was increased by some 10 feet. The fuselage was made 6 feet longer, had a deeper belly, and now carried twelve passengers. Powered by two 750-hp Pratt and Whitney "Hornet" engines, the L–14 came close to equaling the Douglas DC–2 in size. In addition, it added such innovations as Fowler flaps, which permitted slower landing and take-off speeds, two-speed superchargers, full-feathering propellers, and underfloor freight holds. First flown in July 1937, the L–14 began airline service in September 1937. Eventually, 112 L–14s were built.

Over the next two years, Lockheed was also to work on two highly specialized aircraft, which influenced the future of the company in ways no one could have foreseen. The first of these two projects came to be known as the XC–35 and was a result of a U.S. Army Air Corps request. The XC–35 project was the outgrowth of a problem that had been plaguing aviation for quite some time. As humans attempted to fly at ever higher altitudes, it was discovered that the reduced amount of oxygen in the atmosphere robbed the engines of large amounts of power. In addition, the rarefied atmosphere and cold temperatures of the higher altitudes also made human survival an ever-present problem. Yet it was recognized that some very real advantages existed if flight could be achieved at 20,000 feet and higher. For one thing, at such heights, aircraft could fly over much of the weather. For another, the reduced air resistance permitted aircraft to fly faster with less power.

The problem of supplying sufficient oxygen to the engines was solved by an invention known as a turbo-supercharger. Developed by Dr. Sanford A. Moss in 1918, the turbo-supercharger made it possible for reciprocating engines to function at close to their normal power rating at altitudes of up to 40,000 feet. But long before a plane reached such an altitude, its crew and passengers would be unconscious from the thin air, and oxygen masks were only a partial answer. What was required was the ability to maintain a higher pressure inside the cabin than the pressure of the air outside.

The U.S. Army Air Corps was greatly concerned about the problem because they already foresaw future aerial combat at high altitudes. In 1936 Lockheed received a government contract for converting an L–10 Electra for experimental high-altitude flights. The result was the XC–35, which first flew in May 1937. During the tests that followed, it flew successfully at altitudes of up to 30,000 feet while the crew inside remained comfortable and safe, breathing normally without oxygen masks. Although the XC–35 was not financially that important to Lockheed, the design and manufacturing experience gained soon proved invaluable in the development of the Constellation.

It was also during this period that Lockheed became involved in preparing a Model 14 for an attempt at an around-the-world speed record. The client in this case was none other than the famous Howard Hughes. In 1938, Hughes was only 33 years old and already a famous millionaire. His wealth was inherited from his family and consisted of total ownership of the Hughes Tool Company, which made drill bits for oil well drilling. His fame arose from such things as his aeronautical and flying skills, the fact that in 1937 he purchased outright Trans Western Airlines, and his flamboyant life among Hollywood celebrities.

In his attempt at a record, Hughes was challenging the time set by Wiley Post in 1933 of 7 days, 18 hours, 50 minutes. Hughes approached Lockheed and asked them to prepare a Model 14 custom-tailored to his specifications. This they did, and on July 10, 1938, Hughes left New York with a crew of four. Flying by way of Paris, Moscow, over Siberia, Alaska, and Canada, he completed the trip of almost 15,000 miles in 3 days, 19 hours, 8 minutes, a new around-the-world record! It is interesting to note that the previous records set by Wiley Post, and this latest one, were both set in Lockheed aircraft.

The joint effort of Hughes and Lockheed in preparation for this around-the-world flight was actually only the beginning of what would turn out to be a very long association. In fact, Hughes had a tremendous influence on the entire Constellation program.

During 1938–39, Lockheed also embarked on two large-scale production runs that permanently altered the very structure of the corporation. From this time on, Lockheed became and remained a very large firm, even in times of relatively little business. These two programs both involved military aircraft, but despite that, both programs shortly had a significant effect on the soon-to-be-born Constellation program.

In June 1938, after many months of difficult and frustrating negotiations, Lockheed obtained a contract to supply to the British government a bomber version of the Model 14. Known as the Hudson medium bomber, the aircraft was an extensive modification of the standard Model 14. The fuselage was 2 feet shorter, and the engines used were upgraded to 1,100 hp each. Able to carry 2,000 pounds of bombs and armed with both a gun turret and forward firing guns, the Hudson proved to be a highly versatile weapon during the dark days of Britain's war against Hitler. Lockheed built 250 Hudsons under the initial order, and by the war's end had delivered over 3,000 of this aircraft. The importance of the Hudson in Lockheed's history is that it provided the impetus and opportunity for the company to increase their production capacity manyfold. This, in turn, put Lockheed in a position for the first time to manufacture large aircraft in quantity. Without this capability, the Constellation program might have been started only with the greatest difficulty, if at all.

Also during this same busy period Lockheed became involved with the famous P–38 Lightning fighter. The U.S. Army Air Corps issued requests to bid on a new fighter plane in February 1937. Johnson and Hibbard came up with a radical design involving a twin-engine fighter with twin booms. The idea was accepted, Lockheed won the contract, and construction of the prototype was started in July 1938. It first flew in January 1939, and only two weeks later made headlines when it set a coast-to-coast record of 7 hours, 48 minutes.

The P–38 had a number of significant firsts to its credit, including:

1. The only fighter that was in production both at the beginning of the war and at the end.
2. The first fighter to use tricycle landing gear.
3. The first to use a bubble canopy for better visibility.
4. The first to be powered by Allison engines with turbo-superchargers, each engine producing 1,350 to 1,500 hp.
5. The first production fighter to exceed 400 mph in level flight.
6. The first successful twin-boom design.

True, the P–38 had some problems, including engine malfunctions and tail flutter. Both of these problems were corrected, and the P–38 went on to become an extremely versatile and effective military aircraft, so much so, that all told, some 10,000 were produced.

In terms of the Constellation program, the value of the P–38 lay in its aerodynamic design features. A number of these, originally designed for the P–38, found application on the Constellation.

There was one more aircraft that Lockheed brought forth during this period— the Model 18 Lodestar, a further refinement of the L–10 and L–14 series. Its longer fuselage accommodated 16 passengers and a stewardess, thus making it a real competitor of the Douglas DC–2. First flown in September 1939 and in airline service by March 1940, the L–18 was slightly larger than the L–14. Although only a few were sold for commercial use, a military version called the Ventura was brought out in 1941 and used by both the British and the U.S. Navy as a patrol bomber. All told, some 624 L–18s were produced. After World War II, a considerable number were converted for use as corporate aircraft, and Lodestars are still flying today in that capacity.

However, the Lodestar was actually a last-gasp effort by Lockheed to try to compete in the commercial aircraft market of the late 1930s. By 1939, larger and faster aircraft dominated the market. Certain problems arose that plagued the L–14 and temporarily grounded all such Lockheeds. The fact was that the basic Electra design had been developed to its fullest potential. In none of its versions was it able to compete with the Douglas DC–3, which had been flying from 1936 on. Such aircraft as the Boeing Model 307 Stratoliner, introduced in airline service in mid-1940, clearly indicated the coming trend in commercial aircraft. Once again, as in 1932, Lockheed needed a new design to put it back in contention for the high stakes waiting in the commercial aircraft market. But unlike 1932, Lockheed was in an excellent financial position, thanks in part to its growing military orders. Furthermore, Lockheed now had a solid reputation second to none for building high-quality aircraft. The design staff, led by Kelly Johnson and Hall Hibbard, had clearly demonstrated their genius and talent with such aircraft as the P–38. Meanwhile, various forces were in motion that would soon result in the aircraft design known to the world as the Lockheed Constellation.

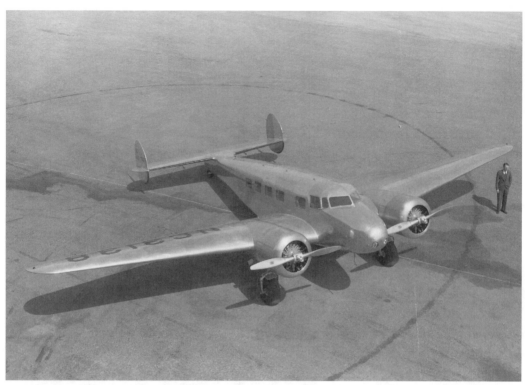

1-1 The Lockheed L–10 prototype transport that first flew in 1934. This airplane embodied a number of features new to aviation. (Lockheed Martin)

1-2 A successor to the L–10, the slightly larger L–12, November 1936. (Lockheed Martin)

1-3 An L–12 in the foreground, flying formation with an L–14. The difference in size is quite visible. (Lockheed Martin)

1-4 A KLM Royal Dutch Airline L–14 loading passengers. (Lockheed Martin)

1-5 A shot of the XC–35. Note the turbo supercharger visible on the engine nacelle, which gave the aircraft the ability to reach high altitudes. The technology developed with the XC–35 was later incorporated into the Constellation. (Lockheed Martin)

1-6 A flight of Royal Air Force Hudson bombers. The Hudson was an outgrowth of the L–14 and was sold in quantity to Great Britain. (Lockheed Martin)

Chapter 2

THE BIRTH OF AN IDEA

The concept for the Constellation did not spring suddenly full-blown from a drafting board. Rather, it was the result of various circumstances and events of the late 1930s combined with the ideas and philosophies of the Lockheed Aircraft Corporation.

Retracing the steps that led to the design and construction of the first Constellation is a fascinating journey through the byways of big business in general and commercial aviation in particular. This is especially true in the case of the Constellation because seldom in the annals of aviation was an aircraft brought forth that represented such a quantum jump in design and performance.

COMMERCIAL AVIATION COMES OF AGE

Possibly the single most important circumstance leading to the development of the Constellation was the phenomenal growth of commercial aviation in the 1930s. Commercial aviation may be said to have reached the level of a viable industry sometime between 1927 and 1930, and then grew very rapidly between 1930 and 1938. This growth pattern is easily perceived merely by examining the revenue passenger-miles flown during the period.

Year	Revenue
	(passenger miles in millions)
1927	2
1930	93
1935	328
1938	618

Another index of this growth was the average trip length per passenger. In 1931 this figure stood at 226 miles, whereas by 1937 it had mushroomed to 432 miles. This burgeoning growth was the result of three separate and distinct factors.

The first of these factors was the restructuring of the many small airline companies existing up to 1930. The then–Postmaster General of the United States, Walter Brown, in an attempt to improve the existing air mail system, forced the creation of a few larger companies. Although a highly controversial move at the time, it did result in airlines that were in a far better condition to operate efficiently and safely.

The second factor was an outgrowth of the first and involved the design and manufacture of larger, faster aircraft, which could carry not only the mail but paying passengers as well. This technical progress would undoubtedly have been far slower if relatively large airlines having strong financial backing had not been created. These airlines provided the potential market, which spurred aircraft manufacturers to undertake the necessary development.

The final factor was safety. As commercial aviation developed and grew, its safety record improved at an impressive rate. This is shown in the following table.

Year	No. Passenger Fatalities
	(per 100 million passenger miles flown)
1932	15
1937	6
1938	2.8
1939	1.2
1940	3.1

In fact, during a 17-month period from March 1939 to August 1940, the scheduled airlines did not have a single accident.

These three basic factors developed in the minds of the public an increasing feeling of a growing industry having stability and safety, as well as providing speedy and reliable transportation.

This entire process of growth was further stimulated and channeled by the

Federal Government. In a historic effort to further strengthen the growing aviation industry, in 1938 Congress passed the Civil Aeronautics Act. This legislation provided for setting up an authority that established aviation policies on air transportation safety and economics. It also provided for an Air Safety Board to investigate accidents. This constituted the first time a firm regulatory system existed that could oversee and coordinate the growth, operations, and safety of the airlines.

The authority was set up in part to prevent too much route duplication and cutthroat competition, which would only lead to airline companies becoming bankrupt. A second important function of the authority consisted of improving airports as well as the infant airway system. It can be truly said that the 17-month period of accident-free flying previously mentioned was partly attributable to the safety program being carried out by the Civil Aeronautics Authority (CAA).

MANUFACTURING COMPETITION

In 1938, the time was ripe for Lockheed to seriously consider entering the sales competition for a new generation of passenger transports. Lockheed was aware of the developing interest for a larger, faster transport, and it was keeping an eye on various large plane developments. In fact, by 1938, Lockheed's design people were actively investigating various possibilities for new designs. They were being spurred on by the knowledge that although they had more orders to fill for both the L–14 Super Electra and the L–18 Lodestar, it had by this time become obvious that the basic Electra twin-engine design had little (if any) growth left. What was needed to compete was an aircraft with considerably more seating capacity, and this almost automatically put any new designs into the four-engine category.

In 1938 and early 1939, Hibbard, Johnson, and their crew brainstormed a number of potential designs. An interesting one, the Model 27, was a twin-engine aircraft with the horizontal control surface forward of the wing, near the nose. This type of design in time came to be known as one employing canard surfaces. Development on this model was halted when wind tunnel testing indicated potential control problems.

Lockheed's design team continued their search for a viable new aircraft. The company's management had by this time come to the realization that just as in 1932, Lockheed was again badly in need of something new to build and sell if it were to remain competitive. Lockheed's next design was more promising. It was for a four-engine aircraft capable of carrying 21 passengers at a top speed of 240 mph. Known as the Model 44, this design then was upgraded to a 30-passenger aircraft with a 270 mph top speed. During this period, Lockheed had been discussing the Model 44 with Pan American Airways (Pan Am), and at their urging the Model 44 grew once more, this time to a 34-passenger, 300-mph aircraft.

With this latest design version of the Model 44, Lockheed was finally becoming competitive with such aircraft as the Douglas DC-4E and the Boeing Model 307 Stratoliner and Model 314 Clipper Flying Boat. But somehow the Model 44, now known as the Excalibur, as finally evolved in mid-1939, failed to spark much enthusiasm among potential customers. It was just another design, from a company that had no experience with large aircraft manufacturing. However, unbeknownst to Lockheed, certain corporate maneuvers within the world of the scheduled airlines would shortly catapult them into the big plane race. Once in that market, Lockheed would remain in it for a very long time.

HOWARD HUGHES AND TWA

The events just described pertaining to the growth of commercial aviation were by no means the only circumstance that directly brought about the Constellation design. During the late 1930s another drama of the business world was being enacted that would impact on this program. TWA, which then stood for Transcontinental Western Airlines, was one of the larger companies to come out of the reorganization of 1930. In 1935 the Lehman Brothers Banking Firm purchased a controlling interest in TWA. Shortly thereafter they promoted to the position of president a TWA captain who had been the Vice President for Operations. This man was Jack Frye, and he was to play an important part in the future of TWA. Over the next four years Frye and his co-workers worked hard to develop and improve TWA. Unfortunately, their viewpoints as former pilots differed considerably from those of the Lehman Brothers, who, after all, were bankers. By 1939 the differences between the two groups reached such proportions that Frye announced he would resign, and many of his chief aides indicated they would do likewise.

Frye had a good friend who was none other than Howard Hughes. Hughes heard of the proposed resignations, and, with his usual flair for the dramatic, he went to Frye and offered to buy a controlling interest in TWA, and then reappoint Frye as president. This was exactly what happened, and by April 1939 Hughes, Frye and Paul Richter had bought controlling interest in TWA from the Lehmans, with Hughes owning 12%.

Hughes, of course, was not only a pilot but an engineer, inventor, and generally an enthusiast of aviation and high-performance aircraft. He agreed with Frye's philosophy that TWA needed larger, faster aircraft to compete successfully against the other large airlines.

Hughes's first step was to buy some Boeing Model 307 Stratoliners. Although these four-engine pressurized aircraft were a definite improvement over TWA's DC–3s, it was generally felt by the airline's management that actually none of the then existing or proposed passenger aircraft had sufficient performance. Hughes still remembered the highly successful L–14 Super Electra, which Lockheed had prepared for his 1938 around-the-world record flight. Remembering that, Hughes wondered whether this wasn't the company to bring to reality the dream that he and Frye had of a larger and faster plane that could overfly most of the weather plus have the range to cross the United States nonstop. Actually, Hughes first went to Consolidated Vultee and asked if they were interested in such a project. But Consolidated was busy developing the B–24 Liberator heavy bomber, and turned him down.

In May 1939 Hughes first approached Lockheed regarding the possibility of TWA purchasing the Model 44 Excalibur. At this time the Model 44 had grown (on paper) to a gross weight of 44,000 pounds. Hughes felt that to meet his requirements of operating non-stop coast-to-coast such an aircraft should gross at least 52,000 pounds. This final step, however, proved to be an impossibility with the Excalibur due to both the basic design, which somewhat resembled an oversized Model 18 Lodestar, and its power plants. So this particular discussion came to an unproductive end, as Lockheed began to realize that the Excalibur was not the answer they were seeking.

Hughes, however, had by no means given up on what he considered to be Lockheed's real value—their design ability. So it was that in June 1939 three Lockheed officials were invited to the Hughes home. The three were Robert Gross, the president, Hall Hibbard, the chief engineer, and Kelly Johnson, the chief design engineer. They met with Hughes and Frye only, because Hughes had already realized that secrecy was an overriding concern if TWA was to really get the jump on its competition.

A NEW DESIGN

At that first meeting, Hughes and Frye brought forth a rough specification for an aircraft capable of carrying a payload of 6,000 pounds, a distance of 3,600 miles at a cruising speed of 275 to 300 mph, and an altitude of 20,000 feet. Such an aircraft would have to carry at least 20 berths or 36 seated passengers in luxury and comfort. The Lockheed officials promised to submit a preliminary design in short order. The three first huddled with a special team of six design engineers, then drew up a set of approximate dimensions and performance figures. A week later they sat down with Hughes and Frye again. These two found to their joy that Lockheed had already surpassed their own optimistic figures. The latest set of numbers showed an aircraft that had grown in size to where it could now carry up to 57 passengers cross-country in only 8.5 hours, a full hour and a half faster than demanded initially by Hughes.

The new transport would gross 68,000 pounds and cruise at 300 mph with a top speed of 350 mph, as fast as fighter aircraft of that day. Fully pressurized, it would have a ceiling of 30,000 feet but would require the very largest reciprocating engines available. In fact, the engines being considered weren't even in existence but were only a goal for engine builders to reach next.

Thus, during even the very preliminary conversations, it became apparent to the Lockheed officials that what Hughes wanted was a far cry from the designs then being readied for flight. To merely compete with such designs the Model 44 would have sufficed. But Hughes wanted an aircraft that would allow TWA to steal a march on the entire industry. To do this, Lockheed would have to bring forth a revolutionary plane that completely skipped a whole generation of aircraft. But if this could be achieved, then the new aircraft would revolutionize commercial aviation overnight.

The preliminary design concepts shown to Hughes and Frye during June were so well received that Hughes quickly decided to sign a contract. This meant taking quite a gamble, because these designs were a far cry from the finished product. But Hughes had already established a reputation for taking calculated risks and usually winning.

At that time TWA was not in a particularly favorable position to obtain the necessary bank credit required to start the project on its way. So Hughes, through his wholly owned company, Hughes Tool, signed a historic contract with Lockheed. This took place on July 10, 1939, and called for the delivery of five aircraft, at that time identified as Excalibur A models. As part of the contract, it was specified that Hughes Tool would own the planes but that TWA would operate them. Much later, in 1942, the contract was assigned to TWA. Simultaneously, Hughes Tool reserved the option to buy a total of 25 aircraft, and this was later increased to 40 aircraft.

It is interesting to note that news of this agreement did not reach the press until January 1945, some five years later. This secrecy was to become routine in all of the early dealings between Hughes and Lockheed concerning the Constellation program. But the reasons went considerably deeper than merely Hughes's mania for secrecy.

Once the plan's basic specifications had been pretty well determined, it became apparent exactly what kind of a giant step forward this airplane would signify. If such information were to reach the ears of other manufacturers and airlines, the competitive advantage that Hughes wanted so badly would evaporate. So

Hughes decided that regardless of the difficulties involved, no information must be allowed to leak out.

Frye bluntly told Hughes that there was only one way to guarantee secrecy. That involved Hughes personally signing the contract, as well as being responsible for its execution. As part of this subterfuge, it was decided that no TWA employees would visit or contact Lockheed under any circumstances. This alone was totally contrary to the way a customer airline usually dealt with a manufacturer. Normally the TWA engineering staff would have its personnel practically living at the Burbank plant.

But not this time! Initially, only two persons at TWA, Hughes and Frye, knew of the proposed airplane, and because Hughes was paying and no TWA funds were being used, it was somewhat easier to maintain absolute secrecy.

Additional subterfuges were also used. The new aircraft was identified by various names both at Lockheed and in short releases given the industry press. The name most commonly used was the Excalibur A, thus further extending the illusion that the aircraft in question was nothing more than another version of the basic Excalibur design. Subcontractors were given no aircraft model numbers or names to go by. The obvious result of all these security measures was that Hughes and Frye were, for a period of time, incredibly busy. So, by the same token, were Hibbard and Johnson.

Nevertheless, this curtain of secrecy was totally successful for more than six months. Even after the secrecy was partially penetrated, as we shall later see, it remained a total secret from the industry at large. Only rumors floated about, nothing truly substantial. Later on in the project the secrecy was further aided by the U.S. entry into World War II and the total control of all aircraft plants by the War Department.

But in the middle of July 1939, war was still distant from our shores, even though Lockheed was already heavily involved in war plane production. For now Hibbard and Johnson and all the other designers at Burbank had a very large assignment to complete. To bring to life, first on paper and then in metal, a new and almost revolutionary transport. A transport that had been bought and paid for sight unseen. A plane that was to be powered by engines that did not yet exist. An aircraft larger than almost any other then in production, and with a performance far exceeding anything then in the air or on the drawing board. All this would have to be done in total secrecy and by a company that had never designed or built any aircraft with more than one-fourth the gross weight of this new plane! Here indeed was a miracle that had to be fashioned by human hands.

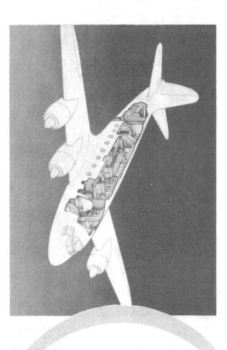

the *Excalibur*...
Forerunner of the Constellation

In April 1939 Lockheed revealed plans for the Excalibur, a four engine transport that had one, two, then three tails in various designs. Gross weight grew from 27,500 to 36,000 pounds and passenger capacity from 21 to 36.

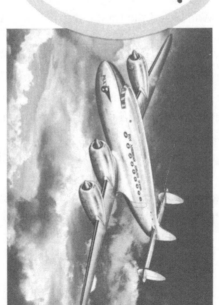

2-1 A sketch of the proposed Excalibur L–44 transport, a design that was later abandoned. (Lockheed Martin)

Chapter 3

THE FIRST ONE

The true wonder of the original Constellation design is not, as some might suppose, the mere design of an aircraft that large that can rise into the air and come down again safely. After all, Lockheed's design people, from Hall Hibbard and Kelly Johnson on down, had already more than shown their ability at designing flying machines. The true wonder was in the future. It lay in the fact that this new design would remain competitive for a full 20 years and, in the fact that its gross weight would double over that period of time. Above all, almost 40 years later people still flew an outgrowth of the basic Constellation design and were able to say that there was absolutely nothing wrong with their birds. Their only problem was that previous shoddy maintenance procedures had caused parts to wear out prematurely! Here, indeed, was a well-conceived and -executed design. Let us now follow the path that led to the final design.

Our brief look at the history of Lockheed does not automatically indicate any great potential for bringing about such a design as the Constellation. True, Lockheed had built a whole family of highly successful small and medium-size twin-engine transports between 1934 and 1939. But the largest of these was the Model 18 Lodestar, which seated only 17 and grossed a modest 17,500 pounds. Compared to the other large aircraft manufacturers, it can be seen that by 1939 Lockheed had not accumulated any large aircraft manufacturing experience. This was in marked contrast to Boeing, with its B–15 bomber prototype (70,000 pounds), and its Model 314 Flying Clipper (84,000 pounds). Consolidated Vultee had already flown its B–24 heavy bomber, and Douglas was readying a new prototype known as the B–19. It was also Douglas that had seemingly stolen a march on the rest of the industry by developing and flying the DC–4E prototype in mid-1938. Now, in 1939, this aircraft was already certificated for commercial use, although the final production version was to be the slightly smaller DC–4.

Yet here was Lockheed, blithely promising to build a larger, faster aircraft, in fact one which would be almost five times the gross weight of any previously built by them and that would require systems not yet even developed by anyone. Gutsy folks, those people over at Burbank!

The basic Constellation design that eventually emerged was, in keeping with virtually all aircraft before or since, the end result of a number of compromises. The starting point had to be the basic specifications as laid down by the customer, Howard Hughes and TWA. These had in turn been somewhat increased by Lockheed themselves just a week after the initial meeting. These specifications and other more detailed ones had been hurriedly put together into a document titled "Airline Equipment Agreement," which was dated July 8, 1939, was signed by Hughes on July 10, and officially issued, in secret, on July 11.

In the case of commercial aircraft, the detailed operating specifications that dictate the design begin with such items as range, cruising and top speed, service and top ceiling, and take-off and landing speeds and distances. To these must be added available payload for passengers and baggage, cargo capacity, and total passenger area. Then one must further add fuel consumption at cruise speed, direct operating costs, expected maintenance costs, and, of course, purchase price.

To quickly review the initial specifications for the new design, they were as follows:

- Payload: 6,000 pounds
- Seated passengers: 57
- Range: 3,000 statute miles
- Cruising speed: 300 mph
- Top speed: 350 mph
- Ceiling: 30,000 feet
- Crew: 6

(Lockheed)

The combined requirement of high cruising speed and low operating cost virtually dictated that the very first item Kelly Johnson consider be the power plants. Accordingly, an analysis was made comparing an existing 1,800-hp engine with a projected 2,200-hp engine. The results were, to say the least, highly interesting if not downright startling. The lower horsepower engines were considerably lighter by some 345 pounds each, or 1,385 pounds total for four, and thus would allow an increase in the amount of fuel carried. However—and this was the real surprise—the bigger, more powerful engines operating at a considerably lower percentage of full power, used less fuel per hour. The 2,200-hp engine used 440 pounds of fuel per hour versus 560 pounds for the 1,800-hp engines. Thus, the four 2,200-hp engines used a total of 480 pounds less fuel per hour! This is turn meant that for a given distance the lower fuel consumption of the larger engines would offset the weight advantage of the smaller engines. At a distance of 2,500 miles, the larger engines would carry a larger payload by some 3,000 pounds. Therefore, on this basis alone, the 2,200-hp engines were indicated.

Another consideration in the choice of the larger engines was the fact that it was felt that only with the largest available power plants could Hughes's requirements for speed and altitude be adequately met. Still another reason was the fact that only very powerful engines operating at a low percentage of full power (at cruise speeds) would give the desired result of 1 mile per gallon of fuel used. This last item met the requirement for low operating cost.

However, there were still other important reasons to use the larger 2,200-hp power plants. These included:

1. Shorter take-off runs. This was an important consideration for TWA if they were to be able to operate the aircraft into many different cities, some with small airports.
2. A greater margin of safety if an engine failed, especially during or shortly after take-off.
3. Simpler engine installations.
4. Longer engine life and reduced maintenance due to the engines being operated at lower percentages of full power.
5. Higher maximum performance if needed.

Thus, the choice was made, and Lockheed designed the Constellation around the Wright R3350 Cyclone engine, a power plant not yet actually designed, let alone built. This was the one very obvious drawback in the choice of an engine, namely, that a totally unproven engine was picked. Actually, the 3350 did exist, but not in a 2,200-hp version. The basic engine was an 18-cylinder radial with two banks of 9 cylinders each and a total displacement of 3,350 cubic inches, hence its familiar designation as the Wright 3350. Formerly, it was the Wright Cyclone and was first built experimentally in 1937. The first engine developed 1,700 hp at 2,200 rpm (take-off rating at sea level). Later engines built in 1939/40/41 and 42 boosted this gradually to 2,400 hp at 2,600 rpm. Although tested on such large aircraft as the Douglas B–19, only a grand total of 72 actual engines were built through 1943 covering seven different models, none truly successful.

However, the decision was undoubtedly the correct one, as proved again and again during the lifetime of the Constellation. But as we shall shortly see, the decision also resulted in some far-reaching and unfortunate consequences. Having decided on the power plant, Kelly Johnson and company were now free to turn their attention to the next major step in the design, the fuselage. It had already been decided to use a low-wing design. It was also obvious from the specifications not only that the fuselage would have to be pressurized but also that the cabin air would require refrigeration, dehumidifying, and general purification of fumes and odors. Because a perfectly round cross-section fuselage is the easiest to pressurize, the fuselage had such a cross-section from the beginning. But the camber line of the fuselage was not straight, unlike many large aircraft where it is.

To understand the reasons for the dolphin-shaped fuselage that finally emerged, we must backtrack slightly. We have already talked about the engine selection. To harness the power of those mighty engines at low engine revolutions required propellers with a diameter of 15 feet, 2 inches. So that the propeller tips could clear the ground, the fuselage and wing would have to be placed on landing gear of unusual length. But the resulting nose landing gear was so long that it was felt it would cause various problems. So the mean camber line of the fuselage was dropped forward of the wing to reduce the length of the nose gear. Then the fuselage just behind the wing was also given a small amount of downward curve. The reason for this was to reduce the drag at the maximum low drag ratio of the aircraft.

Last, the designers realized that for the triple vertical tail surfaces to clear the ground as the aircraft was rotated for take-off, more clearance from the ground would be needed. For this reason the fuselage camber line at the rear of the fuselage was raised.

All this tinkering with the fuselage camber line resulted in a number of consequences. First, the drag coefficient of the fuselage proved to be lower than expected. This was first indicated in wind tunnel tests and then dramatically demonstrated in flight. In fact, despite the size of the Constellation, it is significant that although its "flat plate area," or head-on wind resistance, of approximately 33.8 square feet is the same as the Douglas DC–4's, the Constellation had 13% less drag—despite having a 13% larger wing and bigger engines.

Second, because the vertical tail surfaces were placed higher relative to the rest of the aircraft, they were less exposed to propeller turbulence and thus provided better control.

Third, the fuselage shape that resulted was extremely distinctive, undeniably graceful, and even beautiful to some. But a price was to be paid by Lockheed for all this. As Hall Hibbard put it succinctly, "You know, that airplane didn't have a straight line in it anywhere except the passenger floor. And so, the poor guys in the shop, oh my, they really had a problem!" (Hall Hibbard, phone interview, 1977).

Once the basic fuselage shape had been determined, there remained the nose and the tail to be considered. The nose, particularly the windshield, surprisingly enough, required a considerable amount of work before a final design was deemed acceptable. Six different designs were developed, of which five reached the mock-up stage. The six designs (Fig. 3-2), as shown in the accompanying sketches, were:

1. Use of the basic fuselage shape, with double-curved glass. This arrangement resulted in poor visibility and was quickly discarded, even though it was thought to give a minimum of drag. No mock-up was made.
2. A rounded nose with the cockpit below the main floor. This design increased drag, unduly endangered the crew in a crash landing, and made for a poor nose gear design.
3. A layout that consisted of two individual bug eyes. It was considered an unusable approach, creating such problems as cockpit instrument and control arrangements and poor communications between pilots.
4. This was a follow-on to the number 3 layout and had one large bug eye. This layout again had too much drag and also would have caused grave problems when pressurized.
5. This lay out used the standard V windshield but was not practical because of the large fuselage width.
6. The final design was based on a conical shape and utilized a number of small windshield panels. Visibility was generally good, and the windshields were the lightest of all the designs studied. One of the considerations weighed in the nose design was the basic cockpit layout. This was designed for a crew of four, namely pilot, copilot, flight engineer, and a radioman/navigator position. *(Lockheed)*

The tail configuration adopted had an appearance that was pure Lockheed. It will be remembered that this company had previously incorporated twin tails on a number of their aircraft. Kelly Johnson felt strongly that where an aircraft had powerful engines for its size, as the Constellation did, then directional control becomes more crucial than directional stability. Johnson opted to use triple vertical surfaces to provide optimum directional control. Actually, Johnson had no choice but to use a third, central vertical surface because one of TWA's specifications was that the aircraft be low enough to the ground to fit into their existing hangars. Only with a third vertical surface could Johnson lower the tail surfaces to fit TWA's hangars and still obtain the high degree of maneuverability considered necessary.

However, use of the triple tail required that the horizontal surface be placed high on the tail. Despite the upward curve of the rear fuselage, the horizontal portion of the tail was still negatively affected by the propeller wind stream, and this necessitated the use of a very large surface. Although the total tail design was shown to be most effective in providing very good control, it was nevertheless a large and complex assembly. Accordingly, it was decided that hydraulic control boosters would be needed, and these were incorporated.

The vertical tail surfaces were of a shape already familiar to many observers. Because the operating speed of the Constellation was close to that of the P–38 Lightning fighter designed by Lockheed, and because that fighter's vertical surfaces had proven highly effective, it was decided to use the same shape scaled up to handle the larger size and weight of the Constellation. If the reader feels these tail surfaces have been seen elsewhere than on the P–38, you are right, as the Lockheed Model 14 also had vertical surfaces of virtually the same shape.

The wing shape selection was based on the results of testing various wing sections in a wind tunnel. Among these were various laminar flow designs as well as a more conventional design used on the P–38. Once again, the basic Lightning design was used and borrowed from. This particular design was chosen because, although it had more drag than many other wings, it also had a very high maximum lift coefficient and excellent stall characteristics. These last two characteristics were not true of the low-drag laminar flow designs.

The wing section and plan form chosen were to result in certain flight characteristics that would be of great value to the whole Constellation series, with the exception of the very last model, which had a new laminar flow wing. These characteristics were a low take-off and landing speed, great stability even in turbulence, and very fast spin recovery. These were the very characteristics that were to endear the aircraft to flight crews, passengers, and operators throughout its lifetime. The wing also had integral fuel tanks, the first aircraft so equipped.

Thus, the wing design, as finally evolved, was almost identical to the P–38 wing except, naturally, larger. It featured two main spars, with a third so-called false spar from which were hung the flaps and ailerons. The basic framework was covered with flush-riveted stressed skin. The Lockheed Fowler flaps were of the same highly successful design as used first on the Model 14 and were instrumental in giving the Constellation its low landing and take-off speeds.

The tail assembly, which we've already seen was designed with the triple vertical surfaces, also used a horizontal surface that had a large chord. The elevator was designed to overcome the possibility of stall at the relatively low landing speeds.

Once the basic airframe had been designed, the next concern of the designers was the total control system. This, of course, is made up of the ailerons, rudder, and elevators. The design of these surfaces would be greatly influenced by the type of control system adopted. The design team was strongly motivated toward the use of a power booster control system because of such factors as a very large speed range (for that time) and the need to increase minimum control speeds and reduce pilot workloads.

Thus, a system of hydraulic boosters that would operate in the same fashion as a car's power steering would be extremely important in improving not only the aircraft's controllability performance but also its ease of operation. However, because such a system had never before been tried on an aircraft of this size, Kelly Johnson approached the problem with great care and thoroughness.

Lockheed had actually undertaken the development of such booster systems in 1939 before the Constellation project was ever started. The development of the system continued for a long five years before it was felt that most of the problems had been satisfactorily solved. The design team had in mind a number of specific advantages that would accrue if the system were successfully developed. These were:

1. Greater control than with any aerodynamic balance system for the same given control surface area.
2. A reduction in minimum drag of 12–30% at speeds of 250–350 mph.
3. Control forces of any specific amount without the danger of overbalance.
4. Doing away with overbalance during serious icing conditions.
5. The use of control surface shapes that are far less subject to compressibility factors.
6. The ability to successfully oppose dangerous aerodynamic and flutter forces.
7. The possibility to easily alter control forces required to move the surfaces, to some extent even in flight.
8. The possibility of using an acceleration limiter.

9. A considerable weight savings in the control surfaces themselves.
10. Less need for manufacturing tolerances and reduced sensitivity to service damage.

Readers should keep in mind that in 1939, when the original decision was made to equip the Constellation with hydraulic boosters, their use was by no means universal. Only a few applications had been tried, and some had been subsequently discontinued. But because all previous failures could be traced directly to design weaknesses, Johnson felt there was an excellent chance such boosters could be made to work successfully. Furthermore, the known disadvantages to any such system were far outweighed by the advantages and actually could be avoided entirely by good design.

Among the disadvantages of control surface boosters that Johnson and his crew had to watch out for were:

1. Need for a redundant or back-up system to substitute for the main booster system in case of failure.
2. The added work requited in servicing and maintaining the system.
3. The friction caused by the entire mechanism which made it more difficult for the control surfaces to center themselves in a neutral position.

It should be remembered that in designing this booster system, Lockheed was once again breaking new ground. There was really very little in the way of history on such systems that could be used to help in the design. For example, one of the things that was not known was what boost ratio would be most desirable on each of the three main control surfaces. If you have a boost ratio of 19 to 1, this means that the pilot is applying 1 unit of force and the booster applies 19 times as much force. It was this very boost ratio, or the optimum boost ratio, that was not known at that time. However, after a certain amount of trial and error it was decided that elevator forces should have a desirable force of 50–80 pounds, rudder pedals 150 pounds, and ailerons 10 pounds.

At this point it might be well to digress and explain a very important point relating to control surfaces in general and to booster systems in particular. When aircraft are flying at cruise altitudes and cruise speeds, there is relatively little control surface movement; by the same token, only relatively low forces are required. But control surfaces are designed to function at critical speeds when, for example, a four-engine aircraft has two engines out on the same side. At such times powerful forces are required to move the control surfaces, and furthermore they must be moved rather quickly to achieve safe landings. In fact, generally speaking, this very same aircraft could have done without power control or booster controls if minimum control speeds of 20–30 mph higher than what is the case had been acceptable. However, Lockheed did not want such a situation. They felt it was very important that the Constellation be able to land and take off at slow speeds, and thus it was necessary to have the control at those low speeds in all conditions. It is interesting to note that here, once again, the basic thinking that went into the original Constellation bore fruit over the years. Airlines and air crews for many years were very satisfied and appreciative of the fact that the Constellation could land and take off at slower speeds than competitive designs.

At any rate, after a certain amount of trial and error, the final boost ratios were determined for the Constellation control surfaces. These ratios turned out to be (1) for the elevators 9.33 to 1, (2) for the rudder 23 to 1, and (3) for the ailerons 26 to 1. However, it should be remembered that these final ratios were by no means the only ones tested. On the contrary, a large range of boost ratios were tried before the final ones were accepted. The Constellation control surfaces were the plain, unbalanced type, although three other types were considered at one time.

The engineers gave a great deal of thought to the actual way in which the pilots would be using the system. One of their concerns was that if external forces were applied to the control surfaces, the system must not work backward, allowing the control surfaces to be moved by the outside forces, and therefore also moving the controls. To achieve this took a great deal of careful study, and as a matter of fact required the time of a highly trained mathematician for a whole year. The system also had to be designed so that the airplane could be flown safely to a landing without the boost controls functioning. The accompanying figures clearly show how the basic system operates (Fig. 3-3, 3-5, 3-6).

To check out the entire boost system, a complete full-scale model was built in a laboratory. Large springs on the simulated control surfaces were used to take the place of air loads. The system was operated many, many times with gradual improvements being made. In fact, the entire mock-up was tested for more than three years. To study the effect of low temperatures on the booster system, the entire tail assembly was enclosed and the temperature lowered to −70°F. Because the Constellations were designed to fly at very high altitudes, it was imperative that all control systems function absolutely normally and with total reliability at very low temperatures. Later on we shall come across a couple of anecdotes that relate directly to this hydraulic booster system.

What finally emerged from all this design work was a large, extremely graceful, low-wing aircraft. The birdlike cylindrical body sat high on the long, somewhat spindly looking, tricycle landing gear. The large radial engines were mounted slightly underslung on the thick, rounded wing. The combination of underslung engines and large-diameter propellers were the main reasons why the fuselage sat high on its landing gear with a considerable amount of ground clearance beneath the belly. The massive triple tail with its large horizontal stabilizer was probably the single most distinctive visual feature. The resulting aircraft gave the appearance of being very large—in fact, larger than its true size. Even compared to today's aircraft, the Constellation's overall size is still very noticeable.

The prototype L–49, as well as the first few aircraft built, were to be powered by the sixth version of the R–3350 known as the 711C18BA2/3350–35. This engine was built during the period August 1942 to October 1944, and a total of 58 were produced. This was followed by the 711C18BA4/3350–35A, of which 181 were manufactured between October 1944 and September 1945. Both engine models produced 2,200 hp at 2,800 rpm, and weighed close to 2,700 pounds each.

Although the engine in its many versions was familiarly referred to as the 3350, each version had at least one (and sometimes two) formal designations. For example, the engine powering the prototype was known at the 711C18BA2 commercially and as the R–3350–35 in the military. Some versions lacked the military designation.

To adequately test the original R–3350 engines, Lockheed borrowed a Navy P2V Ventura and replaced its two engines with two of the Wrights. In-house, this aircraft became known as the Ven-Tellation. The two engines performed well and confirmed the engineers' belief that using this power plant on the newly designed Constellation was the way to go.

Another area in which the Lockheed design team had to do some pioneering was the pressurization system. Lockheed, of course, had been the first in this field with their experimental XC–35. Boeing also did some work in this arena and produced their pressurized Model 307 Stratoliner in early 1940. However, no cabin of such dimensions had ever been pressurized before. Furthermore, pressurization was not the only thing involved. The system had to cool, purify, and circulate the total mass of air in the cabin at altitudes of up to 35,000 feet. About the only thing left out was humidification. The lack of humidity caused by altitude combined with air conditioning was a factor that was not dealt with until the first jet transports came along. Interestingly enough, the original prototype did not have pressurization. But the next three aircraft off the assembly line, which were all used in the test flight program, did.

The Constellation prototype, which was later delivered to the Army Air Force as the first C–69, had a design gross weight of 86,250 pounds. This was a significant figure, not only as compared to other planes of that time but also in terms of the growth of the design from its very inception. The predecessor to the L–49, the L–44 Excalibur, had a 40,000-pound gross weight. When Hughes first approached Lockheed, he had in mind an airplane with a gross weight of around 52,000 pounds. By June 1939 Hughes and Frye had upped this figure to 55,000 pounds. Then, the initial Lockheed study, which took only a week, recommended a weight of 59,200 pounds, but with a more powerful engine than that originally specified by Hughes.

The agreement that Lockheed and Hughes entered into called for a further increase, with the gross weight now at 72,000 pounds. Then, over the next three years, while the future of the Constellation was debated back and forth between Lockheed and the U.S. government, wind tunnel tests showed that the prototype design allowed for still more growth. Initial flight tests then revealed that a weight of 86,000 pounds was entirely feasible. This greater weight was to make the military C–69 a far more efficient aircraft, one that would be more attractive to the Air Force planners. So it was that 86,250 pounds became the standard gross weight of the L–49/C–69.

This rather stupendous growth in the load-carrying capacity of the basic airplane was in time to become a trademark of all Constellations. As much as anything that can be identified, this potential for growth was an excellent indication of exactly how advanced the basic design actually was. It was possibly the single largest factor that enabled Lockheed to manufacture the Constellation in its various versions uninterruptedly from 1946 to 1958, a 12-year span!

By March 1940 the detailed design of the aircraft was well under way, and more people had become involved in the tightly kept secret. At Lockheed, in addition to Gross, Hibbard, and Johnson, who had been in the know from the very beginning, there were Donald Palmer, the chief project engineer, and Ed Tripani, assistant project engineer. At TWA, three more company employees had been brought into the picture. These were Paul Richter, executive VP, Tommy Tomlinson, chief engineer, and Ralph Ellinger, engineer.

However, once the basic design of the Constellation had been determined, it was deemed necessary to have someone from TWA present on a daily basis. This ruled out any of the previously mentioned TWA people because their positions made it impractical to move any of them to the West Coast for an extended period of time. Furthermore, their faces might be too familiar and thus excite comment and rumor. So it was that in March 1940 John E. Guy of TWA was summoned to Paul Richter's office. Guy had been TWA's representative at the Boeing plant in Seattle working on the Model 307 Stratoliner contract.

The meeting with Richter contained some surprises for Guy. First, he was asked for a promise that he would not resign from TWA without the permission of Richter. Given such a promise, Richter then proceeded to lay out the story of the Constellation up to that time. Guy would be assigned on the West Coast as TWA's representative at Douglas Aircraft on a contract for ten DC–3 aircraft. But this would be a cover assignment. His major task would be to act as liaison on the Constellation project. Guy was further instructed to rent a house in Burbank that had an extra large room that was in effect to become the office for the Constellation project. Furthermore, the house was to be in such a location that none of the adjacent homes or those across the street housed Lockheed employees.

Because Guy was to act as liaison on all matters relating to the new Constellation contract, this meant he would be the middle man between Lockheed, Howard Hughes, and Jack Frye at TWA. Thus, all mail between Lockheed and TWA would be transmitted through him. As part of the security procedures, he had to destroy all envelopes by burning and remove all Lockheed letterheads with a razor blade before passing the information on. In transmitting information, a simple code was arranged, with Hughes identified as H, Jack Frye as F, and Hall Hibbard as HH.

Because Guy's cover was the TWA DC–3 contract with Douglas, a major part of each day was spent in Santa Monica at the Douglas plant. But once back home, he had to handle matters dealing with the secret Constellation project. Due to Hughes's nocturnal working habits, Guy would often not be able to reach him until 2 A.M., and return calls might be later than that! When phone or mail communications with the Lockheed design team did not suffice, Guy would take time off from the Douglas project and meet with them either at his home or in some city park.

Guy remained on this project for almost two years, from spring 1940 to late 1941, but the extreme need for secrecy was alleviated somewhat by the turn of events in world affairs. In 1941, as the War Department realized the imminence of the United States entering the war, a visit by military leaders to the Burbank plant forced the total secrecy of the Constellation project to be torn apart. The aircraft was to remain under military security, but there was enough information released that the other aircraft manufacturers became aware of the general design involved. In fact, shortly thereafter TWA set up an office in Burbank to oversee the project. Unfortunately, various events conspired that delayed the initial flights and put off the introduction of the Constellation into commercial use.

The prototype Constellation was already being fabricated at the time John Guy first became involved in March 1940. The aircraft was being built in an experimental shop using temporary wooden jigs. The security surrounding the building was extreme, reminiscent of actual wartime security—in fact, even Lockheed plant personnel not directly involved in the project were unaware of its existence. At this time, fabrication of the fuselage was well along, as were the wings and tail sections.

At the beginning of the actual construction, Lockheed had scheduled the first flight for February 1942. But by late summer 1940 this date was already beginning to slip, and there was really nothing in Lockheed's power to remedy this situation. As you will learn in Chapter 4, the entire project was about to be deeply influenced by the events transpiring overseas, namely, World War II. In addition, Wright was having serious difficulties in developing the 3350 engine. The net result of all this would be a delay of one year in the initial flight of the Constellation and its subsequent testing. In light of later events, this initial delay proved crucial to the future of the Constellation program.

During the middle of 1941 the first official confirmation of the existence of the Constellation appeared in print. In June 1941 *Aviation Week* magazine carried a small item mentioning that the Office of Production Management had authorized Lockheed to build its first Constellation prototype. Actually, as we know, the aircraft fabrication was already well under way. The item also mentioned its projected gross weight of 86,000 pounds and the fact that Pratt and Whitney was developing 2,300–2,500-hp engines for the new transport. This last may have been an indication that Lockheed, unsure of exactly when Wright would finish development of the Cyclone, had talked to P&W about a replacement engine.

A month later *Aviation Week* revealed that TWA had ordered an additional 40 Constellations, and that among other performance parameters, the aircraft would have a ceiling of 30,000 feet. That, of course, would turn out to be a bit of a dream, but was nevertheless interesting. Later, in April 1942, *Aviation Week* carried a photograph showing the prototype fuselage under construction. Finally, in February 1943, the same publication carried a photo of the new transport in flight. Thus, it can be appreciated that the combined needs of Howard Hughes and the military establishment managed to maintain an almost total veil of secrecy surrounding the Constellation until well after its first flight.

Late in 1942 the prototype was finally moved from the assembly building to the Burbank Airport proper in preparation for its first flight. At this point a great number of people saw the graceful airplane for the first time, and much conversation started in the aviation industry about this large transport. By early January 1943 the first Constellation was ready to fly.

Lockheed had decided that it would load the dice in its own favor, because flying a brand-new model for the first time always has an element of risk to it. In addition to their own chief test pilot, Milo Burcham, Lockheed arranged to borrow the famous Eddie Allen from Boeing. This was not in any sense a reflection on Burcham. Allen was considered possibly the foremost test pilot of his time. He also had a great deal of big plane experience, which Burcham did not, and he was also famous for bringing his aeronautical engineering expertise into play and being able to analyze why an airplane behaved the way it did. To cap it off, Lockheed had learned that by using Allen their insurance coverage for the first test flights would cost considerably less.

On January 9, 1943, Allen, Burcham, and the Constellation were ready to go. Also aboard on the first flight were Kelly Johnson, Rudy Thorem, and Dick Stanton. Allen and Burcham made the initial take-off with absolutely no trouble and flew around a while before bringing the big bird back down. The first flight was so totally uneventful that another was immediately scheduled. Before the end of the first day, the rather amazing total of six flights had been successfully completed! At the end of the last one, Allen turned to Bob Gross, who had been in anxious attendance all day and said, "Mr. Gross, this plane flies perfectly. You don't need me anymore. I'm going back home to Seattle." *(Lockheed)* To say that these initial flights were an outstanding success would be a huge understatement. Today, a new aircraft design flies only after lengthy taxi tests, and then often for a single, short, flight. Instead, the Constellation, in one short day, showed the genius of its designers, from "Kelly" Johnson on down, as well as the excellence of the people who built it!

It was a very sad day in the annals of American aviation when less than six weeks later Eddie Allen and 29 others died in the fiery crash of the No. 2 Boeing B-29 prototype. The cause was an engine fire in one of its Wright R-3350s, and the same basic problem plagued the early months of the Constellation test program, until finally Wright solved the problem once and for all.

After the initial airworthiness of the Constellation had been proven, it was flown to Muroc Dry Lake (now Edwards Air Force Base) for its extended flight testing.

One of the more interesting aspects of the Constellation design dealt with the ground rules under which the aircraft was designed. Just prior to the inception of the project, in 1938–39, the CAA, predecessor to the current Federal Aviation Administration (FAA), had developed some changes to the requirements for an airworthiness certificate for large commercial aircraft. Among other things, these dealt with take-off performance, both with all engines running and with one or more engines failing, climb performance, and other aspects. The L–49 was designed and performed in full compliance with these requirements, even though they had not been approved at the time the aircraft design was begun. Immediately after World War II there was a race to prepare new transports for commercial use. At that time, the Douglas DC–4 and Boeing 377 Stratocruiser were allowed to enter service without meeting the new criteria. The L–49 alone, among all the transports flying in 1946–47, complied fully with the new specifications.

Thus, by early 1943 Lockheed's triple-tailed transport of was flying and exciting everyone. But the entire project was about to fall on hard times. The war and other factors were about to deeply affect the project, and it would be years before the Constellation would begin to fly commercially.

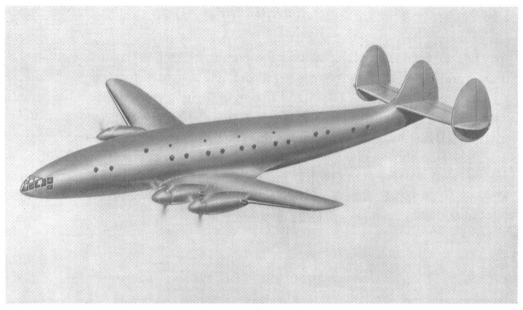

3-1 The Constellation as originally designed in 1939, with reverse-flow cowlings on the engines and a smooth windshield. (Lockheed Martin)

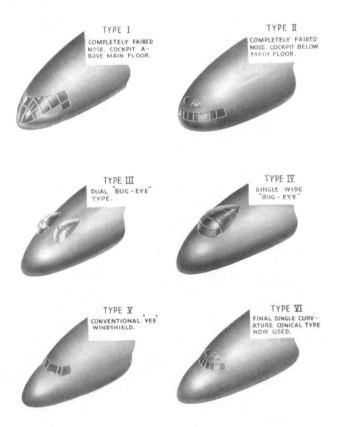

3-2 Sketches of the various nose designs investigated during the Constellation design phase. (Lockheed Martin)

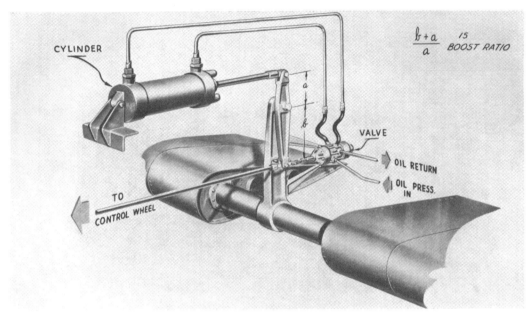

3-3 The basic design of the Constellations's hydraulic booster system. (Lockheed Martin)

3-4 The L–18 Ventura aircraft, on which the Curtiss-Wright power plants destined for the Constellation were flight tested. Among Lockheed employees it was referred to as the "Ventellation." (Lockheed Martin)

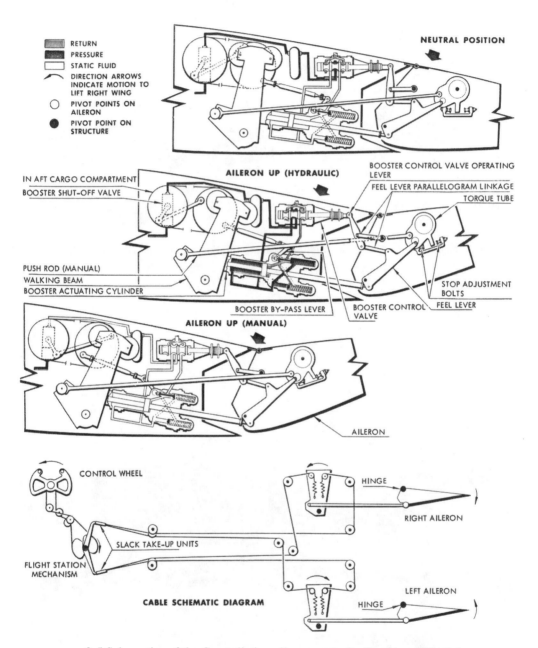

3-5 Schematics of the Constellation aileron controls. (Lockheed Martin)

VIEW A illustrates the rudder booster mechanism with the rudder approximately 15 degrees to right. The parallelogram linkage (1) is positioned to hold control valve (2) in neutral. Any movement of lever (8) from alignment with rudder-operating arm (9) will open the control valve.

VIEW B illustrates opening of the control valve by force initiated by the pilot. The control cables have rotated rudder quadrant (3) and by pulling push-pull feel bar (4), have rotated lever (8) about the actuating-cylinder piston-rod attaching bearing. The rudder moves slightly as the control valve is opened.

Hydraulic pressure is directed by the control valve to the actuating-cylinder, as long as the rudder quadrant is rotated in advance of the rudder-operating arm, or as long as force is necessary to overcome air load on the rudder. Hydraulic pressure, acting upon the cylinder piston, creates a force proportional to that applied to the push-pull feel bar (4) by the pilot. These combined forces move the rudder, and because the pilot must furnish a part of the force to move the rudder, he has a continuous "feel" of the air load on the rudder.

When the movement of the rudder quadrant is discontinued the hydraulic pressure continues the movement of the rudder-operating arm (9) until the arm is aligned with lever (8) and the valve is thereby returned to neutral.

VIEW C illustrates the operating of the rudder by manual force alone. The cable-controlled shut-off valve (5) has been closed and the bypass valve (6) opened, leaving the cylinder piston free to move. Rotation of the rudder quadrant by the cables has moved lever (8) until it has taken up the lost motion in the oversize hole (10) in the rudder-operating arm. Direct force is then applied in moving the rudder-operating arm and the rudder to the right.

WITH THE TRAIL CENTER CONTROL VALUE CENTERED AS SHOWN IN VIEW "A," RESIDUAL EQUAL PRESSURE IS PRESENT ON BOTH SIDES OF THE ACTUATED CYLINDER PISTON.

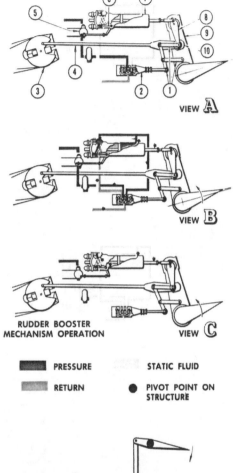

RUDDER BOOSTER MECHANISM OPERATION

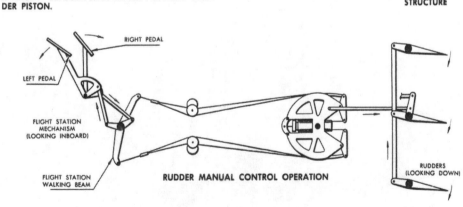

3-6 Schematics of the Constellation rudder controls. (Lockheed Martin)

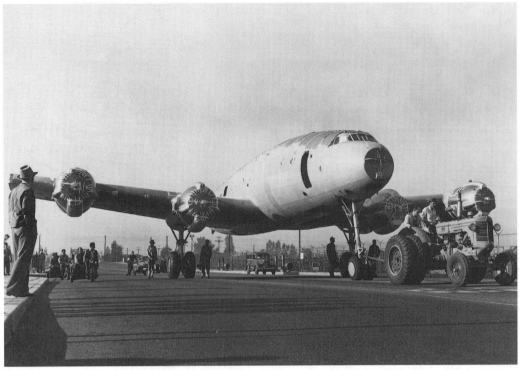

3-7 The L–49 prototype being towed to the Burbank Air Terminal from the Lockheed factory, 1942. Note the missing wing-tips and engines. (Lockheed Martin)

3-8 The L–49 prototype taxiing out for its first flight, Jan. 5, 1943. The famous test pilot, Eddie Allen, borrowed from Boeing, is flying left seat, and Milo Burcham, Lockheed test pilot, is flying right seat. (Lockheed Martin)

3-9 Anxious Lockheed employees watch the L–49 prototype approach for its first landing, January 9, 1943. (Lockheed Martin)

3-10 The L–49 prototype flaring out over the runway just prior to touchdown, January 9, 1943. (Lockheed Martin)

3-11 Interior view of the L–49 prototype heavily instrumented for its series of test flights, August 1944. Note the large amount of test equipment as well as the parachutes being worn by the test personnel. (Lockheed Martin)

3-12 A rather spectacular head-on view of a Connie. (Lockheed Martin)

3-13 An interior view of an L–049 being manufactured. The view is looking aft along three barrel sections of the fuselage. (Lockheed Martin)

3-14 Interior of the Connie prototype during construction, looking forward in the cabin from rear bulkhead, January 1943. Inside surface of pressure fuselage is lined with aluminum foil covered with Kapok Unisorb felt for heat and sound insulation. (Lockheed Martin)

Chapter 4

WWII AND THE CONSTELLATION ENLISTS

The first six years in the life of the Constellation—as measured from the time Hughes signed the initial contract—were a curious mixture of high hopes and vast disappointments. The initial Constellation design period, its construction, and the early flying phases were all carried out against a backdrop of momentous and frightening world events. World War II, which started in September 1939, engulfed the majority of the planet and affected virtually all of its inhabitants. Lockheed in general and the Constellation program in particular were no exception. In fact, as readers may remember, Lockheed had early on become involved in the manufacture of military aircraft with its large order of Hudson bombers for Great Britain. They then followed this up with their highly unorthodox but tremendously successful P–38 Lightning fighter. The War Department was very impressed with the P–38, and it was ordered in quantity.

During the latter part of 1939 and on into 1940, the design of the Constellation was carried forward, all within the strictest secrecy imaginable, per the injunctions of Howard Hughes. But all the security measures applied were to no avail. For in some manner Pan Am was able to penetrate the veil of secrecy and obtain the specifications of the newly conceived transport. This information whetted the curiosity and appetite of Pan Am's President Juan Trippe, who promptly contacted Lockheed and indicated a desire to order a number of the aircraft. Lockheed now found themselves in a very awkward position. They certainly did not want to turn their backs on a potentially large customer, such as Pan Am. On the other hand, their contract with Hughes bound them not only to initial secrecy but also to deliver the first aircraft to any other domestic operator not less than eight months after the last aircraft was delivered to TWA. To add to the growing problem, the Royal Dutch Airlines (KLM) also found out about the super-secret (?) project. They, too, wished to buy a number of the new aircraft then under design.

What Lockheed did was to simply go to Hughes with the problem and ask what they should do. It turned out to be just the right move. For Hughes did not feel threatened by either Pan Am or KLM, because Pan Am did not provide domestic services, and TWA was not operating overseas at that time. KLM, of course, also did not fly domestically in the United States. So he approved the additional sales of aircraft to both airlines. Actually, both he and TWA, as well as Lockheed, felt that further endorsements of the Constellation would be highly beneficial in the long run.

On January 29, 1940, Lockheed signed a contract with KLM to deliver four Model 49 airplanes. However, unlike the previously ordered aircraft, these called for them to be powered by Wright GR–2600 engines, which had less horsepower. The deliveries were to be made in May, June, and July 1941, with the airplanes priced at $430,000 each.

Then, on June 11, 1940, Lockheed contracted to sell Pan Am 20 Model 49 planes and 10 Model 149 planes, with an option for 10 more of either model. The Model 149 was a new designation for a Constellation with more range, a feature necessary to meet Pan Am's operational requirements. By this time the price of a Model 49 had increased to $450,000, and the new Model 149 was quoted at $550,000.

On that same June day, Hughes and TWA amended their contract to call for an additional 21 Model 49s, for a total now of 30 aircraft, with each of the additional 21 costing $425,000.

Thus, by the summer of 1940 Lockheed found itself, on paper, with firm orders for a total of 64 Constellations, with an option for 10 more. All this on an aircraft whose prototype had barely begun construction!

But unfortunately, Lockheed didn't really have all those orders. A month before a little man with a brush mustache and a very loud voice had drastically changed these plans from his headquarters in Berlin, Germany. Adolf Hitler decided to bring the well-known Phony War of 1939–40 to a shattering end. In the early morning hours of May 10, 1940, German armed forces invaded Europe's Low Countries: Belgium, Holland, and Luxembourg, as well as France. By the middle of June, it was all over. Not only was Holland occupied, but so was a large part of

Western Europe. The immediate consequence was that the KLM contract was now only worthless paper.

But a far more long-range consequence was also taking place concurrently. The war had suddenly spread and threatened to spread still further. The issue now was what effect would all this have on Lockheed in general, and the Constellation program in particular.

The first noticeable effect was the increased urgency for war plane production. Both the British and the Australians wanted Hudson bombers, and they wanted them *now*! So successful was the design that the original order of 250 mushroomed to a total production run of 3,000!

The highly successful P–38 was ordered in quantity by both the United States and Great Britain. The U.S. Navy wanted Ventura patrol bombers, an offshoot of the L–18. What with tooling up for these aircraft and expanding existing production, Lockheed's financial resources were becoming strained. Then, in September 1940, following President Franklin Roosevelt's call for producing 50,000 airplanes a year, the War Department issued an industry-wide alert that all companies should tool up for mass production of military aircraft!

Thus, it can be easily seen how, a full year before the Japanese bombing of Pearl Harbor, the U.S. government was already preparing for war. This may or may not have been apparent to the man in the street, but it was all too obvious to Lockheed, as they constantly grew and expanded and hired still more workers. Unfortunately, all this activity slowed down the tooling and manufacturing of the Connie prototype.

In Fall 1940 Lockheed considered it necessary, in view of the situation, to notify its customer airlines that the original delivery dates for Constellations would not be met, and that the extent of further delays was virtually impossible to predict. Thus, there began a period which was to stretch from fall 1940 to late 1944, during which the entire Constellation program was in a constant state of confusion and change. This was due primarily to the following four specific circumstances:

1. The termination of all commercial aircraft production.
2. The continuing difficulties experienced by Wright Aeronautical Company in developing and perfecting the R–3350 power plant.
3. The government's various manufacturing priorities that Lockheed had to comply with.
4. The government's seeming difficulty in deciding what part the Constellation should play in the overall war effort.

The specifics of what happened during this difficult period can best be presented in capsule form and chronological order.

Chronology from December 1940 to February 1946

- **December 1940**: War Department informs Lockheed that all commercial aircraft production will probably be shortly terminated.
- **January 1941**: War Department urges Lockheed to increase their P–38 program. It also intimates that the Constellation project is slowing down needed war plane production. Lockheed replies this is simply not the case, but that to cooperate with the government as much as possible, they will indefinitely postpone production of the Constellation, and will engineer and build only three prototypes. This constituted the death knell of the Constellation production at this time.
- **February 1941**: Wright Aeronautical Corporation informs Lockheed that the GR–3350 B-version prototype has failed to produce either the promised power or fuel consumption. Wright indicates it will substitute a newly designed C-version, which is being developed for the Boeing B–29 heavy bomber under development. (This piece of news meant that not only would there be a further delay on engine delivery but also Lockheed would have to engineer a totally new power plant installation.)
- **May 4, 1941**: The Office of Production Management (OPM) notifies Lockheed that they don't object to the construction of three prototypes, but any decision on quantity production is deferred. Furthermore, prototype construction must not interfere with military orders. Of the three prototypes, one is to be a Model 49 and one a Model 349. (The Model 349 is actually a military version of the longer-range Model 149, identical except with a large cargo door and reinforced flooring.)
- **September 13, 1941**: OPM advises Lockheed that 10 additional aircraft may be produced during 1943, but none were to be released to the airlines.
- **October 10, 1941**: OPM countermands directive of September 13, 1941.
- **December 22, 1941**: OPM indicates that production of as many as 80 aircraft may be authorized. However, these will have to meet specifications of U.S. government, TWA, and Pan Am. No delivery to airlines is authorized.
- **February 20, 1942**: Government notifies Lockheed it intends to place a formal contract for 180 Model C–69 (L–49) aircraft.
- **March 30, 1942**: Lockheed notified that government will own all Constellations to be produced. TWA and Pan Am will operate all aircraft for the government. Production to total 260 aircraft broken down as follows:

50 Model 49s and 30 Model 349s on airline contract; 180 C–69s on Army contract.
- **April 30, 1942**: Army indicates it now intends to buy initial 80 aircraft directly.
- **May 20, 1942**: Lockheed schedules first flight of prototype for August 31, 1942.
- **May 20, 1942**: Prototype Model 49 is inspected by Army. Percent of completion of main assemblies is as follows:

    1. Fuselage and wings, 90%
    2. Tail, 60%
    3. Tail controls, 40%
    4. Power plant installation, 5%
    5. Hydraulic system, 50%
    6. Landing gear, 75%

- **May 21, 1942**: Army issues clarification of government identification of Constellation models as follows:

    1. C–69: original civilian order for 50 aircraft (does not include KLM order).
    2. C–69A: additional civilian order of 30 aircraft.
    3. C–69B: Army order for 180 aircraft (Model 349).

- **June 8, 1942**: Lockheed, in a very long and detailed communication to the Army, points out how various government directives have resulted in long delays to Constellation program. This, together with vast financial outlays by Lockheed related to increased military production, means that they can no longer manufacture initial 80 aircraft for original price. Because these 80 airplanes are actually to be built to Army standards and are to be operated only by the airlines for the Army, Lockheed feels it cannot build them unless a new price per airplane is determined. Lockheed suggests distributing research and development costs over all 260 aircraft, with new prices to be:

    50 Model 49s at $408,800 each
    210 Model 349s at $583,600 each

- **June 26, 1942**: Army initiates procurement of first 80 aircraft.
- **July 2, 1942**: Assistant Secretary of War makes final decision that original contract between Lockheed and TWA is to be honored. Remaining 251 aircraft are to be purchased directly by government. TWA and Pan Am both

will have repurchase rights. Contracts for the two airlines, which make up balance of first 80 aircraft, are to be assigned to government.

- **July 14, 1942**: Army issues new production breakdown as follows:

    1. 20 C–69s of 65,000 pounds gross weight
    2. 30 C–69As of 67,000 pounds gross weight and with large cargo door
    3. 210 C–69Bs, Lockheed Model 349s of 86,000 pounds gross weight. This directive drops all Model 149s from the order.

- **August 31, 1942**: Date for first flight of prototype; flight is delayed.
- **September 21, 1942**: First flight of Boeing XB–29 prototype, which is equipped with virtually identical R–3350 type C engines. In the next 26 hours of test flying of the B–29, there were 16 engine changes and 22 carburetor changes.
- **December 8, 1942**: Wright advises Lockheed that it is unsafe to fly either the Constellation or the Ventura Ventellation, both equipped with R–3350s, until certain changes are made.
- **December 30, 1942**: The Number 2 XB–29 makes a successful emergency landing with number four engine on fire and with an uncontrollable runaway propeller.
- **January 8, 1943**: Constellation prototype makes first flight. Six flights on first day are all completed successfully.
- **February 18, 1943**: Number 1 XB–29, with Eddie Allen at the controls, crashes due to engine fire. Eleven on board and 19 on the ground are killed. (This crash constituted a loud warning to everyone that the Wright 3350 was simply not ready for mass production.)
- **February 20, 1943**: The C–69 is grounded by Army pending investigation of R–3350 fires.
- **April 13, 1943**: C–69 is cleared for further flight testing after engine modifications by Wright.
- **May 18, 1943**: Army determines that 210 C–69Bs cannot be produced until early in 1945 due to engine unavailability. The Army now considers having only initial 20 C–69s built and no more. It is believed this would allow increase of P–38 production as well as free up material for production of Douglas C–54A aircraft.
- **June 3, 1943**: Lockheed agrees to build only 3 C–69 airplanes, and not more than 10 C–69's per month through 1944, totaling 80 airplanes.
- **June 16, 1943**: Army states original contract for a total of 260 aircraft is still in force.

- **June 24, 1943**: Army indicates contract to be altered, and 207 C–69B aircraft will now be C–69 model.
- **August 1943**: Army verbally directs Lockheed to stop all C–69 production work and concentrate on the P–38.
- **October 6, 1943**: Army confirms that all Lockheed production personnel assigned to the C–69 project have been temporarily reassigned to P–38 assembly line to increase rate of production.
- **October 14, 1943**: Lockheed confirms verbal agreement of September 18, 1943, to cease all C–69 work except on first two airplanes.
- **December 17, 1943**: Lockheed indicates seriousness of delays caused by problems with the R–3350. Pinpoints problems as (a) high-tension ignition cable failure (which occurred on the B–29 also) and unscrewing cylinder heads during flight. For these reasons, Number 1 Constellation flew only three months in 1943.
- **April 7, 1944**: Army directs Lockheed to cease development of C–69B model and to produce three C–69B airplanes on contract as C–69 airplanes.
- **April 17, 1944**: Number 2 Constellation sets coast-to-coast record.
- **July 12, 1944**: Right main landing gear of number 3 airplane collapses during taxiing. Cause is welding failure. New design using forgings eliminates much welding.
- **August 30, 1944**: Lockheed requests airplane weight increase to improve utility. Recommends 100,000-pound take-off weight, 87,000-pound landing weight, and fuel capacity increase to 5,200 gallons total.
- **September 5, 1944**: Ten crews from Air Transport Command (ATC) assigned TDY on West Coast for C–69 transition training.
- **October 27, 1944**: Army approves 100,000-pound take-off weight starting with number 111 airplane.
- **November 13, 1944**: Crews, now 15 in number, permanently assigned to West Coast to continue C–69 training.
- **December 8, 1944**: Lockheed proposes amending contract so as to total only 101 C–69 airplanes, 10 C–69C (100,000-pound) airplanes, and 9 C–69 airplanes on original TWA contract, for a total of 120 airplanes.
- **December 22, 1944**: Army memo indicates that shifting production personnel to the P–38 line has indeed curtailed C–69 production with only 10 airplanes completed as of this date. No aircraft in excess of 120 airplanes are expected to be built for the Army.
- **January 2, 1945**: Army proposes to limit production to 223 airplanes.

Crews are assigned to newly formed 159th AAF Base Unit, the first C–69 squadron.

- **January 23, 1945**: TWA's Intercontinental Division assigned job of testing and proving C–69 by the Army.
- **February 3, 1945**: 159th AAF Base Unit disbanded and personnel reassigned.
- **February 15, 1945**: Army formally amends contract and reduces total number of C–69s to 73.
- **April 17, 1945**: Lockheed proposes building last 53 airplanes (out of 73) at a fixed price of $706,845 each.
- **August 3, 1945**: Lockheed informed that their P–80 jet fighter now has priority over both the P–38 and the C–69.
- **August 15, 1945**: Army terminates C–69 contract at 14 aircraft.
- **August 20, 1945**: Army questions need for C–69s beyond 14 C–69s accepted to date. Six additional airplanes are nearing completion.
- **August 20, 1945**: Lockheed removes production personnel from six C–69s under construction and assigns them to number 21 airplane, which is to be delivered to commercial airlines.
- **August 23, 1945**: Government reinstates six undelivered airplanes.
- **August 27, 1945**: Army terminates 50 more airplanes from total order.
- **September 19, 1945**: Army indicates intention of retaining 20 C–69s already delivered or about to be.
- **September 20, 1945**: All C–69s are grounded as a result of Constellation accident at Topeka, Kansas.
- **September 26, 1945**: Army recommends termination of 3 C–69D (100,000-pound version) airplanes that are still on contract and are in addition to 20 C–69's.
- **October 11, 1945**: Investigation of Topeka accident results in 28 safety changes by Lockheed on undelivered C–69s.
- **October 19, 1945**: Formal cancellation of 3 C–69D airplanes (100,000-pound version), leaving total of 20 on contract, of which 15 now delivered.
- **November 12, 1945**: Army decides to offer five undelivered C–69s to Lockheed for sale.
- November 23, 1945: Offer to Lockheed for five C–69s made officially.
- **December 26, 1945**: Lockheed makes counteroffer to Army for five-C–69s, provided it is accepted before January 4, 1946.
- **December 27, 1945**: Army terminates remaining five C–69s on contract. (This, in effect, means that they had been sold to Lockheed.)

- **January 21, 1946**: Lockheed indicates that 4 of Army's 15 aircraft have been offered to KLM. (These were later delivered to KLM.)
- **February 1, 1946**: Army decides to retain remaining 11 C–69s and use them within United States. *(Lockheed)*

And so, after more than five years of war-induced confusion, Lockheed could once again look at their Constellation program in terms of peacetime sales. But there is no question that the Lockheed management knew full well that their position in 1946 was not the same as it had been in 1940. The original element of surprise had long since been lost, and now the competition had some idea as to what it would take to catch up with Lockheed.

Throughout this long, difficult, and frustrating period, the future of the Constellation program was being affected in a number of ways. From reading the correspondence between Lockheed and the government, it was obvious that Lockheed management was acutely aware of this fact and was desperately trying to ensure that future success would be the eventual result. The two basic circumstances continually threatening the Constellation program during this period were the extremely serious engine problems on the one hand and the seeming indecisiveness of the government on the other.

As to the former circumstance, by the middle of 1944 the major problems with the R–3350 had been essentially resolved. This can be surmised by noting that the Air Force had by then deployed substantial numbers of R–3350-powered Boeing B–29 heavy bombers halfway around the world to India. From here the B–29s were successfully conducting long-range bombing missions that most certainly could not have been carried out unless the R–3350 engines were functioning with a considerable amount of reliability. The extremely high priority put on the B–29 program obviously had much to do with the R–3350's problems being resolved in relatively short order. But back in early 1943, when the Constellation prototype was grounded because of the engine problems, Lockheed could not have predicted when, if at all, the R–3350 would reach the point where it was a proven, dependable engine. The mere fact that Lockheed themselves on December 9, 1942, had requested permission of the Army to study the feasibility of using Pratt & Whitney R–2800s highlights their acute concern. Switching to the R–2800 would have not only materially reduced performance but in all probability seriously curtailed future development of successive models. So the reader can picture how, for almost two years, Lockheed kept seeing large question marks in the future of their transport.

The other major circumstance, that of the government's indecisiveness in the procurement and utilization of the aircraft was not only more subtle but also potentially more significant in terms of the long-range future. In the first place, the Air Force seemed to feel that the C–69 should carry more payload. But this was not, in any sense, a weakness of the airplane. On the contrary, the original design had managed to emerge with more payload that Hughes had called for. Furthermore, the C–69 had far greater speed and range as well as more sophisticated systems than other military transports of that day. But these very capabilities resulted in a heavier airframe and a somewhat reduced payload than might have otherwise been the case. The Air Force did not seem to realize this rather basic fact.

In a letter dated June 19, 1944, Hall Hibbard compared the C–69 with the Douglas C–54A as follows (information courtesy of Lockheed):

	C–54A			C–69	
Take-Off Weight *(pounds)*	67,100	73,000	82,000	86,250	93,000
Useful Load *(pounds)*	27,952	33,852	31,700	35,950	42,700
% Useful Load	41.5	46.3	38.6	41.6	46.0

Hibbard goes on to note that the 93,000-pound version of the C–69, with virtually the same percent useful load, not only carries some 4.5 tons more but over a 65 percent greater range. Combined with some 50 mph higher speed, cabin pressurization, and a greater ability to climb over the weather, the net result puts the C–69 in a totally different category than the C–54A. But correspondence of the time emanating from various military and government sources indicates no such awareness on the part of the government.

Further complicating the already muddy waters was the recurring change of numbers of aircraft to be built of each model version as well as the total. The priority of the total program also appeared to change almost on a daily basis.

Without a top priority, there was no way Lockheed could begin building the C–69s, either in quantity or with some dispatch. The absence of necessary materials alone, allotted in some cases to the C–54A program, saw to that.

All this changing of direction and priority had the net result that by the war's end only 15 C–69s had been completed and delivered to the Air Force. Of these, only 11 actually saw service.

This in turn meant two things. First, Lockheed was unable to supply the Air Force with a large fleet of transports, which, if continued in service, would have also meant a tidy spare parts business. Second, if such a fleet had been declared surplus after the war, either wholly or in part, then Lockheed could have converted and resold them to the airlines in a relatively short time.

"What-ifs" are essentially a meaningless exercise. But this writer believes that it can be said, with a fair degree of confidence, that if the government had placed a higher priority on the C–69 program, then Lockheed would in all likelihood have had considerably larger total sales of their L–049 models in 1946–47.

The Air Force's effort to organize a C–69 operational unit is an excellent example of the vacillating priorities that existed during this period. A rather bizarre effort by the Air Force to form the first C–69 operational unit occurred in late summer of 1944. The Air Force rather suddenly decided that it would be highly advantageous to quickly organize Air Transport Command (ATC) units to operate the C–69 transport. By this time the invasion of France was moving more quickly than had been expected, and many military men felt that the end of the war in Europe was already in sight. But the Pacific was another story. With the Japanese still seemingly strong, the speed and range of the C–69 were particularly attractive features over the long reaches of the Pacific.

As part of this overall effort to organize and train an initial C–69 unit, Lockheed was advised that C–69 deliveries must henceforth be expedited and should eventually reach 10 airplanes per month. Considering the size and complexity of the aircraft, as well as the fact that Lockheed was involved in producing four other military aircraft (P–38s, B–17s, PV search planes, and the new P–80), this was a very tall order. In addition, some 1100 men were assigned as part of the cadre of personnel to train and support the transitioning Air Force crews.

In early September 1944, the Air Transport Command of the Air Force chose 10 five-man crews, two each from five ferrying bases, and sent them to Long Beach, California, and thence to Burbank to begin C–69 transitioning, at this time consisting of ground school.

Co-pilot on one of the crews from the 588th Base Unit at Presque Isle, Maine, was First Lieutenant Manley Holt. Holt, now a retired Pan Am 747 captain, still remembers those days with an Alice-in-Wonderland kind of view. Holt had been a C–54 driver operating out of Presque Isle. The crews picked went to Burbank in September 1944 for 30-day TDY spent in C–69 ground school. They returned to Presque Isle, and 48 hours later were airborne again for Burbank. The second 30-day TDY was to have been for the purpose of starting the actual transitioning into the C–69, but no aircraft were available, and the entire month was wasted.

During the month of October, while the student crews sat around, the first C–69 destined for the program was being flight-tested by Lockheed pilots. Various problems continually arose to delay its use by the waiting crews. First it was engine trouble, the same trouble plaguing the B–29 program, which was eventually traced to the ignition system. Then it was vibration in the nose wheel steering, which necessitated steering the big plane by means of brakes and engines. The net result of all this was that the crews returned to their respective home bases without ever having flown a single hour in the C–69.

In November the various crews were once again ordered to Burbank, this time on a permanent basis. All personnel were assigned to the 556th AAF Base Unit, 6th Ferrying Group, Ferrying Division, ATC, based in Long Beach, California.

Starting in the middle of November, a total of 15 crews finally began boring holes in the skies over southern California with the new C–69. An oddity in the make-up of these crews was the presence of second lieutenants functioning as flight engineers, believed to be the only such instance either in ATC or MATS (Military Air Transport Service). At the beginning of January 1945, the crews were transferred once again, but this time only on paper. The new orders made them a part of the newly constituted 1597th AAF Base Unit, 3rd Foreign Transport Group, Ferrying Division, ATC, based at Long Beach but operating from Burbank. This unit was known as the Joint Service Test of C–69.

Unfortunately, the new C–69 unit did not last very long, for on January 24, 1945, all personnel were recalled to Long Beach for reassignment. On February 3 the crews were reassigned to other bases. This marked the formal termination of the short-lived effort to phase the C–69 into regular Air Force use.

Holt recalls that in the space of the five months that this effort was going on he actually flew the C–69 less than 100 hours. Obviously, the number of aircraft needed to train this unit was simply not available.

Ironically, the biggest factor against the C–69 program was Lockheed's own P–38! Kelly Johnson and his boys had indeed designed too well! To add to the irony, some years later, the military would become by far the largest single customer of certain versions of the Constellation.

But now it was 1946, and Lockheed was anxious and eager to see what the dream of Hughes and Fry, Hibbard and Johnson could do in an unrestricted business environment.

4-1 View of the cockpit of a USAAF C–69, August 1944. Pilot and co-pilot instrument panels are identical. Center panel displays engine instruments. Center pedestal holds throttles in center, elevator trim wheels at edges, rudder trim in forefront of pedestal. Flight engineer's panel is partly seen at right. (Lockheed Martin)

4-2 The rather spartan interior of a USAAF C–69, typical of military transports, February 1945. (Lockheed Martin)

4-3 The Lockheed B–6 assembly building, with C–69 Constellations moving down the assembly line, May 1944. (Lockheed Martin)

4-4 The original Curtiss-Wright 3350 engines being worked on, October 1945. (Lockheed Martin)

4-5 The first C–69 to enter USAAF service with the Air Transport Command in November 1944. These crews were probably TWA Inter-Continental Division personnel wearing USAAF uniforms. (Lockheed Martin)

4-6 An overhead view of one of the first C–69's to be delivered to the USAAF, August 1945. Note the glass dome on the front upper part of the fuselage for use by navigators taking star sights. (Lockheed Martin)

4-7 "Leading Particulars" (Lockheed Martin)

Chapter 5

THE CONSTELLATION SPREADS ITS WINGS

By early 1945, it had become obvious to many in this country that World War II was fast approaching an end. In Europe, Hitler's Wermacht was becoming increasingly demoralized as it was relentlessly crushed between the Soviet juggernaut on the east and the combined Allied might on the West. In fact, the end was only weeks away. In the Pacific, Japan was still holding out tenaciously, despite the immense damage and havoc created by the B–29 bomber fleet. However, many military leaders still hoped to bring that country to its knees without the necessity of a bloody invasion of the Japanese home islands.

The gradual winding down of the war was evidenced by the reduction in the size of the orders for airplanes and the subsequent decrease in employment. Lockheed had already begun to feel this in 1944. Employment there was at an all-time high of 94,000 in 1943, but was down to 60,000 by December 1944. In April 1945 it was only 45,000 and by August 1945 had shrunk to 35,000. The Army order for the C–69 had also been gradually reduced from 210, first to 113, and finally to eleven (see Chapter 4).

With this reduction in government work, Lockheed could once again seriously think about peacetime production. Actually, they probably never stopped thinking about what lay ahead after the war, and this is easily seen in the fact that starting back in August 1944 Lockheed regularly advertised the virtues of the

Constellation in four-color multipage ads in *Aviation Week*, the aviation industry's most widely read publication.

The scheduled airlines were also seriously giving thought to postwar passenger services and to what their individual equipment needs would be. But some of the airlines were thinking about more than the domestic services that they had offered prior to World War II. The Air Force's use of long-range aircraft such as the Douglas C–54 and the Lockheed C–69 had opened their eyes to the possibilities for long nonstop flights. This in turn had directed the attention of some airlines to the business opportunities available in flying overseas. This thinking resulted in some interesting events during 1944–45.

Just prior to the breaking out of World War II, both Pan Am and British Overseas Airline Company (BOAC) had begun transatlantic service using the large Boeing Clippers. But this had brought no more than a mere trickle of traffic. Now two other U.S. companies decided to move in on what appeared to them could be a lucrative postwar field. In June 1943 TWA filed an application with the Civil Aeronautics Board (CAB) to permit it to fly around the world, serving Europe, North Africa, the Middle East, India, China, Japan, Alaska, and the West Coast. Here indeed was an ambitious scheme for an airline that had previously flown only domestically.

Actually, a particular circumstance brought about by the war made such a move not at all surprising, as we shall shortly see. On July 5, 1945, the CAB granted TWA the right to fly its intended route eastward as far as India. Another entry in this overseas competition was that of American Export Airlines, later to become American Overseas Airlines (AOA) when it was taken over by American Airlines. AOA had also received CAB authority to fly overseas, in their case to Scandinavia, Germany, and the British Isles.

The various airlines that felt they would have need for a long-range high-speed aircraft were in most cases already highly impressed with the Constellation on the basis of a number of record-breaking proving runs that took place in 1944–45. Prior to these, the airline industry had been aware of the engine problems that hounded the Constellation in 1943 and early 1944. But the word had gone around that the Boeing B–29 had finally managed to achieve trouble-free flight using the same power plant, and this together with the problem solving done by Lockheed itself, as well as Wright, of course, reassured airline managements.

In April 1944 the Army elected to have their first C–69 delivered to TWA. Readers must remember that TWA and Pan Am had been previously selected by the Army as the two organizations that were to first prove the C–69 in actual military use and then operate the growing fleet both domestically and overseas on military airlift missions. At this point Howard Hughes, from whom precious little had been heard regarding the Constellation during the difficult days of 1942 and 1943, stepped back into the picture. He requested of the government that this first C–69 be permitted to make its delivery flight painted in TWA colors, and further, that he and Jack Frye of TWA be at the controls. This permission was given, and the rather strange combination was set up.

In preparation for the flight, both Hughes and Frye spent a few days in the middle of April at Lockheed's Burbank facility flying the C–69. Frye made two flights totaling 3.4 hours, and Hughes also made two flights, totaling only 2.9 hours. On Sunday, April 16, 1944, Hughes and Frye felt that weather conditions across the United States were such as to favor a record attempt. Accordingly, the big C–69 was fueled up and prepared. Departure was scheduled for the early morning hours. There would be 12 passengers and a total of 7 crew members, with Hughes and Frye each flying half the trip in the left seat.

At 3:56 A.M. Pacific time on April 17, Hughes gunned the four big Wright engines and sent the C–69 rolling down the runway at Burbank and into the air. Cruising at 15,000 feet, their course took them over New Mexico, Kansas, Missouri, Ohio, and on into Washington. Over Kansas the altitude was increased to 18,500 feet due to light icing conditions. Six hours, 58 minutes after leaving Burbank, they were on the ground at Washington National Airport, having achieved an average speed of over 340 mph! Their time broke the existing record, set by a TWA Boeing 307 Stratoliner in July 1940, by an astonishing 5 hours! The speed potential of the Connie had been proven beyond all doubt!

At this point a word of explanation is probably in order. As the reader progresses thru these pages, it will become obvious that the Constellation design became progressively heavier and able to carry bigger loads further. However, one operating parameter remained basically the same. And that was the cruising speed. The speed of any airplane is based on a number of factors, and is not a constant, but rather falls within a relatively narrow range.
The airspeed is a function of:

1. The aerodynamics of the aircraft structure; that is, the wings and fuselage.
2. The power of the engines.
3. The amount of load it is carrying.
4. The altitude at which it is operating.
5. The outside air temperature at that altitude.

Thus, the reader can easily see how these variables will affect the actual True Air Speed (TAS) of any aircraft on any particular flight. Furthermore, on long flights, where a large percent of the gross weight of the aircraft is made up by fuel, the total aircraft weight diminishes greatly as fuel is burned off, with a resulting increase in speed without the addition of any power. The Constellations and Super Constellations, except for their last variant, the L–1649A, all had the same wing. This alone pretty much determined the speed range for the whole family of airplanes.

Basically, the Connies and Super Connies cruised at True Air Speeds between 275 and 340 mph, or 240–295 knots, TAS. Ground Speed (GS) depends on the direction and speed of winds at the particular cruising altitude. In addition the reader should keep in mind that the range of the aircraft is dependent not only on fuel load and fuel consumption, but also on the weight of the aircraft at take-off.

Additionally commercial airlines try hard to keep aircraft operating and maintenance costs down. This is achieved in part by flying at what is commonly referred to as "long-range power settings" which result in lower cruising speeds.

The question is also often asked as to the service ceiling of the various Constellations and Super Constellations. All these aircraft had a service ceiling of 24,000 feet imposed on propeller-driven reciprocating-engined aircraft of that period. This ceiling was a function of both the power of the engines as well as the amount of pressurization within the cabin. However, a lightly-loaded Connie or Super Connie could climb higher. Capt. Schnaubelt of TWA clearly remembers taking an empty Connie on a ferry flight to above 30,000 feet! But in regular service, 24,000 feet was the legal limit.

Other record flights followed. In August 1944, a C–69 flew from New York to Paris non-stop in only 14 hours, 12 minutes. These flights, together with the service reliability being achieved by the Air Force in the use of the few C–69s they had received, went a long way toward convincing airline executives that the Constellation was the aircraft needed for postwar service where range and speed were important. There was one fly in the ointment during this period of 1944–45. On September 18, 1945, a C–69 made a safe emergency belly landing in Topeka, Kansas, after an uncontrollable fire in number one engine caused the entire engine to drop off. No specific cause was found at this time, and the incident did not appear to have an adverse effect on airline customers. No one was injured in the landing, and the cause—overheating of the supercharger drive shaft—was not determined until nine months later, when a similar event took place.

The various long-range record flights achieved by Constellations during 1944–45 had a definite impact on the immediate future of the aircraft. Airline executives began to make their postwar plans on the basis of this one aircraft and its performance. Although interest was shown by both long-haul and short-haul airlines, those companies operating or planning transoceanic and transcontinental routes were the ones who felt they just had to obtain this aircraft. The three original customers, TWA, Pan Am, and KLM, were all operators of very long routes. This in turn led airlines with competing route structures to want to jump on the bandwagon and procure Constellations also, which would then enable them to compete.

Actually, Lockheed had foreseen the forthcoming enthusiasm for their airplane and, furthermore, knew that even before it was ever put into commercial use they must look ahead to more advanced models. In this they were spurred on by the knowledge that just across town Douglas was already hard at work on a virtual redesign of the DC–4 to be known as the DC–6. Up in Seattle, Boeing had already unveiled a military transport known as the C–97. With the wings, engines, and tail of the B–29 but a completely new fuselage design, the C–97 set a Seattle–Washington, D.C., record in January 1945 by flying the distance non-stop in 6 hours, 3 minutes, 50 seconds at an average speed of 383 mph. True, the C–97 may have had the advantage of stronger tailwinds than were available to Hughes and Frye a few months earlier. Nevertheless, it was an impressive performance that put Lockheed on notice.

So it was that in May 1945 Lockheed began designing a new version of the Constellation known as the L–649, which was to be powered by the first truly commercial version of the R–3350 engine just then being developed by Wright. Note that this new model design began before even one L–049 had been built or delivered to the airlines. In addition, Lockheed had already come to the conclusion that at the end of the war the Air Force might more than likely make available for repurchase and resale the relatively few C–69s they had received. So that such military versions would be usable by airlines, Lockheed engineered a conversion of the C–69 to L–049 standards that was known as the L–149.

This interest shown in mid-1945 by various airlines came not a moment too soon. In early August the Japanese empire surrendered, still reeling from the double disasters wrought by two atomic bombs, and World War II came to a sudden end. The military production that had caused Lockheed to grow ceased virtually overnight as the government canceled almost all its contracts. Bob Gross shut down all of Lockheed's many buildings and immediately entered into discussions of the future with his chief executives. Out of these meetings came the courageous decision to keep Lockheed going with the orders on hand and to try and carry forward in the uncertain economy ahead. It was their view that with a shorter work week and only a few layoffs, the company would have enough work to keep it going. After only a five-day shutdown, Lockheed reopened its doors, to the vast relief of its employees and the local community.

At that time, in mid-August 1945, Bob Gross made a dramatic announcement in which he revealed that Lockheed had already received orders for 103 Constellations! Worth some $75.5 million, the backlog was the largest ever experienced by any manufacturer in the commercial airplane market up to that time. It permitted Lockheed to retain a sizable percentage of its employees, and in fact, was the one production line that kept the company from shutting down entirely for at least a few months.

The 103 aircraft on order actually consisted of three distinct models. Sixty-six were new L–049 models yet to be built, although some of these were already in the production pipeline having been originated as Air Force C–69s. Another 18 were actually Air Force C–69s, which were repurchased and converted by Lockheed. Because these were all low-time aircraft, the customers receiving these particular aircraft were in effect obtaining like-new Constellations at a somewhat reduced price. Another 14 aircraft were an advanced model, the L–649, on which design work had been started in May 1945. Finally, the last five were ones for which the airlines had not fully decided what model they wanted.

Readers should keep in mind when reading about aircraft orders that some of them were changed and others were canceled. Thus, the original orders do not coincide fully with the actual aircraft delivered. The table in the back of this book gives a full list of Constellation deliveries.

Lockheed was able to approach this huge production order with a justifiable measure of confidence. Their design ability stretched back in time from the very origins of the company. Their workforce was skilled and experienced, especially after the trial and tribulations of World War II, and Bob Gross had an excellent team composed of:

- Courtland S. Gross, vice president and general manager (Bob Gross's younger brother)
- Cyril Chapnellet, vice president/administration
- Hall Hibbard, vice president and chief engineer
- Carl Squier, vice president/sales and service
- Charles Barker, vice president and treasurer
- Kelly Johnson, chief of research and development

In August 1945, as World War II came to its dramatic close, Lockheed emerged from its wartime era as one of the largest manufacturers of airplanes in this country. A full 6 percent of all wartime aircraft production had been by

Lockheed, and even this was misleading because many of the aircraft were multi-engined. Its production score at that time read:

2600 Ventura patrol bombers
2700 B–17 Flying Fortresses (built under license from Boeing)
2900 Hudson medium bombers (1298 for the Royal Air Force)
<u>9000 P–38 fighters</u>

17,200 Total aircraft built
(Lockheed)

All of this meant that Lockheed could look forward to peacetime work with at least two things going for it. First, it had successfully grown as an airplane manufacturer and was now in the position of being able to build large and complex airplanes in quantity. This could not truly have been said back in 1938–39. Second, their top management team was of such caliber and experience that investors could believe in their ability to sell airplanes and then fill the orders on time and at the estimated cost. These capabilities put the company in an excellent competitive position versus other aircraft manufacturers. At this time Lockheed had stabilized its work force at 32,000 employees, many of which were to work on continuing military contracts rather than on the Constellation line.

It is interesting to note that by early October 1945, Lockheed's firm orders for Constellations now stood at only 86, broken down as follows (courtesy of Lockheed):

- TWA, 36 planes
- Pan Am, 21 planes
- Pan Am-Grace, 2 planes
- AOA, 7 planes
- Eastern, 20 planes

All orders were for the L–049 model, with the exception of Eastern, who had ordered the L–649 model for later delivery.

In fall 1945, as the airlines were working and planning for peacetime service, certain other significant events took place. On September 3, the State Department officially restricted travel across the North Atlantic. There were, no doubt, many reasons for this order. For one thing, all westbound ship crossings, as well as ATC flights, were completely filled with returning servicemen. There was also considerable official travel of U.S. citizens, as well as others, going to Europe on missions relating to bringing order out of the chaos that was Europe after World War

II. Thus, the airlines intending to fly the North Atlantic did not really feel great compulsion to rush into a market that was so small.

Another important event took place in December when Pan Am reduced their one-way fare from New York to London from $572 to $275, with the round trip becoming $495. Although the reduction was certainly great, in terms of 1945–46 dollars, this was still a fare only a few could afford and in fact was equal to first class fare on a ship.

Lest the reader be misled, regular commercial airline service across the North Atlantic started a number of months before the Constellations entered service. On September 3, 1945, both Pan Am and AOA started commercial flights to Europe using Douglas DC–4 Skymasters, many still equipped with military ATC interiors. At the end of November, AOA inaugurated Chicago–London flights by way of Gander and Shannon with a flight time of 27 hours. Also started at that time were Washington–Philadelphia–London flights by AOA and Washington–London flights by Pan Am. Thus, readers can see that Pan Am and AOA wasted no time getting into the middle of the battle for superiority in this yet-to-be-proven market. TWA, on the other hand, elected to delay starting until they could do so with their shining hope, the Lockheed Constellation.

It should also be noted that at this time there was great confusion in the matter of fares. Thus, although Pan Am was charging only $275 one-way for New York–London, AOA was still asking $572, and BOAC, who had started postwar service with their venerable Boeing B–314 flying boats, was charging a whopping $647 one-way. Luckily for everyone involved, sanity shortly entered the arena, and all nations flying internationally agreed to abide by the fare structure established by the International Air Transport Association (IATA). The IATA represented 24 nations and 44 airlines, and the fares established were on the basis of common international agreements.

So it was in this mixed atmosphere of hope and anxiety, plans and confusion, that the Lockheed Constellation was to enter commercial airline service in early 1946.

December 1945 saw the certification of the L–049 by the CAA. This was accomplished after only 27 hours of flight tests. It is likely that the CAA's effort was expedited by the fact that the almost identical C–69 of the Air Force had been flying successfully on long flights since 1944. The flight hours amassed by the Army in effect served in part as a proving ground for the commercial L–049.

December also saw the delivery of the last of the first nine aircraft to come off the assembly line, all to TWA. The reason why TWA was the only airline to receive aircraft during November and December dates back to the original contract between Howard Hughes and Lockheed. Dated July 10, 1939, that contract stipulated that TWA would buy the first nine airplanes produced, regardless of who else ordered the Constellation. Six years later, Lockheed was finally able to honor that stipulation.

TWA had received the first of the nine aircraft back on November 15, 1945. Although there was a certain amount of fanfare and excitement at Kansas City, where formal delivery took place, TWA had actually been flying Army C–69s for almost a year, since February 15, 1945. All of these aircraft now being delivered were brand-new L–049 models, and TWA lost no time starting crew training, with an eye to introducing their fast, attractive airplanes as soon as possible.

TWA's activity as part of the Air Transport Command dated back to December 1941, shortly after the bombing of Pearl Harbor. At that time TWA created their Inter-continental Division (ICD) through a government contract. Operating as an integral part of ATC, the ICD trained aircrews and later also operated aircraft overseas. They operated the Boeing B–307 Stratoliners, formerly used domestically by TWA, C–54s, C–87s, and eventually C–69s. The ICD had been given the job of testing and proving the C–69 on January 23, 1945, and their first C–69 was delivered on February 15, 1945.

It should be remembered that Pan Am and American Export Airline (later AOA, a division of American Airlines), also were performing similar overseas functions as part of ATC. Pan Am was to also fly C–69s during 1945.

The operations carried out by the essentially civilian components of ATC during World War II actually proved absolutely invaluable in the establishment of safe, reliable air transportation across the North Atlantic. The many thousands of flights across this body of water enabled substantial advances to be made in weather forecasting, flying techniques in weather penetration, celestial and radio navigation, long-range fuel management, pressure pattern flying (which took advantage of tailwinds), and bad-weather approaches to airports. It appears safe to say that without these five years of flying across the Atlantic, the introduction of large-scale passenger flights might not have been possible during 1945–46.

Pilots transitioning to the Constellation in 1945–46 found themselves waxing enthusiastic about the airplane. And well they might, for here was a larger, faster, more reliable aircraft with a greater payload and range, yet easier to handle.

The Constellation cockpit was another area that received high marks from the pilots. This part of the design had received much attention by the Lockheed design staff. True, it was relatively narrow, but on the other hand, crew members could reach any control or switch with ease. The visibility through the multifaceted windshield was good. The cockpit instrument lighting was a vast improvement over the DC–3 and made night instrument flying far less of a strain. The hydraulic control boost system, once the pilots became accustomed to it, provided a high degree of control while requiring little physical input. Much appreciated also were the full-feathering, reversible-pitch propellers, the first to be licensed on a commercial transport. Associated with the propellers was a propeller reversing system operated through the throttles with a mechanical linkage designed so that it was impossible to reverse the propellers inadvertently. Pilots discovered, to their great delight, how much this feature contributed to the short landing distance required by the Constellation.

In actual fact, the design and performance of the L–049 was advanced over other contemporary transports by the same order of magnitude that the Boeing 707 jet transport was advanced over contemporary reciprocating and turboprop airplanes in 1959. So it is little wonder that pilots were eager to fly the Constellation; once proficient in its operation, they found it a real pleasure.

These initial deliveries of commercial Constellations had a gross weight of 96,000 pounds, thanks to the work done previously by Lockheed, in part at the constant instigation of the government. However, it should be remembered that all L–049 aircraft showed their history during World War II as concerned their interiors. The C–69s were, naturally, austere and grim-looking aircraft inside, as were virtually all World War II transports. Even though Lockheed attempted to bring forth an aircraft that would be attractive to passengers of the 1946–47 era, they did not have much time to spend in interior design work. Compounding the problem was the fact that manufacturers of cabin interiors and seats in 1945 were turning out products almost identical to that found in 1939–40. Anyone who bought a new car of 1946–47 vintage was acutely aware that almost nothing had changed from six years prior.

The orders for Constellations that were on Lockheed's books in fall 1945 were almost exclusively for airlines with long-haul routes. This is hardly surprising considering that the Constellation was the longest-range aircraft in production at that time. This circumstance turned out to be a double-edged sword for Lockheed. On one hand, it firmly established the Constellation as the leader on long-haul routes. But the huge backlog of orders at this time gave Douglas a golden opportunity to sell its new DC–6, sight unseen, to domestic operators of medium-length routes. Douglas seized a majority of this market and never relinquished it thereafter during the era of the DC–6/DC–7.

In January 1946, Pan Am began to receive its deliveries, with the first Constellation being delivered on January 5. A total of three aircraft were delivered in January and another four in February. Pan Am was able to match TWA's entry with the Constellation despite its later deliveries because of its ATC contracts that permitted at least some of its crews to have prior experience in flying the type.

February 1946 was the moment of truth for TWA, for Pan Am, and for the Constellation. Six and a half years after inception of the Constellation concept, and some five full years after the date that Hughes thought he would introduce the L–049 into service, the time had finally come for the Constellation to spread its wings and begin doing the job it had been originally conceived and designed to do.

Pan Am and TWA had certain distinct advantages over any other carriers when it came to starting regular transatlantic passenger service. Not only were both airlines the first to receive delivery of the L–049 models, but both had been flying the military version, the C–69, across the Atlantic for some time. This, of course, was part of the civilian effort of the ATC. However, both airlines had to do much work to begin their respective services in early February 1946. Facilities in Europe were almost non-existent with the countries there still struggling to recover from the war.

Although there was a considerable amount of publicity and press coverage associated with the new service and with TWA's transcontinental Constellation flights, a review of what was printed back then reveals a surprising lack of genuine excitement. There appear to be two major reasons for this. The first is that the United States was beset by many difficult and disturbing problems, including a sluggish economy and a series of major strikes. Added to this was the overwhelming fact that the American people in this period were waking up to the fact that a wrecked and starving world was looking to them for leadership and assistance. The other factor to be remembered is that both carriers were initially flying only a few trips a week. This decision was really not theirs, because not enough Constellations had been delivered for more than token service. But both airlines also knew that they would not be besieged by passengers at this early date. For one thing, the State Department was allowing only a few individuals to fly to Europe, and these usually were on government business. The fares being charged were so high as to discourage all but the relatively well-to-do. As far as tourists were concerned, Europe was simply not ready to deal with them and would not be for quite some time. So the reader must try to visualize things as they were in early 1946 and understand that this new service, though in no way an experiment from the operational or flying point of view, was a step that only a very few people would or could take at this time.

Ironically, the honor of operating the very first scheduled passenger flight in regular service fell not to TWA, which had helped pioneer the Constellation design, but to Pan Am.

On January 14, 1946 a Pan Am L–049 departed New York to begin a daily New York–Bermuda service. Although possibly not quite as dramatic as a transoceanic service, the fact was that at last here was the Constellation, finally in regular service some five years later than anyone had originally expected.

Then, in the three weeks following, a number of highly publicized survey and preview flights took place that carried aboard members of the press and officials of the airlines involved. Actually, the first of these flights had taken place back on December 3, 1945, when a TWA Constellation flew Washington, D.C.–Paris with fuel stops at Gander and Shannon, in 14 hours, 48 minutes. On January 20, Pan Am made a survey flight from New York to Lisbon in 9 hours, 58 minutes. Compared to the 24 hours required by one of the Pan Am Boeing B–314 flying boats, or the 19 hours needed by the DC–4, the flight was, to say the least, an eye opener!

On February 1, TWA flew an L–049 New York to Los Angeles in 10 hours, 49 minutes, including a brief fuel stop at Kansas City. Carrying 32 passengers and a crew of 10 and bucking 40–60 mph headwinds, the flight established a new east–west record, breaking the record set almost six years previously by a TWA Boeing B–307 Stratoliner of 11 hours, 55 minutes. The next day the same plane flew San Francisco–Los Angeles in 1 hour, 14 minutes with a total of 56 people aboard. Both flying time and passenger load constituted new records. On February 3 the same aircraft again set records. With Jack Frye in command, it flew from Los Angeles to New York in only 7 hours, 27 minutes nonstop, with a total of 56 passengers aboard. Again, both were new records. This flight time was almost 4.5 hours less than the record set by TWA in July 1940.

Thus, by February 1946 both TWA and Pan Am were operating the Constellations regularly, and passengers could take them across the United States, to Bermuda, and across the North Atlantic to London and Paris.

In those days of early commercial flights across the Atlantic, the initial flights were treated by the *New York Times* newspaper, for one, the same as trans-Atlantic sailings of the major passenger liners. Departures and arrivals were listed each day, which was not difficult to do since there were so few each day. This was a far cry from today, when overseas flights into New York can run into the hundreds. (See Figure 5-7.)

On February 3, 1946, Pan Am began the first regular transatlantic Constellation service with a flight from New York to Bournemouth, England, the temporary terminus until London Airport was finished. Flown in 12 hours, 9 minutes, the flight set records for the New York–Gander and Gander–Shannon legs. Two days later it was TWA's turn. Their flight was Washington–New

York–Gander–Shannon–Paris. Carrying 36 passengers and 8 crew members, the flight took only 16 hours, 21 minutes. On February 15 TWA started its transcontinental Constellation service, flying Los Angeles–New York.

So at last the Constellations were truly in service, even if on a modest basis. As more aircraft were added to TWA's and Pan Am's fleets, additional services were introduced. In addition, a third airline began to receive delivery of the L–049. This was American Overseas Airlines, the transoceanic division of American Airlines, which had ordered seven Constellations.

At the end of May 1946 Lockheed delivered their first Model 149 conversion of the Air Force C–69 aircraft, which had been repurchased by Lockheed. These conversions were to go to various airlines, some directly and some indirectly by way of aircraft brokers. The airlines that began using these conversions were BOAC, El Al, and TWA, with the very first Constellation built going back to Lockheed to be used as a prototype for future developments.

By July, Lockheed was rolling out the last of their new L–049s. The last batches went to KLM, Air France, LAV, and TWA, with TWA receiving the very last one manufactured. At this point the Lockheed assembly line began working on the 20 L–649 models for Eastern. But July also brought a major crisis in the life of the Constellation.

Almost from the beginning of its flying career, the Connie had been the victim in a number of accidents, both major and minor. However, except for some initial engine problems as experienced by the C–69, no pattern of major weakness had been found in the airplane. This was all changed on July 11, 1946. A TWA training flight had just taken off from Reading, Pennsylvania, for some crew training. Shortly after take-off, the smell of burning insulation was noticed, followed shortly thereafter by smoke entering the cockpit from the lower cargo compartment, although at the time it was thought to come from the main cabin. The crew immediately took action to return to the airport. As the smoke became thicker, a side window was opened in an attempt to keep forward visibility from being completely obscured. The cabin fire extinguisher was activated, but to no avail. Visibility by now had become zero, and the crew could hardly breathe. The pilot in command elected to attempt a blind landing, which took place on a farm. The aircraft was demolished by the landing, and further destroyed by the fire. Of a total of six crew members aboard, only the pilot in command survived.

The reverberations of this accident were massive and very quick. The CAA, using the power given it by its enabling legislation, immediately grounded all Constellations. The event was naturally bad news for the airlines involved, although they all had considerable numbers of DC–4s that could be substituted on the schedules. But for Lockheed, who had pinned their hopes for postwar production on this one aircraft, it was tantamount to a major earthquake. However, Bob Gross was determined to use all the facilities at hand to try and unravel the problem. In this he and Lockheed were greatly helped by the investigation carried out by the Civil Aeronautics Authority.

The results of all this work were multifaceted. First, it was discovered that the fire had been the result of electrical arcing that took place at the wing root. It was caused by a combination of events. To bring electrical power from the generators, near the engines, to the cabin, a type of insulated bolt is used known as a through-stud. These must be well insulated to carry the electricity through the skin of the pressurized fuselage. The through-studs were proven to be improperly insulated, with the result that they arced and created very high temperatures in a short period of time. It was also found that adjacent to the location of these insulators, glass wool insulation lining the fuselage had become impregnated with leaking hydraulic fluid from lines passing in the vicinity. The combination of high temperatures with the hydraulic fluid resulted in fire and smoke.

As a direct result of these and other findings, all Constellations underwent a number of modifications, some of which were not actually considered mandatory. The through-studs were completely redesigned, and the insulation of certain wiring was modified so that it would not chafe. Copper cables replaced aluminum conductors in the generators, and steps were taken to prevent short-circuiting in circuit breakers, fuses, and control switches. The power plants also underwent some safety modifications.

Fire extinguishers were provided for the accessory section of the nacelles, and more total extinguishing power was supplied to the whole system. Lines carrying hydraulic fluid were made more fire resistant as well as less likely to leak because of rubbing against other adjacent metal parts. A long-range program was initiated to develop a hydraulic fluid that would be less flammable. At the same time, all aircraft were equipped with direct fuel injection instead of carburetors, which resulted in better control of fuel flow and fuel savings. Finally, actual tests showed that the best way to keep smoke from the cockpit was to open a door or hatch further back in the fuselage, thus setting up an air current that would draw any and all smoke away from the flight crew.

The Constellations that started flying after this grounding were considerably better aircraft, because the modifications made were not only the ones necessary to resolve the problems brought to light by the Reading crash but also a number that made the plane not only safer but also reduced maintenance and potential equipment failures. The CAA required a 50-hour accelerated service test before it permitted the Constellation to return to regular service. Finally, on August 24, 1946, the first Constellation returned to service, some six weeks after the accident. In the case of TWA, their first L–049 did not take to the air again until September 20, this across the North Atlantic, and service in the United States was resumed on October 2.

The grounding had affected a total of 58 Constellations, had cost Lockheed and the airlines considerable amounts of money, and generally caused much consternation in the aviation field. However, no airlines with Constellations on order changed their minds, and even passengers seemed to feel for the most part that the problems had indeed been solved. It was to be the first and last time in the history of the Constellations that a problem of this magnitude went unnoticed until a crash brought it to light. It was also true that it took a combination of both faulty through-studs and a nearby leak in a hydraulic line to cause the problem. As later crashes in the years to follow showed beyond a shadow of a doubt, this was the old snowball phenomenon, wherein one event leads to a second event and so forth, eventually causing a crash. Except in cases of sabotage or midair collisions, few commercial aircraft crashes are caused by only a single circumstance.

After returning to service, the Constellations flew smoothly and trouble-free. But, unfortunately, the same could not be said for the airlines. As 1946 became 1947, it was obvious that the hoped-for masses of people clamoring to fly across the United States and over the North Atlantic were simply not materializing. But this was certainly not the fault of the Constellation. Airlines flying the airplane noted many happy passengers and generally high load factors.

Approximately one year after entering service, there were a total of 67 Constellations delivered to 7 airlines. Including the Army's C–69s, these had amassed a total of over 63,000 flying hours and produced some 600 million passenger miles. The fatality rate was a low 1.66 passenger fatalities for every 100 million passenger miles. So the first year of the Constellation drew to a close. There had been many noteworthy records set and some setbacks, but there was no doubt in anyone's mind that the Constellation was now a very real part of commercial aviation—one that its competitors would have to view with respect.

5-1 The first C–69 delivered to the USAAF makes a night take-off from Burbank with Howard Hughes and Jack Frye at the controls, April 17, 1944. The flight to Washington, D.C., took a record-breaking 6 hours and 58 minutes. Note the TWA markings authorized by the War Department. (Lockheed Martin)

5-2 A view of the Lockheed ramp at Burbank, with 5 USAAF C–69 Connies awaiting delivery, March 1945. (Lockheed Martin)

5-3 R. E. Gross, President of Lockheed Aircraft Corp., (left) and Jack Frye, President of TWA, sign contract for purchase of additional Constellations for TWA, August 1945. (Lockheed Martin)

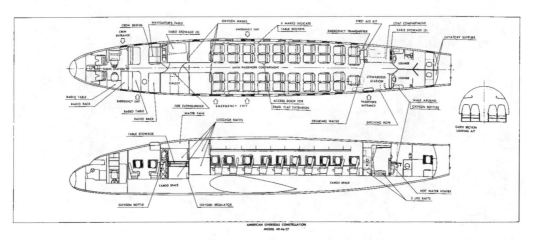

5-4 A schematic of the Model L–049 Constellation as configured for American Overseas Airlines, a division of American Airlines. (Lockheed Martin)

5-5 Interior view of a typical L–049, 1946. (Lockheed Martin)

5-6 A Pan Am Clipper, L–049 Connie, 1946. (Lockheed Martin)

Marine and Aviation Reports

Transport and other shipping schedules still are subject to changes and frequently are incomplete. Dates are considered tentative. All arrival and departure times given are Daylight Saving.

SHIPS

NEW YORK

ARRIVED YESTERDAY

Sea Ray, Elizabeth Blackwell, Argentina, Peter de Smet, Stephen Johnson Field, Cinch Knot, Waltham Victory, passengers; General John R. Brooke, Blanche F. Sigman, troops.

DUE TODAY

Stavangerfjord (Oslo, Bergen)—744 passengers; due 7:30 A. M.; Pier 8, E. R. (Norwegian America Line).
Edward Ripley (Port Said)—20 passengers; time and pier not given. (American Export).
Joshua Leach (Marseille)—12 passengers; time and pier not given. (American Export).
George Washington (Bermuda, Puerto Rico)—277 passengers; noon; 34, N. R. (Alcoa-Agwi).
Antinous (Antwerp)—10 passengers; 9 A. M.; 6, Bush Terminal. (Waterman).
Cape Trafalgar (Venezuela)—10 passengers; time not given; 65, N. R. (Grace).
Colby Victory (Havre)—1,052 troops; 3:30 P. M.; 15, S. I.; troops to Camp Kilmer.
Blue Ridge Victory (Southampton)—616 troops; 8 A. M.; 15, S. I.; Kilmer.
Peter Minuit (Havre)—9 troops; 3 P. M.; instream off Rosebank; Kilmer.

DUE TOMORROW

James J. Hill (Glasgow)—10 passengers. (U. S. Lines).

Greece Victory (Chile)—Passengers. (Grace).
Vulcania (Alexandria, Naples)—855 passengers, including war brides and children. (American Export).
Tufts Victory (Havre)—977 troops.
Lewiston Victory (Havre)—962 troops.
Hood Victory (Havre)—978 troops.

DEPARTED YESTERDAY

Uruguay, Fort Royal, Madaket, Magallanes, passengers; Zebulon B. Vance, Army and Navy dependents.

DEPARTING TODAY

Sea Stallion (Shanghai)—12 passengers; time not given; 29th St., Brooklyn. (Isthmian).

DEPARTING TOMORROW

San Mateo Victory (Shanghai)—10 passengers. (American President).
Mormacgulf (Buenos Aires)—12 passengers. (Moore McCormack).
Kenyon Victory (Honolulu)—3 passengers. (Isthmian).
Titus (Venezuela, Curacao)—7 passengers. (Royal Netherlands Line).
Santa Leonor (Venezuela)—Passengers. (Grace).

AIRLINES

All airline arrivals and departures are from La Guardia Field unless otherwise noted.

ARRIVED YESTERDAY

Star of Madrid (Paris)—5:30 P. M. (TWA).
Flagship America (Stockholm)—2:45 P. M. (American Airlines).
Flagship Amsterdam (London)—Late last night. (American Airlines).
Clipper America (Leopoldville)—8:30 A. M. (Pan American).
Clipper Europe (London)—11:58 A. M. (Pan American).
Clipper Africa (Bermuda)—4 P. M. (Pan American).
Clipper Congo (Bermuda)—9:30 P. M. (Pan American).

DUE TODAY

Star of Cairo (Paris)—6:30 A. M. (TWA).
Star of Paris (Paris)—1:30 P. M. (TWA).
Clipper Bermuda (London) — 6:35 A. M. (Pan American).
Clipper Lisbon (London)—10:35 A. M. (Pan American).
Clipper London (Lisbon)—11 A. M. (Pan American).
Clipper Congo (Bermuda)—9:30 P. M. (Pan American).
R. M. A. Bangor (Bermuda)—3 P. M. (Baltimore Airport). (British Overseas).

DEPARTED YESTERDAY

Star of Lisbon (Paris)—11 A. M. (TWA).
Clipper Africa (Bermuda)—9 A. M. (Pan American).
Clipper Congo (Bermuda)—2 P. M. (Pan American).
Clipper Atlantic (London)—5 P. M. (Pan American).
Clipper Eire (Leopoldville)—7 P. M. (Pan American).
Clipper America (London)—9 P. M. (Pan American).
R. M. A. Bangor (Bermuda)—Noon. (Baltimore Airport). (British Overseas).

DEPARTING TODAY

Star of Madrid (Paris)—9 A. M. (TWA).
Star of Athens (Geneva)—11 A. M. (TWA).
Acropolis (Cairo)—3 P. M. (TWA).
Flagship Boston (Berlin)—11 A. M. (American Airlines).
Flagship America (London)—2 P. M. (American Airlines).
Clipper Congo (Bermuda)—2 P. M. (Pan American).
Clipper Eire (London)—5 P. M. (Pan American).

5-7 Marine and Aviation reports from the *New York Times*. (June 15, 1946)

5-8 "Fuselage" (Lockheed Martin)

5-9 "Wing and Empennage" (Lockheed Martin)

Chapter 6

HORSEPOWER, GIVE ME MORE HORSEPOWER!

If early 1947 saw the end of the first chapter in the commercial life of the Constellation, it also saw the beginning of a chapter in which commercial aviation truly grew and prospered. In this growth lay the opportunity that Lockheed badly needed to continue the further development and sales of the Constellation family of aircraft. The term *family* is used advisedly here, because by this time Lockheed was coming to the firm conclusion that the basic Constellation design was such as to have a large measure of growth built into it. The issue now was to develop this potential for growth, and then to find the markets that would buy it.

Late 1946 and early 1947 was an extremely difficult period for Lockheed in particular and the airlines in general. Lockheed had no sooner completed its modifications of the Model 049s (as a result of the Reading crash) than it was hit with a large order cancellation on the part of TWA. This cancellation covered 8 L–049s and no less than 18 L–649s. The cancellation was in no way a reflection of the previous problems of the Constellation. It was entirely the result of the financial situation in which TWA found itself. This in turn was caused by far lower than expected passenger loads, especially on domestic service, a fall pilot strike, and of course the extra costs caused by the Constellation grounding in summer 1946. However, Lockheed managed to stagger through those winter months, and some of the canceled L–049s were sold off to other operators. But better times were just ahead, and they were in part made possible by the vision that Lockheed showed when it began design on the Model 649.

Two basic factors led to the Model 649. One was the built-in capacity for growth that existed in the basic Constellation design, and the other was the more powerful engine developed by Wright. Tests carried out at Burbank early on convinced the engineers that with a relatively modest number of changes the Connie's gross weight could be increased considerably beyond the 86,000 pounds at which the L–049 had been certified for commercial use.

Actually two factors catalyzed the development of the L–649. The first was the promise of more horsepower, which Wright demonstrated in early 1945. The second was the interest shown by Eddie Rickenbacker of Eastern Airlines (EAL) in a Constellation version having more payload and luxury than the basic L–049. For these two reasons, in May 1945 Lockheed had begun development of the L–649.

The power plant advancement by Wright came about, as it often does, because of expanded requirements by the military. In 1945 Wright had begun production of the R–3350-24W, an engine capable of putting out 2500 hp at 2900 RPM at take-off, and 2100 hp at 2400 RPM at cruise setting. This engine powered the famous Navy Lockheed series of patrol bombers known as the P2V Neptunes, an aircraft famous, among other things, for the fact that it was in continuous production from 1945 to 1961. In fact, some Neptunes are still being flown today by private operators using them as fire-fighting aircraft.

With Lockheed developing a sense of confidence in the new power plant, it was decided to design the L–649 around the commercial version of this engine. This engine was officially known as the 749C18BD1, more familiarly as the BD–1. It was designed by Wright exclusively for commercial use and was considerably different in design from the power plants used on the C–69 and the L–049. For one thing, it featured forged cylinder heads to replace the cast aluminum heads previously used.

So in 1945, as Lockheed's engineers began their redesign of the basic Connie, their objectives, in the words of Kelly Johnson, were:

1. To install improved heating, cooling, and ventilation systems.
2. To increase economy of operation with the efficiency and additional 300 hp available per engine.
3. To provide more luxurious and quieter cabins through the use of improved insulation and advanced interior seating.
4. To increase the payload.

When Lockheed rolled out their first L–649 in mid-1946, there were no noticeable differences apparent to casual bystanders. The overall dimensions and appearance were virtually identical to the L–049. Actually, the aircraft had many new features, although the basic frame and wings were, in fact, identical. First and foremost, of course, were those new engines commonly referred to as the BD–1s. With 300 hp more apiece, or a total of 1200 more hp, a number of performance changes took place. The gross weight was now 94,000 pounds, or 8000 pounds more than on the L–049. The empty weight went up only some 6500 pounds. Thus, there was a net gain of 1500 pounds of payload. Speed went up too, with some 25 mph added to the cruise speed, pushing it up to approximately 325 mph. The landing gear was beefed up to safely handle the 4 tons of additional weight.

The assembly surrounding the engines was also redesigned. Built by Rohr, the entire nacelle was so fabricated that merely by disconnecting the wiring and oil and fuel connections, the entire engine, mountings, and oil system became removable as a unit. This of course proved a real advantage when an operator wished to replace an entire engine without delaying an flight unduly. Another innovation was the sectioned cowling, which opened up like orange peel. This type of design allowed maintenance to be performed with considerably more ease and also more quickly.

The cabin came in for a number of significant changes. The internal cabin wall, not including the floor, was shock-mounted on rubber lining installed between the cabin and the fuselage. This "floating" cabin was built to appreciably reduce noise and vibration. The entire interior was given a new treatment that enhanced the somewhat Spartan appearance of the L–049. A redesigned air conditioning system by Air Research was installed, operated by superchargers hydraulically coupled to the outboard engines. The cooling assembly was placed in the wing, and provided 70 cubic feet per minute of air per passenger, compared to the 40 cubic feet provided in the L–049. The internal temperature was maintained at a constant 75 degrees Fahrenheit, and if one outboard engine was operated while the aircraft was on the ground, then cabin cooling became available even then.

With a somewhat greater fuel capacity, the L–649 also had a slightly longer range, although some of the extra fuel weight was traded off by the greater fuel consumption of the more powerful engines. All in all, this model was a successful refinement of the L–049, and Lockheed was extremely enthusiastic as to its sales potential. EAL and Rickenbacker had touched off the early ordering when they signed up for 14 aircraft, and TWA followed up with 18 more. But then, in October 1946, when TWA was forced by economic conditions to cancel their order, Lockheed was left with a brand-new design on the assembly line that at that moment looked like an unmitigated sales disaster!

When Lockheed was still in the design stage of the L–649, someone made the comment, "Man, this is going to be a real gold-plated Constellation." The nickname stuck, and it became known unofficially as the Gold Plate Constellation. When the first one was delivered to EAL in April 1947, it flew from Burbank to Miami in 6 hours, 55 minutes, averaging 340 mph and setting a new record. The previous record had been set by a Panagra DC–6 only weeks earlier, but that flight took some 20 minutes longer. Immediately after its arrival in Miami, the Gold Plate L–649 was refueled and took off for New York City. It covered this leg in 3 hours, 30 minutes, breaking the previous record, set by EAL in December 1946 with a DC–4, by some 30 minutes. These L–649s delivered to EAL were all in 60-passenger configurations and carried some 4690 gallons of fuel.

The first L–649 had a Lockheed serial number of 2501, and on October 18, 1946, it first flew, with Lockheed's Tony LeVier as pilot, Rudy Thoren as co-pilot, C. E. Smith as flight engineer ,and John Stockdale as flight test engineer. The very first flight proved that the aircraft was indeed an improvement over the L–049, but considerable propeller vibration was discerned. The propellers were a new design from Curtiss. On the second test flight, with Kelly Johnson aboard, they created so much vibration that Johnson simply wrote on his pad, "Completely unsatisfactory." Various propellers were tried thereafter, with aircraft 2501 and 2502 trying out five different types of propellers in a single week. Eventually, with the help of both Hamilton-Standard and Curtiss, the problem was resolved.

Another problem area encountered was icing of the fuel master control, which on the Constellation power plants was the equivalent of a carburetor. Readers may remember that one of the modifications that took place as a result of the various findings of the Reading crash investigation was the replacement of engine carburetors with fuel injection. The icing of this system was a serious matter. Roy Wimmer, test pilot on the particular flight, took an L–649 down to west Texas to fly in severe icing conditions. Near Laredo all four engines abruptly quit, and what ensued was that famous silence that all pilots find more frightening than any very loud noise. The tech rep for the fuel control manufacturer was aboard this flight. When the crew looked for him to get some very quick advice, they found him near the back of the airplane adjusting his parachute harness! So the crew tried their own fix, namely, pumping alcohol to the control, which thawed the ice and allowed the engines to be restarted. Needless to say, the problem was eventually resolved. However, it is not recorded whether the crew was still talking to the tech rep when the aircraft landed, or what Lockheed may have said to that particular manufacturer!

The reasons for the lack of L–649 sales go beyond the simple fact that domestic airlines were not doing very well financially. Because the basic reason is one that affected the entire Constellation program throughout its lifetime, it's worth examining here. The L–049 sales that Lockheed made in 1945–46 fell into two basic categories: the U.S. lines that flew overseas and a number of foreign overseas operators. But of the initial complement of buyers, only TWA flew domestically, and it used only a few of its Constellation fleet for its domestic schedules in 1946–47. Because the entire Constellation production for the first 18 months was completely taken up with orders, the other domestic operators were faced with the double problem of long delivery delays coupled with the fact that any operator in direct competition with TWA might be faced with even longer delays caused by the provisions of the original contract with Hughes. In addition, there was the consideration that most domestic operators did not, at that time, feel a real need to obtain aircraft with a range as long as that possessed by the Constellation. So, these companies all went to Douglas and first used their DC–4, and later began receiving deliveries of the new DC–6, an aircraft developed as a specific response to the challenge laid down by the Constellation. Thus, in 1946, no domestic operator was actually in the market for any Lockheed airplanes. It is interesting to note that to a marked degree the operators that initially ordered Constellations came back to buy more in later years, whereas those that went in for Douglas aircraft stayed with Douglas for their reorders.

Ironically, the Constellation would have been an excellent buy for domestic airlines eager to reestablish themselves in the U.S. postwar markets. This would have been particularly true for airlines with fairly long, highly competitive routes. The L–049 would not only have enabled them to fly coast to coast nonstop, but would have allowed them to do so at speeds that were not matched until 1951 when the Douglas DC–6B went into commercial service. But as it happened, aside from the problems mentioned, the main trunk lines did not at that time see a big market for long, nonstop flights. Furthermore, there was a strong feeling shared by all the major trunks that passengers would rebel against flights of 8–10 hours. In time this particular attitude was disproved, but in 1946 it most certainly must have affected the airlines' thinking.

The L–649, although a very real refinement of the basic Constellation design, did not actually take full advantage of the potential the 2500-hp Cyclones gave it. So it seemed to Lockheed, during the long winter of 1946–47, that not only was the Constellation possibly doomed to a quick extinction but that Lockheed itself was facing the possibility of having to shut its plants down. But as it happened, various events taking place in the background were about to turn things around in a rather dramatic fashion.

The first break came when Kelly Johnson and his people realized that certain modifications of the L–649 could lead to an almost identical aircraft with considerably more range. This might just be what overseas carriers, both U.S. and foreign, required. In meetings with some of their L–049 customers, this turned out to be exactly the case. The reasons for this bears looking into, because they bespoke of a whole aviation revolution affecting aviation to this day.

The technical development, continued sales, and increased use of the Connies in the late 1940s and the 1950s was much more than merely a combination of engineering improvements and marketing successes. The life cycle of the Connies is actually a generally accurate reflection of certain trends that occurred after World War II. These trends can be summarized into the following three categories:

1. Growing dependency of business on commercial air transportation.
2. A boom in long-haul tourist traffic that utilized air transport to an ever increasing degree.
3. The development of Western and Communist country blocs, and the resulting cold war.

Each of these trends helped develop a market for certain classes of large aircraft. But in addition, the results of these trends also produced an interplay that resulted in innovations developed for a certain market finding applications in another market.

In order to obtain a clear perception of the various causes and effects that provided the impetus for the entire Connie production program, it becomes necessary to identify these various events and their results.

Various circumstances greatly influenced the success of the Connies in the period 1946–1956. None of these circumstances could possibly have been foreseen during the Connie's initial developmental period because they all came about as a direct result of World War II. Prior to World War II, there had been a beginning of regularly scheduled transatlantic service by both Pan Am and British Imperial Airways, the predecessor to British Overseas Airline Company (BOAC), now known as British Airways. Only flying boats were used, because aircraft reliability was such that no one felt quite secure operating land-based aircraft on long, over-water routes. Further, because these flying boats were not pressurized and accordingly flew lower, they were routed by way of Bermuda and the Azores. This ensured better weather but also resulted in an increase of many miles on a New York–London trip.

World War II saw an impressive series of advances take place. It began with the ATC C–47s flying as far as Iceland, by way of Gander, Newfoundland or Goose Bay, Labrador, and then the west coast of Greenland. This was followed by thousands of delivery ferry flights to England. The aircraft included both two- and four-engine bombers, and later even single- and twin-engine fighters with long-range fuel tanks. Finally, ATC Douglas C–54 Skymasters began year-round service to England by way of Gander or Goose Bay on the west bank of the Atlantic and Shannon, Ireland, or Prestwick, Scotland, on the east side. To accommodate this vast amount of traffic, new airfields with long runways were built equipped with such landing aids as ground control approach (GCA). It was also during this time that long-range navigation (LORAN) equipment began to be installed in the larger aircraft. All of this flying resulted in more dependable equipment, firmly established navigational techniques, an increase in weather forecasting reliability, and finally crews with far more confidence in their aircraft and themselves.

Another result of World War II was the increased familiarity of Americans with foreign lands in general and Europe in particular. The fact that so many U.S. military men traveled to Europe in wartime helps explain, at least in part, the constantly increasing volume of both tourists and business people that developed in the late 1940s and early 1950s. Tourism in particular grew rapidly because Americans had accumulated substantial savings during the war. Combined with low prices abroad, the net results were truly phenomenal.

Large U.S. companies began to expand their holdings and operations to Europe. This in turn created a market for managers, salespeople, technical representatives, engineers, and so on who found it necessary to travel to Europe frequently, often for only a few days.

Starting in 1946, the Soviet Union and the United States found themselves in the position of two adversaries who are at war in everything except the actual fighting. Known as the Cold War, this strange kind of battle had an effect on many things going on in this country. For one thing, it led to closer ties with Western Europe, which in turn led to a far greater volume of official government trips overseas. All of this affected overseas flying, and in the period 1946–49 the airlines flying across the Atlantic doubled the amount of traffic carried. This complex and varied background paved the way for the increased sales and use of the Constellation in 1947.

The aircraft that was the outgrowth of the L–649 was known as the L–749, and was not, in fact, very different. What Lockheed did was simply take advantage of the unrealized potential shown by those Wright BD–1 engines. Careful analysis and testing had revealed that the basic L–649 structure could accept an additional 8000 pounds, and it was decided that this increased payload capability should be used for greater range. Accordingly, the Engineering Department came up with integral fuel tanks, which became part of the outer wings. In the L–649 model, only the inner portion of the wings carried fuel.

The resulting L–749 thus had a gross weight of 102,000 pounds, 45 percent more than the original L–049. The useful load, which includes passengers, crew, cargo, and fuel, rose by a whopping 22 percent over the L–049. This now meant that the L–749 could handle flights of up to 5000 statute miles, although at that range there was some reduction in payload. But the airlines became very interested in this model, as proven by the sales that soon came Lockheed's way.

The L–749 was to garner a total of 59 aircraft sold. Ten different companies were to buy then. Some were previous customers, such as Pan Am who only wanted 4, or TWA, who ordered 12. KLM was also a repeat customer, and they ordered the biggest number with 13. Air India ordered three as they made plans to expand their service to accommodate the needs of their country, which was about to earn its independence. The Venezuelan LAV and the Australian Qantas became new customers, as did the Irish Airline. Air France expanded their fleet with 8 more, and somewhat surprisingly, EAL ordered 7 to go with the 14 L–649s they were operating.

In May 1947 EAL put the first of their brand-new Model L–649s into service to the accompaniment of a considerable amount of publicity. Eastern served the extremely competitive New York–Florida market, and Eddie Rickenbacker hoped that his new Gold Plate Special would give Eastern a badly needed edge. True, Spring was not the time when traffic to Florida was particularly heavy, but on the other hand, starting at this time gave crews and maintenance personnel an excellent chance to learn how to best utilize their new, expensive birds.

Initial schedules included nonstop Washington–Miami, Newark–Miami, and Newark–Houston flights, the latter taking advantage of the Constellation's range. Then, once all the aircraft on order had been delivered, additional schedules were phased in. It is interesting to note that although Eastern used the L–649 on some of their longest routes nonstop, they had absolutely no hesitation in also using the aircraft on such short segments as New York–Washington. Here, once again, the dual ability of the Constellation to handle either long flights or short legs with operations out of relatively small fields was shown. In fact, Eastern was so pleased with their L–649s that they came right back with the order for seven Model L–749 aircraft in May 1948.

The line-up of customers for the L–749 was a dead giveaway as to the major use of that aircraft. Airlines like Air India, Air France, Pan Am, TWA, KLM, Qantas, and LAV used it. It was rather obvious that the newly lengthened range of the aircraft was going to be put to use by these companies. Once again Lockheed had garnered the major share of the long-range market. Once again Lockheed was not in a good position to make domestic sales because their production line was filled for some time to come. It was also true that Douglas was aggressively selling their DC–6 and filling the void left by Lockheed.

By now, in 1948, Lockheed was continually reexamining the growth potential of the Constellation. With some 59 Model 749 airplanes on the order books, the engineering people sat down to take another hard look at the basic Constellation. The intuitive feeling that the aircraft powered by 2500-hp engines could easily handle a greater load was borne out by careful analysis. On the basis of these studies, Lockheed proposed to bring out a Model 749A that would have 5000 pounds more take-off weight. This extra 2.5 tons was then translated directly into an identical increase in both landing and zero fuel weights. Thus, the airlines could look forward to 5000 pounds more payload.

To achieve this weight gain, the existing L–749 was equipped with brakes of greater capacity, landing gear tires of more ply rating were added, the landing gear structural members were beefed up, and some strengthening of the wings and fuselage was also undertaken. The resulting airplane was most attractive to the airlines, who obtained more payload without sacrificing range or speed and also at the basically identical specific fuel consumption. The first L–749A aircraft were delivered in October 1949, some 2.5 years after the first delivery of the L–749. South African Airways was the first customer to receive a delivery, although Air India also received an L–749A in the same month. The two big customers were TWA, who, because of booming overseas traffic ordered 25 planes, and Air France who ordered 10 of the model. All told some 70 L–749As were sold.

Two of the customers were of particular interest, these being the U.S. Air Force and U.S. Navy. This was the first time the military had shown an interest in the Constellation since the World War II days of the C–69 and its attendant confusion. The Air Force ordered 10 of the Model 749A with military interiors and Navy bought just 2 as prototypes and test beds for use as early warning aircraft. These two orders shortly became very significant to Lockheed, even though they were quite small (see Chapter 8).

These military orders were preceded by a special test flight, which had considerable impact on the future of the Constellation. Before the military services were willing to sign on the dotted line, they wanted some assurances that the

L–749A version they were considering would fly at heavier gross weights if so required. Flying airplanes considerably in excess of the design maximum gross take-off weight is an old military custom that goes back to at least World War II. This author can still remember reading with considerable amazement and consternation how the Boeing B–29 was flown early in its career at successively greater weights, until it was operated routinely at 145,000 pounds, even though it had originally been designed to have a maximum gross take-off weight of some 120,000 pounds. Thus, it's obvious that the military did this kind of thing rather routinely.

The pilot chosen to fly these overload tests was Lockheed's Herman "Fish" Salmon, a test pilot with a distinguished career. A L–749A was flown up to Muroc AFB for the test, and was loaded with 26,000 pounds of water in special tanks placed in the fuselage. Fish took the aircraft off the ground at a staggering 133,000 pounds! After the flight his comment was, "Rate of climb wasn't all that it might have been, but it sure flew with an overload!" (Lockheed) To say this was an understatement is merely stating the obvious. The rate of climb, which on a L-749A is normally over 1000 feet/minute, must have been a great deal less in this case. At any rate, the military was impressed with what they saw, and the Navy and Air Force orders went through.

Some years later "Fish" Salmon gained nationwide TV exposure, no doubt somewhat to his surprise. Salmon had been flying tests on the Lockheed F–104 Starfighter, sometimes referred to as the missile with a man in it. On a particular test flight he fired a newly developed 20mm cannon that operated in a manner similar to the Civil War Gatling gun. Known as the Vulcan, the cannon had a number of barrels that rotated into place in rapid sequence. Salmon fired the cannon while flying at altitude, and the next thing he knew he was gently floating down from the sky in his parachute. He landed safely, except for minor scratches and bruises, but when questioned as to what had happened, he could not remember anything. His memory had wrapped protective amnesia around itself. In an attempt to find out what had happened, it was suggested that Salmon undergo questioning while under the influence of sodium pentothal. This he agreed to, and the entire session was filmed and taped, and later shown on national TV. While under the effect of the pentothal, "Fish" remembered that as he fired off the cannon the cockpit filled with acrid smoke. At that point he wisely elected to eject. From his description of what happened, the engineers were able to determine that smoke emitted from the gun barrels was being drawn directly into the cockpit. The problem was resolved, and Salmon no doubt had to undergo a certain amount of good-natured kidding from his co-workers about his TV debut!

6-1 Cabin interior work underway on a Model L–649/749, 1950. (Lockheed Martin)

6-2 Eddie Rickenbacker, President of Eastern Air Lines and flight crew with first "Gold Plate" L–649 Connie, S/N 2501, prior to departing Burbank on record-setting 6 hour 55 minute flight to Miami, Florida, April 1947. (Lockheed Martin)

6-3 Some Air France L–749A's had sleeping berths. Those so equipped were scheduled non-stop eastbound New York-Paris in 1949. (Lockheed Martin)

6-4 An Air India L–749A, a model the airline began receiving in Fall 1949. (Lockheed Martin)

6-5 TWA, which purchased numerous L–749A's, began using a "SPEEDPAK," which made luggage loading/unloading faster, in 1949. (Lockheed Martin)

6-6 A South African Airways L–749A, an aircraft whose range capability was well suited to the long haul from Johannesburg, 1950. (Lockheed Martin)

6-7 "Surface Controls" (Lockheed Martin)

Chapter 7

THE CONSTELLATION STRETCH

If the 1940s was the decade of the Constellation, then the 1950s was certainly the decade of the Super Constellation. This became true despite the competition from the Douglas and Boeing contemporary designs, the British turboprops, and finally the De Havilland, Boeing, and Douglas turbojets. It was a decade that brought forth a number of surprises for Lockheed and the Constellation program.

In February 1950, Lockheed began design work on a new version of the Constellation. It was to be a larger and heavier aircraft with a stretched fuselage. Although this aircraft was one more step in the orderly progression of growth of the basic Constellation aircraft, it was actually an airplane with a considerable number of significant changes. In fact, from this time on, it can be said that a new subfamily of Constellations came into existence, all generally known as Super Constellations.

The initial design was specifically identified as the Model 1049. It was the direct result of a new need, on the one hand, and the availability of improved technology, on the other. This, of course, was the same combination essentially as had brought about all the earlier model changes. But this time the differences in the need were a little greater and the new aircraft that resulted reflected a somewhat larger step forward.

THE NEED

Since the inception of normal commercial air service after World War II, airlines everywhere had been waiting for the often predicted traffic boom.

Unfortunately, the traffic figures for the years 1946–48 did not seem to show any such occurrence taking place, either in the United States or internationally. What had come about was a general and gradual increase in the number of passengers, but nowhere near as many as had been hoped for. However, by late 1949 the airlines of the world believed that a sharp increase in traffic was in the making. This optimism was generated by a number of factors. The postwar recession, which had affected the U.S. economy so markedly, was easing, and more money was available. As business gradually improved, companies everywhere stepped up the amount of traveling required of their employees. This was the first indication of what was to come. Another factor was the considerably improved situation in Europe, where the various nations of Western Europe, assisted in considerable measure by the U.S. Marshall Plan, were working themselves out of the almost total physical and economic collapse brought on by World War II. Business travel there also began to increase, and even more important, the beginning of a resurgent tourist industry became visible.

Still another area the airlines had to be aware of was that the gradually but steadily increasing traffic had now reached a level where certain flights would be totally filled, and potential riders had to be turned away. This growth is most clearly discernible when one examines the table below, which was provided by the IATA.

Traffic of U.S. Carriers *(in 1000s)*

Year	Domestic Passengers	% Change	International Passengers	% Change
1946	12,164	—	1091	—
1947	12,822	+ 5.4	1428	+30.9
1948	13,094	+ 2.1	1447	+1.3
1949	15,121	+15.5	1599	+10.5
1950	17,468	+15.5	1752	+9.6

Traffic of International Carriers *(in 1000s)*

Year	Passengers	% Change
1946	18	—
1947	21	+16.7
1948	24	+14.3
1949	27	+12.5
1950	31	+14.8

It was also during this period that a number of countries initiated flag service beyond their own boundaries, in many cases to the United States. U.S. carriers, by the same token, began flying to various cities all over the world as part of the reciprocity agreements that were constantly being added to.

All of this added up to a couple of specific needs as enunciated by the airlines. One was the need for more aircraft, generally of a type to have long range and considerable payload. The other was the requirement for airplanes that could carry more passengers and at a lower seat-mile cost than what was currently available. Focusing and sharpening this latter need was the fact that the first reduced airfares had been tried by some companies, notably TWA. The results were such that forecasters were convinced that the combination of larger aircraft with lower seat-mile operating costs and additional fare reductions could easily result in far larger numbers of people flying. Thus, the airlines brought a sense of urgency to the aircraft manufacturers in fall 1949.

THE TECHNOLOGY

In 1949, when Lockheed had test-flown its L–749A at a gross weight of 133,000 pounds, it had become obvious that the basic Constellation airframe still had a great deal of growth left in it. But there was a real question in everyone's mind at Burbank as to how all this potential growth was to be utilized. The idea of more speed resulting from larger power plants was quickly dropped. Aside from the fact that a moderate increase in horsepower would result in very little additional speed, more speed was not what the airlines seemed to feel they needed just then. Greater payload for the same basic airplane was found not to be the answer either. The airlines were generally content with the very considerable range available to the L–749 and L–749A models. As far as more payload in the form of either passengers or freight, where was one to put either? The existing fuselage was completely used. This rather automatically led to the next logical step. Because the basic airframe could withstand greater loads, how about stretching the fuselage, thus accommodating more passengers, baggage, mail, and freight? True, there was one pitfall. With the existing 2500-hp engines, a considerable increase in weight would reduce the Constellation's performance substantially. Of even greater concern to the engineers was the fact that the considerable safety margins that were such an important feature of the Constellation and that had greatly helped in selling it would virtually disappear.

Fortunately for all, the Wright Company had developed still another version of their 3350 in the meantime. This one was known as the 956C18CA1, with a refinement known as the 975C18CB1. Developing 2700 hp in the CA1 and 2800 in the

CB1, this gave the Lockheed design staff just about the amount of power they needed. Once again these engines had already been tested in military service in their similar military versions. Known as the R3350-26W, 26WA, and 26WB, the engine was produced to power a number of military aircraft, the biggest application being in the Douglas AD–1, -3, -4, -5, -6, and -7 single-engine attack aircraft. With production of the military versions starting in early 1947 and over 3750 being built by 1956, the engine was already a proven product.

Actually, during the early sessions among the Lockheed design people, there was still another consideration that arose. This one could have terminated the entire Constellation program right then and there. At that time, the application of jet power to transport aircraft was actually under way. De Havilland in England was actively working on its famous Comet prototype, and up in Canada, our resourceful neighbors were designing a jet transport known as the Avro Jetliner. But these were untried aircraft. Even if they were to turn out to be totally successful, both Lockheed and many of the airline people felt that their high fuel consumption would result in prohibitive operating costs. There was in the background also the feeling that jet aircraft in general, and jet engines in particular, had not yet reached the level of safety that would warrant their introduction into commercial use. So the people at Lockheed decided to once again gamble and proceed with the new design.

THE SUPER CONSTELLATION: PART ONE

When Lockheed decided to lengthen the basic Constellation fuselage and go to the Super Constellation series, they were actually continuing a growth process that had begun before the first Constellation ever flew. Readers may remember that the original Constellation had grown in landing and take-off weight a number of times prior to ever flying. Then, of course, after the war the basic Constellation grew in weight, if not in size, through the 649, 749, and 749A models. So, when the go-ahead had been given, Kelly Johnson and the other design people tackled the question of the design of this new bird in earnest.

The design of this new model, to be known as the L–1049, started in February 1950. In the 18 months prior to that date, Lockheed had done some preliminary work on two other models. In early 1948 the L–849 model was considered, this being a Constellation with heavier weight and powered by the then-new Turbo-Compound 3350 (more on that later). Then, in mid-1949, Lockheed was looking at a Model 949, which would have had a 12-foot longer fuselage and again the Turbo-Compound engines.

When the formal design program on the L–1049 started, the idea of more passengers and lower seat-mile costs had been clearly defined. Then the designers, looking over wind tunnel results of models being tested, found that once again, the basic potential of the Constellation had been underestimated. These results clearly showed that an aircraft with more than a 12-foot stretch could easily be accommodated. The final result was that a decision was made to insert two separate new sections of fuselage, one in front of the wing, and one behind.

A front section measuring 128.8 inches long by 139.3 inches in diameter was inserted just forward of the front spar. A second, or rear section, 92 inches long by 136.6 inches in diameter was inserted some 55 inches behind the rear spar. Both sections were of constant diameter, unlike the rest of the original Constellation fuselage, and altogether increased the length of the fuselage by 18.4 feet. Actually, the designers had little choice but to build the extra fuselage length in two sections, because only by splitting it into two parts, one forward of the wing and one behind, could a fairly long total lengthening take place without destroying the weight and balance of the aircraft. In later years, a great many aircraft received the same type of treatment, both commercial and military, and in almost all cases, the plug sections were in the same fashion, one forward of and one behind the wing.

Kelly Johnson was anxious to try out the new concept. But building a brand-new fuselage of this design would take many months and a considerable amount of money. Then Johnson remembered a spare Connie that could be converted to the new proposed configuration. Just across town, at Culver City, was the private field of Howard Hughes, and on it, sitting idle, was the Model L–049 he had bought some years before. This aircraft was no less than the original Constellation prototype. After its original testing, it had gone into service with the Army for a fairly short period of time. After the war, it was declared surplus, and Hughes purchased it. But for some reason, he had hardly ever used it. Lockheed purchased the aircraft and brought it to Burbank.

At that point it is said that the airplane had been flown only three times since its Army days back in 1944–45; once, on its ferry flight from Burbank to Culver City, again on a single flight by Hughes out of his field, and finally the return flight to Burbank. So it was that in 1950 the Constellation prototype returned once more to its place of birth. Now carrying the serial number 1961, the aircraft began a career that must be considered unique in the annals of large aircraft.

The first item on the agenda at Lockheed was proving out the new fuselage for the proposed Super Constellation series. Accordingly, 1961 was pulled into the plant and the fuselage was actually sawed into three distinct parts, with the cuts taking place both forward and behind the wing. Then, new barrel plug sections were inserted in those two locations, and the entire five-piece fuselage was put together again. With new engines of 2700 hp, old 1961 was ready to fly again.

The interior of the aircraft, including the cockpit, hardly looked like the predecessor of a line of luxury airplanes. The airplane had no permanent air conditioning or pressurization systems. The cabin was stripped and had nothing more than a plywood floor. The cockpit was filled with a number of rigged-up instruments for carefully recording the aircraft's performance.

But the strangeness did not stop there. A wood and metal brow was attached directly above the cockpit windows to simulate the new, larger windshield planned for the Super Connies. Inside, the ample fuselage was filled with a maze of tanks, piping, and valves. The purpose of this Rube Goldberg–like arrangement was to load the airplane to various gross weights, shift the center of gravity in flight, and even lighten the load while flying by dumping a portion of the water ballast. No such system of a similar size or complexity had ever been tried before.

When the aircraft first flew on October 13, 1950, Lockheed had itself a brand-new prototype airplane at a saving of millions of dollars and many months. Old 1961, soon to become known as the Beast of Burbank, was to go on to many firsts in the next few years. But all that was in the future at that point. Flight tests proved beyond a shadow of a doubt that the extra length did not alter the flight characteristics to any appreciable degree, and the plane flew over a year proving out various modifications, all of which related to the Model 1049A.

However, there were other changes in the aircraft. The round windows were replaced by rectangular ones that measured 16 by 18 inches. These afforded far better visibility to the passengers. The cockpit enclosure was also changed, with the roof line now appearing to have a beetle-browed appearance. As part of this modification, the cockpit windows were enlarged, now being some 3.5 inches higher and with some seven panels replacing the previous nine. Furthermore, the windscreen was no longer a smooth semicircle but was now more squared off.

In addition to the lengthened fuselage and the CA1 power plants, the L–1049 had changes to the main landing gear damper plates. Moreover, the vertical tail fins were made higher by some 2.5 feet to improve longitudinal stability. The increased height resulted in some 25 percent greater rudder-fin area. The longer fuselage required a 92-inch greater moment arm. Thus, the amount of control both longitudinally and laterally remained about the same as on the standard Constellation. Interestingly enough, one avowed purpose of the improved control was to provide for the greater torque of turboprop power plants, which at that time were already being considered as a likely future source of power.

In addition to these highly visible changes, the designers and engineers made some unseen ones. The newly lengthened fuselage needed more strength; accordingly, the basic fuselage frame was reinforced. This not only made allowances for the greater weight but also stiffened the longer fuselage and so prevented it from doing what was known as "nodding" in turbulent air. This, in turn, provided a smoother, more comfortable ride for the passengers. The new L–1049 was a different aircraft operationally than its predecessor. It carried up to 92 passengers, versus only 69 for the L–749A. The fuel load had been increased by some 5000 pounds, with a corresponding range increase of almost 300 miles. The cost per seat-mile was lower, which was precisely the goal originally set. However, the airplane cruised considerably slower, generally giving away some 25–40 mph as compared with the earlier Constellations. The reason for this is rather simple. The weight of the aircraft grew more proportionately than the horsepower, and thus the performance decreased slightly.

Lockheed might possibly have gone to the more powerful Turbo-Compound engines that were then becoming available, but correctly judging that there were unsolved problems with that power plant, decided to use the 2700-hp version instead. The net result of all this was that although the L–1049 was a very attractive airplane in terms of its operating economics, the airlines, with their public relations orientation, felt that less speed would lose passengers. Whether this was actually the case is debatable, but the fact remains that for this reason the L–1049 sold only in small quantities and was actually an interim aircraft. It was the first of two steps between the standard Constellation and the Super Constellation.

A total of only 24 aircraft were built, 14 for EAL and 10 for TWA. The EAL 1049 and the TWA L–1049 differed somewhat, as might be expected in view of their differing route structures. EAL originally took delivery of an aircraft with a gross weight of 116,000 pounds, whereas TWA's planes grossed 120,000 pounds. The difference was due to the center section fuel tanks of the TWA aircraft, which provided an additional 730 gallons of fuel. EAL, with its relatively short stage lengths, did not suffer as much from the lower speed and badly needed the carrying capacity in winter on its routes to Florida. Concerning TWA, a curious story has circulated over the years. It is said that Hughes ordered the 10 planes to keep the Constellation production line open and thus help Lockheed get through a difficult financial period. However, TWA was also having its problems, and thus it has been rumored that some of these aircraft were left on the ramp at Burbank for a considerable length of time before TWA took delivery. The first production L–1049 was delivered to EAL and went into service in December 1951. The airplane cost some $1,250,000 in late 1951. TWA introduced their L–1049 in September 1952.

The introduction of the rectangular windows in the L–1049 Super Constellation has an interesting and amusing story behind it. Charles Thomas of Lockheed was a sales engineer in the late 1940s at the time the L–1049 was being considered. One of the airlines he called on regularly was Northwest (NWA). At NWA, he often dealt with their vice president of operations, Ken Ferguson, who headed the negotiations for NWA on new equipment. Ferguson was a very tall, very large, and imposing figure, well known for his friendliness. Every time Thomas met with Ferguson, the latter would mention that NWA felt that square (rectangular) windows were an absolute must. Thomas would go back to Burbank with these requests, but with little success; and in time, Lockheed engineering became very tired of hearing this repeated request. In fact, one day, Hall Hibbard, the Lockheed vice president of engineering, finally told Thomas that square windows were simply not to be and that there would be "no change!" in the current round windows.

Shortly thereafter, a Lockheed team, led by Hibbard, went to NWA headquarters in Minneapolis to try and work out a contract with NWA. At the meeting, attended by quite a number of people, Hibbard and Ferguson sat next to each other, and the latter opened the meeting by asking, "Hal, we simply must have square windows!"

Hibbard immediately said, "Okay, that's fine. What's next?" Everyone around the table looked at Hibbard and Ferguson, because Thomas had been insisting all along that NWA must accept round windows.

Thomas exclaimed, "Well, that's very interesting! It's a good thing that you came, Mr. Hibbard. Now they can have their square windows!" (Charles Thomas)

And that is supposed to be the way that the square windows came to be. Ironically, NWA did not purchase any Constellations until the L–1049G was introduced, and then only bought four, which were used for a relatively short time before being sold.

In passing, it is interesting as well as ironic to note that part of Lockheed's concern with square windows was caused by the stress concentrations at the corners and the feeling that the pressurization cycles could lead to metal fatigue at those points. Some four or five years later, in 1954, the crashes and subsequent grounding of the De Havilland Comet I jet transport was found to have been caused by just that problem!

Although the L–1049 did not enjoy much success, it was a preview of things to come. Major events were afoot in the world that would impact directly on the

Constellation program and would give Lockheed more business than it had believed could possibly exist for their airplane.

Before we move ahead to the unexpected events surrounding the Constellation in the 1950s, readers might be interested to take a look at a specific step in the growth of the L–1049. We have already discussed how the fuselage was stretched. It is interesting to note, however, that this stretching and growth of the original aircraft was not a new phenomenon. In the first place, Lockheed had done this to some extent with their original L–10, L–12, and L–14 Electra aircraft. But there was an even more startling example of this growth process in which Lockheed had been involved. In 1944 and 1945, Kelly Johnson had developed and designed the first U.S. operational jet fighter, the famous F–80 Shooting Star. This aircraft, in its original A model, and later in its B and C models, was the U.S. Air Force's first line fighter in the late 1940s, and some 1773 aircraft were produced and delivered. Then the Air Force came up with a need for a jet trainer. Johnson took the basic F–80, stretched the fuselage, added a second seat with a complete set of controls, and came up with the famous T–33A jet trainer. This plane soon came to be known as the T-bird and trained thousands of pilots. The T-bird was fantastically successful, and in fact, Lockheed sold a whopping 5800 of the T-birds to the US Air Force, with 656 more built under license in Canada and another 210 in Japan. In addition, Lockheed built 217 of a Navy version used for carrier training.

By this time, what with the Korean War and the concern of a Soviet aircraft attack on the United States, the Air Force was looking for a day/night all-weather interceptor that it could obtain not only in quantity but quickly. Lockheed took their T–33 and turned it into the F–94 Starfire. Built in A, B, and C models, the aircraft proved to be the mainstay of the Air Defense Command for a number of years. In its final version, it was equipped with a nose radar that could track enemy aircraft, an afterburner, and air-to-air missiles housed in a semicircle around the nose. It was facetiously said to have a TV, overdrive, and built-in fireworks. Some 839 aircraft were built all told. Thus, over a period of some 10 years, Lockheed managed to take a basic design and expand it to the point where a grand total of 9500 aircraft were built in various models! Although Lockheed was not the only one to use this means of retaining a basic design, it was possibly the only company that refined the concept to the point it did, with very large rewards resulting.

THE SUPER CONSTELLATION: PART TWO

The second part of the basic Super Constellation development began some six months after the first in summer 1950. The events that led to this further and highly significant development will be examined in some detail in the next chapter. For now, we should take a look at a number of technological advances that led directly to the full development of the Super Constellation. These developments affected all of the models following the L–1049 and thus can be described without reference to any particular model application.

In July 1950, Kelly Johnson and his design team sat down to develop what was in some ways a completely new series of airplanes. The pressure was on from the military establishment for fast and significant results. Luckily, it happened that one of Johnson's attributes was his ability to examine the latest technology available and then use it to its fullest extent. The aircraft technology current or newly developed in July 1950 was certainly one of the chief factors leading to the further successful development of the Super Constellation family of airplanes. Within that technology, a certain few specific items played a major role in the designs that flowed from Burbank in the next few months.

The designs that Lockheed was beginning to work on were in answer to new requirements issued by the Navy. The Navy was looking for a fleet defense aircraft which would be a further development of its previously acquired prototypes, the PO–1W aircraft, which were basically L–749A aircraft with modifications. The Navy was also seeking to acquire a new transport aircraft able to carry with equal ease, cargo, passengers, or medical evacuation litters. Both airplanes had in common a need for more payload, cabin space, and range than had been available up to that time. Thus, the new designs would have some basic parameters in common.

Hibbard and Johnson were already pretty sure they knew what was needed. The L–1049 taking shape at Burbank provided a large cabin, with considerably more space available than the standard Constellation. What they set out to create was an airplane with more payload, more range, and somewhat more speed. They felt that the basic Constellation design had considerable growth left in it, provided that certain things came to pass. The first item they had to consider was the engine.

By a fortuitous circumstance, Lockheed was in a particularly good position when it came to power plants. For some years they had been building and delivering to the Navy a variety of versions of the P2V Neptune patrol bomber. This airplane was destined to set some kind of record for continuous production, with Lockheed producing them continuously for a full 20 years. As the type developed, its twin engines were constantly being upgraded, particularly since advanced electronic equipment was making the P2V heavier and heavier. Now, in spring 1950, Lockheed was about to try something new in power plants, known as the Turbo-Compound engine.

THE TURBO-COMPOUND ENGINE

The development of the Constellation since 1943 had certainly been in part due to the availability of new and more powerful engines. In fact, readers may remember that one reason the original Constellation was so far ahead of other contemporary aircraft was its use of a new engine. Now, the same thing was about to happen again.

Some four years earlier, in June 1946, the Navy had authorized Wright to begin a design study on a new development of their 3350 reciprocating engine. The first test engine was built in 1947, and in May of that year test-stand trials were begun. For the next two years, further development was carried out with company funds only because the government, due to changing priorities, had put a very low funding level on the project. However, in October 1949, Navy interest was revived, no doubt in part because of word from Wright that the new engine gave promise of achieving the same power output as earlier models at a considerably lower fuel consumption. This news came at a time when some of the early enthusiasm for turbine engines was being dampened by their exorbitant fuel consumption. It really didn't matter how fast they were going if they couldn't reach their destination!

With the new funding available, a prototype of the engine was installed in the nose of an old Boeing B–17 Flying Fortress. The engine needed a large-diameter propeller, and this overlapped the radii of the inboard props. For this reason, it was placed in the nose. During take-off this circumstance set up some very undesirable vibrations. The solution was to fly the B–17 with the inboard engines feathered, certainly a sign of the power inherent in this new 3350. The Navy was satisfied it had a power plant that was a large step forward. Final approval of the engine came in March 1950, and it was approved for use in the Lockheed P2V–4 patrol bomber.

Wright began manufacturing the first model of the Turbo-Compound, the R3350–30W, the same month, and the first Neptune flew with these engines in April 1950. By the time Lockheed began to develop the design of the new military Super Constellations, it had more experience, though still limited, on this engine than any other airframe manufacturer and had accumulated some 80,000 hours on the Neptune fleet.

Let us now take a look at precisely what makes up this Turbo-Compound engine. First, readers should keep in mind that over the years, ever larger experimental engines had been built. But it soon became obvious that adding more cylinders to an engine led to not only a very heavy power plant but one so complicated as to make high utilization very doubtful. For this reason Wright began looking around for another solution to the problem of higher power output. The answer they brought forth was that of harnessing the large amount of exhaust from the engine, thus recovering energy normally wasted.

The Turbo-Compound then basically consisted of a standard 3350 engine with a new power recovery section inserted between the power and accessory sections. The power recovery section was made up of three ram air-cooled blow-down turbines called Power Recovery Turbines (PRT) . A total of six cylinders fed their exhaust to each turbine. The turbines were mechanically connected to the main crankshaft through fluid couplings and fed approximately 20 percent additional power, obtained from the exhaust, back to the crankshaft and the propeller. One of the features of this arrangement was that there was practically no back pressure transmitted to the basic engine. The little back pressure generated was said to be about equal to that of the jet exhaust stacks previously used on the 3350s. (See Fig. 7-3).

The total advantages of these power plant were:

1. Up to 20 percent less fuel consumption at the same power output of the basic engine.
2. Up to 20 percent total power increase.
3. A 5 percent decrease in specific engine weight. Specific weight about 1 pound/hp.
4. No increase in cowl diameter. Actually, there was a 2.3-inch increase, but this was considered minimal in terms of installation and drag increase.
5. No additional controls for the pilot.

This, then, was the heart of the new airplanes. With a maximum horsepower rating of 3250 hp (dry), and 3500 hp (wet), the wet engines used water injection for one or two minutes on take-off to increase power. The designers now found themselves with enough power to allow appreciable weight increases without loss of performance. True, the new power plant was to cause certain problems, which we will examine later, but the fact remains that it was the magic key that opened new doors to the future of the Super Constellation.

It is interesting to note that Wright was the first company to carry out a Turbo-Compound development, and that it turned out to be the only such design to go into production. Before Wright was finished, it was to manufacture a total of 11,221 units over a period of 10 years, and, in addition to powering the Super Constellations (all except the 24 L–1049s), they also powered the Neptune, the

Fairchild C–119 Flying Boxcar, the entire family of Douglas DC–7 transports, and even a few Martin flying boats.

The Turbo-Compound was, obviously, a somewhat more complex piece of machinery than the regular 3350. Like all advances in technology, certain problems had to be resolved. One early difficulty that arose was caused by the disintegration of the PRT buckets or blades. If the PRT simply ceased to function, the basic engine could still continue to perform, albeit with considerably reduced power. But if the turbine wheel started to come apart, then it became a much different story—those turbine wheels spun at 17,000 rpm. A turbine wheel that begins to disintegrate, for whatever reason, and sheds its blades, then as these fly off in all directions, causes terminal damage to the rest of the engine and in some cases to the adjacent power plant. The solution to this problem was, initially, to strengthen the casing around the PRT. By switching to cast metal, the blades were prevented from leaving the PRT assembly. In time this problem with the PRT's was eliminated.

One of the positive by-products of the PRT was the noise suppression achieved. This was due in part to the different exhaust stacks. The noise reduction was apparent both within and outside the aircraft and was a feature much appreciated by the airlines, who were becoming defensive about noise in the vicinity of airports. It also became obvious that the new engine delivered its power more smoothly, much to the satisfaction of the passengers.

Another problem that arose early in the application of the Turbo-Compound to the Super Constellation had to do with the exhaust. The long and very hot exhaust flames (600–800 degrees Fahrenheit) caused major difficulties with the wing trailing edges. The continued operation of the engines resulted in a marked weakening of the wing structure near the exhaust, due to the heat being applied. The problem was so severe that Lockheed put a special team to work resolving it. It took 9 months and almost $2 million, but eventually the problem was cured, and this particular difficulty was never again encountered.

This problem delayed delivery of the L–1049A and B models to the military and. in fact, set back the entire Super Constellation program. Nevertheless, in time the Turbo-Compound became the finest reciprocating engine of its size and powered many well-known aircraft. It can be speculated that because of this single engine design, the large-scale introduction of turboprop and turbojet powered aircraft in commercial use was probably delayed by some years.

The Turbo-Compound has been viewed by many as a huge, complex relic that should never have been introduced in large quantities. But the fact remains that these engines performed wonderfully well for many years and did so at a fraction of the fuel consumption of their newer, noisier brethren, the turbo jets.

INTEGRALLY STIFFENED SKIN

With these new power plants in hand, Lockheed could now meet the military's requirements for payloads considerably greater than those of the L–1049. With the greater payloads came greater gross weights, up from the 120,000 pounds of the L–1049 to between 133,000 and 145,000 pounds. This meant a total weight increase of some 20 percent. Kelly Johnson wanted to keep the existing wing design and all the excellent flying characteristics inherent in the plane. But this wing had already been reinforced a number of times as the Constellation's gross weights grew from 86,000 to 120,000 pounds. Further reinforcing the wing would impose a severe weight penalty, which no one was really willing to accept. So, once again, Johnson and the other engineers turned to a piece of new technology. Up to this time, the bottom of the wing was made up of skin reinforced with riveted stiffeners. Now a new system of machining offered more strength with less weight. It consisted of integrally stiffened pieces of aluminum alloy.

Such a piece, measuring over 32 feet in length by 4 feet wide, weighed only 323 pounds when finished. The original slab of aluminum weighed 10 times as much. The slab was machined by a huge new skin mill, which cut channels down the length of the 1.75-inch slab, leaving standing ribs 3/16th of an inch thick. There were six such panels in each wing. Compared to the previous method of construction, these new units were one piece, whereas previously there had been 1500 parts which required some 300 man-hours to rivet into an assembly. These panels were machined from a new aluminum alloy known as 75ST. Lockheed's ability to machine such large pieces measuring over 30 feet in length was due to new, improved milling equipment. At that time Lockheed purchased a new Giddings and Lewis skin mill, which allowed the important manufacturing change to take place.

OTHER IMPROVEMENTS

There were other innovations in these latest Super Constellations. A wingtip tank design was developed that carried some 600 gallons in each tank, 1200 gallons total. The use of these tanks was made possible in part by the new wing construction, which permitted the addition of such considerable weights at the extreme ends of the wings. For the cargo versions, a new floor made of extruded magnesium planks was used. Equipped with tie-down rings, seat attachments, and litter fittings and able to withstand loads of 300 pounds per square foot, the new floor made cargo handling far easier.

This, then, was the basis of the fully developed Super Constellation. The immediate results of the total design effort were four separate models—two for the military and two for commercial use. The L–1049A and B models were delivered exclusively to the Air Force and Navy, the A version being the Airborne Early Warning and Control (AEW&C) radar-equipped aircraft, and the B version the long-range cargo/combination model. From these designs there followed shortly thereafter the C model, which was a purely passenger-carrying commercial aircraft, and the first such equipped with the Turbo-Compound engines. Immediately after the C model came the D, which was exclusively a cargo plane and an offshoot of the military B model. The first of each of these four models were delivered within a period of 17 months, between March 1953 and August 1954. Shortly before the D model was delivered, in June 1954, the passenger E model delivery also began.

The design of these aircraft was strongly tied together, even though the type of use for each model dictated some basic differences in the finished product. Actually, from the L–1049A through the L–1049F was a continuous development effort, and it often becomes difficult to distinguish precisely where an idea came from. It should also be clearly understood that the aircraft were not necessarily developed entirely in the sequence of their model numbers.

The B model was delivered before the A model, the reason being that the A model, with its extremely sophisticated radar equipment, took longer to develop and manufacture. Likewise, the E model was delivered before the D model. Actually, in terms of the design, there was one more model that fits into the initial phase of this Super Constellation development, and this was the F model, although the first F aircraft was not delivered until mid-1955. More will be said in later chapters concerning the various models developed. For now, it is sufficient to cover what major ideas went into the Super Constellation.

The Super Constellations, starting with the A model, were used for very different purposes. The reasons that led to their specific development also varied greatly.

Let us now look at what led to the first two, the L–1049A and B, and to what uses they were put. Because those two aircraft were to become an integral part of the U.S. defense establishment and were, in their own unique ways, to break new ground in terms of ways in which airplanes could be used.

7-1 Interior view of the first L–1049, used as a test aircraft, August 1951. The view is looking forward, and shows the various water ballast tanks used to test the basic aircraft with various loads. (Lockheed Martin)

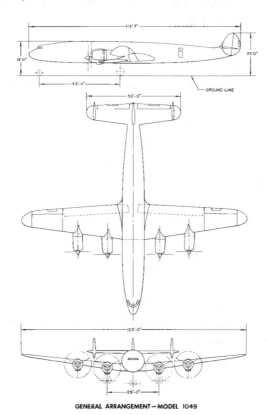

7-2 A schematic view of the L–1049 Super Constellation, 1951. The lengthened fuselage is clearly discernible. (Lockheed Martin)

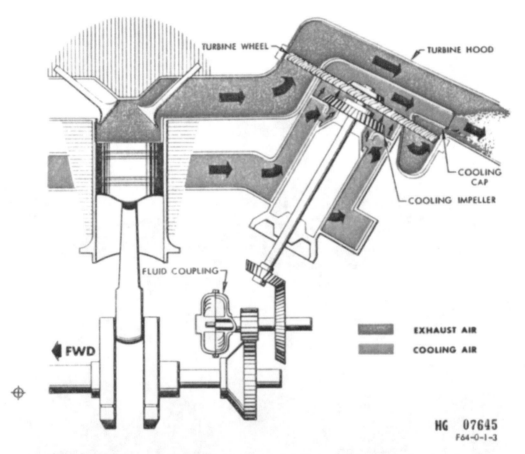

7-3 A cut-away view of the Curtiss-Wright Turbo-Compound engine showing the Power Recovery Turbine (PRT), 1951. The additional horsepower of this engine is what made the Super Constellation concept possible. (Lockheed Martin)

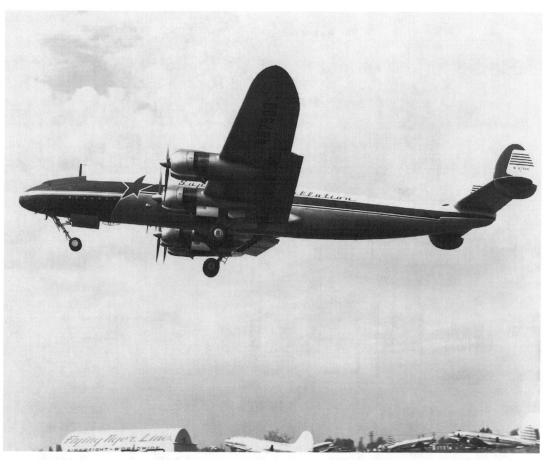
7-4 The original L–1049 Super Constellation test-bed aircraft, 1950. (Lockheed Martin)

7-5 A wing panel made from integrally stiffened skin used on the Super Constellations, 1950. The basic Connie wing had to be strengthened in order to carry the extra weight of the Super Connie models. (Lockheed Martin)

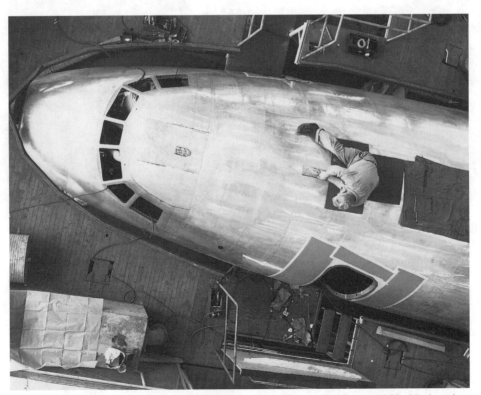

7-6 An overhead view of a Super Constellation being manufactured, 1950. Notice the redesigned cockpit windshield with an eyebrow protusion above the center windows. (Lockheed Martin)

7-7 L–1049 Super Constellations on the Lockheed ramp awaiting delivery to TWA, 1952. (Lockheed Martin)

Chapter 8

A NEW MEMBER OF THE FAMILY: THE WARNING STAR

In 1950 a new chapter began in the long history of the Constellation, for in that year Lockheed began production of a new and unique version of the airplane. Known as an Airborne Early Warning and Control (AEW&C) aircraft, the production of this version for the military services would eventually total over 25 percent of the total number of Constellations built in all its models over the entire production history, including both Constellations and Super Constellations.

But the total quantity of these aircraft procured was only one of a number of unusual facts and events associated with this model. The previous history and the circumstances that led to this design were in themselves intriguing. The AEW&C was the first of its kind to go into production and be deployed anywhere in the world. Its design, functions, and applications were all aviation firsts. The aircraft played a significant part in the air defense system of the United States and then confounded its detractors and the experts by literally coming back from the scrap heap to be used in new applications. The entire AEW&C program from beginning to end was shrouded in various degrees of secrecy, and to this day few people fully realize what the AEW&C Super Constellation did for the United States.

In summer 1950, the military began discussing some possible new models of the Constellation with Lockheed, and it marked the beginning of a new chapter in the long history of this aircraft. Lockheed then was already looking ahead to further developments of the Super Constellation for commercial uses. But as the military services took the first of what would be a number of significant steps affecting the Constellation program, the entire developmental program began to move at a much faster rate. For despite the fact that some months would pass before Lockheed would begin developmental work on their new L–1049 Super Constellation, the discussions with the military services acted as a catalyst and resulted in the total development of the Super Constellation concept.

Although the original circumstances that helped bring about the development of the Super Constellation (the L–1049) were essentially tied to commercial aviation, the second part of the evolution of the Super Constellation was without doubt greatly hastened and influenced by the needs of the Navy and Air Force. True, the results were quickly adapted to commercial use. Nevertheless, the initial stimulus was from the defense establishment, and it is entirely possible that without that prodding the later versions of the Super Constellation might have either come about much more slowly or not at all.

Granted, Kelly Johnson and his crew were already looking hard at various improvements of the original L–1049 to make it more attractive to the commercial market. But extensive changes such as those that eventually took place cost a great deal of money; without firm orders, Lockheed's management would have to think twice before committing the company to a lengthy research and development program. Instead, with military orders in hand, Lockheed could complete this further step forward at little added cost.

There was another reason why without the military orders the later Super Constellations might never have seen the light of day. By the early and mid-1950s, the new power plants available were stimulating much discussion about commercial aircraft powered by either turbojet or turboprop engines. Certain weaknesses of these engines, especially their high fuel consumption, tended to discourage their use. Nevertheless, if the later models of the Super Constellations had not appeared when they did, this author believes one of two things might well have occurred. Either Douglas would have completely dominated the commercial market with reciprocating propeller transports, or turboprop airplanes would have made a large-scale appearance. The combination of availability of funds and the placing of deadlines by the defense establishment was the one-two punch that changed the future of the Constellation to a very large degree. Thus it was that these military requirements caused Lockheed to complete the two-step transition from the standard Constellation to the Super Constellation.

In early 1950, as Lockheed was developing the original L–1049, the needs of the airlines were such that very large increases in either payload or range were not of a magnitude as to require such radical improvements. But in July of that year, when the Navy approached Lockheed, that was precisely what they did require, and this naturally sped up the normal step-by-step growth of the airplane considerably. Once again, military needs affected commercial performance, and once again the entire process accurately reflected the events of the time.

THE NAVY STEPS IN

The Navy had been considering a follow-on design to the PO–1W radar picket aircraft for some time. Although the two aircraft built of this model had proven very successful, the Navy wanted an aircraft with more range and on-station loiter time, more cabin space, and higher payload and gross weights. Kelly Johnson and company met with the Navy representatives and brought forth a preliminary design that aroused much interest. Shortly thereafter, the Navy Department placed an order for six prototypes of this design. Known at Lockheed as the L–1049A, it was identified by the Navy as a WV–2 fleet defense aircraft. At this time, the Navy viewed this airplane's role as mainly defensive while supporting a fleet operating far off-shore. Its true role was not identified until considerably later.

Soon thereafter, the Navy asked Lockheed whether a version of their Super Constellation could be used as a long-range aircraft capable of a multipurpose role carrying cargo/passengers/medical litters. The airplane would have to meet the requirement of rapid conversion to any of the three configurations, namely, carrying cargo, passengers, or air evacuation medical cases. It would also need to have a long range. Again, Lockheed came up with a preliminary design, and this model was identified as the L–1049B.

Not long after the Navy had approved the preliminary design of the L–1049B, it placed an initial order for nine aircraft. Although the L–1049B design was initiated shortly after the L–1049A, the B model would fly and become operational considerably sooner than the A. This was the case because the development, procurement, and manufacture of the B model was considerably simpler and more straightforward than the A, with its highly sophisticated electronic payload. However, much of the airframe, systems, and power plant technology was common to both, and the two designs can be said to have been developed simultaneously.

Let us now examine, with some care, not only the design and operation of this new version of the Super Constellation, identified as the L–1049A, but also, and very important, certain historical events that led to the need for this particular aircraft. Because, as always, aircraft designs are almost entirely the end result of design processes that are in turn begun in response to very specific needs. Thus, if the L–1049A is viewed as the beginning of a totally new design and production cycle of the Constellation family, it was also the end result of a series of events that began some six years earlier. These events resulted directly in the need for a radar picket aircraft, and the end product came to be known as the oddest-looking airplane ever flown at that time. Although the events are quite involved and intricate, they are worth examining, because they resulted in a total production of over 200 AEW&C aircraft. Furthermore, the events form a capsule version of world events of that period.

EVENTS LEADING UP TO THE AEW AIRCRAFT

During World War II, the Soviet Union was officially an ally of the United States and, to be sure, fought valiantly against Nazi Germany. But the Soviet government considered the Western nations their natural enemies, and thus did everything in its power to obtain all the military intelligence it could from both the United States and Great Britain. As part of this effort, Soviet spies were able to acquire a great deal of information relating to the design and manufacture of the early atomic bombs. In what proved to be a surprisingly short time, the Soviets applied this information to their own nuclear program, and sometime in August 1949 exploded their first nuclear device.

Although this piece of information was serious enough for the Western alliance, especially in view of the Cold War, which was quickly escalating at that time, this new weapon still did not pose a serious threat for the United States, because the Soviets were not believed to have a suitable delivery system. But shortly thereafter, this hope was dashed, and the presence of a growing Soviet strategic aircraft fleet was confirmed. Herein lies another strange tale.

In spring and summer 1944, the United States was beginning heavy bombardment of the Japanese home islands with Boeing B–29 Superfortress heavy bombers. These B–29s were based in China, and thus had a long way to go to reach their targets. The Japanese defenses were varied in their effectiveness, but on at least some raids, American losses were high. On July 29, 1944, some 60 B–29s struck at the steel plants located at Anshan, Manchuria. The target was defended by both fighters and heavy flak. One of the aircraft, commanded by Captain Howard R. Jarrell, had just dropped its bomb load and was making its turn away from the target when it received a direct flak hit below the starboard wing. With one engine out and a second losing oil, Jarrell elected to head for the Soviet Union, a decision that was based on the briefings he had previously received. The B–29 reached the vicinity of Vladivostok and was met by Soviet fighters. The aircraft safely landed, and the crew was interned.

Then, on November 10, during a night raid over the Japanese island of Kyushu, a B–29 commanded by Captain Weston H. Price found itself coming off the target with insufficient fuel to return to base. Price also decided to head for

Soviet territory and landed safely at Vladivostok. This crew was also interned, and their B–29 was never seen again. On November 21, 1944, a third B–29 flown by Lieutenant William J. Mickish, who, after bombing Kyushu, also found he could not make it back to base. Heading for the same Soviet city, this airplane again made it safely.

The crews were eventually returned safely to the United States, but nothing more was heard about the aircraft. Then, some two years later, in November 1946, the German press reported that the Soviets were producing a carbon copy of the B–29. This report was not believed by the West, but in August 1947, copies of the B–29 were seen flying over Moscow. The Soviets had disassembled the three captured aircraft, and, through reverse engineering, had managed to develop drawings and production tooling for manufacturing these aircraft. The Soviets identified this airplane as the TU–4, and by summer 1949 some 300 of these aircraft were operational with Soviet strategic bombing units.

At that time, the United States believed that these aircraft, launched from far northern bases, could strike our largest centers of population on one-way suicide missions. This, then, was the initial act in the development of the Soviet Union's strategic bombing fleet.

The TU–4 was followed by further designs that were larger, faster, and had considerably longer range. By the mid-1950s, the Soviets were putting into operational use a turboprop bomber known as the TU–20, also sometimes referred to as the TU–95. This aircraft was in the general category of the Convair B–36, and although it had less range, it boasted considerably greater speed. It could easily carry multiple nuclear devices, and had the necessary range to reach almost any part of the continental United States and return to base. The TU–20's design philosophy was in great part based on the TU–4 and can be traced directly back to those captured B–29s. Thus, by the late 1950s, the Soviets were directly threatening the continental United States with their equivalent of the U.S. Air Force Strategic Air Command (SAC).

This potentially awesome threat by the Soviet bombers carrying nuclear weapons was the motivator for the creation of a radar picket fleet of aircraft. But there were still more ingredients that led to this aircraft, and once again it is necessary to go back to the cataclysmic days of World War II. In 1944 and 1945, the U.S. Navy was subjected to a deadly assault from the Japanese weapon known as the kamikaze, or "divine wind." These were the infamous piloted suicide attacks, and, especially in 1945, they proved highly effective in reaching American ships and either sinking them or putting them completely out of action. Out of this period there grew a need for airborne radar. The reason for this is simply that radar, until recently, could see only as far as the horizon. Putting radar in an airplane allowed its range to increase dramatically and enabled warning of approaching aircraft to be given much earlier. This in turn permitted defending aircraft to be in a far better position to meet and destroy the threat.

After World War II, the famed Massachusetts Institute of Technology undertook developing a satisfactory airborne radar. In doing so, they also provided the Navy with another use for the sophisticated electronic gear, namely, that of helping monitor and control various units of a surface fleet, as well as providing warning of approaching enemy ships.

In May 1948, the Navy was attempting to find the right aircraft for carrying the airborne radar that had been developed. The Douglas DC–6 was considered but left something to be desired. Then along came Lockheed's C. G. Vogeley of the sales department. He showed the Navy how the L–749A could easily accommodate the necessary electronics because of its long landing gear, payload capability, range, and the famous triple tail to give it directional control in spite of the huge radome planned which would be mounted on the cabin roof. The Navy ordered two of the aircraft, known as the PO–1W, and the first one flew on June 17, 1949. The aircraft had a certain resemblance to a humpbacked porpoise, but it flew well, and the electronic gear inside performed its wizardry much to the satisfaction of the Navy.

The two PO–1Ws being tested by the Navy were strictly experimental models and were designed, among other things, to help prove the value of the radar picket concept. This they did successfully. Actually, these were not the first such aircraft acquired by the Navy. Starting in 1950, before the PO–1W's were operational, the Navy had been flying two converted Boeing B–17 Flying Fortresses, each carrying early warning radar in a belly radome mounted below the bomb bay. Known as PBW-17s, these two aircraft flew on radar picket duty for almost two years and then were declared surplus. But these two B-17s had more adventures in store for them. Purchased and reconditioned in 1961, they were flown across the Atlantic Ocean to England, along with a third B–17, and were used in the filming of the movie *The War Lover*. The story of this transoceanic flight by the three war-weary birds is told by Martin Caidin in his book *Everything but the Flak*, published in 1964.

THE AEW CONCEPT TAKES FORM

As is often the case in human affairs, the government's thinking process that eventually led to the acquisition of an entire fleet of AEW&C airplanes was by no means direct. The Navy ordered the first of these aircraft in mid-1950, but for a different purpose altogether. The Navy's original interest in radar picket aircraft was in:

1. Providing early warning of enemy aircraft attacking fleet units.
2. Acting as an airborne Combat Information Center (CIC) that could vector fighters against enemy aircraft, and
3. Directing antisubmarine warfare, as well as other various duties, from its carriers.

As long as a fleet was operating 1000 to 1500 miles from a friendly air base, the new plane could fly out to sea and protect it by orbiting in the area for a number of hours.

At this time, in mid-1950, protecting the mainland from enemy air attacks was just beginning to be identified as a specific air defense requirement. This did not occur earlier because intelligence information being received was not such as to convince military planners of the Soviet potential for launching a successful major air attack on the continental United States. But by late 1950, the stories being told by German scientists who had worked in the Soviet Union since 1945 and were now being repatriated, gave cause for some real alarm. They spoke of large, powerful turboprop engines and of new long-range strategic bombers. Coupled with the overall tension caused by the Korean War, this news set off a massive defense effort aimed at preventing any meaningful successful penetration of continental air space by Soviet strategic aircraft. As it happened, the intelligence reports were in part misleading and led military planners to erroneous conclusions. For the Soviet main threat, the Tupolev TU–20, later to become known as the TU–95 Bear, rather than becoming operational in the early 1950s, did not reach this stage until 1957. Nevertheless, all the frantic work that followed the early reports of late 1950 were essentially based on this preliminary information.

The need for AEW&C units to augment the air defenses of the continental United States was specifically identified and emphasized in 1951 by the release of the Charles Report. This report was drafted by personnel at MIT working under an Air Force contract to study the entire air defense picture. The Charles Report, followed by a second report released in August 1952, showed the need for in-depth radar nets located far to the north of potential U.S. targets, with said nets able to provide 3 to 6 hours of warning of an impending enemy air attack. In addition, due to the long-range capability ascribed to the Soviet strategic bomber fleet being built around the TU–95 Bear turboprop bomber, it was shown to be necessary to defend against an end-around sneak attack bypassing the northern radar nets. Such an attack could come over water from the northeast or northwest approaches to the continental United States.

The overall plan that evolved grew and developed over a considerable length of time. It began with numerous mainland radar stations coupled with local fighter interceptor units. The number of these radar sites grew to 44 by 1950. Many of these sites were then woven into a nationwide integrated defense system by 1954. This was expanded by 1957 into a double line of radar sites covering the northern approaches. Following this, military planners came up with a formidable barrier consisting of three separate radar nets.

The first, known as the Pinetree Line, stretched generally along the U.S.–Canadian border from the Pacific Ocean to Maine. This line was finished in 1955. The second line, known as the Mid-Canada Line, stretched from coast to coast along the 55th parallel and entered service in 1957. The third, and by far most expensive line, was the Distant Early Warning (DEW) Line. Built north of the Arctic Circle, it extended from Alaska to Greenland across the northern reaches of Canada. This line also became operational in 1957 at a cost of over $400 million, and was finished in spite of unbelievably difficult working conditions. It took four years to build the DEW line.

Unfortunately, this radar coverage did not give any defense whatsoever against aircraft approaching the U.S. coasts from the northwest or northeast over the ocean approaches. True, these routes were considerably longer. However, by the early 1950s, the Soviets were already flying prototypes of turboprop bombers with the range to fly just such mission profiles. Therefore, adjuncts to these electronic radar barriers, radar picket ships, were to patrol off-shore of both coasts to prevent long-range aircraft from completely bypassing all of the radar nets and reaching the continental United States without any advance warning. Off the Atlantic coast there were also placed three radar stations built on structures not unlike off-shore oil-drilling rigs, and appropriately named Texas Towers. Finally, further out to sea, the Navy and Air Force were to operate radar picket airplanes officially designated as AEW&C aircraft.

The basic concept that envisioned using AEW&C aircraft was simplicity itself, but the realization of that concept was anything but simple to carry out. As originally drawn up in summer 1951, the concept developed by the Air Force saw a need for two seaward extensions of the land-based radar networks. It is interesting to note that back in August 1947, General George C. Kenney, U.S. Air Force, then Commander of SAC, made a strong pitch for equipping some of the new Corvair B–36 long-range, heavy bombers with radar for off-shore patrol duty. This could be said to have been a forerunner of the AEW&C idea and was strangely prophetic.

This original planning envisioned a need for augmenting the basic radar nets because they would not give any real warning of enemy aircraft approaching from the east or west toward the American coastlines, and nets along the coasts would improve this situation only slightly. Thus, the original thinking called for two lines of warning, sometimes called barriers, to be set up off-shore of the two coasts. Each barrier would be made up of a number of stations, and at each station an aircraft would orbit in a long, race track pattern.

The barriers were to be some 800 miles long each and located approximately 225 miles off-shore. A barrier might be made up of four or more stations, with the aircraft flying on station some 150 miles apart. This was estimated to provide a 90 percent coverage. In addition, Navy picket ships were to assist the whole operation with their seaborne radar sets.

The barrier, in effect, would be an electronic wall some 800 miles long and 5 miles high, with the airborne radar able to detect not only any aircraft moving through at any altitude from near sea level to 40,000 feet but also suspicious ship movements. The theoretical range of the radar sets was 240 miles, and this dictated the distance between stations of 150 miles, because a considerable overlap was considered necessary. The actual effective range of radar sets can vary with such factors as weather, the state of a particular radar set, and the size and nature of the radar return. Based on this plan, the Air Force initially saw a need for 56 AEW&C aircraft in late 1951.

The application of the AEW&C concept came about when someone realized the obvious: namely, that an airplane capable of loitering over a fleet located a great distance from land and able to spot attacking aircraft at almost any altitude while they were still up to 200 miles away could perform the same defensive function for a land mass. In this case, the land mass turned out to be the continental United States.

THE CONCEPT IS REFINED

A second part of this concept was actually formalized later, and it saw a need for more radar barriers further away from the continental coasts, which would provide even greater warning time. This additional need was in part a reaction to the August 1953 explosion of a thermonuclear device by the Soviet Union, coupled with intelligence reports indicating a fast-developing Soviet capability to deliver bombing attacks with turboprop-powered long-range aircraft.

At this time, an interesting rivalry developed between the Navy and the Air

Force concerning the proposed new radar picket operations. The Air Force had the primary responsibility for continental air defense, including the proposed radar nets far to the north. The Navy's only clear responsibility at that time was providing some few radar picket ships which would patrol off-shore, and with their radar pinpoint enemy aircraft trying to sneak in very low. Although the Air Force also felt it had a responsibility for the off-shore airborne radar picket operations, the Navy happened to have the right airplane at the right time.

The solution arrived at provided for the Air Force to staff airborne picket lines some few hundred miles off each coast, while the Navy would handle similar operations considerably further out over the oceans. The Air Force would operate from mainland bases, and the Navy would fly from bases in Newfoundland and the Azores over the Atlantic and Alaska, Midway Island, and the Hawaiian Islands over the Pacific. This arrangement not only satisfied the honor of each service but also created a double line of defense. The only fly in the ointment for the Air Force was that the only AEW&C design that looked promising was already being procured by the Navy.

At this point the Navy's experience with airborne radar was seen as the answer to the threat of air attacks approaching from off-shore. The planners in the Pentagon began looking around for the airframe and hardware necessary to implement a viable airborne early warning system. They took a long, hard look at the Navy, which had done a great majority of the development work on the AEW&C concept. The Navy had already begun to procure some of the new aircraft for fleet defense purposes. Under the circumstances, the top military planners and decision makers felt that it would make sense, both militarily and politically, to direct the Navy to establish the new barriers located farther out to sea. So it came about that Lockheed found itself with simultaneous orders for these intricate and sophisticated aircraft from both the Air Force and the Navy and, in fact, with a competition betweens the two services for delivery positions, as both services scrambled to put these aircraft into service by 1954.

The maps at the end of this chapter show the approximate locations of both the Air Force and Navy barriers, as well as the various radar nets the barriers were augmenting. The aircraft, which were to man the barriers of both services, were ordered and delivered over a period of time, not only because of the obvious need for production time but also because of budgetary constraints coupled with the fact that the total need of both services became fully apparent only over a number of years.

The original planning was based on a 24-hour/day coverage of all barrier stations. The airplane Lockheed was proposing would have sufficient fuel to remain in the air over 20 hours if need be. Thus, two aircraft each remaining on station 12 hours could fully staff a station. Naturally, the planners included the need for extra aircraft, because at any one time a certain percentage of the total fleet would always be tied up in training or would be on the ground undergoing major maintenance. Based on this, it was determined that some 40 airplanes would be required to fully staff each barrier.

INITIAL PROCUREMENT OF THE WARNING STAR

The Air Force actually was the first military service whose role in this mission was clearly defined, namely, the manning of the two barriers which were closer to shore. The Navy was to staff the two barriers further off-shore, but their total mission was spelled out after the Air Force's, even though, ironically, it was the Navy that had pioneered the type of aircraft, tested it, helped design the production aircraft, and had placed the first orders. So, when the Air Force placed their initial orders, they were in one hell of a hurry to get quick delivery. This led to the suggestion by Lockheed to change the order for Super Constellation C–121C transports to one for RC–121C AEW&C aircraft.

The airplane that the Navy began talking to Lockheed about in the summer of 1950 became known initially as the PO–2W. After a short time this was changed to the designation WV–2. Lockheed gave it the name Warning Star, a name familiarly used by all for both these airplanes as well as the general program. The WV–2 was a direct outgrowth of the PO–1W prototype airplanes, which the Navy had helped develop together with Lockheed only a couple of years earlier. The results of the operations with the two prototypes had been highly successful, and the Navy had been considering ordering the PO–1W airplane into quantity production when another Lockheed representative came on the scene. He was Henry Rempt, known by his co-workers as Hank Radar.

Rempt was an electronics and armament engineer and as such had many dealings with the military. The Navy had developed a 17.5-foot search radar to be mounted on blimps. Rempt immediately recognized the tremendous advantage such a large antenna would provide over the six-foot model then in use on the PO–1W. Rempt was, as he put it in a letter to the author, "uninhibited by any excessive knowledge of aerodynamics!" So he suggested that the new 17.5-foot antenna be mounted on the bottom of the new Super Constellation fuselage. The engineers at Lockheed thought he was crazy, but after some further consideration, realized that he had come up with the answer to a lot of problems. Thus it was suggested to the Navy that they purchase a new radar picket aircraft based on the then–newly designed Super Constellation and mount the larger antenna.

Because the effectiveness and range of a radar unit relates directly to the size of the antenna, the new one recommended by Rempt was a tremendous improvement, what with its being almost triple in size. In addition, the use of the new Super Constellation concept, including the Turbo-Compound engines able to lift much greater weights, permitted the Navy to realize an aircraft design that would have more internal space for electronics and crew and a greater fuel load for a much increased loiter capability. The Navy was definitely interested. They had had considerable experience with Lockheed in the form of the P2V Neptune patrol bomber, that famous airplane built continuously for 20 years! They knew the quality of Lockheed products, and the PO–1Ws were currently demonstrating what the concept could do in real situations. So it was that in mid-1950, the Navy began contractual talks with Lockheed on the procurement of quantities of the new radar picket airplane.

Meanwhile, by early 1951, the Air Defense Command (ADC) of the Air Force began to pinpoint a need for AEW aircraft to protect ocean approaches. This need was reinforced by the Navy's announcement that radar picket ships that could partially accomplish the same job would not be available before 1954. By mid-1951, a decision had been made that the Air Force go ahead with procurement of the only AEW aircraft that was then actually available. This, of course, was the Navy WV–2 Fleet Defense Aircraft, which could actually be used as both an offensive and a defensive weapons system. This decision led in January 1951 to the conversion of the Air Force order for 10 C–121C cargo aircraft to RC–121C AEW&C aircraft.

Actually, the Air Force's decision to convert the previously ordered C–121C airplanes was not their initial decision. When they first determined that they would have to rather quickly procure at least an initial complement of AEW aircraft, they were thinking in terms of using some rather old B–29s converted to this purpose. The development work on the first B–29 was being carried out at Wright Field, Ohio, when Rempt happened to visit the project. He quickly pointed out to the Air Force project people that the end result of all their labors would be an aircraft whose capabilities would be no better than the existing Lockheed P2V ASW Neptune and that these capabilities were not really adequate for the AEW function. The B–29 project was under the sponsorship of the ADC, which was also procuring Lockheed's F–104 as a first-line aircraft. Thus, Rempt already knew the people involved at ADC, and he elected to go talk to them.

ADC indicated their acute need for AEW airplanes and mentioned the Navy PO–1W as an airplane they felt could do the job if available. But Rempt pointed out to them the inferiority of this prototype as compared to the 17.5-foot antenna on then newly proposed WV–2.

The Air Force quickly saw Rempt's point, and in late 1950 they asked if they could obtain an aircraft equivalent to the WV–2 in short order. After some investigation, it was determined that the controllers' consoles were going to be a bottleneck. These consoles are the very heart of the system, and the Air Force would not be able to obtain ready-to-operate aircraft until some two years after the Navy planes flew. This was simply unacceptable to the Air Force and precipitated some intense discussions in a desperate effort to solve the problem.

The solution that resulted was an ingenious one indeed. Lockheed would take 10 L–1049B Super Constellations that the Air Force had ordered as cargo-passenger C–121 aircraft. These planes would then be built as the radar picket version and would carry the same height finder and search radars as the WV–2 Navy birds, because these items of equipment were available from the manufacturer. To substitute for the long-lead controller consoles, Lockheed would design and build these consoles themselves. These units, however, would have to be fitted with older scopes, which were smaller than those the Navy was going to obtain. This particular deficiency bothered the Air Force, but once again, resourcefulness won the day.

Lockheed went to Ed Land of Polaroid, the inventor of the Land Camera and many other devices. A unit was developed that would take a photograph of the radar scope. Each photograph carried the image of four sweeps of the radar antenna. The film was then quickly developed by the Polaroid instant development system, after which it was projected on a 24-inch circular screen. The radar tracks showed up as four blips, and with the use of filters, the first two blips showed up in green, and the last two were red. This gave the operator an instantaneous picture of the direction of the target. The resulting presentations were considerably brighter than the typical radar scopes, and because the picture showed four complete sweeps at one time, it was no longer necessary for the operator to maintain a continuous observation of the scope.

The Air Force was pleased with the proposed solution, and the initial order for C–121Cs became instead an order for RC–121C radar picket airplanes. As it turned out, the Air Force planes would fly before the Navy WV–2.

THE WARNING STAR FLEET GROWS

Because the decisions as to the actual responsibility for the AEW operation came over a period of time, the aircraft acquired by the Navy and Air Force were placed on order at various dates. For this reason, the delivery of aircraft took place over an extended period of time, and the total AEW concept was implemented in pieces over three years.

The initial Navy order was for an aircraft to carry out fleet defense operations and had nothing to do with the continental U.S. air defense mission. The same appears to have been true of the second and third orders by the Navy. The last two Navy orders were definitely in support of the projected air defense missions. The Air Force, on the other hand, ordered all of its aircraft with the air defense mission in mind. It should be pointed out that the specific part to be played by the Navy in the air defense of the continental United States was not fully formalized until late 1954. It was this decision that resulted in the large Navy orders in fiscal years 1955 and 1956. However, readers should keep in mind that at no time were all the Navy WV–2s committed to air defense. A portion were always on call for a variety of assignments around the world, often relating directly to fleet movements and missions, as well as to trouble spots that developed.

The table below presents a graphic picture of the procurement history of the Warning Star airplanes.

AEW&C Aircraft Order Recap

Ordered FY (Date)	Type	Quantity	Acceptance Dates
USN (7/50)	WV–2	6	10/53 to 4/54
USAF 51 (7/50)*	RC–121C	10	10/53 to 11/54
USN 51	WV–2	6	6/54 to 7/54
USAF 52 (1/52)	RC–121D	15	8/54 to 1/55
USN 52	WV–2	20	8/54 to 4/55
USAF 53	RC–121D	30	2/55 to 4/56
USAF 54	RC–121D	5	5/56
USN 55**	WV–3	8	3/55 to 6/55
USN 55	WV–2	45	2/56 to 12/56
USAF 55	RC–121D	22	5/56 to 10/56
USN 56	WV–2	47	2/57 to 12/57
USN 57	WV–2	18	1/58 to 9/58
Total:		232	

* This order originally for C–121C cargo aircraft was converted to RC–121C AEW&C aircraft in 5-51.

** The USN WV–3 aircraft had the regular AEW&C capability, plus additional equipment to aid in weather reconnaissance, especially hurricane tracking and analysis. (See Chapter 9.)

The table shows the sequence in which the Warning Stars were ordered and delivered. It quite accurately reflects the relative importance of the Air Force and Navy in the AEW&C program and the various decisions made at the highest levels concerning this program.

Thus we see how at the beginning of FY 51 (mid-1950), the Navy placed its initial order for six of the WV–2s, with which it planned to develop the concept of fleet defense aircraft. Shortly thereafter, the Air Force placed its initial order for 10 C–121C cargo aircraft, which were essentially identical to the just-ordered Navy planes. In May 1951, the Air Force, as a result of the efforts of Lockheed in general and Henry Rempt in particular, was able to convert this order to RC–121C picket aircraft. Later in fiscal year 1951, the Navy ordered six more WV–2s, as it evidently saw more need for this type of aircraft in support of its worldwide fleet operations, especially with the police action in Korea. By fiscal year 1952, the need for AEW&C aircraft was gaining some urgency, and both services placed additional orders; the Navy for 20 more, and the Air Force for 15 RC–121Ds, which were essentially identical to the Navy WV–2s. These 15, together with the previous 10 RC–121Cs would give the Air Force an initial minimum capability to operate a picket patrol off one of the coasts. This order was also in response to an Air Force requirement established in late 1951 for 56 AEW aircraft. The Air Force followed this up in fiscal year 1953 with an order for 30 RC 121Ds and in FY 54 with an order for 5 more of the same.

These additional 35 aircraft in effect completed the original Air Force requirement for 58 airplanes and further gave this service the means to operate a second coastal picket patrol. By 1954, the Navy's role in all of this had finally been resolved at the highest policy levels, and accordingly, in FY 1955, the Navy ordered a whopping 45 WV–2s, which would suffice to man one complete Ocean Barrier. At the same time the Navy also placed an order for eight WV–3s, which were basically WV–2s, but with the additional capability for carrying out extensive and varied weather reconnaissance, including penetration of hurricanes. In the same fiscal year, the Air Force, whose part in all this now appeared somewhat larger, ordered an additional and final quantity of 22 RC–121Ds. Then in FY 1956, the Navy, still striving to complete their AEW fleet, placed a final order for 47 WV–2s, this being the largest order of this type of aircraft ever placed up to that time or since. The Navy, it must be remembered, used a sizable portion of their AEW force in fleet support. When they initially deployed airplanes for the Atlantic Barrier, they temporarily used aircraft destined for fleet use, which were later replaced as more airplanes were delivered in 1956 and 1957. This, then, is the procurement history of the airplane, and ironically, shows that although it was the Air

Force that played catch-up initially, it was the Navy that was forced by top-level decisions to do the same at the end.

DESCRIPTION OF THE WARNING STAR

In the previous chapter we looked at some of the new technology that went into the basic Super Constellation model, starting with the L–1049A. Now, let us take a look at what this radar picket airplane was like that was about to start down the production line.

The L–1049A/WV–2/RC–121D aircraft bears some careful scrutiny, inasmuch as it was a truly unique airplane in a number of ways. The basic airplane was identical in its dimensions to all other Super Constellations, except the last model, the 1649A. These dimensions were a wing span of 123 feet, a fuselage length (including the nose weather radar) of 116 feet, 2 inches, and an overall height of 24 feet, 8 inches at the top of the tail fins. The external appearance, however, was certainly different from all other Super Constellations and, in fact, from all other airplanes except the two prototype Lockheed/USN PO–1Ws. Above the fuselage, directly over the wing, jutted a majestic plastic radome not unlike a shark's fin in appearance. This structure housed the APS–45 height finder radar, and measured eight feet high, with a teardrop-shaped cross-section to reduce drag. Directly underneath the wing was attached a bathtub or bowl-shaped radome, built by Zenith Plastics of Los Angeles and said to be the largest plastic part ever manufactured up to that time. It housed the APS–20B search radar and measured some 19 feet by 29 feet by 4 feet deep, with a mere 14 inches ground clearance.

In addition to these very noticeable radar housings, the aircraft also had the first application of wingtip tanks on a large airplane. These tip tanks gave the aircraft an unusually rakish appearance, especially if the aircraft was photographed in a bank or turn.

The two highly noticeable protuberances on the fuselage led to a number of nicknames. For example, ADC at one time coined and used the name the Hunchback of ADC for this aircraft. Kelly Johnson himself made the following comment during a speech in the mid-1950s. He said, "Speaking of protuberances, these bulges have appeared so illogical to the layman, that we have been suspected of designing an airplane to carry giraffes. The lower radome, approximately 19 feet by 29 feet on the underside resembles a medium-sized swimming pool. The eight-foot-high dome on the top of the fuselage appears adequate for the upper extremity!" On a more serious note, either Lockheed or the Navy officially dubbed the aircraft Warning Star, a most fitting name, often used to refer to the entire AEW&C program, both Navy and Air Force.

We have already discussed the presence of new technology items such as the Curtiss-Wright Turbo-Compound engines, the integrally stiffened aluminum skin panels on the wings, and the 600-gallon wingtip tanks. Other changes and additions were also incorporated in the A model. Some of these were actually incorporated first on the B or cargo model, which, as previously mentioned, came off the assembly line before the A model. Those features common to both included fuselage and inner wing reinforcing; new, heavier main landing gear; aft cargo door; center wing section fuel cells; no cabin step; integrally stiffened wing lower surface; a few round windows; and a new oil transfer system. In addition to these items, the following changes were instituted on the A model only: The fuselage was redesigned to better accommodate the upper and lower radomes, known as the dorsal and ventral radomes; the outer wing was integrally stiffened so as to handle the extra weight of the tip tanks; a fuselage fuel tank was installed for extra range; the wingtip tanks were made standard, although detachable; and the floor installed was lighter than the cargo floor on the B model. Note that the L–1049B/RC–121C did not have the tip tanks.

This aircraft had a maximum overload take-off weight of 143,600 pounds, 12 tons heavier than the L–1049 model, which was certainly a notable growth, considering that the same basic structure was being used. The 10 fuel tanks, including the wingtip tanks, carried a grand total of 8,750 gallons of fuel.

THE WARNING STAR PROGRAM TAKES OFF

As first the Air Force RC–121Cs and then the Navy WV–2s began coming off the Burbank assembly lines, the respective services had to start the complex process that would culminate in operational units carrying out designated missions. However, a number of problems faced both the Air Force and the Navy. The AEW&C program involved a brand-new weapons system of considerable sophistication. This meant a training program for operating both the aircraft and its various systems, as well as all the complex and necessary maintenance. The maintenance aspect was complicated by the fact that both the electronics and the Curtiss-Wright engines were new to the Air Force. The Navy had accumulated some experience with the Turbo-Compounds (on the Lockheed P2V Neptune patrol bomber), but it, too, had to assimilate the new and complex electronics systems.

The Navy also found itself without an adequate available force of manpower experienced in either flying the big birds or operating the electronic gear. To top it all off, there was the double whammy of the extreme weather frequently encountered over the North Atlantic and North Pacific areas where the patrols would operate coupled with various equipment problems inherent in any new and complex airplane. It is not an exaggeration to say that all personnel involved found themselves facing a challenge of awesome proportions.

The two services had highly competent officers to lead their respective programs, the Air Force assigning Brigadier General Kenneth Gibson to command the newly formed 8th Air Division, and the Navy Captain (later Rear Admiral) Wes Bying to command the Airborne Early Warning Wing, Atlantic.

Although, as previously noted, the Navy had placed the earlier orders for AEW&C aircraft, the Air Force played a successful game of catch-up through the strategy of converting their orders for C–121C cargo aircraft to RC–121Cs. The success of this maneuver was due also to the technical ingenuity of Henry Rempt and his Lockheed cohorts working together with Polaroid. By this time, Lockheed was beginning to appreciate the possibility that the total orders for this type of aircraft could amount to very substantial numbers.

The first AEW&C airplane flying was an Air Force RC–121C in March 1953, with first acceptance by the Air Force in October 1953. Simultaneously, the Air Force established the 4701st AEW&C Squadron at McClellan Air Force Base outside of Sacramento, California.

Also in October 1953, Lockheed began delivering WV–2s to the Navy. The Navy formed a VW-1 Squadron at Pearl Harbor in April 1954, with which to begin operational test flying and procedural developments. Not only was it necessary to write a whole new operational manual on the best uses of the Warning Stars, but the fact was that without sufficient aircraft on hand, neither service could begin to set up even a single off-shore barrier.

A month later, in May 1954, the first RC–121D flew, and in June, the Air Force accepted their first one. In August the Air Force began the same type of operational test flights as the Navy from McClellan AFB. This was followed in December by the activation of the West Coast counterpart, the 552nd Wing at McClellan.

The Navy commissioned the Airborne Early Warning Wing, Atlantic, at Patuxent River, Maryland, on July 1, 1955, with the three member squadrons activated on August 1, September 1, and October 1. On May 1, 1956, the wing moved to Argentia NAS, Newfoundland, and on July 1, 1956, the Atlantic Barrier was initiated on a full-time basis. From this date on, for more than six years, there was never a time when the Atlantic approaches to the continental United States were not guarded by at least one aircraft from either the Navy or the Air Force. Actually, except for the very beginning phase, both of the two Atlantic Barriers had aircraft on station maintaining their vigilance.

While the Navy began its full-time operational AEW flights over the Atlantic, the Air Force began its portion over the Pacific. Each service then initiated its second phase on the opposite side of the North American continent, with the Air Force beginning the Atlantic operation from Otis AFB on Cape Cod, Massachusetts, and the Navy starting its Pacific Barrier from Oahu, Hawaii.

Gearing up these operational units involved a great deal of difficult and hurried work on the part of many thousands. The Barrier Patrols had considerable urgency behind them, but the priority placed on this overall function was really not that high. The SAC of the Air Force and the Polaris program of the Navy had far more immediacy and therefore also more immediate funds. Yet the Barrier Patrols were not dissimilar to SAC's operation, in that they, too, were on an around-the-clock basis. Once begun, the barriers had to be properly manned no matter what the circumstances. The circumstances proved to be quite grim at times.

To begin with, there was a shortage of trained personnel to handle both the operation and maintenance of the electronics, without which the entire operation was totally worthless. The Navy for one, took newly commissioned ensigns and newly enlisted personnel and trained them right on the job. Though highly unorthodox, this move proved to be very effective and successful. Flight crews had to be transitioned into the big Warning Stars, including some who had no previous experience in multi-engine reciprocating aircraft.

During the initial period of operations, a number of problems arose under the stresses of day-in, day-out operations. The Turbo-Compound engines were shown to be basically strong, reliable power plants, provided they were operated and maintained according to the manufacturer's directions. If they weren't, then in-flight problems multiplied quickly, and time between overhauls was reduced accordingly. This later became a continuing problem for some of the commercial operators also and was true throughout their lifetime. Pilots and flight engineers who had been used to dealing with less powerful engines quickly discovered they couldn't just bang throttles open or operate at maximum take-off power for periods longer than specifically stipulated in the operating manuals. Human nature being what it is, it took some overheating problems, premature in-flight shutdowns, and blown engines before some of the flight personnel became true believers in the proper method of engine operation.

A second problem dealt with unreliable spark plugs. The pilot who found himself over the North Atlantic at night in heavy weather and severe icing conditions, flying at 14,000 feet and unable to climb above the worst of the weather because the plugs would not tolerate climb power settings, must have had numerous choice words to utter. In time, the failure rate of spark plugs was reduced to an acceptable number. But, as an example, in May and June 1956, just prior to starting the 24-hour operation of the Atlantic Barrier, the Navy experienced a failure of nearly 2000 spark plugs. This number gives some small indication of the severity of the problem. One difficulty that remained for years was that of leaking fuel tanks. The Warning Stars unfortunately were not equipped with self-sealing tanks.

However, as it turned out, problems related to the basic airplane that occurred in-flight did not necessarily cause mission aborts. On the other hand, a serious malfunction with the radar equipment could and did cause aborts, because there was no point in keeping an airplane on station if its mission of surveillance was seriously impaired. Thus, during the first six months of 1957, the Air Force experienced aborts caused by radar malfunctions, as compared to aircraft malfunctions, at about a three to one ratio.

Problems relating to the human factor also arose. The Barrier Patrols routinely required missions lasting up to 16 hours, sometimes longer. This resulted in serious fatigue problems, especially when severe weather was encountered, which was all too often. A typical crew could count on flying every fourth or fifth day, and piling up well over 100 hours per month. This, of course, was in addition to the other duties many of the men had to carry out. One solution was that employed by the Air Force, which took a page from SAC's book, and required all crews to undergo a postflight massage and body conditioning period as part of the debriefing. The results of this step were excellent.

Because the basic mission of the combined AEW&C fleet involved orbiting on station within a relatively restricted area, the Air Force and Navy crews all too often found themselves flying an entire mission within the same storm area. This, of course, was in marked contrast to typical point-to-point operations where normally one flew through or around severe weather, but would not be forced to remain in it for an entire 16-hour flight. The problem of weather was considerably aggravated by the fact that the Warning Stars normally flew at altitudes of between 12,000 and 18,000 feet. Above this altitude, fuel consumption increased markedly. Below this level, radar range decreased. But this also meant flying where the very worst icing conditions existed, in addition to often severe and continuous turbulence.

Of the various operating areas used to maintain the Barrier Patrols, the very worst was probably the North Atlantic Ocean, extending southeast from Newfoundland. This was the area where the Navy flew its Atlantic Barrier Patrol. The North Atlantic Ocean is generally considered to be the stormiest large body of water in the world, and the weather above it is no better. Thus, when the AEW&C Wing, Atlantic, began flying out of Argentia, Newfoundland, in July 1956, it was confronted by a very special challenge in the form of the weather.

This, of course, was the proverbial frosting on the cake in reverse for the Navy. Here they were with relatively inexperienced crews, flying new airplanes whose bugs were still being discovered, operating untried electronic equipment of a high level of sophistication, and flying a vital air defense mission that was still in the embryonic stages! On top of it all, they were facing some of the worst flying weather encountered anywhere on the face of this planet!

How bad was the weather? The statistics for the first few months speak for themselves. From October 1, 1956, to March 1, 1957, a total of 17,634 hours were flown with 483 Barrier launches being made, or an average of 3.22 launches per 24-hour period. During this period, 410 GCA approaches were made under actual IFR conditions. Over 11 percent of the departures were instrument take-offs, and over 11 percent were with a cross-wind greater than 25 knots. There was freezing rain 17 percent of this period, and the average ceiling and visibility were 600 feet and 1.5-mile visibility. Keep in mind, that's an *average*! Take-offs were made with cross-winds up to 68 knots at 45 degrees and landings with winds up to a 45 knot cross-wind component. One memorable take-off was into a 73-knot wind gusting to 92 knots at 25 degrees to the runway! Icing of all types was encountered 61 percent of the time, and turbulence during 53 percent of the flights. Obviously it required skillful flying to maintain the Barrier!

The Navy's Pacific Barrier, with its northernmost terminus in the Aleutians, also had its goodly share of weather. The Aleutians have long been known for their particular brand of weather, and they did not disappoint the Navy in mixing a highly variable and lethal combination with which to bedevil the Warning Stars and their crews.

The Air Force, flying from mainland bases (McClellan and Otis), did not have to contend with such severe terminal weather. On the other hand, both bases were among the worst in the country for frequent and severe fogs.

There is a story that humorously illustrates the deplorable weather conditions in which the Barrier Patrols operated. It seems that one day an Air Force air inspector was flying in to make an inspection of the Wing at Otis AFB. Otis, being adjacent to the Atlantic Ocean and often affected by the infamous fog generated around the Grand Banks off the New England coast, frequently had to operate in conditions of marginal visibility. Such was the case on this day. The air inspector's pilot, flying a small North American T–39 Sabreliner twin-jet, managed to put down safely after repeated unsuccessful attempts to penetrate the thick fog. After being duly welcomed by various base officials, the air inspector (AI) proceeded to expound on the difficulty of their approach and landing. Obviously, in his eyes, he and his people had just put their lives on the line to carry out the inspection. While standing on the flight line in the damp, impenetrable mist, the AI was suddenly interrupted by the very loud noise of reciprocating engines at maximum take-off power. Startled, he broke off his self-congratulatory dissertation, spun around toward the noise, then wheeled back and asked the base commander in an incredulous tone what the hell was going on. The commander hesitated briefly, and then off-handedly explained that the noise was from an RC–121D whose crew was practicing touch-and-gos in the marginal weather! The AI gaped and then began walking rapidly toward Base Operations. During the rest of his stay, no further word was heard from him concerning his "death-defying" arrival at Otis. The story may be apocryphal, but the fact remains that Barrier Patrol crews in both services routinely took off in conditions that would preclude driving, let alone flying. (Lockheed)

LTC Eugene Halbach, U.S. Air Force, who flew for a time from McClellan AFB, clearly remembers his zero-zero take-offs. His aircraft would be towed out to the active runway with all engines shut down. The tug would carefully align the plane with the runway center line and disconnect. The crew would then start the engines and complete all their checks. At this point, Hallbach and his crew would proceed to make a completely blind take-off on instruments without once having seen the ground from the time they climbed into their aircraft! (LTC Halbach) This was the caliber of flying that was routinely expected of crews on AEW&C operations.

The Warning Stars all operated at take-off weights that were extremely high for the size of the aircraft. The maximum overload take-off weight was 156,000 pounds, and it was common to operate at this figure. But at this weight, if one lost an engine shortly after take-off, fast action became a necessity if a disaster was to be averted. The crew would have to reach a minimum altitude, then fly to the nearest uninhabited area, dump the majority of the fuel, and then return to base and land safely. All this while operating the three remaining engines at maximum except take-off power and hoping nothing would let go!

The AEW&C fleets of the Navy and Air Force were used simultaneously as two separate but complementary parts of the complete air defense system. The Air Force staffed patrol lines some 150–200 miles offshore from each coast, with the Pacific Ocean operation based at McClellan. The Navy manned the Pacific and Atlantic Barrier Lines, both of which were much farther out from the continental United States. The Pacific Barrier Line lay roughly between Hawaii and the Aleutian Islands, with aircraft based in both those locations, as well as sometimes operating from Midway Island. The Atlantic Barrier Line lay between Newfoundland and the Azores with Argentia as the main operating base.

Between the inception of these four air defense lines of warning in the mid-1950s and the gradual reduction and eventual abolition in the mid-1960s, a number of changes took place. The actual location of the basic lines, as well as the location of the specific bases, were moved a number of times. Also, the Navy's

Atlantic Barrier Patrol was moved in 1961. The operation out of Argentia was replaced with a jawbreaker known as the GIUK Line, which stands for Greenland–Iceland–United Kingdom Line. This line did double duty, because it not only protected the North Atlantic approaches to the American continent but also operated in support of NATO forces and gave warning of aircraft flying toward Western Europe. In particular, it gave warning of Soviet forces operating from northern Russian bases and flying around the northern tip of Scandinavia. One reason for the establishment of this line was the lack of proper radar coverage in the area known as the GIUK gap.

The Barrier Patrols of both services were operated for over six years without let-up. Base personnel and nearby residents learned to set their watches by the roar of the four Turbo-Compounds at take-off power, as the Warning Stars went aloft at regular intervals. The reliability was nothing short of phenomenal, and together with this tangible proof of superior maintenance, there was built an enviable safety record—a tribute to training and proficiency. Although statistics are not available, it is known that both services accumulated almost perfect safety records in their operation of the Warning Stars.

As a postscript to the Barrier Patrols, the reader might be reminded that this period, roughly 1955–65, coincided with the Cold War reaching new heights of international tension. During this period, the USAF Strategic Air Command (SAC) was maintaining airborne bombers 24 hours a day. Simultaneously, the Air Force and Navy were doing precisely the same thing with the Barrier Patrols, although with a much smaller total fleet of aircraft. And just as some people living adjacent to SAC bases could set their watches by the noise of B–47 and B–52 jet bombers taking off, so could those individuals living near the Warning Star bases.

But while the SAC operation was generally well recognized by the public, the Warning Stars and their crews flew in almost total obscurity. And yet their contribution to the overall security of the United States was hardly less, and their missions almost universally flew in much worse weather, since the Warning Stars could not climb above the majority of the weather the way the SAC jets could.

THE WV–2E/RC–121L

Although 1958 was the end of acquisitions of Super Constellation airframes as AEW&C aircraft, a large number of them underwent conversion in the 1960s, which will be detailed later. But there was a single AEW&C aircraft converted that merits special attention.

The actual airplane was the very first WV–2 built. This was Navy tail number

126512, which was originally delivered in October 1953. Some time later, in late 1954, this particular airplane was returned to Lockheed under a special Navy contract for conversion. What was being contemplated was no less than a completely new concept of AEW&C aircraft.

The converted aircraft was called the WV–2E, and the man behind the idea was the very same man we've already met on the RC–121/WV–2 project, Henry Rempt of Lockheed. Rempt proposed combining both search and height finder radar antennas into one single structure. He further proposed using a search antenna of no less than 37.5 feet in diameter! This was a full 20 feet larger diameter than that used in the belly or lower radome of the RC–121/WV–2. This antenna was designed to fit inside a saucer-shaped radome known as a Rotodome. A vertical structure called a fin acted as a mount for this huge Rotodome. The Rotodome, with the search antenna inside, rotated as one unit. Thus, the two were tailored to match. The fin on which the Rotodome was mounted also housed the height-finding radar antenna.

The WV–2E had another distinction. Its radar equipment operated at much lower frequencies, and as a result, gave better performance over the water. Sea waves reflect radar energy, but because the waves are relatively small, the high-frequency, short-wave length are reflected more than the low-frequency, longer wavelengths. Hence, with the lower frequencies of the WV–2E, much less water return showed on the radar displays, and therefore specific objects on the water's surface or near it became more visible and distinct.

With the new "flying saucer" antenna, the WV–2E could cover an area 50 percent greater than any airborne radar of its day. The height finder could cover from sea level to 100,000 feet. The new radar was designated APS–70 and was developed by the Lincoln Laboratory of MIT and was produced by General Electric. The 37.5-foot-diameter search antenna was built by Hughes Aircraft, and the futuristic radome made of resin-bonded glass fiber was produced by Zenith Plastics.

To accommodate the weight and rotation of the Rotodome, special bearings were needed. Kelly Johnson, who was very good at locating and adapting existing components to do a job, picked the large bearings used from a catalog of bearings for steel mills. They worked very well indeed! The Rotodome was driven by a Vickers hydraulic motor

The WV–2E was ready for taxi tests in August 1956, and it flew shortly thereafter. No particular problems were encountered with the aerodynamics of the strange-looking airplane. In fact, the single integrated structure provided a better structure for cutting through the air. On the Warning Star, the radomes kept the maximum speeds down to about 185 knots indicated air speed (IAS), so as not to rip off the height finder dorsal radome.

The aircraft was tested at length by the Navy and met or exceeded all of Lockheed's and Rempt's high expectations. As Rempt put it to this author in a letter, "In my opinion there has been no AEW&C aircraft built that could match the WV–2E radar performance. Of course, today's radars, computers and displays are better, but they all could be used on the WV–2E. The secret of radar efficiency is antenna size, and no other aircraft has carried a rotating 37.5 foot antenna!"

In December 1957, Lockheed set up a special project to develop a WV–2E follow-on. A few months later it was rumored that the Westinghouse J34 jet engine was a possible auxiliary power plant for the new picket aircraft, which had in the meantime picked up the designation W2V–1. Then, in May 1957, Lockheed presented a firm proposal to the Pentagon for a CL–257 picket aircraft. The aircraft would have a new 150-foot thin wing, which had been designed for the passenger carrying L–1649A, and would be powered by Allison T56 turboprop engines, the same power plants used in the Lockheed C–130 Hercules. But in August of that year the project was canceled by the Pentagon "for the time being"; not long after Congress voted to cancel the project permanently because of lack of funds.

The total weapons system that Lockheed proposed to the Pentagon in May 1957 would have been a formidable aircraft indeed. Among its features were:

1. The newly proven radar capabilities of the WV–2E with its exclusive Rotodome.
2. The large fuel capacity of the 150-foot thin wing. This would have provided long range and excellent loiter capability.
3. The power, fuel efficiency, reliability, and low maintenance of turboprops.

It would have meant high cruise speeds, high altitude capability for overflying the weather, and far better fuel efficiency at low altitudes than with turbojets. In addition, while on station, the aircraft could have operated on either three or two engines, for even greater fuel savings. With a fleet of these AEW aircraft, half the size of the then-existing RC–121/WV–2 fleet, the armed services could have carried out all their previous assigned tasks with better overall results. Not only would such a fleet have expanded the military's capabilities, but the operating costs would have been considerably lower. Furthermore, such a fleet would have had a very long useful life, because the power plants of that type last longer and were not about to go out of production.

Proof of the soundness of the overall concept lies in two events that followed. The first is the successful production use of the Rotodome concept in newer, smaller AEW aircraft, such as the Navy Grumman E-2C Hawkeye. The second is the current deployment of the Air Force Boeing E-3A Airborne Warning and Control System (AWACS) aircraft, which also uses the Rotodome. This aircraft, which had been talked about for a good many years, began undergoing operational proving flights and crew training in 1959. But AWACS became operational 22 years after the WV–2E and at the astronomical cost of $130 million per aircraft!

Even if one makes allowances for the possibly lower operating altitudes of the turboprop-powered Lockheed version versus the turbofan E-3A, the WV–2E follow-on actually had the same, or better, radar range capabilities. Its Rotodome constituted a real breakthrough in airborne antenna technology. Congress and the Pentagon could not (or did not) wish to understand the value this weapons system represented to the United States. As a result, a truly impressive technical achievement died in its infancy, much to the later cost to this country's defense capabilities.

THE WV-3 WEATHER RECONNAISSANCE VERSION

One further and extremely interesting use of the WV–2 Super Constellations was in weather tracking and reconnaissance. The aircraft used were L–1049As, which were basically Navy WV–2s, but with additional specialized equipment. Even though their activities were totally divorced from those of the AEW&C squadrons, these aircraft could still be quickly pressed into service as AEW&C planes.

The eight special aircraft known as WV–3s were ordered by the Navy in 1954, and delivery took place in the second quarter of 1955. The program dealt with weather reconnaissance in general and specifically with data gathering on severe tropical storms. These storms are variously known as hurricanes, typhoons, and cyclones, depending on their location on Earth.

All of these storms are identical in make-up. They are huge, low-pressure areas that develop wind speeds of anywhere from 75 to over 250 miles per hour, along with torrential rains and tornadoes. These storms get their fantastic energy from the interaction of the ocean with very warm air masses above it. For reasons not known to this writer, these storms are called hurricanes in the Atlantic Ocean and the Caribbean Sea, typhoons in the Pacific Ocean, and cyclones in the Indian Ocean. Their winds are counterclockwise, and there is usually a small circle of clear, calm air in their very center, known as the "eye."

The origin of this aerial reconnaissance program can be traced back not to any events in aviation but rather to an occurrence in sea operations. Specifically, the Navy became extremely interested in this area of activity after December 1944 as the result of a catastrophic event that occurred. A very large and unpredictable typhoon hit the Navy's Third Fleet while it was engaged in operations supporting the landings on the Philippine Islands against the Japanese. The typhoon hit the huge spread-out fleet with very little warning. It capsized 3 destroyers, damaged 28 other vessels, caused fires to break out on 3 aircraft carriers, and destroyed some 146 airplanes. A total of 790 men lost their lives, and 80 more were injured.

As a result of this disaster, the Navy came to the conclusion that in the future it would be necessary to track these tropical storms accurately. Because they were spawned and lived out their short lives almost totally at sea, airplanes would have to be used for this type of operation.

In 1945 the Navy began flying a limited typhoon-tracking operation in the western Pacific. After the end of World War II this operation languished for a number of years. But then in 1959, this type of reconnaissance began again on a bigger scale. It involved both Navy and Air Force aircraft, and as part of this operation, the eight WV–3s acquired by the Navy were flown for a number of years well into the 1960s.

The structure of the WV–3 was just about identical to the WV–2, and so was its performance. However, it is interesting to note that official Navy publications indicate that the WV–3 had a lighter empty weight and that its maximum take-off weight (overload) was some 11,000 pounds less. It's possible there is some confusion on this point, because some documents reflect theoretical or design weights, whereas others show actual weights carried during real missions. If this is the case, then it would appear that all L–1049A models, regardless of mission, were generally limited to 145,000 pounds maximum take-off weight.

All of the major internal equipment found in the WV–2 was also carried by the WV–3. In addition, the WV–3 also carried specialized meteorological equipment for analyzing the make-up and vital symptoms of large storms. This equipment consisted of the following: vortex thermometer, psychrometer, aneroid barometer, flight recorder, icing rate meter, and a radiosonde. Certain search radar–related items of equipment were omitted from the WV–3. However, this aircraft could in fact carry out almost all missions that the WV–2s performed and at times did just that.

THE WARNING STARS AND THE CUBAN MISSILE CRISIS

October 1962 was a month that will probably go down in American history as the first time the United States was threatened with impending nuclear attack, from not just one source but two. As readers might remember, the Soviet Union was discovered to have been deploying intermediate-range nuclear missiles in

Cuba, and by the middle of October, these installations were very close to becoming operational. In the ensuing international crisis, the United States was facing the strong possibility of missile attack from both the Cuban installations and the Soviet Union.

The United States responded with large-scale military mobilization as forces were gathered for the possible invasion of Cuba. Reconnaissance flights over Cuba became frequent. In the midst of all this rather frenetic activity came the RC–121s of the 552nd Wing flying out of Otis AFB. Information on their role is still basically wrapped in secrecy, but nevertheless this author was able to determine certain facts.

The 121s were used first to monitor and vector the high-altitude Lockheed U–2s on vital photo reconnaissance flights. At the same time, the 121s could also keep track of any and all air activity originating in Cuba or coming into that island from outside, such as Soviet airlift transports. The communication capability of the 121s was utilized to maintain contact with the Guantanamo Naval Base on Cuba's southern shore, where U.S. personnel must have been feeling thoroughly nervous by that time. Finally, the 121s were also used to monitor ocean traffic approaching Cuba as the United States imposed a quarantine on all vessels coming into the area.

The Warning Stars were on 24-hour/day operations during this time. It is entirely possible that some of the flying was done by Navy WV–2s, although this could not be confirmed. An interesting sidelight to all of this was the way the 121s were able to vector the U–2s, despite the fact the latter were operating at extremely high altitudes, probably in excess of 80,000 feet and possibly as high as 100,000 feet. The 121s' search radar could not, under normal conditions, find anything that high. The ingenious solution was to fly at almost wave-top height over the ocean. The search radar beams would bounce off the water and be reflected at much steeper angles. In this manner, the U–2s were tracked. The height finder was also used in a special way, in that it had the capability of tracking in addition to determining height. A direct result of the operations carried out at this time was the conversion of some of the 121s into EC–121Q aircraft, which had special capabilities.

Although the Cuban Missile Crisis was short-lived, the 121s played a meaningful part, and more to the point, may well have demonstrated to various high-level military figures that these aircraft had additional potential that had not even been remotely exploited. Little did anyone realize in 1962 that new, grim duties lay ahead for the Warning Stars.

CONCLUSION

The offshore barrier patrols flown by the WV–2 and RC–121C and D aircraft of the Navy and Air Force were certainly a very real and integral part of the total U.S. air defense system. From their inception in 1955 until the early 1960s, this was every bit as much a real mission as was SAC's airborne alert force carrying nuclear weapons.

In retrospect, it could be argued that the barrier patrols, along with some of the radar nets built, had never really been necessary. Because the Soviets were not able to put the TU–95 into operation in meaningful numbers until the late 1950s, by which time the international picture was changing, arguably no real threat had ever existed. But we really don't know this to be true. For, if the air defense system had not been developed and implemented to the level it was, might not the Soviets have given serious consideration to a preemptive attack, even though they might have had to do so with less than optimum forces? We shall never know, but it appears safe to say that the air defense system in general, and the barrier patrols staffed by a highly effective and flexible fleet of AEW&C aircraft in particular, acted as a deterrent and a restraining force on the Soviet Union.

To give readers an idea of the relative strength of the AEW&C fleet, it should be mentioned that from August 1956 to November 1969 the Air Force portion of the fleet never numbered fewer than 70 aircraft. The peak was reached in December 1964 when 83 RC–121Ds were in commission.

One of the interesting aspects of the Curtiss-Wright R–3350 Turbo-Compound engine that powered the Warning Stars was the fact that as time went by, and with the proper maintenance, the time between overhauls (TBO) became longer and longer. In fact the 552nd Early Warning and Control Wing at McClellan set a truly stupendous record for TBO.

A R–3350-95 engine, which was remanufactured by Curtiss-Wright, was then installed on an RC–121 Warning Star on September 23, 1962. The engine received routine maintenance with some minor components changed as needed. It served on three different Warning Stars, and on November 20, 1964 was finally taken out of service. During that period of 26 months, the engine had accumulated 3009 hours of continuous use! After it was deactivated and torn down, the engine was found to be in basically excellent condition except for a minor oil leak! Considering how many of these engines, both in commercial and military use, were only lasting around 1000 hours TBO, this was a truly impressive performance, with great credit due Curtiss-Wright, the Air Force maintenance crews, and the Warning Star flight crews who treated their engines with care.

In the early 1960s, the total number of aircraft supporting the Navy and Air

Force barrier patrols was gradually reduced. True, an additional mission had been established with the creation of the 966th AEW&C Squadron, 551st Wing, at McCoy AFB, Florida, on May 1, 1963. This unit was formed to maintain watch over the activities of the Castro regime in Cuba. But overall, the Warning Stars appeared to be reaching the end of the road. This in spite of the fact that in 1963–64, many of the RC–121Ds (but not the older RC–121Cs) and some WV–2s had been brought back to Burbank for upgrading the electronic systems. This involved, among other things, the installation of an on-board computer on the Air Force aircraft that could communicate information from the radar scope read-outs directly to NORAD's newly installed SAGE computers via data links. The resulting modified aircraft all received new designations at this time. The Air Force birds became EC–121Hs, and the USN WV–2s became EC–121Ks. The WV–2Qs were called EC–121M, and the weather reconnaissance WV–3s became WC–121N. Later on, some of the Navy 121Ks were further modified and were then known as 121Ps.

This general downgrading of the entire AEW&C program appears to have been due to a number of factors. One may have been the newly developed reliance on intercontinental ballistic missiles (ICBMs) as the first line of offense, and the new radar defense against them, the Ballistic Missile Early Warning Stations (BMEWS). A second may have been the realization by the Pentagon planners that the bomber fleet the Soviets were supposed to have developed and implemented, and which was the original reason for the Atlantic and Pacific Ocean Barriers and much of the AEW&C program, was now being perceived as being much smaller and far less of a threat. In fact, the Soviets, too, were implementing an ICBM force. Also, relations between Soviet Russia and the United States after the Cuban Missile Crisis appeared to be slowly improving.

Finally, the operation of the Warning Stars was progressively becoming more expensive. Many of these airplanes had accumulated a great deal of flying time and were beginning to require considerable maintenance. The power plants were also a problem, because no new ones were manufactured after 1957.

The result of all this was that Barrier Patrol crews no longer felt as motivated while carrying out their long flights on station. Their professionalism enabled them to carry out the mission at an undiminished level of competence, but their morale dropped noticeably. By 1963–64 the patrols were looked on as continuous training flights more than anything else. One reason they were continued was the realization by the military that this large number of AEW&C aircraft was very much a force capable of carrying out other important duties as long as the aircraft were fully operational and the crews proficient.

The most revealing indication of the downgrading of the AEW&C program occurred in June 1965 when the Navy flew its last official barrier flight on either the Atlantic or the Pacific Barriers. However, as we shall see later, this particular date may have had an altogether different significance.

Many of the Navy 121Ks were flown to Davis-Montham AFB in Arizona for retirement and mothballing. The Air Force was starting to retire its RC–121Cs, which, in any case, as the oldest segment of the early warning fleets, were naturally the aircraft with the highest total airframe time.

At this point, it certainly seemed as though the end was in sight for all of the remaining EC–121H and K Warning Stars. Little known to the crews, a new mission was about to develop that would tax their airplanes and themselves to the utmost.

8-1 A USN PO–1W Radar Picket Aircraft. This L–749A was the test-bed for the entire Warning Star concept. Two were delivered to the Navy in 1949. (Lockheed Martin)

8-2 The prototype test-bed Super Constellation converted by the addition of radar domes and more powerful engines. Standing in front, left to right, are Dick Stanton, engineer; Rudy Thorsen, test-pilot; Clarence "Kelly" Johnson, the man behind many of Lockheed's designs, which were among the most innovative in aviation at the time. (Lockheed Martin)

8-3 A USAF RC–121C Warning Star Airborne Early Warning and Control Aircraft (AEW&C) taxiing out for take-off. This aircraft was the first model to carry the Turbo-Compound PRT engines. Notice the height-finding radar on top of the fuselage and the search radar protruding from the bottom. (Lockheed Martin)

8-4 Diagram showing how a AEW&C aircraft operates by seeing incoming enemy aircraft on its radar and passing the information to defense forces. (U.S. Air Force)

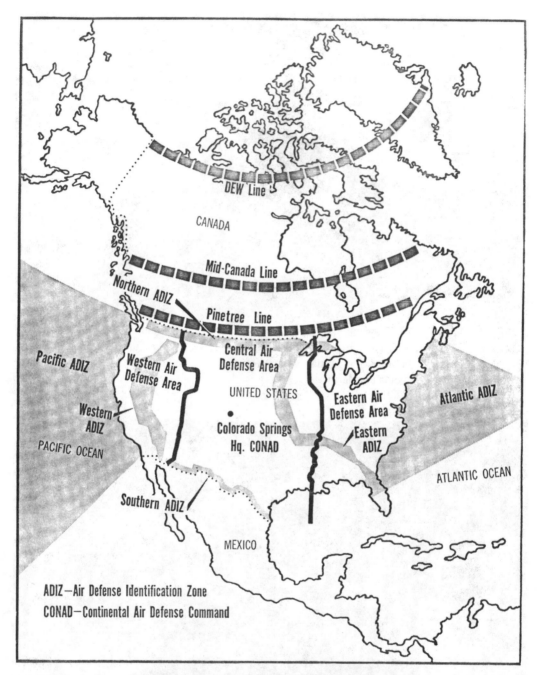

8-5 Map showing the 3 radar fences deployed in Canada in the 1950s which gave protection from enemy bomber fleets striking over the Polar area. Note that there is no protection against long-range aircraft coming in over either the East or West Coast. (U.S. Air Force)

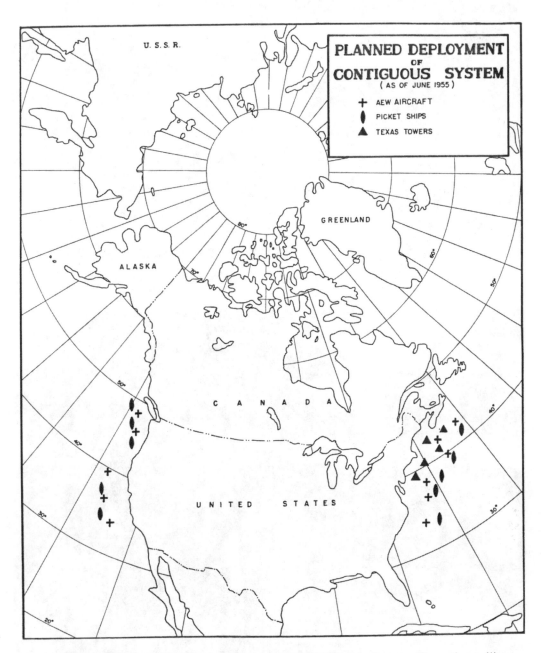

8-6 Diagram showing the planned deployment of AE&W aircraft, as well as other military assets, off the coasts of the U.S. in the 1950s. (U.S. Air Force)

8-7 An overhead view of a U.S. Navy WV–2 AEW aircraft. (Lockheed Martin)

8-8 Interior view of a U. S. Navy WV–2 AEW aircraft showing some of the radar receivers. (Lockheed Martin)

8-9 A tip tank used on the U.S. Air Force RC–121s with lightning protectors shown. (Lockheed Martin)

8-10 A view of the U.S. Navy WV–2E about to touch down. Note the very large 37 1/2 foot radome. This antenna configuration was employed many years later in the USAF Boeing AWACS aircraft which were the successors to the Lockheed airplanes, and which fly to this day. (Lockheed Martin)

8-11 "Landing Gear, Wheels, and Brakes" (Lockheed Martin)

Chapter 9

THE CONSTELLATION IN VARIOUS MILITARY VERSIONS

As mentioned in the previous chapter, the military input into the Constellation program resulted in not one but two new designs. One was the AEW&C picket aircraft, and the other was the R7V–1/C–121C cargo aircraft. Although this cargo aircraft was a considerable improvement over anything then being operated by the military services, it was actually the third such acquisition by the military services of the Constellation family.

The first such effort was, of course, the short-lived C–69 program of World War II. That particular program, as readers may remember, resulted in some headline-making pioneering flights, but not much else. In fact, the C–69 never saw regular service, as such, with the U.S. Army Air Force.

The second such program began in 1948. At this time, the newly constituted U.S. Air Force saw a need for some high-speed airplanes to be used either to transport personnel or critical cargo over long distances. Lockheed had recently introduced their L–749A Constellation, and its combination of speed and range appealed to the Air Force planners. Accordingly, in February 1948 ten such aircraft were ordered and identified as C–121As.

The C–121A program was, to be sure, very small, but the various uses that these aircraft were to be put to over a number of years made it interesting. The aircraft themselves were not basically different from their civilian counterparts, the L–749As. They had the same fuselage and wing design, the same power plants with 2500-hp take-off rating, and the same 107,000 pounds maximum take-off weight. It is interesting to note that the official Air Force pamphlet showing the basic aircraft characteristics indicates an overload take-off weight of 132,000 pounds, which is a huge increase over the normal weight.

Under the original contract, nine of these aircraft were built to identical specifications, and the tenth was called a VC–121B and was internally configured from the beginning as a VIP transport. On delivery beginning in late 1948, seven of the C–121As were assigned to Military Air Transport Service (MATS) at Westover AFB, Massachusetts. Here they were initially utilized to fly personnel or supplies from Westover to Rhein-Main AB, West Germany. This operation served as a supply effort for the famed Berlin Airlift then in progress, and the supplies were transshipped to C–54s at Rhein-Main for immediate forwarding to West Berlin. These seven planes only flew on this particular operation for some four weeks, but during this time managed to fly some 5.9 million passenger miles, which opened some eyes and minds to the possibilities inherent in using large, fast transports on very long routes, where large air shipments had heretofore not been considered to be very practical. The well-known Lockheed reliability also helped carry the message home.

However, this small fleet of aircraft was not destined to remain at Westover for very long. In 1950, these airplanes were transferred to the 1254th Special Air Missions Squadron (SAMS) initially based at Washington National Airport and later at Andrews AFB, Maryland, just outside of Washington, D.C. Here, these aircraft, now equipped with very comfortable interiors, began carrying government personnel and visiting dignitaries all over the world. One was based for a period of time in Iceland, where it gave support to U.S. activities there. In early 1951, one of the C–121As was brought to Europe, where it became the personal aircraft of General Dwight D. Eisenhower, at that time Commander of SHAPE, with headquarters in France. This aircraft became known as *Columbine*, the first of three different airplanes to carry this name. When Eisenhower was elected president in 1952, a second C–121A was specially outfitted for his use and became known as *Columbine II*. It was this aircraft that carried him to Korea in November 1952. This particular airplane remained in presidential service until November 1954, at which time it was replaced by a Super Constellation. The entire fleet of C–121As and Bs were retrofitted with various improvements over the years, including weather radar. The mere fact that they were used for such important and delicate work for a considerable period of time attests to the reliability of the Constellation.

In summer 1950, the Navy began discussing with Lockheed a transport design that could be used for a number of applications. Earlier, as readers may remember, the Navy representatives had begun serious talks with Lockheed on the need for a AEW&C aircraft, and the L–1049A model was being conceptually formulated as the answer to this need. It was only a short step to see the large load-carrying ability of the A model as being also the answer for a transport version.

At this time, the Navy was being affected by world events that made the need for a long-range transport have some real urgency. For when, in July 1950, North Korea invaded South Korea, the Navy found itself fighting a war that was many thousands of miles away. Along with the Air Force, the Navy quickly realized an acute need to be able to move personnel, critical materials, and injured men in a matter of hours over distances that had not heretofore been commonly transversed by transport aircraft. The L–1049B seemed to fit the bill with its payload, speed, and ability to convert the interior in a short time.

As it happened, the Navy decided to hedge its bets, and at the time it began procuring new transports, it ordered almost equal numbers of the Lockheed L–1049B and the Douglas DC–6A, known as the C–118 in the Air Force, or the R6D in the Navy.

The Navy originally ordered 11 of the transports in mid-1950, either August or September. It was initially identified as an ROV–1, but prior to delivery, the Navy changed this to the designation R7V–1. Later, in fiscal year 1951, the Navy ordered an additional 40 of the big aircraft, in great part due to the extreme airlift requirements being imposed by the Korean War.

Shortly after the first Navy order, the Air Force also placed an order, this one for 10 of the L–1049Bs, which they called the C–121C. However, this was the order mentioned in the preceding chapter that was changed after a few months to RC–121C AEW&C airplanes. Thus, these particular 10 airplanes never flew as cargo aircraft, only as radar picket planes.

The new aircraft that Lockheed proposed to the Navy in July 1950 was their L–1049B, which was a natural outgrowth of the current technology the company had been studying for application on the L–1049A AEW version. The overall dimensions were the same as the L–1049A, but the aircraft had a slightly lower gross weight, and its general structure was not beefed up to the extent that the A model's had been.

The basic aircraft structure of the L–1049B was essentially identical to the L–1049A/WV–2 as far as external dimensions, general layout, and overall construction, with the obvious exception that the very large and visible upper and lower radar domes were missing. However, there were certain other fairly significant differences. Only the inner wing was integrally stiffened, whereas the outer wing had the same basic structure as the original L–1049 series. The fuselage also lacked as much reinforcing. These differences were due first to the lack of both wingtip fuel tanks and a fuselage fuel tank, and second, to the absence of the heavy radar equipment. However, as compared to the original L–1049, it did have a strengthened main landing gear. In addition, two large cargo doors were provided on the left side, the forward one having dimensions of 5 feet, 1.5 inches wide by 6 feet 2.5 inches high, and the rear one measuring 9 feet, 4.5 inches wide by 6 feet, 2.5 inches high. These cargo doors were important not only for easily and quickly handling large pieces of cargo but also for easy entry and exit of patient litters.

The aircraft had the same 3250-hp engines as the A model but managed a somewhat higher cruise speed due to the lower gross weight and the reduced drag resulting from the lack of the huge radomes. The reason for the smaller total fuel supply was the fact that this aircraft had no requirement for extremely long loiter capability, and some of the fuel weight was traded off for payload.

When carrying cargo, the L–1049B had a capacity of 5568 cubic feet. Converted to the medevac version, 80 litter patients could be accommodated; in the passenger configuration, between 62 and 97 seats could be fitted depending on leg room needed, and so on. Maximum payload was 38,570 pounds, and maximum still air range was on the order of 4000 nautical miles, although at this distance the payload would decrease to 31,640 pounds. Typical cruise speeds were 225 knots IAS, which was some 30 knots faster than the A model.

Delivery of the R7V–1s to the Navy began in November 1953 and all 50 aircraft were delivered by December 1954. The 51st aircraft on this order was completed as a VC–121E, was delivered in September 1954 to the Air Force and became famous as President Eisenhower's personal aircraft, the *Columbine III*.

This author found some documentation that indicated that Lockheed actually produced the L–1049B in two versions. The second version differed from the first in that it had a reinforced fuselage, changes in the fuel management system, and wing reinforcements to permit a take-off weight of 150,000 pounds. It also had a normal gross take-off weight of 133,000 pounds, or 3000 pounds more than the earlier L–1049B version. However, it was not possible to verify that the Navy actually took delivery of their R7V–1s in both versions. Records indicate that all these aircraft had take-off weights of 133,000 pounds.

This Navy order for 51 aircraft was the only one placed for the L–1049B model. By 1953 Lockheed was offering a L–1049F cargo version. This aircraft was identical to the L–1049B but was reinforced for 150,000-pounds take-off weight. This increase in take-off weight appears to have been incorporated in case the fleet was ever retrofitted with turboprop engines, in which case a greater payload could have been carried. In December 1953 the Air Force, feeling that it had to upgrade the capabilities of MATS, placed an order for 33 of this F model, which it identified as C–121C aircraft. Delivery of this order began in July 1955. During this period MATS was actively considering using turboprops on the C–121 fleet but eventually discarded the idea.

To clarify the question of the relative weight and performance of the L–1049B/R7V–1 and the L–1049F/C–121C, there is conclusive evidence that both aircraft types were operated at the same identical take-off weights and with essentially the same cargo capacities and ranges.

The Navy R7V–1s and the Air Force C–121Cs were used to help man the various divisions of MATS, which later became the Military Airlift Command (MAC). MATS was divided into three distinct divisions. The Continental Division served the needs totally within the continental United States, the Eastern or Atlantic Division flew from the East Coast across the Atlantic to Europe and as far as Iran and North Africa as well as south to South America, and the Western or Pacific Division made the long jump from the West Coast across the Pacific Ocean, serving Japan, and then south and west to the Philippines, India, and Saudi Arabia, where it met up with the Eastern Division. The big Lockheed transports were used exclusively on the Atlantic and Pacific Divisions. The Pacific Division was generally manned by the Navy operating from Moffet Field, California, and the Eastern Division was handled by the Air Force flying out of Charleston, South Carolina. The Navy operated from Moffett Field with their VR–7 squadron. This unit actually flew two different routes. The northern route flew to Hawaii, Wake Island, and Tokyo, with return via Midway Island. The southern route was via Hawaii, Kwajalein, Guam, Manila, Saigon, Bangkok, Calcutta, New Delhi, and Karachi, to Dahran in Saudi Arabia.

The Air Force flew a main route east from Charleston AFB, SC to Lajes Field, Azores (refueling), then to Rhein-Main in Frankfurt, West Germany. Other flights operated through the Azores to North Africa, Cairo, Egypt, and on to Dahran. The L–1049Bs and Fs were basically reliable, long-legged birds, and the kind of flying they did for MATS proved this point day in and day out. For example, the Air Force would dispatch one of their 121s from Charleston AFB to West Germany and return. The aircraft would stop in the Azores to refuel, at Rhein-Main for crew change, unload at Munich Riem in 1 hour, return to the Azores to refuel, then to McGuire AFB, New Jersey, to offload, and back to Charleston. At no time would the aircraft be on the ground much more than 90 minutes. The trip would mean covering a distance of over 9000 nautical miles.

In fall 1956, Operation Safe Haven rather dramatically showed the passenger airlifting capabilities of these airplanes. At that time, the United States had decided to permit refugees of the Hungarian uprising who had fled to Austria to enter this country. To help bring some of these people across, Operation Safe Haven was begun. Operating from December 11, 1956, to January 2, 1957, a mixed fleet of

C–121Cs and Douglas C–118s brought back almost 10,000 refugees—all this with only one or two flights a day, although in total, 107 trips were carried out.

Between them, the Navy and the Air Force ordered a total of 84 of the R7V–1/C–121C Super Constellations. During 1958, this combined fleet reached a peak, with 76 aircraft in service. In the five-year period of 1956–61, there were never fewer than a combined total of 70 of these aircraft in the active MATS inventory. By way of comparison, during the same period, MATS was also operating up to a maximum of 126 C–118 (DC–6) aircraft. These, of course, were Lockheed's main competition in both civilian and military use.

In 1958, a decision was made by the Department of Defense to transfer 32 of the Navy R7V–1s to the Air Force. This move was accomplished by the latter half of 1958, with these airplanes receiving a new designation of C–121G to distinguish them from the C–121C aircraft that the Air Force was already operating.

After 1962, the MATS Super Constellation fleet was rapidly phased out, as new Lockheed C–130 Hercules and Boeing C–135s were introduced into the fleet. After 1963 only a handful of C–121s were left in MATS service. This, however, was not the end of the line for these big birds. Some 28 of these C–121Gs were transferred to Air National Guard (ANG) units beginning in June 1962. The four ANG squadrons were the 183rd at Jackson, Mississippi; the 156th at Charlotte, North Carolina; the 150th at Newark, New jersey; and the 140th at Olmstead AFB (Harrisburg), Pennsylvania. All four units were Aeromedical Evacuation Squadrons, and each received an initial quantity of seven of the C–121Gs. The aircraft were configured to carry 18 litters and 30 ambulatory patients.

Together, these units assisted regular MATS aircraft in performing worldwide AirEvac missions. During the period of 1965–70, these C–121Gs carried out AirEvac of wounded servicemen from Southeast Asia, in addition to flying other missions over the North Atlantic, the Caribbean, and some patient feeder flights within the continental United States. Most of these aircraft were retired from the inventory by the early 1970's.

THE COLUMBINE III

One of the L–1049B/R7V–1 aircraft ordered by the Navy's Bureau of Aeronautics was destined to have a far more glamorous career than the rest of her sisters. This was Navy aircraft 131650, which had been ordered as part of a lot of 28 in FY 1951 under Contract 51-655. Shortly after this particular aircraft started down the Lockheed assembly line, it was decided that President Eisenhower needed a replacement for his *Columbine II*, a L–749A/C–121A, which by now had accumulated considerable air time. Accordingly, it was decided that a modified

L–1049B would be used as the replacement, and a special supplementary contract was let. This airplane actually became part of the Air Force inventory and was identified by them as a VC–121E, the only such aircraft in existence, with tail number 53-7885A.

Being the president's plane, this VC–121E naturally differed in many ways from both the L–1049B military version and the forthcoming L–1049C passenger version. To begin with, this particular lot of L–1049Bs had additional fuselage and wing reinforcement, which permitted the standard take-off weight to go up to 133,000 pounds (from 130,000 on the original L–1049Bs) and the overload take-off weight to 145,000 pounds when powered by turboprop engines. In addition, the fuel management system was improved. The fuselage was fitted with rectangular windows, the same as the commercial Super Constellations.

But the most visible changes were within the cabin. The cockpit itself was essentially unchanged from other Super Constellations. But starting from the rear bulkhead of the crew compartment, the main cabin was subdivided into compartments designed to provide comfort, privacy, and convenience for the president, his family, guests, and various assorted other staff members. A separate compartment was filled with sophisticated communications consoles that enabled the president to be in communication with anyone anywhere in the world. Among the communications gear installed was an airborne teletype machine that connected to the White House, and an air-to-ground radio-telephone.

The *Columbine III* was delivered to Washington on September 10, 1954, and for the next six years traveled hundreds of thousands of miles all over the world on official business. When not carrying the president, it was used to carry Cabinet members or other high government officials and also was used to transport chiefs of state of foreign nations.

The *Columbine III* was retired as the official presidential airplane on January 20, 1961, and became a part of the same fleet of the 1254th squadron. In April 1966, the aircraft was decommissioned and was flown to Wright-Patterson AFB, where today it is on display as part of the Air Force Museum.

THE FASTEST CONSTELLATION

During the period that the L–1049 series was being developed to its ultimate potential with reciprocating engines, Lockheed was also attempting to design and sell a turboprop-powered version. Although this particular development never sold a single aircraft commercially—and in fact only four such test aircraft were ever built—it was a potentially exciting project that bears description.

Lockheed started its formal quest for a turboprop-powered L–1049 in

September 1951 when it unveiled the idea for a commercial, cargo version of the L–1049B/R7V–1, and announced that a similar aircraft with turboprop engines and called the L–1049D would also be available. It appeared that serious thoughts on such a design actually began in November 1951, and the conversion of the L–1049 was known as the L–1149. At about the same time the Navy expressed an interest in such a design and ordered four prototypes powered with Pratt & Whitney T–34 turbo-prop engines. This became the L–1249 model. Some time after the order was placed, it was decided that two of the four aircraft would go to the Air Force, with each service carrying out its own test program.

The four prototypes were flown at length by the Navy and Air Force, and the results were certainly interesting. In the early testing during January 1955, company test pilots R. E. Wimmer and J. F. Ware achieved a speed of 479 mph with a Navy L–1249/R7V–2, which was flown at low power settings at a 20° angle of descent from 25,000 feet to 8000 feet. Shortly thereafter, a take-off was made at a weight of 166,400 pounds. The two R7V–2s were used by Lockheed for a variety of comprehensive testing before being turned over to the Navy. The Navy in turn used them on various routes to accurately evaluate their capabilities.

The first Air Force L–1249/YC–121F was delivered to the 1700th Test Squadron of MATS at Kelly AFB, Texas, in February 1956, with the second one delivered in April 1956. From then until June 1957, both aircraft were operated by the 1700th squadron on various MATS routes.

The Model L–1249/YC–121F/R7V–2, which evolved from the L–1049B/R7V–1, had the same basic structure, but differed in a number of important aspects. These were:

1. Pratt & Whitney T–34–P6 turboprop engines of 6000 equivalent shaft horsepower.
2. New, slimmer, longer engine nacelles to fit the smaller-diameter engines.
3. A shorter wing span (by 6 feet) with tip tanks optional. With the tip tanks the wing span increased by 2 feet to 119 feet.
4. Strengthened wings to accommodate a 150,000-pound take-off weight.
5. A fuselage fuel tank carrying 1000 gallons. This gave it the same arrangement and fuel load as the L–1049A/WV–2.
6. Heavier main landing gear with high heat treatment and a strengthened fuselage.
7. Modified internal systems (hydraulic, electric, etc.) to mate with the new power plants.

The performance envelope of the aircraft clearly reflected the additional power and capabilities of the turboprop engines. For example, at a weight of 145,000 pounds at 20,000 feet, the airplane would cruise at 380 knots IAS. Its limiting cruise speed was a very respectable Mach 0.63 anywhere from between 20,000 and 40,000 feet. At full load, its ceiling was still over 30,000 feet, and its range with a 35,000-pound payload was 3000 nautical miles at 25,000 feet. Thus, readers can see what a powerful performer the L–1249 was for its time.

In the approximately year and a half that the two YC–121Fs were flown by the Air Force, a great deal was learned about their operational capabilities, problems, etc. With the aircraft being flown from Texas all the way to Europe where highly varied weather conditions were encountered, this helped in fully evaluating the engines and systems. One serious problem that showed up was the cracking of propeller pump housings with the subsequent loss of oil. The problem became serious enough to cause the grounding of both aircraft for some weeks.

A measure of the great potential of the design was demonstrated on January 23, 1957, when a YC–121F was flown from Long Beach, California, to Washington, D.C., in 4 hours, 43 minutes, an unofficial speed record.

By June 1957, when the test program flown by the 1700th Test Squadron was brought to a successful close, a number of significant goals had been achieved. The Time Between Overhauls for the T–34 engines had been increased from 150 hours to a respectable 1250 hours. During March 1957, the two aircraft had been flown an average of 6.9 hours per day—over 200 hours per month each.

In conclusion, it would appear that it was adequately demonstrated that the potential for this design was every bit as good as originally indicated by Lockheed. The commercial version of the L–1249 could have carried 106 passengers in economy class and would almost certainly have been the finest long-range transport built in the United States prior to the introduction of the Boeing 707. But as previously explained, it simply was not to be.

However, there was one last attempt to use this basic design in some way. That would have been a turboprop version of the Navy WV–2E radar picket plane described in Chapter 8. Such an aircraft would indeed have been a tremendous addition to the nation's defenses. The greatly improved radar gear of the WV–2E mated with a flying platform such as the L–1249 would have resulted in a much larger area being defended by fewer aircraft, because the greater range of the new radar would have been further enhanced by the 10–15,000-foot higher cruise altitude of the L–1249. This additional altitude capability would also have permitted crews to operate over the majority of bad weather and icing conditions.

Unfortunately, in June 1957, the project was terminated due to lack of funds.

So the entire turboprop concept of the Super Constellation died without ever having the opportunity to reach the production stage.

In a sense, it might be said that what befell the turboprop Super Constellation concept was the exact opposite of what happened at the inception of the Constellation project itself. Back then, the fortuitous existence of a new, advanced power plant, namely, the Curtiss-Wright 3350, made possible the bringing into existence an aircraft design that could take advantage of the increased power, and mated with it bring about a quantum jump in large aircraft performance. Some 15 years later, a refinement of that same design could not be put into production when Lockheed obviously felt that the proper engine was not readily available. The only unanswered question is whether a British power plant could have been substituted, and then, whether it would have been available in quantity and soon enough. Thus are some dreams realized, while others fade away.

9-1 A USAF C–121A used by General Douglas MacArthur during the Korean conflict in the 1950s. (Lockheed Martin)

9-2 A USAF VC–121B Connie known as the "Columbine" and used by President Eisenhower in the early 1950s. (Lockheed Martin)

9-3 The interior of a USN R7V–1 transport showing the litter installations used for medical evacuation missions. (Lockheed Martin)

9-4 A USN R7V–1 Lockheed L–1049B transport. (Lockheed Martin)

9-5 A USN R7V–1 interior showing the seating arrangement for personnel transport. (Lockheed Martin)

9-6 A view of the USAF VC–121C "Columbine III" used by President Eisenhower in the late 1950s. (Lockheed Martin)

9-7 The turbo-prop powered L–1249/YC–121F prototype, one of 4 built, which set many speed records. (Lockheed Martin)

Chapter 10

THE SUPER G CONSTELLATION

As we have seen in the preceding two chapters, the L–1049A and B models could be said to have been the first true Super Constellations. However, both were used entirely for military applications. It was not until the L–1049C was introduced in service in summer 1953 did the commercial airlines began operating equipment on a par with that being produced for the military. All the technology used in the L–1049A and B models was certainly not applicable only to the military. Commercial airlines were also looking for greater payload, longer range, and faster cruising speeds. Thus, it was only logical that much of the basic technology would be applied very quickly for commercial purposes.

The initial model of the Super Constellation series had been the L–1049, a purely commercial design that did not prove to be successful. Now, Lockheed proposed to bring out a much improved model that could more readily reap the potential benefits of the larger Super Constellation fuselage.

In late 1951, Lockheed's design people began once again working on a commercial design. At this time, design work on the L–1049A and B models had progressed to the point where the basic aircraft was firmed up, and many of the technological innovations were being tried on the faithful "Beast of Burbank." Lockheed was hard at work on one particularly aggravating problem that plagued the initial installations of the Turbo-Compound engine. This was the exhaust, which was so hot and stretched so far back from the engine exhaust stacks that its heat was actually weakening the structural integrity of the rear section of the wing. It took Lockheed 9 long months and over $2 million to overcome the problem, but it was an absolute necessity that it be totally and quickly resolved.

Essentially, Lockheed now had a practically new airplane on their hands, one far different from the original L-1049. It came not a minute too soon, because by this time the airplane picture had once again changed. For one thing, bigger and faster transports were now flying; these were the huge Boeing 377 Stratocruiser and the popular Douglas DC-6B. Lockheed had competed successfully as far as cabin size was concerned, with the introduction of the L-1049, but performance was lacking. For another thing, the nature of the airline business was also changing. Average trip length was increasing each year, and the tourist was now becoming almost as big a factor as the businessman. This, then, was the backdrop when Lockheed went back to the airlines with a design they felt was both viable and highly competitive.

THE PREDECESSOR TO THE SUPER G

Lockheed was now proposing a L-1049C model, powered by the more dynamic Turbo-Compound that had somewhat more speed but, at 133,000 pounds gross weight, a real increase in payload.

In February 1951, design work on the L-1049C began in earnest. Kelly Johnson had in hand a design, the L-1049B/USN R7V-1, that was not far from what was required for the airlines. However, a passenger version did not need the heavy cargo floor or the oversized cargo doors of the L-1049B. The L-1049C, as it came off the drawing board, had the following features.

1. An L-1049 fuselage with some structural changes and relocated doors.
2. A new main landing gear designed to take the heavier gross weights and also able to achieve faster retraction times.
3. Inner wing reinforcing and integrally stiffened inner wing lower surface.
4. A new oil transfer system.
5. Revisions to the fuel management system.

The L-1049C was the first true Super Constellation passenger transport. It was possibly the most economical to operate and generally was a match for the Douglas DC-7 and 7B aircraft entering service at approximately the same time.

The prototype L-1049C, which was destined to go to KLM, first flew on February 17, 1953. During the preceding months, Lockheed's sales teams were busy trying to sell the new transport, but they were not very successful within the United States. Only Eastern bought any of this model, in September 1951 ordering 16 aircraft, the largest single order for the L-1049C. All other orders came from foreign airlines, with both Air France and Qantas ordering 10 each, and KLM and TCA 5 each. In all, 51 C models were sold.

The C model featured improved interior design, and, depending on the customer's needs, could carry from 54 to 109 passengers in various configurations and mixes of classes. Its maximum range with a capacity payload was no real improvement over the L–749A. Nevertheless, the total package was attractive to airlines flying long, over-water trips. Its cruising speed was slightly higher than either the L–749 or the original L–1049. So it was that the majority of the L–1049Cs were employed over the North Atlantic route and beyond on the long, desolate legs to the Orient and Australia.

However, though the L–1049C was a distinct model, it was also the first of four models that were closely tied together in design and performance. These four were the L–1049C, E, G, and H. They constituted an orderly progression of refinement in what was essentially the basic Turbo-Compound-powered Super Constellation, as best exemplified by the L–1049C. A clue to the similarity of their design is demonstrated by the fact that a number of C models were upgraded, at their owners' request, to E and even G configuration. E models were upgraded to G models, and a few G models were upgraded to the H configuration.

While Lockheed was busy producing and delivering the L–1049C in the latter half of 1953 and the first half of 1954, it was also designing the changes that were brought out in the E model. Readers should keep in mind that as Lockheed was producing these commercial aircraft, it was simultaneously assembling various military versions on a parallel assembly line. These military orders continued to flow into 1958. At any rate, in April 1954, the first L–1049E was ready to fly and did so on April 6, 1954, some 16 months after its predecessor first took to the air. The major change on the E model was the strengthening of both the fuselage and wings to accommodate a take-off weight of 150,000 pounds in anticipation of the retro-fitting of turboprop engines. However, the landing gear was not reinforced for the higher weight on this model.

There were two additional types of modifications as part of the E model. The E/01 had reinforced inner wing and main landing gear, and its take-off weight was increased by 2400 pounds to 135,400 pounds The E/02 variant had the /01 modifications, plus new main landing gear brakes and wheels, which permitted the landing weight to increase by 3000 pounds or up to 113,000 pounds.

The first L–1049E was delivered in June 1954 to Iberia, the Spanish flag carrier. Only 23 E models were sold, due mainly to the fact that Lockheed very quickly followed this model up with a considerably improved G model. For this reason, a number of orders for the E model were converted to orders for the G model before they had begun going down the assembly line. Readers should also be aware that as far as the E/01 and 02 versions are concerned, this really referred to changes that took place after the aircraft had been delivered to the customer. Thus, the E model was really a transitional model between the original Turbo-Compound Super Constellation, the L–1049C, and the most successful commercial Super Constellation, the G model.

THE SUPER G

The L–1049G model, or as it came to be popularly known, the Super G, was the result of Lockheed's attempt to increase both the payload and the range of the basic Super Constellation. These improvements became possible when Curtis-Wright introduced certain improvements to their 3350 power plant. These included changes to the superchargers that enabled the maximum except take-off power of the engine to go up from 2600 bhp to 2700 bhp. With this additional power, the take-off weight was increased to 137,500 pounds, and the landing weight was increased also to 113,000 pounds. In addition, the zero fuel weight was increased by 4500 pounds, which meant an additional 2+ tons of payload plus a greater flexibility in choosing payload/fuel combinations to best suit various operators' needs. The range of the Super G had been increased over the C and E models, by the addition of two 600-gallon wingtip tanks. This installation was virtually identical to that of the L–1049A radar picket aircraft. These additional 1200 gallons of fuel boosted the still air range of the Super G to 4620 miles, with reserves, or some 700–800 miles longer than its predecessors.

Some 8 months after the first flight of the E model, the first Super G flew on December 17, 1954. The first Super G delivery was to Northwest Orient Airlines on January 22, 1955. Thus, one can easily see the relatively short time interval that transpired between the introduction dates of the E and G models respectively.

The Super G boasted no fewer than 107 design improvements over the E model. Many Super G's were fitted with the new weather radar, either in the factory or later by the customer. A new type of Goodrich de-icer boot was installed in both the wing and tail. The cabin, too, received some improvements with 700 pounds of fiberglass insulation added to the cabin wall in an effort to further reduce the engine noise perceived by the passengers. A new type of GE oven was introduced to speed up serving meals. The interiors, styled by Henry Dreyfuss, the famous industrial designer, generally duplicated those found in the C and E models but were somewhat more colorful and interesting.

The Super G may be considered the most successful of the entire Constellation family only if one differentiates between the L–749 and the L–749A, which together totaled 113 orders. But that would seem justified, considering they had differing gross weights for one thing. The orders for the Super G were to total 104, and the first customer was a newcomer to the Constellation ranks. Northwest Orient Airlines ordered 4 of the aircraft, followed by the oldest Constellation customer, TWA, which initially ordered 20. Later, TWA ordered an additional eight. Lufthansa ordered two lots of 4 each, and Eastern, a frequent client, picked up 10 more. Air France turned out to be the second largest customer, buying 14 altogether. KLM and Varig ordered six each, and Air India five. Other airlines with smaller orders made up the remaining 23 orders. The various orders for the Super G were thus split among 17 airlines in all.

Let us now take an in-depth look at what made up a Super G Constellation—what it looked like and how it was put together. Although it is clear that each model had certain unique features, and in fact even aircraft of the same model might differ because of customer specifications and preferences, nevertheless, in examining this model in some detail, we are in effect looking at any Super Constellation.

FUSELAGE

The fuselage is of semi-monocoque design, with a circular cross-section having a maximum diameter of 11 feet, 7.5 inches. The structure is made of extruded rings connected by longitudinal members, which form a rigid whole. The fuselage is 113 feet, 4 inches long, and the main cabin floor is basically an unbroken level surface. There is a total of 7807 cubic feet of volume within the fuselage, with 744 usable square feet of cabin floor area. The fuselage is sealed and pressurized between the forward and rear bulkheads. The forward bulkhead lies between the cockpit, or flight station, and the nose section. The aft bulkhead acts as the rear wall of the cabin and is located just forward of the tail assembly. There is also a fixed bulkhead between the cabin and the rear of the cockpit areas that is a structural partition. All other partitions are nonstructural and movable, thus permitting considerable flexibility in setting up various cabin configurations.

Blankets of fiberglass insulation are cemented directly to the outer skin of the fuselage. A dead air space exists between this insulation and the inner side panels. A second layer of fiberglass, plus the vinyl trim, completes the side walls. There are three external doors, these being a main passenger door on the left rear at the galley section; a left forward passenger/cargo door located just behind the cockpit at the relief crew and navigator's compartment; and a crew door on the right side at the rear of the cockpit.

Cabin windows are large, rectangular, and double-paned. The inner panel is tinted green. The outer window panel is laminated and is the main surface that withstands the pressurization force. In case of outer panel failure, the inner panel will withstand the full cabin pressure. Pressurized cabin air is passed between the two panels to keep them free of frost or steam. Window emergency exits are provided on both sides of the fuselage, the number varying depending on the customer. In all cases, these exits consist of hatches, which have windows and can be forced open, either from the inside or the outside.

The aft pressure bulkhead is provided with a circular manhole that permits access to the unpressurized rear fuselage area. The main floor is positioned just above the main wing spar, which passes entirely through the fuselage. This wing section divides the lower fuselage lobe into forward and rear cargo compartments.

The floor used in the passenger version is plywood in the main compartment aisle, as well as in the lavatories, galleys, entranceways, and cockpit. But where the passenger seats are located, the flooring is a metal-covered honeycomb. Seat tracks are anchored to this part of the floor, and the passenger seats are anchored in turn to these tracks. Where the customer procures the aircraft in the cargo or cargo-passenger combination versions, the floor is made up of removable extruded aluminum sections that can withstand much heavier loads. The flooring in the passenger version is covered throughout with carpeting held down by double-faced adhesive tape.

The two lower cargo compartments are lined, sealed, and pressurized. Each of these areas can be reached from the cabin through an access hatch in the main cabin floor. These hatches have a plastic wide-angle lens window so that each compartment can be inspected while in flight for such things as smoke or fire. Main access to these cargo compartments is through 30-inch by 40-inch inward opening hatches located in the belly of the fuselage. An optional second hatch to the rear compartment is also available. The rear compartment has 420 cubic feet volume and can be loaded with up to 8480 pounds, whereas the forward one has 274 cubic feet volume and can accept a maximum load of 5380 pounds, thus totaling 694 cubic feet and 13,860 pounds.

The main cabin passenger seats consist of either two- or three-unit seat assemblies, anchored to the tracks and easily movable, which allows the operator to change the passenger seating configuration easily and quickly. The seats have backs that recline to 38° from the vertical.

There is a single galley for storing and heating food trays and for other simple functions. Two identical lavatories are located at the extreme rear of the cabin, just forward of the aft pressure bulkhead. On some aircraft, one or two additional lavatories are located between a small, forward passenger area and the main passenger compartment.

WINGS

The wing is of cantilever design, all metal with stressed-skin design. There are two, rather than one, wing spars, with a main beam and a secondary beam. The wing is subdivided into 15 separate and distinct assemblies. These are the single center section and two each of the inner wing panels, outer wing panels, wingtips, outer tips, flaps, ailerons, and trim tabs. Wingtips are removable so that fuel tanks can be substituted.

The center section is part of the fuselage and contains the center section fuel tank, which has a capacity of 730 gallons, and the reserve oil tank, with a capacity of 67 gallons.

The inner sections each mount two complete engine nacelles, two fuel tanks of 790- and 1555-gallon capacity, respectively, wing flaps, main landing gear, and various related controls. In addition, these sections also contain cabin superchargers, refrigeration unit, and other air conditioning equipment. The inner wing structure consists of a box made up of the two main spars, or beams, connected by chordwise ribs. Aluminum alloy skin internally stiffened with corrugations covers the upper surface, and machined skin integrally stiffened covers the lower surface. A leading edge structure and a trailing edge structure with an auxiliary beam are also part of the inner wing.

The outer wing section makes up the rest of the basic wing structure, except for the wing tips. The outer wing behind the main spar is covered with aluminum alloy skin, stiffened internally with stringers. Forward of the main spar, it is covered with extruded integrally stiffened skin. Each outer wing contains an aileron with booster mechanisms, an integral 565-gallon fuel tank, and a landing light.

The wingtips come in two lengths, with the tips used in aircraft equipped with tip tanks being 30 inches shorter. If no tip tanks are used, an outer tip fits outside the wingtip itself and is equipped with a position light. The tip tanks each carry some 610 gallons of fuel and a position light.

Each wing is equipped with a six-section, high-lift, modified Fowler-type flap. The left and right wing flaps are interconnected to ensure that both flaps extend simultaneously. As with all such type flaps, the first portion of flap extension results in additional lift and further extension adds still more lift but increases drag.

The ailerons extend the full length of the outer wing panels. They are attached to the wing with flush, continuous, anti-icing hinges. Weights placed at various points ensure both static and dynamic balance. Each aileron also has a controllable trailing edge trim tab.

EMPENNAGE

The empennage, or tail assembly, has a 50-foot-wide horizontal stabilizer, with split two-section elevator, three vertical fins that rise 10 feet, 4 inches above the stabilizer, three rudders, and trim tabs on both elevators and on the two outboard rudders only. The entire tail assembly is metal covered, except the rudders and rudder trim tabs, which are covered with dope-impregnated fabric. The elevators are rigidly interconnected to ensure identical movement. The two outer fins extend some 4 feet below the stabilizer. All three rudders are statically balanced, and the center rudder alone is also dynamically balanced.

LANDING GEAR

The landing gear is a fully retractable tricycle gear, with the two main gears retracting into the inboard nacelles and wing, while the nose gear retracts into the forward part of the fuselage. All elements are fully enclosed by mechanically operated flush doors, and all are extended and retracted by hydraulic-driven actuating cylinders. Each main gear has a single oleo-pneumatic strut and dual wheels, 17.00 by 20, one on each side of the strut. The nose gear has the same type of strut and two 34-inch wheels.

The gear doors are actuated by the gear oleo-pneumatic shock struts operated by the secondary hydraulic system. The main gear has both uplocks and downlocks. The uplock prevents the gear from prematurely extending when subjected to G forces during maneuvers or turbulence. The downlock prevents the drag struts from folding while there is a load on the gear, namely, while on the ground. Each of the dual wheels on the main landing gear is equipped with two single-disk brakes. These are connected in pairs, that is, the inner brake on one wheel is connected to the outer brake on the adjacent wheel. The brakes are operated by depressing the brake pedals, which actuates the hydraulically powered pistons in the cylinder assemblies.

POWER PLANTS

The power plants consist of four Curtiss-Wright Turbo-Compound air-cooled 18-cylinder reciprocating engines. Depending on the specific customer, they are identified as the 972TC18-DA-1, EA-3, or EA-6. Each engine has three power recovery turbines (PRT). Each PRT receives the combined exhaust of 6 of the 18 cylinders, with the turbine geared to the engine crankshaft through a fluid coupling. Thus, the exhaust is used to add power by driving the power recovery turbine, which is in turn connected to the crankshaft. A single-stage, two-speed, gear-driven supercharger is contained in the engine rear section. In addition, each engine has a fuel injection system.

The basic engine, together with accessories, cowling, oil cooler and scoop, and propeller, make up a quick-engine-change unit. This unit can be replaced in approximately 3 hours. The basic engine, minus the propeller, is some 90 inches long, 57 inches in diameter, and weighs between 3400 and 3650 pounds, depending on the engine model. The propeller reduction gear ratio is 0.4375:1, and all propellers turn clockwise.

The engine is rated at 3400 hp maximum power at sea level, 2850 hp maximum except take-off power at 5000 feet, and 2600 hp maximum except take-off power at 16,000 feet. Cruise power is 1900 hp at 11,600 feet, and 1800 hp at 20,600 feet.

The engines are equipped with either Curtiss electric or Hamilton Standard hydromatic propellers. Both types are constant-speed full-feathering, with reversible pitch. The propellers are 15 feet in diameter and three-bladed.

HYDRAULIC SYSTEM

There are two hydraulic systems, the primary and the secondary. A hydraulic pressure of 1700 psi is maintained by four engine-driven pumps, one pump per engine. The primary system operates the surface control boosters, the primary return bypass valve, and the left wing secondary heat exchanger fan motor. The two pumps on this system are driven by the number one and two engines. The secondary system operates the landing gear, nose wheel steering mechanism, wing flaps, outer wing and wingtip fuel dumps, the secondary heat exchanger fan motor in the right wing, the engine oil transfer pump, the secondary and aspirator return bypass valves, and the main reservoir pressurizing aspirator. The two pumps on this system are driven by number three and four engines.

Should either hydraulic system fail, a motor-controlled crossover valve between the two systems allows hydraulic fluid to supply either system. Electric motor–driven hydraulic pumps develop auxiliary hydraulic pressure for operating the rudder and elevator booster systems during take-offs and landings.

ELECTRICAL SYSTEM

There are two electrical systems; a 24-volt DC system, and a 115-volt, 400-cycle AC system. These systems provide power for all motors, instruments, communications gear, lighting, and other miscellaneous circuits. The wiring for the various circuits is tied in bundles supported by insulated clamps. All wires are numbered at frequent intervals for easy identification. Wires located forward of the engine firewalls are flameproof. There are four main DC generators, one in each engine nacelle, all of which are connected to the main DC bus. The DC system directly powers the engine starters, propeller feathering pump motors, cowl flap actuators, certain emergency circuits, and energizes the inverters that supply AC power. The DC system also is used for both the internal and external lighting systems, the galley equipment, the air conditioning system, various cockpit warning lights, the auxiliary fuel pumps, windshield wipers and defoggers, and emergency power for a few vital cockpit flight instruments. There are also two storage batteries that are connected into the DC system.

The AC power supply is provided by a minimum of two inverters, although customer preference may dictate more. An emergency inverter or engine-driven alternators supply standby AC power for instruments and radios. This particular inverter is normally located in the nose section of the fuselage, near the equipment it feeds.

The AC system is used to power all cockpit flight and engine instruments, various indicators, all communications and navigation equipment, the weather radar, and the PA system.

AIR CONDITIONING

The air conditioning system provides cabin pressurization, auxiliary ventilation plus air circulation, heating, and cooling. Pressurization is maintained as follows: Up to 12,300 feet flight altitude, cabin pressure is equivalent to sea level. At 20,000 feet flight level, cabin pressure is equal to that at 5000 feet. At 25,000 feet flight altitude, cabin pressure is equal to that at 10,600 feet.

At altitudes over 25,000 feet, cabin pressure will be correspondingly lower than 10,600 feet and is normally forbidden.

Pressurized air is supplied by two engine-driven compressors, or cabin superchargers, located in the number one and four engine nacelles. Additional air is supplied by ram air ducted into the main distribution systems from wing leading edge inlets located near the fuselage. Cabin heating is provided by two internal combustion heaters. The flight deck is supplied with an additional electric heater, due to the greater cooling action experienced by the nose section. Cooling is generated by two cooling units located in the inner wing sections. The entire fuselage, including the cockpit, main cabin, and both cargo compartments, are pressurized. The system as a whole cleverly mixes various amounts of pressurized air, heated and unheated cabin recirculated air, and outside air to achieve the right pressure/temperature combination. This is considerably more complicated than one might realize at first glance. Readers should keep in mind that not only does outside pressure change as the aircraft climbs and descends, so does outside temperature. To heat the main cabin, and also to set up an air curtain that acts as a blanket of insulation against outside temperatures, hot air is passed through ducts that are located between the inner cabin trim and the insulation layer nearest the fuselage wall. Air is also passed between the inner and outer panes of each window to prevent fogging, as previously mentioned.

Due to the importance of this total system for passenger safety, as well as comfort, the system on the Super G represents a considerable improvement over previous ones. The original L–049s in particular left quite a bit to be desired, and the system as a whole was upgraded when the L–649/749 model was developed and again for the Super Constellation models.

COCKPIT

The cockpit, or as it is sometimes called, the flight deck, is of course the nerve center of the entire airplane. Not only is the airplane flown from here, but all the aircraft systems are controlled from here also. Cockpits in the Super Constellations differed somewhat from each other, depending on customer preference and requirements, and therefore, the description given here is of a typical configuration. However, the layout of the cockpits of all Super Constellations, including all military versions, was essentially the same.

In general, the cockpit has space for four crew positions. Forward are the pilot and co-pilot positions, with controls, instruments, and so on. On the right side, behind the co-pilot, is the flight engineer's station with its panels and controls. On the left side, behind the pilot, is a station that can be used by a radio operator or as a jump seat for an observer. This completes the cockpit proper, which has a partition at the rear with a door. Beyond this partition is a compartment that is often used as a crew rest compartment, especially on long flights. It has a set of upper and lower berths on the right side. Across from it is the forward entrance door and vestibule. This space often accommodates a crew station, such as a navigator's position, with desk and instrument panel.

The instruments and controls used by the flight crew are gathered together into clearly delineated groups on various panels and consoles. The pilots have six instrument panels, three control panels, and one control stand. The relative location of these panels is shown in the illustrations at the end of the chapter. Their basic functions are:

- **Overhead panel**: Includes landing light switches, control surface booster switches and circuit breakers, radio frequency selector controls, and engine ignition switches.
- **Glare shield instrument panel**: Course indicator, magnetic indicator, and range indicator.
- **Center instrument panel**: Engine instruments, trim indicators, wing flap position indicator, landing gear lights, outside air temperature indicator, reverse pitch indicator lights, and master fire warning lights.
- **Pilot's and co-pilot's instrument panels**: Flight instruments, including altimeter, airspeed indicator, localizer and glide slope, marker beacon lights, clocks, attitude indicator, turn and slip indicator, and so on.
- **Pilot's and co-pilot's auxiliary instrument panels**: An additional five or six indicators and lights, differing between the two panels.
- **Pilot's side panel**: Various light switches and rheostats and a radio selector switch.
- **Co-pilot's side panel**: Various switches for heaters, defoggers, and de-icers, rheostats, and a radio selector switch.
- **Center control stand**: Throttles, propeller controls, reverse pitch throttles, flap and landing gear controls, three-axis trim tab wheels and controls, and autopilot controls.

The flight engineer's position has a total of four panels, as shown in the illustration. Their basic functions are:

- **Control quadrant and lower switch panel**: Throttles, carburetor air switches, engine supercharger controls, fuel mixture and tank selector levers, oil cooler flaps, cowl flap switches, and ignition analyzers.
- **Lower instrument panel**: Engine, hydraulic, fuel flow, and oil system instruments.
- **Upper instrument panel**: Various system indicators.
- **Upper switch panel**: Propeller feathering controls, electrical system controls, and other miscellaneous switches.

Where a navigator station is provided, the navigator's instrument panel includes azimuth indicator, outside air temperature indicator, sensitive altimeter, Mach air speed indicator, clock, and gyrosun compass repeater.

The radio operator's station would normally be equipped with a low frequency radio transmitter/receiver able to transmit and receive over long distances.

MAIN CABIN LAYOUT

The layout of the main cabin could be arranged in any number of combinations, and individual air carriers did in fact use many different layouts. A typical arrangement used a combination that resulted in a total of 63 seats in a single class configuration. In addition, there were accommodations for 11 crew members, including 4 relief crew. The seats, lavatories, galley, and various coat closets were all interspersed in such a way as to break up the long tunnel effect of the fuselage. This particular circumstance was becoming an active consideration to manufacturers and airlines alike. In the case of the Super G, famous industrial designer Henry Dreyfuss was retained by Lockheed at a cost of $1.5 million, and the Dreyfuss staff generated some 120,000 design and engineering man-hours in the total effort.

A typical result is a fuselage subdivided into four separate and distinct cabins. The forward cabin, just behind the crew rest compartment, seats 12 in 3 rows of seats. Then comes a section of two lavatories and adjoining coat closets, which form a functional divider. Following this is the main cabin, which contains 32 seats in 8 rows. At the far end of this section is another divider, behind which is located a small lounge area, with eight seats in two rows, facing each other. Another partition separates the lounge from the galley on one side and the main passenger entryway on the other, the latter including coat closets and a double seat for cabin attendants. Still another partition, and we come to the aft cabin, seating 11 in 3 rows. Then two more coat closets, two individual attendant seats, and right at the back, a second set of dual lavatories. In addition, overhead racks are located in the three main compartments. The lounge area has a removable table on one side, and, instead of overhead racks, a provision for berths over the seats.

It is easy to visualize how, with all this subdivision of space, what is an almost 100-foot-long cabin is transformed into a number of seemingly isolated compartments that are far more pleasing to the eye. Together with murals, fabrics, leathers, and so on, the final result makes for a more comfortable and attractive airplane. It is a far cry from the original C–69 interior; but then, the times called for some real improvements in interior design, especially in view of the longer nonstop flights that the Super G would make common.

This, then, is what a Super G Constellation is like. It is an airplane design that would play an important part in world commercial aviation. Unlike the earlier Constellation models, the Super Constellations did not participate in dramatic trail-blazing efforts, but the L–1049C/E/G/H models did set a high standard for long-range services routinely operated, and a great many people from countries the world over flew comfortably and safely in these aircraft.

10-1 A view of the Lockheed delivery ramp in 1954. Among the Super Constellations awaiting delivery are military AEW and transport aircraft, L–1049C, D, and E models for commercial carriers, and what appears to be the VC–121C for President Eisenhower in the foreground. (Lockheed Martin)

10-2 Typical Super Connie pilot's panels. This photo shows the layout of an L–1049B/R7V-1 USN transport. (Lockheed Martin)

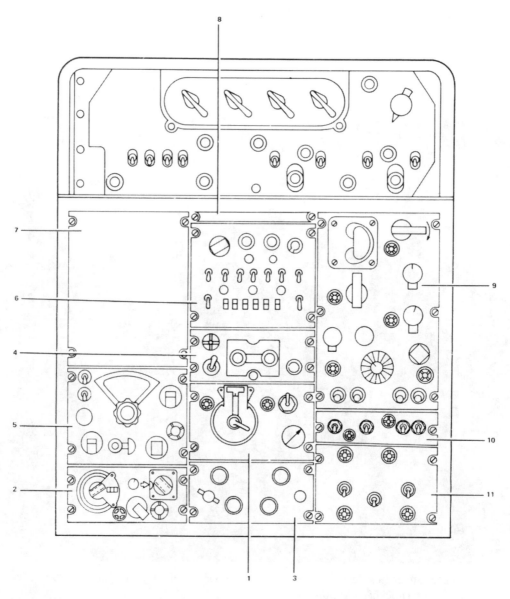

1. AN/ARN-14 VOR RECEIVER CONTROL PANEL
2. AN/ARC-27 UHF CONTROL PANEL
3. 618-T CONTROL PANEL
4. AN/ARN-21 TACAN CONTROL PANEL
5. AN/ARN6 CONTROL PANEL
6. C6280( )/APX IFF CONTROL PANEL
7. COVER PLATE (REF)
8. PANEL, BLANK 60D91678B103
9. AN/APS-42 RADAR CONTROL
10. AUXILIARY INTERCOM CONTROL PANEL
11. P.A. CONTROL SYSTEM

10-3 Typical pilot's overhead panel (EC-121-D). (U.S. Air Force)

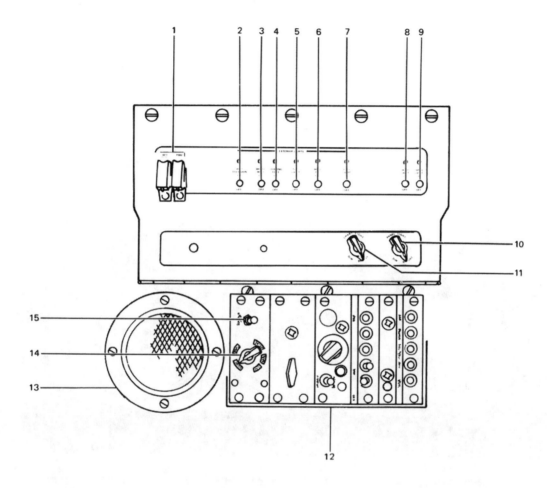

1. FLARE RELEASE SWITCHES
2. ANTI-COLLISION LIGHT SWITCH
3. WHEEL WELL LIGHT SWITCH
4. LEADING EDGE LIGHTS SWITCH
5. TAIL LIGHT SWITCH
6. WING TIP LIGHTS SWITCH
7. TAXI LIGHT SWITCH
8. CHART LIGHT SWITCH
9. PANEL LIGHT SWITCH
10. PANEL LIGHT RHEOSTAT
11. CHART LIGHT RHEOSTAT
12. RADIO AND ICS PANEL
13. LOUDSPEAKER LS-184
14. PANEL LIGHT RHEOSTAT
15. VHF-NAV/ARN-21 SELECTOR SWITCH

10-4 Typical pilot's side panel. (U.S. Air Force)

1 ID-249 COURSE INDICATOR   2 ID-250 RADIO MAGNETIC INDICATOR   3 ID-310 RANGE INDICATOR

10-5 Typical pilot's glareshield panel. (U.S. Air Force)

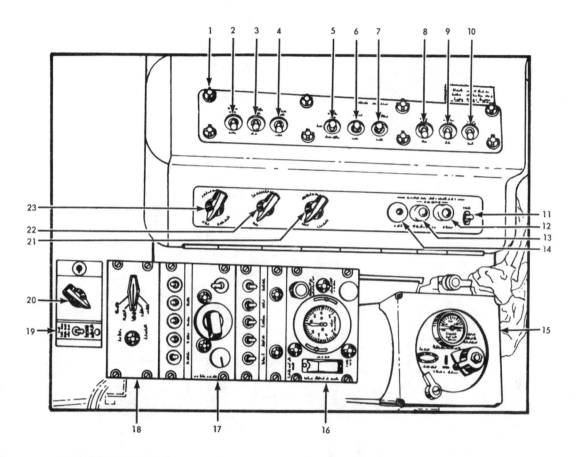

1. EDGE LIGHTS (8 EA)
2. PANEL LIGHT SWITCH
3. CHART LIGHT SWITCH
4. PEDESTAL REAR LIGHT SWITCH
5. IFF ANTENNA SWITCH
6. LEFT PITOT HEATER SWITCH
7. RIGHT PITOT HEATER SWITCH
8. WINDSHIELD DEFOG HEATER SWITCH
9. WINDSHIELD DEFOG BLOWER SWITCH
10. MAST DEICER SWITCH
11. NESA SYSTEM SWITCH
12. NESA SYSTEM POWER ON LIGHT
13. NESA CYCLING LIGHT
14. NESA RESET SWITCH
15. OXYGEN REGULATOR
16. RADAR PRESSURIZATION CONTROL AND INDICATOR
17. COPILOT'S ICS PANEL
18. RANGE FILTER SWITCH PANEL
19. VHF NAV AND ARN-21 SELECTOR SWITCH
20. INPH PANEL LIGHT RHEOSTAT
21. COMPASS LIGHT RHEOSTAT
22. CHART LIGHT RHEOSTAT
23. PANEL LIGHT RHEOSTAT

10-6 Copilot's right hand console. (U.S. Air Force)

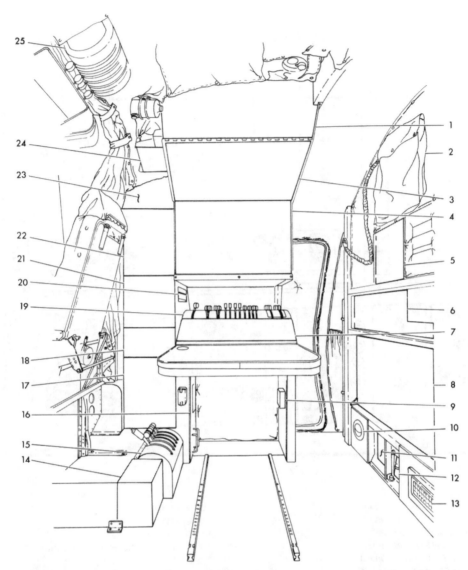

1 UPPER SWITCH PANEL
2 DITCHING ROPE AND CONTAINER
3 UPPER INSTRUMENT PANEL
4 LOWER INSTRUMENT PANEL
5 ENGINE/HEATER FIRE EXTINGUISHER CONTROL PANEL
6 STATION 260 UPPER SWITCH PANEL
7 LOWER SWITCH PANEL
8 AIR CONDITIONING CONTROL PANEL
9 STATION 238 CIRCUIT BREAKER PANEL
10 CREW DOOR LIGHT
11 DITCHING VALVE RELEASE HANDLE
12 CABIN HEATER FIRE EXTINGUISHING CONTROL PANEL/CB PANEL
13 STATION 260 AIR OUTLET
14 IGNITION ANALYZER CONTROL PANEL
15 FLIGHT ENGINEER'S AUXILIARY CONTROL QUADRANT
16 LOWER MJB 212 PANEL
17 MJB NO. 3 PANEL
18 MJB NO. 2A PANEL
19 FLIGHT ENGINEER'S CONTROL QUADRANT
20 UPPER MJB 212 PANEL
21 MJB NO. 2 PANEL
22 MJB NO. 1 PANEL
23 UPPER MJB PANEL
24 RADIO SELECTOR BOX
25 EMERGENCY SHUT-OFF LEVERS AND QUADRANT

10-7 Flight engineer's station. (U.S. Air Force)

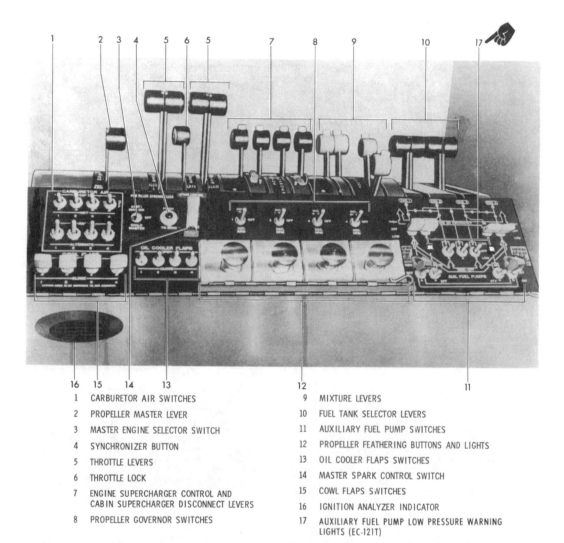

1	CARBURETOR AIR SWITCHES	9	MIXTURE LEVERS
2	PROPELLER MASTER LEVER	10	FUEL TANK SELECTOR LEVERS
3	MASTER ENGINE SELECTOR SWITCH	11	AUXILIARY FUEL PUMP SWITCHES
4	SYNCHRONIZER BUTTON	12	PROPELLER FEATHERING BUTTONS AND LIGHTS
5	THROTTLE LEVERS	13	OIL COOLER FLAPS SWITCHES
6	THROTTLE LOCK	14	MASTER SPARK CONTROL SWITCH
7	ENGINE SUPERCHARGER CONTROL AND CABIN SUPERCHARGER DISCONNECT LEVERS	15	COWL FLAPS SWITCHES
		16	IGNITION ANALYZER INDICATOR
8	PROPELLER GOVERNOR SWITCHES	17	AUXILIARY FUEL PUMP LOW PRESSURE WARNING LIGHTS (EC-121T)

10-8 Typical flight engineer's control quadrant and lower switch panel. (U.S. Air Force)

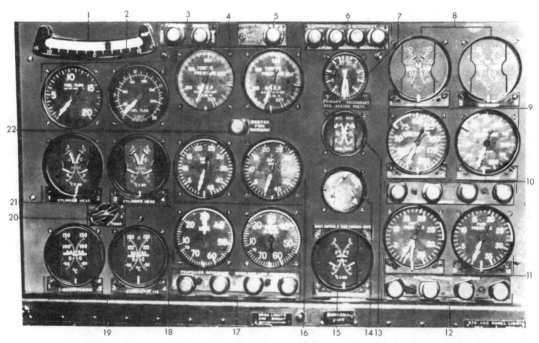

1 INCLINOMETER	13 HYDRAULIC FLUID QUANTITY INDICATOR
2 FUEL FLOW INDICATORS	14 SYNCHROSCOPE
3 DOOR WARNING LIGHTS	15 CABIN SUPERCHARGER DRIVE SHAFT REAR BEARING TEMPERATURE INDICATOR
4 TORQUEMETERS (BMEP INDICATORS)	
5 AC GENERATOR MASTER WARNING LIGHT	16 TACHOMETER INDICATORS
6 HYDRAULIC PUMP LOW PRESSURE WARNING LIGHT	17 PROPELLER GOVERNOR HIGH AND LOW PITCH POSITION INDICATOR LIGHTS
7 HYDRAULIC SYSTEM PRESSURE INDICATOR	
8 OIL TEMPERATURE INDICATORS	18 MANIFOLD PRESSURE INDICATORS
9 OIL PRESSURE INDICATORS	19 CARBURETOR AIR TEMPERATURE INDICATORS
10 OIL LOW-PRESSURE WARNING LIGHTS	20 CYLINDER HEAD TEMPERATURE SELECTOR SWITCH
11 FUEL PRESSURE INDICATORS	21 CYLINDER HEAD TEMPERATURE INDICATORS
12 FUEL LOW-PRESSURE WARNING LIGHTS	22 MASTER FIRE WARNING LIGHT

10-9 Typical flight engineer's lower instrument panel. (U.S. Air Force)

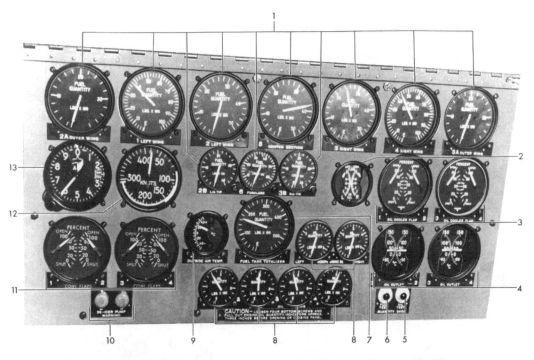

1 FUEL QUANTITY INDICATORS
2 ALCOHOL ANTI-ICING TANK FLUID QUANTITY INDICATOR
3 OIL COOLER FLAP POSITION INDICATORS
4 OIL TEMPERATURE INDICATORS (OIL OUT)
5 OIL QUANTITY INDICATORS TEST SWITCH
6 FUEL QUANTITY INDICATORS TEST SWITCH
7 FUEL QUANTITY TOTALIZER INDICATOR
8 OIL QUANTITY INDICATORS
9 OUTSIDE AIR TEMPERATURE INDICATOR
10 VACUUM WARNING (DE-ICER PUMP) LIGHTS
11 COWL FLAP POSITION INDICATORS
12 AIRSPEED INDICATOR
13 ALTIMETER

10-10 Typical flight engineer's upper instrument panel. (U.S. Air Force)

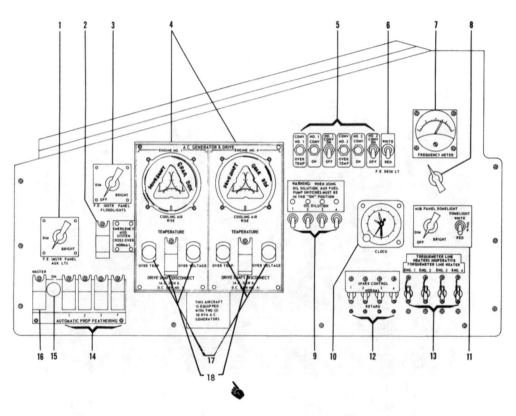

1. FLIGHT ENGINEER'S INSTRUMENT PANEL AUXILIARY LIGHTS RHEOSTAT
2. HYDRAULIC SYSTEM CROSSOVER SWITCH
3. FLIGHT ENGINEER'S INSTRUMENT PANEL FLOODLIGHTS
4. AC GENERATOR TEMPERATURE INDICATORS
5. CONVERTORS NO. 1 AND NO. 2 SWITCHES AND OVER TEMPERATURE LIGHTS
6. FLIGHT ENGINEER'S DESK LIGHT SWITCH
7. FREQUENCY METER
8. FREQUENCY SELECTOR SWITCH
9. OIL DILUTION SWITCHES (INOPERATIVE)
10. CLOCK
11. FLIGHT ENGINEER'S MJB AND DOME LIGHT SWITCHES
12. SPARK CONTROL CIRCUIT BREAKER SWITCHES
13. TORQUEMETER LINE HEATER SWITCHES (INOPERATIVE)
14. AUTOFEATHERING TEST SWITCHES
15. AUTOFEATHERING ARMED LIGHT
16. AUTOFEATHERING MASTER SWITCH
17. OVER TEMP AND OVER VOLTAGE WARNING LIGHTS
18. DRIVE SHAFT DISCONNECT

10-11 Typical flight engineer's upper switch panel. (U.S. Air Force)

10-12 A nose view of a Super Connie. Note the redesigned cockpit windows and roofline just above the windows. (Lockheed Martin)

10-13 A Brazilian Varig Airlines Super G Connie in flight. (Lockheed Martin)

10-14 "Hydraulic System" (Lockheed Martin)

10-15 "Air Conditioning System" (Lockheed Martin)

Chapter 11

BYWORD OF THE AIRLINES

The Constellation design originated as a passenger transport for commercial use. Although a large portion of its total production was destined for the military services, nevertheless it was always first and foremost a commercial aircraft. In that application the general public became familiar with it. It was also in that same application that both its potential and its actual performance over an extended period of time became highly visible and recognized.

The various members of the Lockheed Constellation family of aircraft served the commercial air carriers of the world for almost 20 years. During that period they pioneered new routes and services, gradually extended nonstop distances, and, in general, constituted one of the major forces that helped develop commercial air transportation.

In examining how the various airlines utilized the Constellations and Super Constellations, readers should keep in mind that the continuous development of air routes was basically the result of two distinct forces. The first was the gradual but steady growth of airline passengers, both business and tourists. The second was the gradual development of the airplanes involved, with a resultant increase in performance and capabilities. These two forces have to be viewed together because they occurred simultaneously, and it is often difficult to accurately judge which came first—or for that matter, whether at times one caused the other and in which order.

The way the Constellations and Super Constellations were used by the airlines was dependent, in large measure, on the particular model involved, and as succeeding models with improved performance were introduced, this was readily reflected in the timetables. Thus, one way to better understand what part these airplanes played in air transportation is to examine the schedules they operated.

The Constellations and Super Constellations flew many miles to all corners of the globe during the period 1946–65. The type of schedules they operated varied considerably over the years. This was due to three factors:

1. Equipment capability, performance, and availability.
2. Market needs, growth, and changes.
3. Marketing trends and innovations.

As we follow the progressively expanding schedules operated by Constellations, the influence of these factors will be seen time and time again. However, one portion of the Constellation airline service will not be covered in detail at this time except in passing; namely, the service provided by TWA. This part of the overall history is covered separately in Chapter 13.

The first factor mentioned, equipment capability, performance, and availability, was at all times a major factor. Aircraft reliability, at least in the first few months of the introduction of the Constellations, played a small part in the type of utilization as airlines felt their way somewhat cautiously in scheduling this new, fast, complex airplane. As more experience was gained, and as engine TBO became considerably longer, there was a marked increase in the utilization rate as measured by average hours of actual use per aircraft per 24-hour day.

Payload, or number of passengers that could be carried, was certainly an important consideration, but not in the first couple of years because ridership generally was quite low in the period 1946–47. Range always had to be taken into account. An individual airline also had to expand its Constellation schedules gradually depending on the rate of delivery of additional aircraft.

Thus, as new Constellation models with improved performance were introduced, this was reflected in expanded and changed schedules and in the advertisements carried in newspapers and magazines. All the new features that might be noticed by a potential passenger were highlighted by enthusiastic copywriters. The schedules gradually showed greater frequency, fewer stops, shorter flight times, and periodically, a trail-blazing new route.

Market needs played a large part in determining how best to use the potential of the Constellations. In this regard the airlines generally viewed the aircraft as a long-range, high-speed airplane throughout the majority of its active life. Thus, these aircraft were used most notably on routes where there was strong potential for attracting customers provided the service was fast and comfortable.

The third factor, marketing trends and innovations, was interesting to observe. The ideas, innovations, and attitudes of the airline marketing managers also affected not only the way these airplanes were used but also by such considerations as number of seats offered, the use of lounges and sleeping berths, and the relative size of galleys.

The manner in which the airlines used their Constellations and Super Constellations was partly a function of the specific models they were using at the particular time. For this reason, in analyzing the use of these commercial aircraft, this writer chose to organize this mass of information by the aircraft model. This results in seven distinct phases that, in addition, divide neatly into chronological periods. The beginning and ending dates of each phase correspond generally to the first and last deliveries of that particular model. As a rule, airlines were introducing new model aircraft within two to three months after the deliveries began. This delay was caused by the wish to have more than one aircraft of that model type in service, as well as the need to transition sufficient flight crews and train maintenance personnel.

The seven phases covered are:

- Phase 1, Model 049, November 1945 to October 1946
- Phase 2, Model 649/749, April 1947 to December 1949
- Phase 3, Model 649A/749A, November 1948 to September 1951
- Phase 4, Model 1049, November 1951 to September 1952
- Phase 5, Model 1049C/D/E, June 1953 to March 1955
- Phase 6, Model 1049G/H, January 1955 to October 1958 (September 1959)
- Phase 7, Model 1649A, October 1956 to June 1958

A composite table showing delivery dates of Constellations produced, both commercial and military, can be found in the back of the book as part of the appendices.

Let us now go back to the last days of 1945 and the initial phase in the long and illustrious commercial career of the Constellation.

PHASE 1, MODEL 049, NOVEMBER 1945 TO OCTOBER 1946

This first phase was possibly the most exciting of all the seven phases. Here was an airplane that was a whole generation ahead of anything else flying then or for the next two years. During this period, the Constellation pioneered a number of new routes and schedules, to the accompaniment of a great deal of press coverage. Actually, a case can be made for saying that the entire family of aircraft contributed more in the pioneering of new routes than any other airplane before or since. Granted, various circumstances may have helped make this so. But the inescapable fact remains that the vision of Hughes, Johnson, and Lockheed combined with the aggressiveness of various commercial airlines together made the Constellation the only airplane in its category flying for some two years. During this period a great many new routes were established to the four corners of Earth. In fact, it seemed as though every few days or weeks another speed record was being set or a new service established.

By November 1945, events began to take place that would result in the introduction of the Constellation into commercial airline service at last. That month Lockheed began delivering L–049s to TWA, which immediately started the process of transitioning a number of their more senior crews into the new addition to their fleet. Actually, as previously noted, both TWA and Pan Am had already been flying a very few C–69s as part of ATC operations, but the CAA expected all crews to complete the transition course that they had approved.

TWA was the first, naturally, to begin this transitioning process. Captain Jack Schnaubelt, TWA, now retired, was one of those involved in this process starting that November. Training flights were all flown from Kansas City. He clearly remembers still the difficulty experienced by the initial batches of pilots because of a CAA-imposed procedure. The CAA had never had to certify such a large or complex commercial airliner or the crews to fly it. One aspect of its design, which particularly distressed them, was the hydraulic boost system, again a brand-new piece of technology in commercial airplanes. They felt it only too possible for the boost system to fail, leaving the crew to land this huge aircraft with a control system that would then be physically extremely difficult to operate. Accordingly, the CAA imposed the requirement that all pilots had to make at least one approach and landing with the boost system off.

As Schnaubelt described it, the TWA pilots were almost universally having difficulty with their boost-off landings. They were often landing in cross-winds, and in a number of cases, the actual landings were so rough that it was only by sheer good fortune that no accidents took place. The skies over Kansas were soon filled with a great many loud and colorful expletives as the pilots strained and sweated to line up their balky and recalcitrant Constellations, which had never been designed to be deliberately flown with boost systems turned off! Eventually, after a couple of truly close shaves, the CAA inspectors on hand in the air and on the ground realized the high degree of potential danger and recommended that the practice be discontinued immediately. This was done, accompanied by many sighs of genuine relief from the crews.

December 1945 saw the certification of the L–049 by the CAA. This was accomplished after only 27 hours of flight tests. It is likely that the CAA's effort was expedited by the fact that the almost identical C–69 of the Air Force had been flying successfully on long flights since 1944. The flight hours amassed by the Army in effect served in part as a proving ground for the commercial L–049.

December also saw the delivery of the last of the first batch of nine aircraft to come off the assembly line, all to TWA. The reason why TWA was the only airline to receive aircraft during November and December dates back to the original contract between Howard Hughes and Lockheed. Dated July 10, 1939, that contract stipulated that TWA would receive the first nine airplanes produced regardless of who else ordered the Constellation. Six long years later, Lockheed was finally able to honor that agreement.

TWA had received the first of the nine aircraft back on November 15, 1945. Although there was a certain amount of fanfare and excitement at Kansas City, where formal delivery took place, TWA had actually been flying Army C–69s for almost a year since February 15, 1945. All the aircraft now being delivered were brand-new L–049 models, and TWA lost no time starting crew training, with an eye to introducing their fast, attractive airplanes as soon as possible.

It might be interesting to the reader to note that TWA's activity as part of the ATC dated back to December 1941, shortly after the attack on Pearl Harbor. At that time, TWA created their Inter-Continental Division (ICD) through a government contract. Operating as an integral part of ATC, the ICD trained air crews and later also operated aircraft overseas. They operated the Boeing B–307 Stratoliners formerly used domestically by TWA, C–54s, C–87s, and eventually C–69s. The ICD had been given the job of testing and proving the C–69 on January 23, 1945, and their first C–69 was delivered on February 15, 1945.

It should be remembered that Pan Am and American Export Airline (later to become AOA, a division of American Airlines), also were performing similar overseas functions as part of the ATC. Pan Am also flew C–69s during 1945.

In January 1946, Pan Am began to receive its deliveries, with the first Constellation being delivered on January 5. A total of three aircraft were delivered in January, and another four in February. Pan Am was able to match TWA's entry with the Constellation despite its later deliveries because of its ATC contracts, which permitted at least some of its crews to have prior experience in flying the type.

From a look at Appendix A, it becomes obvious that the airlines with the earliest deliveries managed to be the ones with the quickest introduction of the new, speedy airplane. It is somewhat surprising to note that KLM began to receive their Constellations as late as they did, considering that they were the second customer to order back in 1940, immediately after TWA. The author was not able to determine precisely how this came to be. However, it must be remembered that Holland had been badly damaged during World War II, and its economy all but destroyed. Therefore, it is conceivable that KLM voluntarily accepted later delivery positions while they rebuilt their organization and facilities.

So in November, December, and on into January 1946, the TWA and Pan Am crews trained for the introduction of the new services. Both carriers were aided by Lockheed, who loaned them some C–69s the Air Force had returned to Burbank. These loaners were extremely helpful, especially to Pan Am, who began receiving L–049 deliveries later than TWA.

As the inaugural dates approached, there was considerable publicity by the two air carriers. But a review of the newspapers of that time reveals a surprising lack of general interest and excitement on the part of the general public. At least three reasons come to mind for this phenomenon. First, the United States had come out of a long war only months before, and people were still in the midst of restructuring their lives. Second, the news generally was anything but good, with serious strikes, a recession, and high unemployment vying for newspaper headlines along with the growing threats from Soviet Russia toward European nations. Third, it is likely that relatively few people really understood the significance of the approaching airline services both in terms of the immediate present and of the future.

Both TWA and Pan Am were to initially fly only a few trips a week. This decision was really not theirs, because not enough Constellations had been delivered for more than token service. But both airlines also knew that they would not be besieged by passengers at this early date. For one thing, the State Department was allowing only a few individuals to fly to Europe, and these usually were on government business. The fares being charged were such as to discourage all but the relatively well-to-do. As far as tourists were concerned, Europe was simply not ready to deal with them and would not be for quite some time. So, readers must try to visualize things as they were in early 1946 and understand that this new service, although in no way an experiment from the operational or flying point of view, was a step that only a very few people would or could take at this time.

Pan Am and TWA had certain distinct advantages over any other carriers when it came to starting regular transatlantic passenger service. Not only were both airlines the first to receive delivery of the L–049 models, but both had been flying the military version, the C–69, across the Atlantic for some time. This, of course, was as part of the civilian effort of the ATC. However, both airlines had to do much work to begin their respective services in early February 1946. Facilities in Europe were almost nonexistent with the countries there still struggling to recover from World War II.

Ironically, the honor of operating the very first scheduled passenger flight in regular service fell not to TWA, which had helped pioneer the Constellation design, but to Pan Am. On January 14, 1946, a Pan Am L–049 departed New York to begin a daily New York–Bermuda service. Although possibly not quite as dramatic as a transoceanic service, the fact was that at last here was the Constellation, finally in regular service, some five years later than anyone had originally expected.

February 1946 was the moment of truth for TWA, for Pan Am and for the Constellation. Six and a half years after inception of the Constellation concept, and some five full years after the date that Hughes thought he would introduce the L–049 into service, the time had finally come for the Constellation to spread its wings and begin doing the job it had been originally conceived and designed to do.

In the three weeks following, a number of highly publicized survey and preview flights took place that carried aboard members of the press and officials of the airlines involved. Actually, the first of these flights had taken place back on December 3, 1945, when a TWA Constellation flew from Washington, D.C., to Paris with fuel stops at Gander and Shannon, in 14 hours, 48 minutes. On January 20, Pan Am made a survey flight from New York to Lisbon in 9 hours, 58 minutes. Compared to the 24 hours required by one of the Pan Am Boeing 314 flying boats, or the 19 hours needed by the DC–4, the flight was, to say the least, an eye opener. On February 1, TWA flew an L–049 New York to Los Angeles in 10 hours, 49 minutes, including a brief fuel stop at Kansas City. Carrying 32 passengers and a crew of 10 and bucking 40–60 mph winds, the flight established a new east-to-west record, breaking the record set almost six years previously by a TWA Boeing 307 Stratoliner of 11 hours, 55 minutes. The next day the same plane flew San Francisco to Los Angeles in 1 hour, 14 minutes with a total of 56 people aboard. Both flying time and passenger load constituted new records. On February 3, the same air craft again set records. With Jack Frye in command, it flew Los Angeles to New York in only 7 hours, 27 minutes nonstop and with a total of 56 aboard. Again, both were new records. This flight time was almost four hours less than the record set by TWA in July 1940.

On this same day, February 3, 1946, Pan Am began the first regular transatlantic Constellation service with a flight from New York to Bournemouth, England, the temporary terminus until London Airport was finished. Flown in 12 hours, 9 minutes, the flight set records for the New York–Gander and Gander–Shannon legs. Two days later it was TWA's turn. Their flight was Washington–New York–Gander–Shannon–Paris. Carrying 36 passengers and 8 crew members, it took 16 hours, 21 minutes. On February 15, TWA started its transcontinental Constellation service, flying Los Angeles–New York.

Thus, by February 1946, both TWA and Pan Am were operating the Constellations regularly, and passengers could take them across the United States to Bermuda and across the North Atlantic to London and Paris.

So at last the Constellations were truly in service, even if on a modest basis. As more aircraft were added to TWA's and Pan Am's fleets, additional services were introduced. In addition, a third airline began to receive deliveries of the L–049. This was AOA, the transoceanic division of American Airlines, which had ordered seven Constellations.

At the end of May 1946, Lockheed delivered their first Model L–049 conversion of a Air Force C–69 aircraft that had been repurchased by Lockheed. These conversions were to go to various airlines, some directly, and some indirectly by way of aircraft brokers. The airlines which began using these conversions were BOAC, El Al, and TWA, with the very first Constellation built going back to Lockheed to be used as a prototype for future developments.

By July, Lockheed was rolling out the last of their new L–049s. The last batches went to KLM, Air France, LAV, and TWA, with TWA receiving the very last one manufactured. At this point, the Lockheed assembly line began working on the 20 L–649 models for Eastern.

There is one aspect of these initial operations that is worth looking at in some detail. Namely, although Atlantic crossings in 1946 were being routinely handled, they represented a huge step forward from the few flying boat crossings that had been started in 1939–40 by Pan Am and BOAC. These earlier operations were, to be sure, successful, but of a route-proving nature and with relatively few passenger-miles generated. The 1946 effort represented a far more sophisticated effort. The difference was not merely the equipment. It was more fundamental than that and dealt with the total approach to transoceanic crossings, including even attitude.

The operations carried out by the essentially civilian components of ATC during World War II were actually to prove absolutely invaluable in the establishment of safe, reliable air transportation across the North Atlantic. The many thousands of flights across this body of water enabled substantial advances to be made in weather forecasting, flying techniques in weather penetration, celestial and radio navigation, long-range fuel management, pressure pattern flying (which took advantage of tailwinds), and bad-weather approaches to airports. It appears safe to say that without these five years of military flying across the Atlantic, the introduction of large-scale passenger flights might not have been possible during 1945–46.

The intervening war years between 1940 and 1946 had generated a number of very important specific results directly related to flying over the Atlantic. These were:

1. A greater understanding and more reliable forecasting of weather in general and North Atlantic weather in particular.
2. The existence of a number of new airports built specifically for use by transatlantic flights. These were strategically placed to assist crossings of the Atlantic and had relatively long runways and good navigational facilities.
3. The development of new navigational techniques, perfected by thousands of ocean crossings during World War II. One of these was "pressure pattern" flying, which permitted a pilot to take maximum advantage of available tailwinds, as well as predicting minimum headwinds.
4. The introduction of new and reliable navigational aids and communications equipment, both on the ground and in aircraft.
5. The generally improved TBO of aircraft engines, which resulted, naturally enough, in greatly increased confidence in power plants on the long, nonstop, overwater flights.
6. The existence at the end of World War II of a pool of trained airmen with experience in both four-engined land-planes and long overwater flights.
7. The confidence acquired by all as a result of the thousands of wartime crossings of the North Atlantic, not only by Douglas C–54 Skymasters but also by many military aircraft being ferried overseas.
8. Finally, the overall increase in acceptance by the public of commercial flying, due in part by the fact that so many returning servicemen had flown safely to many far corners of the world during the war.

All of the above factors contributed greatly to the technical success of the 1946–47 flight schedules inaugurated by various air carriers. In addition, during that period of implementation of new routes, the air carriers involved achieved a generally good safety record, which went far to dispel the public's innate fear of flying over seemingly limitless stretches of water.

Comparing typical early Constellation operations with competing aircraft provides a revealing picture. In 1946, Constellations were being scheduled in approximately 3.5 hours less flying time than DC–4s on the New York–Paris trip. The prewar Boeing flying boats required some four to five hours more than the DC–4s.

The significance here is not merely the greater cruise speeds and the higher operating altitudes of the L–049s, which permitted over-the-weather flying. The Constellations had far greater reserve power that could be called on to either circumvent weather or fight headwinds. In addition, the shorter flying time (not the overall trip time) meant lower fuel costs. The Constellation also could be utilized for more total trip-miles per month due to the speed differential. In effect, an airline could now offer faster, more comfortable, more reliable crossings at lower seat-mile costs. All of this was extremely important considering that the airlines, in starting frequent transatlantic services, were taking a large financial gamble.

In 1946, with half the world in a state of near-financial collapse, and the United States itself in economic trouble in the aftermath of the war, these flights could have turned out to be an economic disaster. But the combination of the safety and reliability of these flights, together with a considerable amount of government and business travel across the Atlantic, made the venture a success. Although these long flights would indeed have periods during which revenue was down, they were, almost from the day they started, a fixture of commercial airline services.

With the initial Constellation service under way, more activity began to develop as additional air carriers also received their Constellations. During the progressively increasing tempo of Constellation flights in the spring and summer 1946, the great majority were across the North Atlantic. TWA initially flew New York–Paris and New York–Los Angeles, whereas Pan Am operated New York–London and also to Lisbon. The two carriers were helped in getting their early start by the fact that they were able to borrow additional C–69s from Lockheed for crew training. These were aircraft originally delivered to the Air Force and then returned by them. All flights across the Atlantic to Northern Europe were by way of Gander and Shannon for refueling. This was the normal scheduling in both directions. By March, both airlines were able to increase their flights so as to offer daily service.

In July 1946, Pan Am extended its service from Lisbon into Africa, flying to Dakar, Monrovia, and Leopoldville in the Belgian Congo. Pan Am also began service to Brussels, Prague, and Vienna. By providing some of their Constellation equipment to their subsidiary, Panair do Brasil (PAB), Pan Am began another new route from London to Paris–Lisbon–Dakar–Recife and Rio de Janeiro. This route was noteworthy for its total length of approximately 5,000 miles. With its former widespread experience in flying to many parts of the world, Pan Am was able to capitalize on its head start in equipment deliveries. In that same month they also began daily service from the West Coast to Hawaii.

It is interesting to note that Pan Am actually reduced their flight frequencies across the North Atlantic a few months after the initial introduction of the Constellation. This was no doubt due in part to a wish to use the L–049 in other long-range markets. It may also have been caused by the need to reduce daily aircraft utilization rates slightly because maintenance was requiring more down time than originally expected.

Also in July, AOA began thrice weekly service to London, thus putting a third U.S. flag carrier across the North Atlantic. British Overseas Airways also began service New York–Prestwick–London in the same month. Their aircraft were the first of the converted C–69s. These particular ones had been manufactured just prior to the end of hostilities, and the Air Force had refused delivery. Thereafter they sat in a neat row at Burbank until BOAC purchased them and Lockheed rushed to complete the conversion to L–049 configuration.

The first year of the Constellation was marred by the July 11 crash at Reading, Pennsylvania (see Chapter 5) and the subsequent grounding of all Connies, which lasted a minimum of six weeks. But by fall 1946 modifications had been achieved, and all the Constellations were once again flying.

August saw the beginning of service by those two old and reliable companies, Air France and KLM. Their ability to begin these services some 15 months after the end of a war that ravaged both countries attests to their resourcefulness as well as their ability to rebuild. Although their initial services both over the Atlantic and elsewhere were quite limited, it was nevertheless a strong indication of things to come.

The one other airline to begin Constellation service in this initial year and a half was, surprisingly enough, Linea Aeropostal Venezolana (LAV), the small Venezuelan-flag carrier. With their two L–049s, LAV started a Caracas–New York service in March 1947.

This, then, was the total picture at the end of Phase I, with the only services not discussed being TWA's, which are dealt with in Chapter 13. It was, all in all, a truly mighty collective effort on the part of Lockheed, various airlines, and a number of governments. Phase I was certainly hampered heavily by the war's aftermath, and the Constellation grounding of mid-1946 obviously did nothing to help things along. Nevertheless, by the end of this initial 18-month period, the Constellation was firmly established as the foremost passenger transport of its day. It had pioneered a number of routes, at least in terms of schedules, and had gained the approval not only of flight crews and operating personnel but also, most important, of passengers.

PHASE II, MODEL 649/749, APRIL 1947 TO DECEMBER 1949

Beginning in 1947, as the L–049 deliveries were winding down, the new, improved Model L–649/749 began coming off the assembly line. To be precise, there were two models but they were often identified together because they were identical except for the L–749s being fitted with outer wing panel fuel tanks and having a take-off weight that was greater by 8,000 pounds. This difference made the 749 more of a long-range aircraft than the 649. Otherwise, they were identical in all other respects.

The first L–749 came off the assembly line a month before the first L–649, and the two types were built on the same assembly line with both being delivered simultaneously in 1947. EAL, the only carrier to order the L–649, received all 14 aircraft in that year, 12 of them within the space of only three months. The EAL order for L–649s was the harbinger of things to come. In time, EAL would become the second largest commercial customer of Constellations, exceeded only by TWA. With this large addition to its fleet, EAL was able to initiate Constellation service on a number of its longer, more heavily traveled routes. In the summer of 1947, the EAL Golden Plate Constellations (as they were known) began flying nonstop on such routes as New York–Florida and New York–Houston. With the competition flying DC–3s and some DC–4s, Eastern was able to make much of its new luxury aircraft.

As EAL was receiving their L–649s, Lockheed was also delivering L–749s to Air France, Pan Am, KLM, Airlinte Eireann, LAV, and Qantas. Air France's deliveries were in spring and summer 1947; the others received their L–749s in the latter half of the year. The L–749s longer range and somewhat greater payload were very advantageous to the airlines , all of whom had long, overwater routes.

Air France began their L–749 service in June 1947 across the Atlantic with the eastbound flights having only one fuel stop at Gander on the New York–Paris flight. Westbound, two fuel stops were still scheduled. One eastbound flight each week had luxury sleeper service, and with the lighter payload, was scheduled nonstop New York–Paris! Known as the Golden Parisian, the flight was heavily publicized by Air France. The return flight still made the obligatory two fuel stops. In that same year, Constellation service was also extended eastward to Cairo, Egypt, and Ludda, Palestine. It is interesting to note that the L–749's range allowed a full hour to be saved in doing away with the eastbound Shannon fuel stop. The special weekly New York–Paris nonstop saved a full four hours overall. Actually, the

L–749, though certainly a better overall airplane than the L–049, cruised at a slightly lower speed. The airlines generally benefited from this trade-off of range for speed because their overall flight times were reduced, as was the fuel consumption per trip.

In summer 1947, Pan Am also put its L–749s on the North Atlantic run by flying the New York–London route with a weekly flight going as far as Calcutta, India. This flight connected with a Calcutta–San Francisco flight operated with DC–4s, thus setting up the first around-the-world scheduled service. Pan Am's PAB Division was by this time operating from Rio de Janeiro to Lisbon, Rome, Paris, and London with L–049s formerly used on the North Atlantic.

KLM was next to receive the L–749 and, in the period of August through November 1947, took delivery of 11 of their total of 13. This was the largest single L–749 order. The last two aircraft were not to arrive until October and November 1948, almost a year later. With this expanded fleet, and taking advantage of the additional range of the L–749s, KLM began to expand its operations. The L–749s were put on new routes to South America in the latter half of 1947, first to Montevideo, Uruguay, then to Buenos Aires, Argentina, and Santiago, Chile. At this time also, service was begun to Johannesburg, South Africa.

By October 1948, KLM Constellations were operating Amsterdam–New York–Curacao (Venezuela) and Amsterdam–Batavia (Indonesia) via Cairo, Basra, Karachi, Calcutta, Bangkok, and Singapore. This latter route was certainly proof of the type of intercontinental service that Constellations were capable of handling. This long route to the Far East was operated five days of the week. By 1949, Montreal was added to the Constellation schedules.

Qantas Empire Airways, the Australian-flag carrier, ordered four of the L–749s, all delivered in October 1947. Beginning in December 1947, Qantas initiated through service to London using their big new birds. This was the first time a Qantas flight was operated through to London with Qantas crews. Qantas was impressed enough with the L–749's performance that it purchased two more secondhand from Air India, one in January 1950 and the second in April 1951, thus increasing the fleet to six aircraft. A seventh L–749 was chartered from BOAC from July 1948 to April 1950. With the six L–749s, Qantas was able to maintain flight frequencies to London four times a week. In 1952 a trailblazing route was begun from Australia to Johannesburg with stops at the Cocos Islands and Mauritius. Spanning the Indian Ocean, this was truly a flight over desolate seas and, due to the lack of equipment, was operated only once every three weeks.

Airlinte Eireann, the Irish carrier, received five L–749s in August, September, and October 1947. These aircraft had been ordered to initiate an Ireland–United

States service in 1948, but a change in government policy did away with the plan. For a short time, the L–749s were used on a Dublin–London route for which they were not really suited. In the summer of 1948, all five were sold to BOAC for more than the Irish had paid for them less than a year before.

LAV, the Venezuelan carrier, received two L–749s in September and October 1947. These planes were added to the two L–049s already on the Caracas–New York route with a stop in Havana. The service was operated thrice weekly.

The next airline to receive the L–749 was Air India, another new customer. It accepted delivery of one aircraft in January 1948 and two more in February. With these aircraft, service was started in June 1948 to London with stops in Cairo and Geneva. This was a once-a-week service originating in Bombay, but later more weekly flights were added with stops at Delhi and Calcutta also on the schedule. The L–749s were not to last very long at Air India. As previously mentioned, two were sold to Qantas in December 1949 and April 1951. The third crashed on the slopes of Mount Blanc, France, in November 1950. Nevertheless, these three aircraft did much to make Air India a true international operation.

TWA had placed a large order for 12 L–749's with delivery beginning in the summer of 1948. For more information see Chapter 13.

The last airline to order the L–749 was, strangely enough, the same airline that began the acquisition of this model—EAL. They ordered seven L–749s in mid-1948, received two in February 1949, and the rest in September through December of the same year. Again, these were spread over their longer routes, much in the same way as the L–649s had been. EAL, incidentally, was the only airline to order both L–649s and L–749s and is believed to have received the second or third variant of this type as well as the last.

The role of the L–749 in service with BOAC should also be mentioned here because even though these were secondhand aircraft, they were acquired by BOAC in the same general period as the L–749 was being introduced by other carriers. The purchase of these aircraft by the British constitutes a story all by itself, and the purchase was not decided on until a great deal of political infighting had taken place. At any rate, in summer 1948 when BOAC received the five aircraft from Airlinte Eireann, they were badly in need of that kind of airplane with which to compete successfully with the United States and other flag carriers.

The total of L–649/L–749 production orders was 74, a respectable number for those days considering the cost of the airplane. However, the total production run was less than Lockheed had hoped for, and there were two good reasons for this. First, TWA and EAL were the only U.S. customers. Douglas, with its competitive DC–6, had snared the remaining major U.S. carriers. The foreign carriers, as shown by the L–749 orders, obviously liked the airplane, but they were hampered by their lack of capital and the fact that the economy of all nations was still slowly recovering from World War II. This meant that there was not a truly strong demand for international flights at this time. Tourism would have to wait a bit longer before it began to mushroom.

PHASE III, MODEL 649A/749A, NOVEMBER 1948 TO SEPTEMBER 1951

This next phase was, in a sense, a continuation of Phase II.

In November 1948, Lockheed revealed the existence of their improved Constellation known as the L–649A/L–749A model. This was basically a L–649/L–749 modified to increase the take-off and landing weights. Although the growth was approximately 5,000 pounds or 2.5 tons, its operating and payload characteristics had not actually changed all that much. Operators now had a little more flexibility and, if they wished, greater range instead of more payload.

Basically, the aircraft reflected one more evolutionary step forward, and a relatively small one at that. The design actually had been already put into production at the time it was publicized for Lockheed was already delivering 10 of the L–749As to the Air Force beginning in November 1948, identified as C–121As.

The new design was attractive to many carriers who appreciated the increased payload. Thus it wasn't long before orders for the aircraft began to come in. The commercial sales totals of both the L–649/L–749 and the L–649A/L–749A rather accurately reflected the state of the airline business during the period 1947–50. Domestic U.S. passenger-miles during those four years rose very slowly with the same being true of international passenger-miles flown by U.S. carriers. The same general trend was true of worldwide traffic. This naturally was then reflected in the hesitation shown by the world's major airlines in ordering new and expensive equipment.

Lockheed had managed to sell a total of 74 L–649/L–749 aircraft in about 2.5 years. In the following two years they sold only 58 model L–649A/L–749As. Actually, these were reasonably meaningful quantities for that time, but it is a fact that the Douglas DC–6 and the Boeing Stratocruiser were cutting deeply into the total market.

The first four customers of the L–749A were all repeat orders. For Air France, KLM, and TWA, it meant they had all ordered the first three models of the Constellation. KLM's order enabled them to step up their New York–Amsterdam service to eight flights per week. Air France used some of the aircraft to increase their Paris–Cairo service to six per week. They also put on two luxury New York–Paris flights that operated nonstop eastbound only.

Air India increased their Bombay–London service, also. TWA, with its very large order for 25, quickly placed them in service replacing the aging and by now unpopular Douglas DC–4s. South African Airways, a new customer, used their L–749A's range on the very long Johannesburg–London route.

A U.S. company, Chicago & Southern (C&S), was the only one to place an order for six of the L–649A models. The L–649A had a 98,000-pound take-off weight, thus making it lighter than either the L–749 or L–749A. Basically, it was an intermediate range aircraft, like the earlier L–649, but with the wings reinforced to permit a heavier take-off weight by some 4,000 pounds, thus giving an operator greater flexibility in choosing the optimum range/payload combination. These six aircraft were put in service starting in June 1951 on routes from Chicago, Houston, and New Orleans to Cuba, Venezuela, and Jamaica. In 1953, a new route was begun from New Orleans to Puerto Rico.

The last regular customer was Avianca, the Colombian-flag carrier. Their two aircraft were used to fly a route from Bogotá to Lisbon, Madrid, and on to Paris.

There was one more L–749A sold, this one to none other than Howard Hughes himself in June 1951. This aircraft was supposed to have been turned over to TWA but never was. For over three years the plane was practically never flown. Finally, in September 1954, Hughes sold it to BOAC.

Delivery of the last of Air France's L–749As in September 1951 marked the end of production of the standard Constellation. In a period stretching from January 1943 to September 1951, or some 8.5 years, Lockheed had rolled out a total of 232 Constellations, of which the great majority were for commercial use. The rate of production was relatively slow until the last few years. But as we have seen, a number of circumstances conspired to greatly reduce the total number of Constellations that were sold.

A quick look at some sales statistics on these 232 aircraft reveal some interesting facts. Of this total, 198 were sold directly to commercial customers, the rest to the military. Of this number, 80 percent or 158 were bought by only five air carriers, three U.S. firms and two European. The breakdown is:

- TWA: 62 aircraft
- Pan Am: 26 aircraft
- KLM: 26 aircraft
- Air France: 23 aircraft
- EAL: 21 aircraft

Aside from the fact that relatively few customers bought this many Constellations, the real surprise is that both KLM and Air France managed to buy so many expensive airplanes so soon after the end of World War II. It obviously speaks well for the recuperative powers of these two companies.

It is also significant that only three U.S. air carriers bought relatively large quantities of what was the best aircraft available, at least immediately after World War II. There seems to be little doubt that one overwhelming reason was that air carriers were not willing to accept lengthy delays in obtaining delivery. Another reason may well have been a sense of remaining faithful to manufacturers from whom they had frequently bought aircraft in the past.

As the Constellation production line was phased out, new models were waiting in the wings, ready to come to center stage. Lockheed was about to discover that the basic Constellation design was far from dead and buried. Rather, new and exciting things were about to happen.

PHASE IV, MODEL 1049, NOVEMBER 1951 TO SEPTEMBER 1952

In late 1951, Lockheed began making deliveries of what was in many ways a brand new airplane, namely, the Super Constellation. This was, of course, the first of the line and was identified as the L–1049. The reader should be careful not to confuse this model with the L–1049A, which was a military design and very different (see Chapter 8).

But as explained in Chapter 7, the L–1049 was actually an interim airplane, possessing characteristics of both the previous Constellation design as well as the forthcoming Super Constellation version. Whether for this reason or possibly because the picture concerning future passenger loads was still very murky, the L–1049 was by far the least successful of any of the various Constellation/Super Constellation models. Only 24 were sold, 14 to EAL and 10 to TWA, the two old stand-bys. There was even some question as to whether Hughes authorized the expenditure for the TWA order in part simply to help out his old friend Bob Gross at a time when sales for Lockheed were looking particularly grim.

The entire lot of 24 airplanes was delivered between November 1951 and September 1952 with EAL's order taking up the first six months and TWA's the last five. It is interesting to note that two months after the last L–1049 was delivered, Lockheed began making L–1049B/R7V–1 deliveries to the Navy. Thus, these two orders would appear to have indeed been important to Lockheed in spite of the loss suffered on this model because it permitted the production line to be kept open and prevented the laying off of many skilled workers by bridging the gap between the last of the Constellations and the first of the true Super Constellations.

EAL's use of the L–1049 was similar to what we have seen in their previous orders. EAL did not have any truly long routes. Thus, the big potential that the L–1049 held for EAL was its ability to carry more passengers at a lower seat-mile cost. Accordingly, EAL quickly placed these on the more heavily frequented routes, such as New York–Miami, Detroit–Cleveland–Miami, and Houston–Miami.

TWA, on the other hand, liked the availability of added range and lost no time using their big new birds on coast-to-coast service (see Chapter 13).

PHASE V, MODEL 1049C/D/E, JUNE 1953 TO MARCH 1955

The 1049C can be termed the first true commercial version of the Super Constellation. Powered by the new 3,250-hp Turbo Compound engines developed by Curtiss-Wright primarily for the military, the L–1049C afforded operators new dimensions in range, payload, and speed. These new operating characteristics were clearly reflected in the way the aircraft was used.

The L–1049C had a take-off weight of 133,000 pounds, an increase of more than 2 tons over the original Super Constellations, the L–1049, and some 6 tons over the L–749A model. Cruising speeds were not much different from the L–749/L–749A models, but payload and range were increased by a considerable amount. For with the L–1049C, an air carrier could, for the first time, count on crossing the North Atlantic eastbound nonstop virtually all year without sacrificing too much payload. Westbound, one stop would suffice, depending on the payload.

The larger and more productive L–1049s came on the scene at a most opportune time from the airlines' point of view. During the years after World War II, air traffic generally grew at a very slow rate once the immediate needs had been met. In the United States, the years 1948, 1949, and 1950 each showed revenue passenger-mile increases of less than 7 percent per year on average. Worldwide the increases were on the order of 14 percent per year. This higher figure can be explained in part by the fact that postwar increases in many areas came later than in the United States.

But 1951 and 1952 showed a sudden surge in boardings and passenger-miles. Thus, many carriers were only too glad to avail themselves of the new, larger aircraft. By the time the L–1049C and E models began coming off the assembly lines, some airlines had 100 percent load factors on long flights and badly needed the extra capacity afforded by the Super Constellation.

Of the total of 49 L–1049Cs delivered, 35 were purchased by three airlines. KLM, the first to take delivery, ordered 9, Air France ordered 10, and EAL 16. The remaining 14 aircraft were split among four airlines.

KLM's big new birds were all delivered between June and October 1953. With these, the carrier elected to place them on a variety of routes throughout its far-flung network. Some of the New York–Amsterdam services were with the new L–1049C. But they were also used on the twice-weekly Amsterdam–Johannesburg service, on the Curacao–Amsterdam route via the Azores, and to Jakarta by way of India and Thailand. In all of these markets, except to South Africa, the L–1049Cs were used together with the older Constellations, as well as some Douglas DC–6Bs.

An interesting application of the L–1049C by KLM was their use of the aircraft across the North Atlantic in a first-class configuration only, with other trips handling tourist class. In this specialized service, the aircraft had luxury seats, lounges, and some sleeping type seats.

Air France began receiving its fleet of L–1049Cs simultaneously with KLM, and delivery was completed by November 1953. Air France decided to protect the great majority of their North Atlantic flights with these new aircraft, with some flights actually originating in Mexico City then operating through New York and on to Paris. Many of the eastbound L–1049Cs operated nonstop New York–Paris. Air France also used the same approach as KLM and set up most of its transatlantic flights in a single class configuration. The L–1049Cs were also used on a once-weekly trip, Paris–Caracas–Bogota, via the Azores, and a twice-weekly trip, Paris–Buenos Aires, via Dakar with stops at Madrid, Sao Paolo, and Montevideo.

EAL was able to arrange for a very concentrated delivery period, with all 16 L–1049Cs being delivered in four months, November 1953 through February 1954. The aircraft were different than all other C models in that they lacked a center fuel tank and consequently had a take-off weight of only 128,800 pounds.

This difference made them somewhat more economical to operate and gave them slightly better performance. These aircraft were interspersed all over the Eastern system, taking over flights where loads were especially heavy. This occurred mostly on service to and from Miami. EAL, unlike many airlines, had an enormously complicated route structure and flight schedule, despite the fact that its system was mostly concentrated in the eastern third of the United States. But, for this reason, no single aircraft type ever was used on only a few routes, especially during this period. Furthermore, EAL had a fleet made up of many aircraft types, something that in time came to plague them financially.

Once the last of EAL's Super Cs had been delivered, Lockheed proceeded to begin delivery of the remaining 14 in the period February to June 1954. These were delivered simultaneously among four airlines during the five-month period.

Of the four, Qantas introduced their L–1049Cs first, in May 1954, on the very long overwater route from Australia to Honolulu, San Francisco, and Vancouver.

Later, L–1049Cs were put on other Qantas routes. In June 1954, Air India put their L–1049Cs on the India–United Kingdom route. The same month, the neighboring country of Pakistan began using L–1049Cs to connect east and west Pakistan. They followed this up by then also using their C models to London. Finally, in September 1954, Trans-Canada (TCA) began Toronto–Vancouver service with the L–1049C.

During the last two months of L–1049C production, Lockheed was concurrently rolling out their L–1049E model. The E model differed from the C model in that it had fuselage and wing reinforcing for 150,000-pound take-off weight in anticipation of later conversion to turboprop engines. However, the majority of E models had the same 133,000-pound take-off weight as the C models. The six E models delivered to Qantas differed from the others in that they had strengthened the main landing gear, which allowed the take-off weight to be increased to 135,400 pounds. The E model, although having certain specific improvements over the C model, was a further growth version that did not really possess much of an identity of its own. It was, in a sense, a design link between the C model and the upcoming G model. With only 25 sold, the E model could have been a financial disaster for Lockheed except that its sales must really be combined with those of the C model. Together they represented a total of 74 aircraft and thus provided some small margin of profit for Lockheed.

The E model was purchased by four airlines who had also received C models, these being KLM, TCA, Qantas, and Air India. The other three customers were Iberia, Avianca, and LAV. Of these, Iberia was a new Constellation operator.

Once again their utilization followed the pattern previously established. The E models were used almost exclusively on long, overwater flights, and mostly in the North Atlantic market, where the Constellation reputation helped attract coveted U.S. tourists and businessmen.

One trend that was becoming increasingly apparent was that of relatively small countries acquiring first Constellations and then Super Constellations to be used as overseas flagships of their respective national airlines. No doubt the performance and economics of these aircraft were appealing. But beyond that, there appears to have been a feeling on the part of many small nations that the Connie would represent their national interests in the air well and be an aircraft to be proud of.

In discussing this model series of the Super Constellation, the L–1049D was deliberately left until last. Only four D model aircraft were sold, these to the big cargo carrier Seaboard and Western. The D model was strictly a cargo aircraft and actually was very similar to the L–1049B/R7V–1/C–121C aircraft produced for the military. It was produced concurrently with the E model. It differed from the L–1049B mainly in that it had some of the same improvements as the L–1049C and E models. Thus, its empty and take-off weights had been increased, and it had been structurally reinforced to accept turboprop engines and an eventual take-off weight of 150,000 pounds.

Lockheed had been very optimistic about the sales potential of its L–1049D, but the slow growth of the air cargo market spelled the end of this particular model. As we shall see, a later cargo design proved to be somewhat more successful.

PHASE VI, MODEL 1049G/H, JANUARY 1955 TO SEPTEMBER 1959

This phase was the most successful one from the point of view of Lockheed with more aircraft being sold than in any other phase. Because the company was simultaneously producing a large number of Super Constellations for the military, their assembly line was busy indeed. Phase VI was also the most unique in some ways. It was the longest of any of the seven phases. The aircraft models involved were sold to more airlines than at any time before.

During this period, the Constellation family may be said to have become a symbol of commercial aviation easily recognized the world over.

The basic explanation for the success of the G/H models is quite simple. It was the old formula of a good design appearing at a time when the need was great. The airlines of the world were, in the mid-1950s, becoming very aware of the rapidly increasing passenger traffic, especially tourists. What with the new economy fares spreading quickly, most companies felt that not only were there more passengers, but the potential for the next few years was for additional substantial increases. Thus the stage was set for a Super Constellation model that would not only carry sizeable numbers of passengers but also have the range to permit full loads to be carried over long stage lengths regardless of ambient temperatures at take-off. The G model for the first time gave the airlines that kind of performance. The airlines responded by ordering in quantity.

In discussing this particular phase, it should be noted that Lockheed had plenty of competition from other airframe manufacturers. Douglas was busy selling their highly competitive DC–7 series airplanes. In fact, some of the customers for the L–1049G models also bought DC–7s. In addition, the first long-range turboprop aircraft began to come into service. This was the Bristol Brittania, which entered airline service in 1956. This was indeed real competition. So the Super Constellation had to win its spurs anew all the time.

The new G models began to come off the assembly line at Burbank in January 1955. Those that were equipped with the tip tanks were undoubtedly the most distinctive passenger aircraft seen in the sky then and for many years to come. The first airline to receive the new birds was a brand new customer, Northwest Airlines. They only bought four of the aircraft, put them on their long U.S.–Japan route, and then, after only some four years of service, withdrew them from service due to a program of equipment standardization.

The second customer was also the one who bought the largest number. TWA took delivery of 28 of the G model (see Chapter 13).

Lufthansa received four aircraft in 1955, and ordered four more for 1956 delivery. This fleet enabled the airline to begin their first postwar international service outside of Europe.

Varig, the growing Brazilian carrier, received their six aircraft over a period of some two and a half years, indicating that they actually ordered two lots of three. These went into service on a number of long routes, including New York–Buenos Aires, with six intermediate stops.

Air France, a perennial customer, received a total of 14, which were used on many of their long routes, but mainly to the Far East and over the North Atlantic. With this addition to its fleet, Air France was in a position to strongly challenge the other large carriers on the North Atlantic runs.

KLM received only six of the G model, but this could be misleading because they had already received both C and E model aircraft.

Qantas also improved their competitive position by adding four Super Gs. Their route structure was almost totally unique with routes to Great Britain, the West Coast of the United States, and South Africa. Together with their previously acquired Super Constellations, these additions permitted substantial schedule increases.

Two U.S. air carriers other than TWA ordered large quantities of Super G and H Constellations. Eastern picked up 10 Super Gs, which were used throughout their system. This step was a virtual duplication of what they had done with earlier Constellation models.

The second airline was Flying Tiger, which specialized in air cargo and military charters. They obtained a total of 14 Super H aircraft, and with these were able, over a period of years, to greatly expand their total volume of cargo business.

Speaking of the Super H model, readers should realize that it is somewhat difficult to distinguish between the Super G and Super H models. Both models were originally introduced with the same gross weight. The H was basically the cargo version of the G model and, accordingly, had a large cargo door fitted on the port rear section of the fuselage. The H model also had strengthened floor members and thus a slightly heavier zero fuel weight. Later versions of the H model had an increased gross weight of up to 142,000 pounds. A number of the air carriers that ordered the G model also ordered the H. Among these were Qantas, KLM, TCA, and TWA.

The Super G and H models were in first-line use from their introduction in the mid-1950s until the early 1960s. During this period they amassed a formidable total of passenger-miles and ton-miles flown all over the globe. In this they were assisted, of course, by the earlier versions of Constellations and Super Constellations.

11-1 Aerlinte Eireann, the Irish flag carrier, L–749 Constellations lined up, 1948. (Lockheed Martin)

11-2 An Air France L–049 Connie, 1946. (Lockheed Martin)

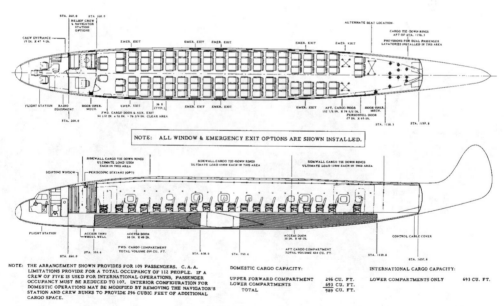

11-3 A high-density all-coach configuration for an L–1049D Super Constellation. Note how many of the seat rows do not have windows. (Lockheed Martin)

11-4 A KLM L–1049C Super Constellation. KLM was one of the earliest airlines in the world to pioneer long routes from Europe to the Middle East and beyond. (Lockheed Martin)

11-5 An Air India L1049C Super Constellation. When Air India moved to other aircraft types, particularly jets, some of these Super Connies went to the Indian Air Force. (Lockheed Martin)

11-6 A National Airlines Super G ready to begin its take-off roll. (Lockheed Martin)

11-7 A dramatic shot of a Super Connie during a night engine run-up. (Lockheed Martin)

11-8 A Northwest Airlines Super G rotating for take-off, with the main landing gear just coming un-stuck. (Lockheed Martin)

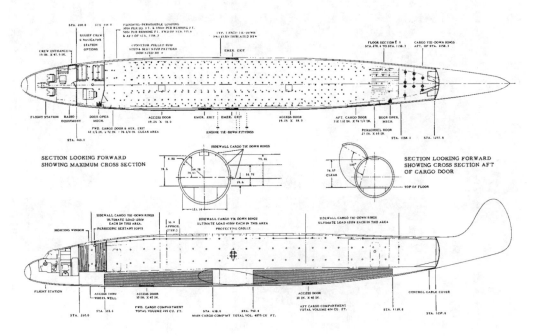

11-9 Typical internal configuration of a cargo Super Constellation. (Lockheed Martin)

11-10 A Real Airlines L–1049H cargo Super Constellation, also convertible to carry passengers. (Lockheed Martin)

11-11 "Utility Systems" (Lockheed Martin)

Chapter 12

THE LAST AND THE GREATEST: THE L–1649A

The last of the entire family of Constellations and Super Constellations was the result of compromise, problems, determination, and shifting priorities and goals. Known as the L–1649A, it was both a success and a disappointment, especially in the financial sense. But for all that, the L–1649A was probably the one aircraft that many feel to this day best epitomized the very peak of large reciprocating, propeller-driven, commercial aircraft. This despite the fact that both larger or faster aircrafts were developed during that period.

While Lockheed had been developing the Super Constellation through the C and E models, it had also been considering a more advanced version. This rather nebulous version had two major goals. One was to successfully compete with the more advanced transports the competition might unveil. The other was a long-standing desire on the part of the transatlantic air carriers to operate an aircraft capable of flying nonstop New York–London in either direction year-round with a full payload. Aircraft such as the Super G Constellation and the Douglas DC–7C could usually operate nonstop eastbound but often not westbound against the prevailing headwinds. And by the early 1950's, with transatlantic passenger totals rising rapidly, the airlines felt that nonstop service would be not only a selling point for passengers but also a feature that would reduce costs in their operations.

From September 1951 to September 1953 little was heard about any such matter as an advanced transport, although it was generally known that Lockheed was building the four prototypes of the Model 1249, the turboprop-powered transport, for the military. Then, in September 1953, Lockheed revealed that it had developed a system to convert L–1049 aircraft coming off the assembly line to turboprop power. Lockheed envisioned using the P&W PT2F–1 power plant rated at 5,600 eshp. With this level of power it was felt that the new English Bristol Brittania turboprop transport could be matched.

In June 1954, Douglas threw down the gauntlet by announcing that it had begun design of its DC–7C, an enlarged version of the DC–7B, which would be capable of crossing the North Atlantic nonstop both ways. This was followed the next month by an order from Pan Am for 25 of the big transports. It became obvious over in Burbank that some fast decisions would have to be made if Lockheed was to remain competitive.

In September 1954 the first turboprop Model 1249 flew, this one a Navy R7V–2. With real hardware now boring holes in the sky, various airlines began showing some interest in the possibility of either converting their Turbo-Compound L–1049s or obtaining new Super Constellations with turboprop engines.

Lockheed's direct response to the DC–7C came in October 1954 when it was announced that the L–1649A concept was now being studied. This was followed in December by the formal offering of a new L–1449 concept to the airlines, with delivery promised by January 1957, and a passenger prototype to be in the air by August 1956.

The Model 1449 (the 1349 was skipped, probably for reasons of superstition) featured a new thin wing; a 4 foot, 7 inch fuselage extension; a gross take-off weight of 177,000 pounds; a 420 mph cruise speed; and a new main landing gear to carry the whole thing. The wing was somewhat similar to the well-known Davis airfoil. Not content with this step forward, the designers followed up with a L–1549 model, which was basically identical to the L–1449 but had a 19 foot, 9 inch fuselage extension and a gross weight of 187,500 pounds. During this same period, Lockheed also began looking at a L–1649 design, which would have a standard Super Constellation fuselage, the new thin wing, and P&W turboprops.

The L–1449 would have been powered by the P&W PT–1, although it could also have used the P&W T52, the Bristol B.E. 25, or the Allison T56. The latter had been considered by Lockheed, but was rejected on the grounds that it would only be available a full year after the PT–1.

Armed with these rather imposing designs, Lockheed's sales team began to make the rounds of the airlines. At least one major airline looked at these designs seriously, that being, not surprisingly, TWA. It was reported that Howard Hughes was having difficulty choosing between the L–1449 and the new Boeing 707 turbojet, whose delivery dates were somewhat in question. At this time, too, Lockheed pointed out that its L–1449 could beat the DeHavilland Comet II across the Atlantic because the Comet needed to refuel once in each direction and the L–1449 did not.

But a few months later in April 1955, the entire question of turboprop-powered transports became academic when Lockheed abruptly terminated the entire L–1449/L–1549 project. The reason was that Pratt & Whitney had suddenly withdrawn their PT–1 power plant from further consideration, saying that they felt that Lockheed's aircraft performance forecasts indicated that more power was going to be pulled from their engines at cruise power settings than P&W felt was reasonably justified. Lockheed indicated no other equivalent power plant was available in sufficient time, and the entire project was scrapped. Months later, in January 1965, TWA revealed that the P&W TP–2 was highly inefficient and suffered from too high a specific fuel consumption.

There is an interesting TWA sidelight to all this. At this time Lockheed was actively working on both the famed Air Force C–130 Hercules assault transport and the L–188 Electra medium-range transport, with both aircraft using the Allison YT–56/501D–13 turboprop engine rated at 3,750 eshp. This engine, of course, had a considerably lower power rating than the P&W power plants previously mentioned. But if we may, let us speculate for a moment.

Suppose a combination had been created of a Super Constellation with a gross weight of some 145,000 pounds mated with Allison turbo-prop engines of around 4,000 eshp? In actual fact, something close to that was tried. One of the Navy R7V–2s was reacquired by Lockheed and fitted with four Allison 501D–13 T/P engines. It flew for a year in 1957–58 as a test bed for the Electra project but admittedly did not really prove whether such an aircraft would or could have been commercially successful. But it is just possible that such an aircraft might have competed quite well.

Another possibility might have been to use the engines of the Bristol Brittania, which at 175,000 pounds gross weight was in the same weight class as the L–1449 model. As a matter of fact, the original model of the Brittania to enter revenue service had a take-off weight of 155,000 pounds, virtually identical to the weight that the L–1649A would have, and was powered by four Proteus turboprop engines of 3,780 eshp. This airplane was flying in mid-1956, a whole year before the L–1649A. At any rate, Lockheed opted to drop the project, and it was openly speculated at the time that this might have been due in large part to some concern on the part of Lockheed that the projected turboprop Super Constellation might have been in direct competition with the new Electra. This author does not believe this would have been the case if the Super Constellation finally developed with turboprops had been that originally envisaged—namely, a very long-range aircraft capable of carrying over 100 passengers. Such an aircraft, if it had been available by 1955–56, would very possibly have sold in sizable quantities and could even have delayed the large-scale entry of the Boeing 707 in passenger service by at least two to three years.

When the Pratt & Whitney turboprop power plants were withdrawn from the market in April 1955 (possibly just before Lockheed made public the fact that it considered them inefficient), Lockheed was left with three paper airplanes that could not go anywhere due to lack of power plants. It was just about this time that Pan Am announced a nonstop luxury service using its Boeing B–377 Stratocruiser Clippers between New York and London/Paris. This was achieved through the combination of 300-mile range extension and a smaller payload.

Readers should also keep in mind that the basic Super Constellation design, starting with the L–1049C model, evolved in fairly small increments through the L–1049H model. The performance figures did not change appreciably, and the basic design was reaching its limits, much the same way the L–749A was the end of the line of the basic Constellation series.

In March 1955 Lockheed began actual design work on the L–1649A. The decision to begin the design of this aircraft was no doubt influenced by the fact that Lockheed's engineers were becoming increasingly disenchanted and frustrated with the P&W PT–1 turboprop. Thus the L–1649A design began just before cancellation of the L–1449 project. Simultaneously, Lockheed was also able to announce that TWA had ordered 24 of the new L–1649As for $70 million. A month later, Pan Am increased their order for Douglas DC–7Cs to 40 aircraft.

At this point, the designers and engineers put together a number of existing elements which would best form a new design. These elements were:

1. A substantial gross weight increase using the same basic fuselage. This particular concept had already been proven on the L–1049A/VW–2/RC–121D aircraft, which had a maximum overload take-off weight of 152,000 pounds.
2. A completely redesigned 150-foot-span wing with changed profile and camber to reduce drag. The new wing had a thickness of 15 percent at the root and 11percent at the tip versus 18 percent and 12 percent, respectively, for the wing used on all the previous Constellations. It also had an increased aspect ratio of 12 as compared with 9.17 on the previous wing. This design was basically a version of the Davis airfoil.

3. Four Curtiss-Wright R–3350, 3,400-hp engines mounted 10 feet further out on the wing to greatly reduce cabin noise. With the engines this far out, the clearance between propeller tip and fuselage becomes 62 inches versus 13.8 inches or 14.8 inches on the Super G.
4. Larger-diameter propellers, these being 16 feet, 10 inches versus 15 feet, 2 inches on the Super G. These propellers had a tip speed some 5 percent slower than the smaller propellers.
5. Electronic synchrophasing of the four propellers to reduce both cabin noise and vibration.
6. A maximum fuel load of 9,600 gallons thanks to the increased capacity provided by the new wing design. This quantity was 1,850 gallons more than the Super G with tip tanks, and a staggering 3,100 gallons more than Super Constellations without tip tanks.
7. Maximum gross take-off weight of 156,000 pounds if equipped with hollow-blade propellers, 160,000 pounds with solid-blade propellers. Maximum landing weight was increased to 123,000 pounds (more than the take-off weight of the original L–1049) and payload up to 24,355 pounds.
8. A maximum long-range cruise speed of 205 knots IAS and a maximum range of over 6,000 miles with reserves.

This, then, was the L–1649A, an airplane generally acknowledged to be the very finest long-range reciprocating commercial transport ever produced. It was certainly a formidable airplane, as its service life clearly demonstrated. Unfortunately, its design and performance were not matched by its market success, and the plane lost a considerable amount of money for Lockheed.

DESIGN FEATURES

The wing, with no sweep-back and a 150-foot span, was by far the most dramatic feature of the airplane. Its design was quite different in two important characteristics: unlimited fatigue life and failsafe properties. To create such a strong and durable wing, a great deal of attention was paid in designing the wing detail to minimize stress concentration. The wing had more integral stiffening than any other commercial design up to that time. The only comparable wing was the Lockheed C–130 Hercules, which proved to be unbelievably durable over many years of extremely demanding service.

The wing had 1,850 square feet of surface, which was a full 200 square feet more than the wing used on all the previous models. This increase in wing area meant that the wing could carry an impressive 9,600 gallons of fuel. The wing was a wet wing, and thus virtually the entire structure could be used as a fuel tank. The standard wing previously used, minus wingtip tanks, carried only 6,500 gallons. This increased fuel load was one of the secrets behind the L–1649A's phenomenal range. In fact, this was probably the largest fuel load carried routinely by any aircraft up to that time and was exceeded only by the coming of the Boeing and Douglas turbojets with their fuel-guzzling engines.

The new wing span permitted the design engineers to move the engines further outboard reducing the noise level in the cabin. The inboard engines were each 5 feet, 5 inches further away from the fuselage. The inboard propeller tips had their clearance from the fuselage increased from 13.8 inches to 62.6 inches, or over 4 feet more, which again reduced the cabin noise level considerably.

The propeller diameter had been increased by 1 foot, 8 inches, and this allowed propeller tip speeds at cruise settings to be some 5 percent lower, again reducing vibration and noise.

The engines were Curtiss-Wright 988TCEA2 Turbo-Compounds developing 3,400 hp maximum at sea level. This was 150 hp more than the power plants of the 1049G. The H model had the 3,400-hp engine. A few G models had been retrofitted with Turbo-Compounds of both 3,400 and 3,440 hp. The additional 600-hp total per aircraft was important in light of the large incremental increase in the aircraft weight.

Kelly Johnson, working together with the Hamilton Standard Propeller Division of United Aircraft and the Curtiss Propeller Division of Curtiss-Wright, had one more trick up his sleeve. Together they developed an electro-hydraulic synchrophasing system that resulted in all four propellers turning in perfect unison. This alone resulted in a cabin noise reduction of some 25 percent!

The gross weight increase was the single largest incremental increase in the history of the Constellation. The L–1049A had grossed 137,500 pounds, whereas the L–1649A grossed 156,00 pounds, an increase of 18,500 pounds or 9.25 tons!

This weight increase combined with the new wing design having the engines spaced farther out necessitated a change in the main landing gear. The main gear trucks were moved outboard some 5 feet each. The landing gear support ribs, which were part of the wing structure, were one-piece forgings made on 35,000- and 50,000-ton presses.

The flap design was also new, with two long span sections on each wing. Still another change was the hydraulic system, where the pressure was increased to 3,000 PSI from the 1,700 PSI used on the L–1049G. By going to this high-pressure system, Lockheed was able to save weight and space on many of the hydraulic components.

This writer can personally attest to how quiet the L–1649A was when flying overhead. After Air France began flying its new L–1649A, a daily flight would depart Chicago Midway airport for Montreal and Paris. This author lived some 8–9 miles due east of the airport at the time. In summer 1958, if outdoors, the Air France flight could be seen climbing out overhead. At that point it could not be at more than 3,000–4,000 feet altitude at most. The aircraft, always easily identified by its huge wing, would slide by quietly, and it was always a surprise how much less noise there was than any other type of large aircraft climbing out.

INTERIOR DESIGN

The interior of the L–1649A was, of necessity, quite similar to the G/H models, because the basic fuselage was identical. But there were also some important differences. The cabin walls were lined with an additional 900 pounds of sound-proofing material. Combined with the other noise-reducing changes instituted in the wing, the result was an amazingly quiet interior. Even when sitting in seats opposite the engines, normal voice levels could be used during take-off. At cruising speeds, one could eavesdrop on conversations quite a distance down the cabin. In fact, except for the turbojets, no plane built since is as quiet inside.

A variety of seating arrangements were available. TWA, which had by far the largest L–1649A fleet, carried 75 passengers in an all-economy configuration. With a mixed first-class economy configuration, 63 could be carried. A new seat, called the Siesta, provided a large degree of comfort when sleeping. Lockheed foresaw the need for more comfortable seating created by the longer nonstop flying times of the L–1649A.

PERFORMANCE

The performance of the 1649A was distinctly better than the 1049H, which had the same power but 18,500 pounds less weight. This was achieved through the careful design of that long, thin wing. The table below gives some idea of how the L–1649A stacked up against the L–1049H as well as the L–1649A's only real competitor, the Douglas DC–7C.

	1049H	1649A (w/ tip tanks)	DC–7C
Max Gross Take-off Weight *(pounds)*	137,500	156,000	139,000
Cruising TAS @ 22,600 feet	282K	297K	—
Max Range @ 10,000 feet *(nautical miles)*	4,750	6,100	4,800
Fuel Capacity (gallons)	6,550	9,600	7,860

DESIGN PERFORMANCE

The performance of the L–1649A differed from that of the L–1049G/H in two important areas: time to altitude and cruise power available.

A L–1049H with 3,400-hp engines at a maximum gross take-off weight of 140,000 pounds on a standard day (57° F), required 56 minutes and 826 gallons of fuel to reach 20,000 feet. A L–1649A at the same weight on a standard day required only 51 minutes and 753 gallons, some 73 gallons less. The L–1049H operated at a long-range cruise speed of 190 KIAS, whereas the L–1649A operated at 205 KIAS, the latter at any weight. At maximum long-range cruise power settings, the L–1649A was still some 15 knots slower than its archrival, the DC–7C. But no other aircraft of its era had the capability to complete long nonstop flights at or close to on time in spite of severe headwinds. For example, a TWA L–1649A departed London for New York carrying a full load of 75 tourist passengers. The headwind on this flight averaged 46 knots, and the aircraft picked up heavy ice on departure, which remained for several hours. The flight landed in New York with 2 hours of fuel reserve left. Not even the DC–7C could boast that kind of performance.

Speaking of the DC–7C, it might be pertinent at this point to broadly compare the DC–6/7 series with the Constellation/Super Constellation airplanes. Competing models of both aircraft had essentially identical power plants and power ratings. However, the Douglas aircraft always had lower gross weights. In addition, the DC–6/7 wing permitted higher speeds, but as a trade-off, required higher take-off and landing speeds.

L-1649A ORDERS

The L–1649A had everything going for it except one thing—its timing. Because of the uncertainty surrounding the possible use of turboprop engines on the L–1249/1449 designs, the L–1649A design was initiated nine months after the DC–7C. The complexity of the all-new wing caused a further 3-month slip in the design schedule, so that the L–1649A was ready for customer delivery a full 12 months after the DC–7C. This was too much for a number of potential customers, who, facing an surge in tourist traffic, needed more aircraft quickly.

Added to this critical problem at the front end was the fact that most of the larger carriers had already or were about to place orders for the new turbojet transports. This was the big problem at the back end; together these two factors spelled the financial death of the L–1649A.

TWA was the first and largest customer with 25. Air France, that old Lockheed customer, ordered 10 aircraft. Lufthansa, a recent satisfied customer, ordered four.

Linee Aeree Italiane ordered four aircraft, but when the company was acquired by Alitalia, who had ordered DC–7Cs, the order was transferred to TWA, who thus had a fleet of 29.

The Brazilian carrier Varig ordered two L–1649As but later changed the order to three L–1049Gs, of which model it had already received three. KLM, another perennial Lockheed customer, considered purchasing L–1649As but decided instead to go with the DC–7C.

TWA, by far the largest L–1649A customer, received 10 airplanes in May 1957, 6 in June, 5 in July, and 2 each in August and September. Air France had eight delivered between June and September 1957, and Lufthansa's four were delivered one each in September and December 1957 and the final two in January 1958. Air France received their final two in February and TWA the last four between March and June 1958. When one remembers that the first Boeing 707s began regular service in December 1958, it becomes obvious how the L–1649A program ran head-on into the jet age.

Thus the total sales for L–1649As came to only 43 airplanes. A 44th aircraft, the prototype that was used for testing and certification, never entered airline service. By way of comparison, Douglas managed to sell 128 DC–7Cs, or almost triple the number. For Lockheed, this meant a sizable financial loss on the L–1649A production run. It is ironic that the aircraft often said to be the finest reciprocating engine transport ever produced was beset by circumstances that drastically reduced its sales potential and cut its active service life short. But while it flew, the L–1649A racked up records never before achieved by comparable type aircraft, and in fact, even set some records that jet aircraft could not match for many years.

AIRLINE UTILIZATION

The airlines acquiring the L–1649A were naturally planning to use its tremendous range potential to the greatest degree possible. Accordingly, the L–1649A was introduced on those high-density routes where range was most important.

TWA initially used the L–1649A on nonstop service in both directions between New York and various European capitals, followed by a new polar route between the West Coast and London (see Chapter 13).

Air France operated their L–1649As between Paris and New York and later on a polar Paris–Tokyo route with a single stop in Anchorage, Alaska. Lufthansa used their aircraft nonstop Frankfurt to New York, their most important long route.

Throughout their relatively short career, the L–1649As demonstrated a high degree of reliability and on-time dependability, as well as a capability to greatly please their passengers. The combination of a quiet ride, comfortable seats, and quicker trips because of fewer fuel stops made the L-1649A the finest long-range passenger airplane in the world up to that time.

The airlines used a number of marketing techniques in introducing the L-1649A. TWA coined the name Jetstream, partly because at times the eastbound L-1649A flights could take advantage of the lower regions of the Northern Hemisphere's jet stream. Thus the public tended to relate the aircraft to jet power. Lufthansa called the aircraft Super Star, which was probably a take-off on Lockheed's own appellation, Starliner.

Air France called it Super Starliner, which distinguished it from Super Constellation. Air France also used a very interesting technique to introduce the aircraft to the French public. A L-1649A was flown some 2,500 miles at an altitude of 1,000 feet from one end of the French coastline to the other. Advertisements in papers of thousands of communities along the route were placed a few days before the flight. Exact times over each beach were shown, and the aircraft was flown in exact accordance with the published schedule. The flight began at Abbeville, near the Belgian border at 0956 hours and ended at Nice at 1905 hours. This flight was repeated a number of times and Air France claimed it was always precisely punctual. These flights took place in summer, so a great number of people must have witnessed the fly-bys. Actually Air France had already tried this advertising gimmick two years earlier in 1955, as a means of introducing the then-new Super G.

Readers may remember that the introduction to this book began with the departure of a TWA Jetstream L-1649A from Los Angeles bound for London. Now we are going to go back and pick up that flight and follow it all the way to London from the vantage point of the cockpit. In this manner we shall observe the flight crew carrying out their duties and thus better understand how such an aircraft operated. This particular flight is also interesting from the viewpoint that polar flights were comparatively new. Scandinavian Airways System had started them in November 1954. Later, airlines using the DC-7C increased the frequency of such operations. But it was only with the introduction of the L-1649A that nonstop flights from the West Coast to Europe via the polar cap became routine. With the DC-7Cs a fuel stop on the westbound leg was generally required.

TWA 770

The following flight is fictional, but is based on actual operations as shown in the L-1649A Operating Manual. The flight plan was developed using actual performance parameters.

It's a Tuesday in August 1958, and TWA is preparing to dispatch Flight 770, nonstop Ambassador service from Los Angeles to London. We are about to meet its flight crew and then look over their shoulders as they carry out their various duties.

Scheduled departure for TWA 770 is 10:15 A.M., and the crew reports in approximately an hour before the flight leaves. The captain today is Brian Edgerton, 41, an 18-year veteran with TWA who joined the company in 1940, and who during World War II, flew co-pilot with TWA's Intercontinental Division. The first officer is Casimir "Cas" Klawinski, 31, who's been with the company since 1953. Klawinski flew jet fighters in Korea before coming to the big transports. Tom O'Malley, 39, is flight engineer. Both he and Edgerton have flown on all of TWA's various Constellation models.

The fourth man on international overwater flights is a navigator. Today that's Frank Busch, 40, who's been pretty much all over the world. Before joining TWA in 1946, Busch had been a navigator with the ATC. In this capacity he flew to many distant corners of the world aboard ATC's Douglas C–54s.

These four would usually make up the total flight crew. But on these long polar flights, the normal crew complement is augmented by two more members. One is a relief pilot who is always rated as a captain, and the other is a second flight engineer. The relief captain today is William (Bill) Bailey, 36, who, due to lack of seniority, is currently flying in this capacity as relief. The second flight engineer is Jason (Jay) Lipschulz, 32, who will split the flight engineer's chores with O'Malley.

The airplane we'll fly on today is TWA's *Star of the Clyde*, registry number N7317C, the 19th L–1649A manufactured, which was delivered to TWA on June 30, 1957. So our aircraft is only some 13 months old.

When O'Malley and Lipschulz reach the airfield, they find out the aircraft assigned to the flight and go directly there. Together they check out the recent recorded history of the aircraft as shown in the log books and satisfy themselves that any outstanding deficiencies or complaints have been resolved. Their next job is to check that all warning lights are functioning, which is done by operating the various push-to-test buttons A check of the various inverters is performed at this time also.

Last, O'Malley checks out the set-up of the 260 panel. This is short-hand for what is formally known as the Station 260 Upper Switch Panel. The Station 260 refers to the position in the aircraft. Actually, the panel is located in the flight engineer's area, mounted on his right-hand side on the bulkhead that separates the flight deck from the cabin. The 260 panel has a number of controls, including heating and air conditioning and a large number of fuses, which affect various systems in the aircraft. O'Malley makes sure that the cabin is being properly cooled with the help of the external power cart, and checks out that all fuses are functional. Then the two flight engineers leave the airplane and go to the dispatch office to meet with the rest of the crew.

The Los Angeles dispatcher for TWA has already made out a tentative flight plan, which is closely examined by the three pilots. Finally, after taking the forecast en route weather into account, Edgerton signs the flight plan.

Today the flight will be following the Great Circle route from Los Angeles to London. On some days, the minimum time track is followed instead, which involves pressure pattern flying. This refers to a technique whereby a route is planned that follows the best winds rather than the shortest distance. It is also known as the shortest time routing, because the flying time can be substantially less than over a shorter route. But today the Great Circle Route seems to be the best bet. Edgerton expects to make it nonstop to London.

For TWA 770 to make this trip nonstop, two things must occur. The number of passengers having reservations must be less than the maximum that can be carried, and sufficient tailwinds must be present. If either of these two factors are not favorable, then the flight must make a refueling stop.

On this day, there are tailwinds that should reach a peak of 55 knots and a passenger load of only 63. Based on this, Edgerton, with the agreement of Bailey, elects to try for a nonstop flight. His flight plan shows a possible fuel stop in Iceland, if it appears that fuel at the final destination, London, is going to be too low.

The final data shows that Flight 770 will be taking off at its maximum weight at 156,000 pounds. This total is made up as follows:

- Operating weight, 91,645 pounds
- Oil (200 gallons), 1,504 pounds
- Fuel reserves (876 gallons), 4,000 pounds
- En route fuel (8,621 gallons), 50,000 pounds
- Passengers (63) and baggage, 9,450 pounds
- Take-off weight, 156,000 pounds

The complete flight plan looks as shown in Fig. 12-14, with a total projected flight time of 16 hours 22 minutes.

The crew receives a complete weather briefing, checks for any last minute Notices to Airmen, and completes the flight plan. With the paperwork complete, the crew trudges out to the Jetstream waiting patiently on the hot concrete apron.

After boarding and depositing their flight gear, Edgerton and O'Malley go back outside. Edgerton quickly but carefully completes a walk-around inspection of the big L–1649A while O'Malley satisfies himself that the fuel tanks are properly filled. Then it's back into the airplane once more.

The cabin crew greets the passengers now boarding and quickly see to it that they are seated and ready for take-off. A cabin attendant closes and seals the rear door, then reports to Edgerton that everything is ready for departure.

In the meantime, the six-man crew goes to their posts. Edgerton and Klawinski, who will fly the airplane initially, are at the controls. O'Malley is at the flight engineer console, and Bailey sits in the radio operator's seat for the take-off. In the crew rest compartment immediately behind, Busch and Lipschulz relax on standard settees.

The rest of the account of this flight is keyed to Greenwich Mean Time (GMT), also known as Zulu time among flight crews. It is the time used for all commercial flights the world over. By using this technique, the reader will better be able to relate various events to the passage of time.

1715Z

Edgerton calls for the Before Starting Engines checklist. Checklists are called out by the first officer and answered by the captain or flight engineer.

FIRST OFFICER	CAPTAIN
1. GEAR LEVER & LIGHTS	DOWN & CHECKED
2. PARKING BRAKE SWITCH	ON
3. AUXILIARY HYDRAULIC PUMP	CHECKED & ON
4. AUX & #1 BRAKE PRESSURE	2800 PSI MINIMUM
5. LANDING LIGHTS	CHECKED & OFF
6. IGNITION	OFF
7. RADIOS	ON & CHECKED
8. NAVIGATION LIGHTS	CHECKED
9. WING DE-ICERS	OFF
10. DE-ICER PUMP SEALS	VACUMN
11. PITOT & MAST HEATERS	CHECKED
12. PITOT PRESS. SELECTOR	ALL ON
13. ALTIMETERS & CLOCKS	CHECKED
14. RMI HEADING SELECTORS	NORMAL
15. DEVIATION SELS	CHECK
16. STATIC CELLS	NORMAL

17. RADAR (IF INSTALLED)   OFF
18. FLIGHT CONTROL SHIFTERS   CK & ON BOOST
19. AUTO PILOT   OFF
20. EFER. HYD. SEL   BRAKE
21. SEAT BELT-NO SMOKING   ON

FIRST OFFICER   **FLIGHT ENGINEER**

1. INVERTERS   CHECK-INSTRUMENTS
                                & RADIOS ON
2. FUEL QUANTITY   54,000 LBS.—CHECKED
3. HYDRAULIC & ENGINE
   OIL QUANTITY   CHECK
4. FIRE WARNING   CHECK
5. CABIN COMPRESSORS   DUMPED
6. CIRCUIT BREAKERS   CK-COWL FLAPS OFF
7. FIREWALL SHUT-OFFS   NOTCH #1
8. FUEL PUMP CONTROLS   CHECK
9. HYDRAULIC PUMP SWITCHES   PRESS ON
10. GENERATORS   ON
11. BATTERY SELECTOR   GROUND POWER
12. ALTERNATE FUEL SOURCE   NORMAL
13. CROSSFEED QUAD. VALVES   CLOSED
14. CARBURATOR AIR   RAM & COLD
15. SPARK CONTROL   RETARD
16. PROP SYNCHRONIZING SEL   CHECK
17. PROPS   FULL INC
18. OIL COOLER FLAPS   OPEN
19. ENG. BLOWERS   LOW
20. MIXTURES   OFF
21. FUEL VALVES   ON 1-2-3-4
22. 260 PANEL   CHECK & SET
23. OXYGEN   CHECK & ON

1720Z

Edgerton indicates he's ready to start the engines, which are always started in numbers 3, 4, 2, and 1 order. The actual engine starting is coordinated with two ramp agents, one of whom stands fire guard with a movable fire extinguisher, while the other communicates with the cockpit via an interphone. For each engine the fuel boost pump is turned to low, then to high. The throttle is set a 1,200 rpm, then:

a. Ground to flight engineer (FE) "Clear to start engines—wing flaps clear."
b. FE to captain, "Ready to start engine—wing flaps clear."
c. Captain to FE, "Start engine" or "Standby."
d. FE to ground, "Clear to start engines."
e. Ground to FE, "Clear all engines."
f. As engine is being turned eight blades mechanic calls out blade count to FE.
g. When eight blades called, FE calls, "Contact number 3."

With number 3 running, Edgerton and Klawinski start the number 4, 2, and 1 engines. As number 4 is started, the flap control is set for 20 percent or take-off position and the flaps checked for asymmetrical extension.

1726Z

With all four power plants running, Edgerton calls for the After Starting Engines check list.

FIRST OFFICER	CAPTAIN
1. BRAKE & HYDRAULIC SYSTEM PRESSURE	3000 PSI
2. FLAP POSITION & SHUT OFF	CHECK
3. ANTI-COLLISION LIGHTS	AS REQUIRED

FIRST OFFICER	FLIGHT ENGINEER
1. GEAR PINS	3 ABOARD
2. DOOR LIGHTS	OUT
3. BATTERY SELECT	ON BATTERY
4. COWL FLAP C.B.'s & POSITION	ON & OPEN
5. FUEL PUMPS	OFF
6. FORWARD CABIN DOOR	CHECK

1728Z

Edgerton turns to Klawinski and requests taxi clearance, and he in turn contacts the tower.

    TWA 770: "L.A. Ground, TWA 770 at Gate G-7, ready to taxi with information Delta."

    Ground: "TWA 770 clear to taxi to Runway 26 Right. Hold short of runway."

    TWA 770: "Runway 26 Right, hold short of runway. Roger, TWA 770."

1729Z

TWA 770 is ready to taxi. Edgerton salutes the ramp agent, who returns the salute, then he releases the parking brake. Edgerton grasps the throttles with his right hand and the nose steering wheel with his left. With minimum RPM on the propellers, TWA 770 turns away from the gate and slowly taxies to its assigned runway. During the taxi, the Auto Feather test switches only are checked. Also, at thie time Klawinski contacts Clearance Delivery on a separate radio frequency and is given the actual flight plan approved by Air Traffic Control.

1740Z

Edgerton rolls the L–1649A onto the run-up pad for Runway 26R. He sets the parking brake, pulls back the throttles to idle, turns to Klawinski, and calls for the Before Run-Up checklist.

FIRST OFFICER	**CAPTAIN**
1. WING FLAPS	INDICATE T.O. & APP
2. TRIM TABS	CHECK
3. RADAR	AS REQUIRED
4. P. PATH COMPASSES	SYNCHRONIZE THEN SLAVE
5. ALTERNATORS	CHECK & NORMAL
6. HORIZONS	ERECT
7. NESA	NORMAL
8. V1 & V2	CHECK

FIRST OFFICER	**FLIGHT ENGINEER**
1. GENERATORS	CHECK
2. A/C POWER	CHECK
3. ENG. RUN-UP	

1742Z

Edgerton, Klawinski, and O'Malley working together go through the engine run-up. The engine alternators are checked. The NESA system, a means of electrically heating the three center cockpit windshield panels to prevent fogging or icing, is checked next. O'Malley sets the engine controls for 1700 RPM and checks the propellers for over-speed control. The automatic propeller synchrophasing system is checked, then the propeller full feathering system. Now the crew check the ignition system on all four engines, as well as the fuel mixture. Finally, the auto-feathering circuits are checked.

1744Z

Edgerton calls for the Before Take-Off Preliminary checklist.

POWER SETTINGS

SETTINGS	RPM	MAP	BMEP
TAKE-OFF	2900	58.5"	277
1ST RED.	2600	51"	@ S.L. 255
CLINB L3	2500	40"	196 @ S.L.
CLIMB HB	2500	43"	199 @14M

FIRST OFFICER	**FLIGHT ENGINEER**
1. PROPS	FULL INC
2. AUTO FEATHER	CK
3. FUEL PUMPS	ON HIGH
4. OIL COOLER FLAPS	CK
5. CABIN FANS & HEATERS	OFF

1745Z

Edgerton asks Klawinski for take-off clearance.

TWA 770: "L.A. Tower, TWA 770 ready for take-off, Runway 26 Right, over."

L.A. Tower: "TWA 770, clear for take-off, Runway 26 Right. Maintain run way heading to 1,000. Right turn approved. Cleared direct Hector VOR."

TWA 770: "Roger, runway heading to 1,000, right turn out, cleared direct Hector. TWA 770."

1745:30Z

Now, moving quickly, Edgerton releases the parking brake, applies minimum power, and gently eases the heavily loaded L–1649A into position at the very beginning of Runway 26 Right. Here he stops the aircraft with his toe brakes and calls for the Before Take-Off Final checklist.

FIRST OFFICER	**CAPTAIN**
1. FLIGHT CONTROLS	FREE

FIRST OFFICER	**FLIGHT ENGINEER**
1. CARB AIR	RAM & COLD
2. MIXTURES	RICH
3. COWL FLAPS	30% ON ROLL

1747Z

TWA 770 is now ready for take-off. Edgerton advances the throttles slowly all the way forward and calls out, "Trim the throttles" over the increasing roar of the engines. O'Malley carefully adjusts the four throttles to 58.5 inches of manifold pressure. As the aircraft slowly gathers speed, Klawinski radios, "TWA 770 rolling." Edgerton has his left hand on the nose steering wheel, his right on the throttles. Klawinski's left hand is just below Edgerton's on the throttle console as a back-up. O'Malley carefully checks the engine gauges in front of him for any indication of power loss or other problem.

Klawinski has been keeping track of the airspeed as the aircraft accelerates. Now he calls out, "Eighty knots." At this speed the rudder becomes effective, and Edgerton moves both hands to the control wheel.

At maximum take-off power the L–1649A continues to gather speed, the landing gear transmitting the shocks of the concrete runway expansion strips to the entire fuselage, the nose bobbing up and down, and the entire aircraft moving sideways against the landing gear snubbers.

Klawinski, still keeping his eyes on the airspeed indicator, now calls out, "V1." This is the maximum speed at which the take-off can still be aborted and the aircraft brought to a safe stop with the remaining length of the runway. With no warnings about any power failures or other problems, Edgerton continues the take-off.

A few more seconds and Klawinski calls out "Rotate." Edgerton eases the control column toward him, the nose wheel comes off the ground, and the long fuselage tilts upward a few degrees.

1748Z

Klawinski now calls out, "V2." Edgerton pulls farther back on the control column, and the big airplane leaves the ground in a flat, gradual climb. Edgerton glances at his rate-of-climb indicator, sees evidence of a definite climb, calls out, "Gear up," simultaneously giving a thumbs-up sign with his right hand. Klawinski replies quickly, "Gear up," and reaches for the landing gear lever and moves it to the UP position. Outside the Turbo-Compounds continue their relentless roar, still at their maximum power settings.

After some 29 seconds the three gear lights flash green. Klawinski has been keeping his eye on them, because Edgerton has his eyes outside the cockpit, and now verbally confirms the light by calling, "Gear is up." Immediately Edgerton calls out "51 inches and 2,600 RPM." O'Malley repeats the command and then reduces the power settings to 51 inches of manifold power and the propeller revolutions to 2,600 RPM. This is taking place some 90 seconds after take-off power was applied, well within the 2-minute maximum generally permitted on the big engines.

1749Z

Edgerton keeps the L–1649A climbing at some 400 feet/min and, as the airspeed increases past 140 knots, he calls, "Up flaps!" and Klawinski activates the flap control lever. As Edgerton feels the aircraft sinking slightly from the effect of the flap retraction, he thumbs more up trim on the trim button set in the control wheel. After a few seconds, Klawinski reports, "Flaps are up."

1750Z

With the landing gear and flaps retracted, the L–1649A now accelerates as it continues to climb. The airspeed reaches 170 knots IAS, and Edgerton calls to O'Malley, "Climb power!" O'Malley repeats the command, and further reduces the power settings.

1752Z

The L–1649A is now climbing through 1,000 feet. Edgerton lowers the nose slightly and begins a gentle right turn. As he reaches a heading of 075 degrees, he rolls the aircraft level and resumes the climb angle, which gives an indicated airspeed of 170 knots. Edgerton cannot fly directly toward his first checkpoint, Hector VOR, because of the mountains northwest of Burbank, which reach up to 10,000 feet. The fully loaded 1649A climbs too slowly to reach such an altitude at that point. Thus, Edgerton is flying a dogleg, first following an 075 degree heading until the last of the peaks are past, and then turning to a heading of 050 degrees and flying directly toward Hector VOR.

1825Z

Over the Hector VOR, the L–1649A has reached an altitude of 10,500 feet. Edgerton gently turns the big aircraft a few degrees left and continues climbing as he heads for Las Vegas, some 100 nautical miles away.

1832Z

As the aircraft is passing through 13,000 feet, O'Malley switches the engine supercharges from low blower to high blower. This is necessary so that a sufficient amount of air is forced into the engines. Even with the high blower operating, the rate of climb averages less than 400 feet/min at these altitudes.

1852Z

TWA 770 flies over Las Vegas, still climbing at 15,000 feet. To the left, Lake Mead can be clearly seen.

1858Z

The initial cruising altitude of 17,000 feet is finally reached some 24 nautical miles beyond Las Vegas. It is as high as Edgerton can go at the current weight, which is now down to just over 153,000 pounds. On a colder day he might have been able to climb to a higher altitude at this stage of the flight. Actually, the airplane is a couple of thousand feet higher than Edgerton would like at their weight, as there is a possibility of marginal engine and turbine cooling. But 17,000 feet was chosen partly because of mountain peaks along the flight path and partly because of local cumulus build-ups in the area.

1927Z

TWA 770 is over Milford VOR, Utah. With a helping wind of some 30 knots, its ground speed is now 272 knots, or 315 mph!

1945Z

We are now 2 hours into the flight and over central Utah. At this time, the first crew change takes place on the flight deck. Klawinski, the first officer, goes off duty. The next five hours will be his own time. He moves back to the crew rest compartment, where he will have his dinner and then sleep until time to go on duty again. He is replaced in the right-hand seat by Bill Bailey, the relief captain.

2004Z

At this time, TWA 770 crosses over Myton, Utah. Ground speed is virtually the same, just over 270 knots. The engines at this altitude burn about 2,900 pounds of fuel per hour, or 493 gallons/hour. This means 123 gallons/hour/engine. At this point in the flight, almost 2.5 hours from take-off, some 10,000 pounds of fuel have been burned off, and the aircraft weight is down to almost 146,000 pounds.

As we fly over Myton, off to the left, the Great Salt Lake is visible.

2025Z

Crossing over Rock Springs VOR, Wyoming, TWA 770 turns onto a more northerly course.

2105Z

At this time, we are over Crazy Woman VOR, Wyoming, and one has to wonder what events in the dim past led to this name. Edgerton now turns almost due north for this next leg. The tailwind has picked up a little more, now boosting speed some 35 knots. This makes the ground speed 282 knots, or 328 mph.

2136Z

TWA 770 reaches Miles City, Montana. The flight now turns on a more easterly course for the next leg to Williston, North Dakota.

2206Z

Reaching Williston, the flight cuts across the northwest corner of the state. In a few minutes it will cross the United States–Canadian border. The ground speed is now up to 286 knots, or 336 mph. At Williston, the flight once again turns to a more northerly heading.

2235Z

This checkpoint, Broadview, is located in the Canadian province of Saskatchewan. Some 90 miles to the west is the city of Regina. Flying through this area at night lights on the ground become farther and farther apart. To the east, about 200 miles, is Winnipeg.

2246Z

Now over Yorkton VOR. This is a very short leg, which was incorporated in the flight plan simply to shorten an otherwise very long leg. The tailwind component has increased to 37 knots for this short leg, making the ground speed 292 knots or 336 mph. Halfway to the next checkpoint, we will cross from Saskatchewan into Manitoba.

2322Z

Crossing over the VOR at the Paj, Edgerton checks with O'Malley, the flight engineer, on the amount of fuel used and the current weight of the aircraft. O'Malley reports almost 20,000 pounds of fuel already used, thus bringing the aircraft weight down to almost 136,000 pounds. Based on this weight plus the fact that stronger tailwinds are forecast at higher altitudes, Edgerton discusses with Bailey the feasibility of asking for a higher altitude clearance at this time. Edgerton's one reservation is that at a higher altitude and at the current weight, airspeed is somewhat more difficult to maintain and engine and turbine cooling becomes marginal. However, if the current altitude of 17,000 feet is maintained, Edgerton feels he may have to divert to Iceland, one of his alternates, to refuel. Bailey agrees that they should try for 21,000 feet but suggests they wait until the next checkpoint, Thompson VOR, when another 1,500 pounds of fuel will have been used. Thus, the likelihood of engine cooling problems would be reduced. Edgerton promptly agrees.

2356Z

Now well into Canada, TWA 770 reaches Thompson VOR, due north of Lake Winnipeg. The flight has just finished crossing the 180-mile-wide Domestic Canadian Air Defense Information Zone (ADIZ), which also delineates the Pinetree Line, the radar line stretching across the center of Canada. Now, with Edgerton's approval, Bailey contacts the Winnipeg ARTCC for permission to climb. This is received, and Edgerton asks O'Malley for climb power. The engines take on a deeper tone, and gradually, the L–1649A climbs toward 21,000 feet. At this altitude and weight, the rate of climb is quite low, only 250 feet/min. The TAS is 224 knots, which works out to a 258 knot ground speed.

0013Z

After 17 minutes of slow climbing, the 1649A reaches 21,000 feet. Edgerton requests a return to cruise power, then carefully trims the aircraft so it is on what pilots like to call the "step." This is the attitude to which an airplane can be trimmed that results in the least drag, and thus the most speed.

It is now time for some crew changes. Frank Busch, the navigator, makes an appearance with the comment, "I guess I'd better come up here or you guys will wind up over the North Pole!" Busch will be doing the navigating on all legs over water from here until the flight approaches the British Isles.

0021Z

Now over Gillam, just 41 nautical miles from where the flight attained its new altitude of 21,000 feet. Beyond this point, our track will be crossing diagonally the southern half of the famed Hudson Bay. But even this far north a very infrequent light can be seen below in some small solitary outpost. Our next two checkpoints are merely latitude/longitude coordinates in the middle of Hudson Bay. So to be on the safe side, Busch waits until we are some 125 miles past Gillam and then takes the first of what will be numerous star sights on this night.

0045Z

We are now 7 hours into the flight, and it is time to play musical chairs once again in the cockpit. Edgerton moves back to the rest area for the next five hours, Bailey moves from the right seat to the left and assumes command of the flight, and Klawinski moves back into the right seat after his rest period. He will be on duty the remainder of the flight.

0056Z

TWA 770 reaches the checkpoint located at 58°N-90°W. At the new altitude of 21,000 feet, the tailwind component has increased to 45 knots. Before us is a 355-nautical-mile stretch over Hudson Bay to the next checkpoint. This leg is the second longest of the entire flight.

0145Z

The flight is now at approximately the halfway point after 8 hours of flying, and it's time for the flight engineers to change places. O'Malley goes back to the rest area to join Edgerton, and Lipschulz takes over as flight engineer.

0203Z

The flight reaches 61°N-80°W, a point close to the eastern edge of Hudson Bay. As we reached 60°N latitude, we crossed from Canada proper into the wilderness area known as the Northwest Territories. On this leg, our TAS was up to 267 knots, and the tailwind pushed us to a ground speed of 312 knots, or 360 statute miles. Without a doubt, we are really moving! The weight of the aircraft is now down to just over 132,000 pounds, which means in eight hours, some 15 tons of fuel have been burned off.

0236Z

The flight crosses over the Ungava Peninsula, which is many hundreds of miles north of Quebec, and reaches the settlement of Deception Bay. A nondirectional beacon located here helps the crew home in on the checkpoint.

0313Z

TWA 770 crosses the Hudson Strait and shortly after passing the coast of Baffin Island, is over the Frobisher Bay VOR. If the original weather forecast had predicted lesser tailwinds, the flight would, in all probability, have landed here for refueling. As it is, most westbound flights with full payloads land here. Frobisher Bay is also close to the halfway point in terms of distance. The flight has already covered 2,638 nautical miles with 2,210 yet to go.

0357Z

TWA 770 reaches its checkpoint at 65°N-60°W. From now on all checkpoints will be at every 10° of longitude. The 65°N latitude puts the flight at its extreme northern point. We are now crossing the Davis Strait and midway between Baffin Island and Greenland. If it were daylight, we would see a considerable amount of ice below us, even though it is August. This particular checkpoint is significant because it is right on the boundary of the DEWIZ, the Distant Early Warning Identification Zone. This zone encompasses the famous DEW Radar Line.

0443Z

TWA 770 reaches the checkpoint at 65°N-50°W, which is located a few miles inland from the west coast of Greenland. North of us some 125 miles is the airport at Sondrestrom. At this point, we are only 90 miles from the Arctic Circle.

0532Z

Reaching 64°N-40°W, TWA 770 has overflown Greenland. Beneath us in the moonlight, the terrain shines ghostly white, for this huge island is totally covered with ice except for a few stretches of coastline. Greenland is a very high land mass, almost a plateau, with the interior having a mean altitude of 9,000 feet. Because Greenland is clearly visible below us, Busch, the navigator, is able to easily confirm our position as we cross the coast.

The air speed has increased again, and is now up to 274 knots. Combined with the strongest tailwind we've encountered yet, 55 knots, our ground speed is now up to 329 knots—a whistling 379 mph!

0545Z

Once again it's time for a crew change. Edgerton steps into the cockpit, yawning hugely, and replaces Bailey in the left seat. He will take over command for the balance of the flight. Busch is busy talking with Weather Ship *Alpha* on the HF radio. *Alpha* is some 130 nautical miles southeast of us and is one of seven weather ships maintained by the United States, Canada, and various European countries. Each ship cruises slowly within a very small area, providing passing aircraft with the latest weather advisories and with radar fixes to assist the navigators and pilots.

0624Z

TWA 770 is now at 63°N-30°W, about halfway between Greenland and Iceland. The weight of the aircraft is down to 116,000 pounds, with 40,000 pounds of fuel having been used. Edgerton consults closely with Lipshulz concerning fuel consumption and with Busch on tailwinds to be expected, as well as terminal weather in London. He must make a decision shortly if he is to divert to Iceland for an unscheduled fuel stop. But it appears that this is unnecessary, and the flight continues as per the flight plan. Busch has confirmed our position at the checkpoint by radio with Weather Ship *Alpha*, which is still within radar range. At this point, we cross into the Iceland Military ADIZ. Below us, in the bright, early morning sunlight, we can see a few scattered icebergs floating in the Denmark Strait.

0705Z

We are now some 120 miles southwest of Reykjavik, Iceland. Edgerton, who is sitting relaxed in the left seat, suddenly straightens and peers through the windshield. Then wordlessly he points to the 10 o'clock position off to the left. Two small dots swiftly grow larger and then pass very quickly by the left wing a half mile away. They are Air Force Lockheed F–94C Starfire all-weather interceptors, a squadron of which is based in Iceland.

TWA 770 drones on over the sun-speckled Atlantic Ocean. A few minutes later it is Klawinski's turn to point. Ahead and slightly below is the unmistakable dolphin shape of a Super Constellation, but this one has clearly visible domes above and below the fuselage.

It is one of the Navy Lockheed WV–2 AEW&Cs, which are also based in Iceland. Klawinski turns around with a grin and cracks, "Seems to be a Lockheed sky around here!" There are appreciative chuckles in the cockpit.

0722Z

Flying over a long 312-nautical-mile leg, we reach the checkpoint at 60°N-20°W. Our ground speed is down slightly due to a reduced tailwind.

0839Z

This is the longest leg of the entire flight, 396 nautical miles. It takes us from a point due south of Iceland to near the Outer Hebrides Islands. The tail wind is down to 40 mph, but our TAS has risen again to 278 knots because of the reduced weight of the aircraft as fuel is burned off.

On this leg Busch is able to cross-check his navigation by talking with Weather Ship *India*, which cruises south of our track about 80 miles. The ship's radar fix confirms the position. Near the end of the leg, Busch also gets a fix on the VOR located on one of the Outer Hebrides Islands.

Edgerton is receiving current weather advisories of terminal weather for London, and these do not make him happy. English weather is living up to its reputation. The warm air over the Gulf Stream meeting the colder air from the North Sea is generating the usual witches' brew of clouds and rain. Edgerton knows he is likely to encounter some delay in his approach to London Airport. So now he consults with Klawinski and Lipschulz concerning fuel status. If it appears advisable, Edgerton can divert to Prestwick, Scotland, which today is only some 60 nautical miles north of our track. But finally, he is satisfied this course of action won't be necessary, and he elects to continue as originally planned.

With almost 15 hours of flying completed, the L–1649A is down to a weight of only 110,500 pounds, having burned off 46,500 pounds of fuel.

0900Z

The flight is now within range of land-based omni stations in Northern Ireland and Scotland, so Busch's navigating chores are finished. He collects his various paraphernalia and moves back to the crew compartment to have some breakfast.

0928Z

Having made landfall near the city of Londonderry, TWA 770 flies over Belfast, Ireland, still at 21,000 feet. The last leg is only 210 nautical miles, and Edgerton now prepares to start his let-down. Below, thickening clouds totally obscure any view of the surface. Without a doubt, it will be a bumpy descent.

0942Z

Edgerton decides it is time to start down. Air Route Traffic Control clears him to descend, and he calls for 1,800 RPM and 120 BMEP, which will result in a 1,000 feet/min rate of descent. Lipschulz makes the necessary adjustments to the propeller controls and the throttles, and the L–1649A dips her nose and starts down. The descent is smooth for the first few minutes, but then, as the aircraft enters the top of the cloud layer, gentle turbulence is encountered. Edgerton asks Klawinski to turn on the "Fasten Seat Belt" light.

0952Z

Approaching 11,000 feet, still in solid cloud, Lipschulz shifts to low blower operation, simultaneously reducing power further to 1,700 RPM and 110 BMEP. Edgerton announces he wants to reduce the rate of descent to 750 feet/min because of the turbulence, and Klawinski trims the aircraft to meet that descent rate.

1001Z

TWA 770 reaches 4,000 feet, and Edgerton levels off in compliance with ATC instructions. The flight is now only 30 nautical miles from Heathrow Airport, and London Approach begins directing TWA 770's approach. Edgerton has reduced airspeed to 180 knots because of the dual factors of increased turbulence and speed limitations imposed by ATC in the crowded London Terminal area.

1003Z

Edgerton now calls for the Before Landing Preliminary Checklist.

FIRST OFFICER	CAPTAIN
1. SEAT BELT SIGN	ON
2. AUX. HYD. PUMP	CHECK & ON
3. BRAKE & HYD. SYSTEM PRESS	3000 PSI
4. AUTO PILOT	AS REQD.
5. WING DE-ICERS	OFF
6. PARKING BRAKE LIGHTS & SW	TEST & OFF
7. TWI (IF INSTALLED)	CHECK
8. ALTIMETERS	SET
9. GEAR LIGHTS	TEST
10. BOUNDARY SPEED	CHECK

FIRST OFFICER	FLIGHT ENGINEER
1. CABIN ALTITUDE	FT
2. HYD. PUMP SWITCHES	PRESS ON
3. FUEL VALVES	ON 1-2-3-4
4. ENGINE BLOWERS	LOW
5. SPARK CONTROL	RETARD
6. ALTERNATE FUEL SOURCE	NORMAL
7. CROSSFEED QUAD. VALVES	CLOSED

With this out of the way, Edgerton is ready for the approach. Heathrow Airport is reporting a 500-foot ceiling variable, half mile visibility variable, with low scud and fog. An ILS approach will be required.

1006Z

London Approach directs TWA 770 to descend to and maintain 1,500 feet. Klawinski acknowledges. Edgerton once more calls for reduced power, and the nose dips as the L–1649A starts sliding down. The aircraft is bouncing around in the clammy clouds, and Klawinski helps Edgerton at the controls as they attempt to dampen the worst of the movements.

1010Z

Edgerton levels off at 1,500 feet, calls for 150 knots, and follows the instructions from London Approach that will bring him to an intersecting point with the ILS radio beams. He calls for the Before Landing Final Checklist.

FIRST OFFICER	**CAPTAIN**
1. LANDING GEAR	DWN-3 GREEN LIGHTS
2. RADAR	OFF
3. SEAT BELT/NO SMOKING	ON

FIRST OFFICER	**FLIGHT ENGINEER**
1. MIXTURE	RICH
2. PROPS	____ RPM
3. CARB. AIR POSITION	_____
4. CABIN FANS & HEATERS	OFF

1012Z

With the checklist completed, Edgerton now calls for 60 percent flaps and 140 knots. Klawinski calls out, "Flaps, 60 percent," and rams down the flap control lever. As the flaps move out and down from the wing trailing edge, the aircraft tries to balloon upward. Edgerton feeds in nose down trim to compensate for this. Klawinski calls out, "Flaps set, 60 percent." Lipschulz adjusts the power levers increasing power to maintain 140 knots.

1013Z

Edgerton intercepts the ILS locator and turns to his final approach. A few seconds pass, then the Outer Marker light flashes and a buzzer rings. Edgerton trims the aircraft nose down and keeps his eyes on the ILS instrument.

1014Z

Still bumping around in the overcast, the L–1649A steadily sinks through the clouds and rain, carefully kept in line with the localizer and glide slope of the ILS.

1015Z

TWA 770 is approaching 500 feet still in the clouds. Klawinski, whose job is to determine when the aircraft has transitioned to visual flight as well as spotting the runway approach and threshold lights, sings out, "Approach lights!" Edgerton looks up from his disciplined scanning of the instruments. Through the rain and haze he sees the flashing runway approach lights and calls out, "130 knots!" Lipschulz reduces the power a fraction, and the L–1649A sinks toward the runway threshold. As the aircraft crosses over the runway threshold, Edgerton pulls the throttles all the way back, pulls back slightly on the wheel, and then lets the airplane float until the main gear hits the runway. He lets the nose down slowly until the nose gear makes contact, then calls, "Reverse power!"

Klawinski activates the propeller reversal system, and to the accompaniment of a loud roar from the engines, the L–1649A quickly decelerates. As the speed falls below 75 knots, Klawinski disengages the propeller reversal system, and the engine noise drops to a low rumble. Edgerton slows the aircraft to taxi speed with the toe brakes, and then turns off the runway onto a taxiway.

Heathrow Ground Control provides directions to the gate, and TWA 770 trundles sedately among aircraft of a dozen or more countries to its parking location. Edgerton carefully turns the L–1649A on the apron, ever mindful of that sweeping 150-foot wing. Once in place, the crew shut down the four big Curtiss-Wrights which have kept up their reassuring roar for 16.5 hours.

The long polar flight is over. Just another routine operation that spanned 5,600 statute miles at an average speed of 320 mph. An everyday occurrence. Yet one not possible until a short time before, when the instrument that made it all possible, the L–1649A, took to the airways!

12-1 The first L–1649A in flight. (Lockheed Martin)

12-2 A view of the L–1649A cockpit, 1957. Compare this instrumentation with that of the original Constellation. (Lockheed Martin)

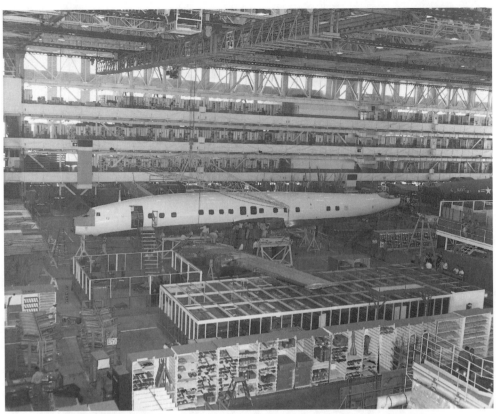
12-3 The Lockheed production line for the L1649A. (Lockheed Martin)

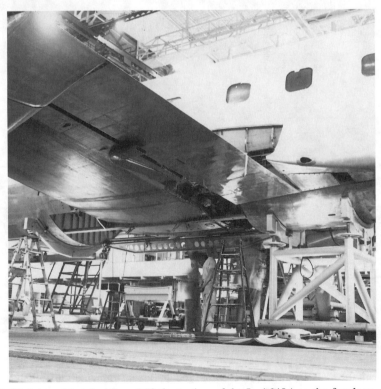
12-4, 12-5, 12-6 Attaching that long 150-foot wing of the L–1649A to the fuselage. (Lockheed Martin)

12-5

12-6

12-7 A wing assembly for the L–1649A being moved by dolly. (Lockheed Martin)

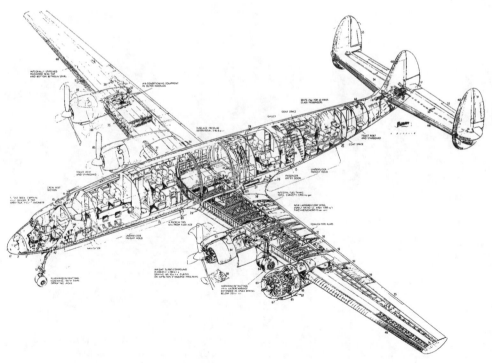

12-8 Schematic of an L–1649A. (Lockheed Martin)

12-9 High-density coach configuration of an L–1649A. (Lockheed Martin)

12-10 An Air France L–1649A used on the Los-Angeles-Paris Polar route. (Lockheed Martin)

12-11 A Lufthansa L–1649A with the mountains near Burbank looming in the background. (Lockheed Martin)

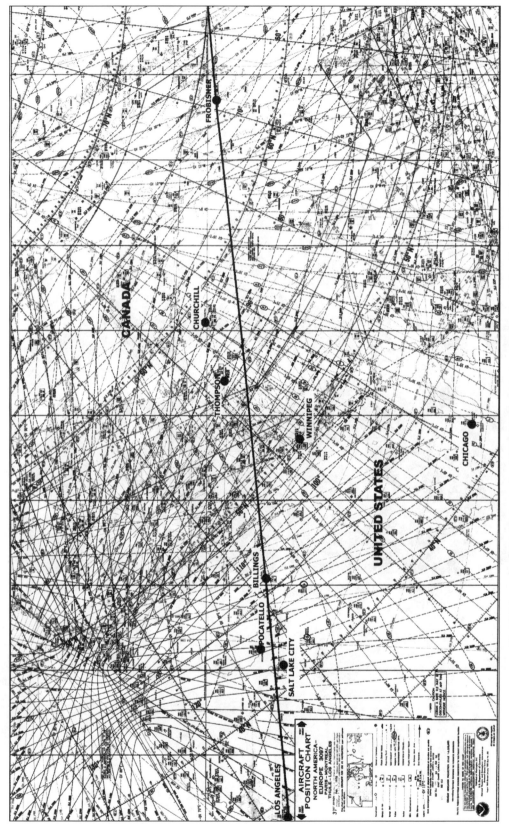

12-12 Chart showing flight path of TWA 770, Los Angeles to Frobisher Bay. (Luisada)

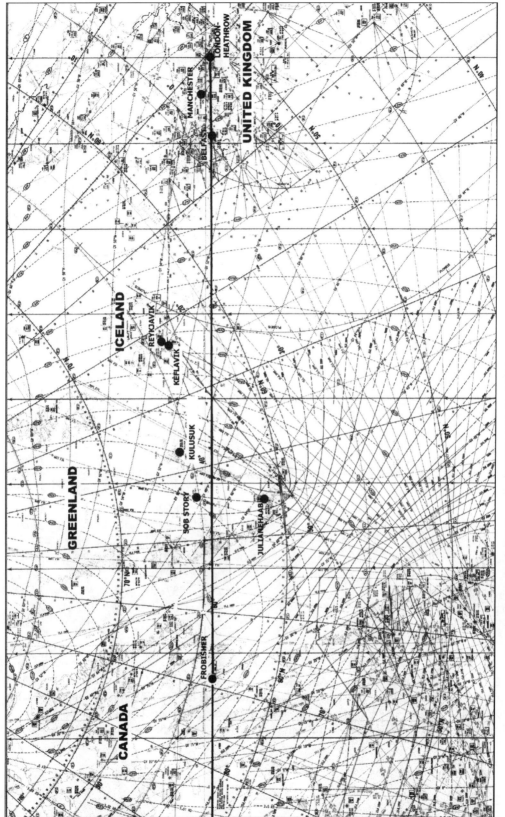

12-13 Chart showing flight path of TWA 770, Frobisher Bay to London, England. (Luisada)

FLIGHT PLAN—TWA 770

Leg	Checkpoint	Altitude (Feet)	Distance (N.M.)	Cumulative Dist. (N.M.)	Dist. To Go (N.M.)	Airspeed IAS/TAS (Knots)
	L.A. INT.	Sea Level	—0—	4,848		—0—
1	Hector	> 10,500	117	117	4731	170/190
2	Las Vegas	> 15,000	100	217	4631	170/200
3	TOC	> 17,000	24	241	4607	170/210
4	Milford		129	370	4478	189/242
5	Myton		168	538	4310	189/242
6	Rock Springs		96	634	4214	193/247
7	Crazy Woman		185	819	4029	193/247
8	Miles City		145	964	3884	194/248
9	Williston		140	1,104	3744	196/251
10	Broadview		134	1238	3610	196/251
11	Yorkton		55	1293	3555	199/255
12	The PAJ		175	1468	3380	199/255
13	Thompson	17,000	160	1628	3220	199/255
14	TOC	21,000	74	1702	3146	170/224
15	Gillam		41	1743	3105	193/263
16	58° N – 90° W		180	1923	2925	193/263
17	61° N – 80° W		355	2278	2570	196/267
18	Deception Bay		168	2246	2402	196/267
19	Frobisher Bay		192	2638	2210	198/270
20	65° N – 60° W		231	2869	1979	198/270
21	65° N – 50° W		255	3124	1724	201/274
22	64° N – 40° W		266	3390	1458	201/274
23	63° N – 30° W		280	3670	1178	203/277
24	60° N – 20° W		312	3982	866	203/277
25	57° N – 10° W		396	4378	470	204/278
26	Belfast	21,000	260	4638	210	205/280
27	London		210	4848	0	225/305

12-14 Flight plan of a typical Los Angeles-London Polar flight. TWA Flight 770, a Lockheed 1649A "Jetstream" Super Constellation. Taxi Weight: 156,455 lbs. Take-off Weight: 156,100 lbs. Total Distance: 4,848 nautical miles. Average speed: 297 knots. Total Time Enroute: 16 hours, 20 minutes. Souls on Board: Flight crew=7, Cabin crew=5, Passengers=63, Total=75. (Luisada)

LOS ANGELES—LONDON

Wind Vector	Ground Speed (Knots) —0—	Elapsed Time (Min.) —0—	Total Time Enroute —0—	Zulu Time 1748	Fuel Used On Leg (Lbs.) —0—	Total Fuel Used (Lbs.) —0—	Fuel Remaining (Lbs.) 54,000
20	210	:37	:37	18:25	3545	3545	50455
25	225	:27	1:04	18:52	2760	6305	47695
30	240	:06	1:10	18:58	435	6740	47260
30	272	:20	1:39	19:27	1421	8161	45839
30	272	:37	2:16	20:04	1835	9996	45004
35	282	:21	2:37	20:25	1036	11032	43968
35	282	:40	3:17	21:05	1983	13015	40985
32	280	:31	3:48	21:36	1539	14554	35446
35	286	:30	4:18	22:06	1480	16034	37966
35	286	:29	4:47	22:35	1421	17445	36545
37	292	:11	4:58	22:46	533	17988	36012
35	290	:36	5:34	23:22	1776	19764	34236
30	285	:34	6:08	23:56	1687	21451	32549
34	258	:17	6:25	0:13	1000	22451	31549
45	308	:08	6:33	0:21	380	22831	31169
45	308	:35	7:08	0:56	1694	24525	25475
45	312	:69	8:17	2:03	3358	27883	26117
40	307	:33	8:50	2:36	1606	29489	24511
45	315	:37	9:27	3:13	1810	31299	22701
45	315	:44	10:11	3:57	2132	33431	20569
55	329	:46	10:57	4:43	2248	35679	18321
55	329	:49	11:46	5:32	2394	38073	15927
50	327	:52	12:38	6:24	1840	39913	14087
45	322	:58	13:36	7:22	2832	42745	11255
40	310	:77	14:53	8:39	3738	46483	71517
40	320	:49	15:44	9:28	2394	48877	5123
30	335	:38	16:20	10:06	1123	50000	4000

12-15 "Power Plant and Propellers" (Lockheed Martin)

12-16 "Fuel and Oil Systems" (Lockheed Martin)

Chapter 13

TWA AND THE CONSTELLATION

No history of the Lockheed Constellation can be considered complete without relating the part this aircraft played in the fortunes of Trans World Airlines. TWA was the single largest commercial buyer and operator of Constellations, exceeded only by the Air Force and Navy. Its total buy/lease of 146 Constellations, Super Constellations and Jetstream Constellations constituted a whopping 17 percent of all such aircraft built.

As a percentage of purely commercial sales, TWA's share becomes an even more impressive 28 percent. Or, to put it another way, TWA operated almost one out of three of all commercial Constellations ever built. Thus it becomes apparent that the interrelationships of TWA and the Lockheed Constellation are a very important part of this story.

TWA's fortunes during the 1940s and '50s were the result of three circumstances:

1. The general state of the economy.
2. The relative competitive position held at any one time as compared to other air carriers.
3. The effectiveness of top management.

As related in Chapter 2, TWA generally, and its principal stockholder, Howard Hughes, in particular, played key roles as catalysts in the development of the original Constellation design in 1939–40. Then, during World War II, neither TWA nor any other private company had much, if anything, to say about the program as the government maintained a tight rein on all aircraft production.

After the war, TWA's influence on further design developments was proportionately far less. For one thing, other air carriers were buying Constellations in quantity; carriers such as Eastern and Air France had a sizable vote in such matters. Another factor was the general economic situation during any given period of time, as well as the availability of new technology. The latter, in turn, was certainly highly influenced by the military's needs in a period of the Cold War and police actions. So, although TWA greatly influenced the Constellation program in 1939–40, from 1946 on the reverse became true; the Constellation was a basic and continuing influence in the fortunes of TWA until the advent of the jet transport in 1959. Because such a very large part of the total TWA fleet was made up of Constellations for over 15 years, it is worthwhile to examine in some detail how TWA used its Constellations, with what results, and how this aircraft may have influenced TWA's fortunes.

GETTING STARTED–1945

First of all, one should remember that before 1942, TWA was basically an east–west trunk carrier flying between the Eastern Seaboard and California, with intermediate stops at such cities as Pittsburgh, Detroit, Chicago, Cincinnati, St. Louis, Kansas City, and Phoenix. When World War II came to these shores, TWA turned over a number of its flight personnel and aircraft to the Air Transport Command (ATC) of the Air Force. The flights TWA operated under ATC auspices were carried out by the Intercontinental Division (ICD) of TWA, which had been formed in December 1941 for just this purpose.

ICD's crews developed a great deal of expertise not only in flying all over the world but also in operating large, four-engine aircraft. ICD initially operated TWA's five Boeing B–307 Stratoliners, which had been originally put into transcontinental passenger service in 1940 and were known during the war as C–75s. Later ICD was assigned a fleet of first Consolidated C–87s (converted B–24 heavy bombers) and, eventually, Douglas C–54 Skymasters. Together with a school that specifically trained airline crews for this type of worldwide flying, ICD became the nucleus of TWA's postwar overseas operations. During 1942–43 alone, ICD crews, flying as part of overall ATC operations, completed over 1,000 transatlantic crossings.

In January 1945, ICD was assigned the additional task of testing and proving the new Lockheed C–69 (L–49) Constellation. Pan Am was also assigned this same task. However, there were so few C–69s in service that ICD actually accumulated relatively little Connie flying time, although some of the flights were across the Atlantic. Again, this was valuable, if limited, experience for TWA.

In July 1945, TWA was granted government sanction to operate internationally as far east as Cairo, Egypt, and Calcutta, India. This was the result of the application made by TWA in June 1944 to operate an around-the-world route. Thus, the stage was set for TWA to become one of the two largest U.S. flag carriers, the other being Pan American.

World War II finally came to an end in August 1945 and, in September, TWA and Lockheed signed a contract calling for the purchase of 36 Constellations. The first 12 were to be delivered to TWA prior to any other deliveries on the basis that TWA had provided a large amount of assistance in the original development of the basic design. Eighteen of these planes were to be delivered during the remainder of 1945, but, as we have already seen, this was not to be. Only eight new L–049s and two converted C–69s were actually turned over in 1945. The first made its delivery flight on November 14, 1945.

During the immediate postwar period, TWA, along with other major air carriers, went through a period of readjustment as it switched from wartime to peacetime operations. When it began to receive its first L–049s in November 1945, it had already decided to use them mainly on the overseas routes just awarded with a few Constellations to be used to start new services in the United States proper. This decision was not surprising in view of the L–049's range and speed. There was also no doubt in the minds of TWA's management that, because overseas traffic was likely to be quite limited, those carriers starting the earliest service stood the best chance of carving out a respectable slice of the market.

So TWA bent every effort to begin service as soon as possible. Part of the effort dealt with the need to create a brand-new organization in various foreign countries. It would have to handle sales, reservations, ticketing, dispatching, communications, maintenance, and all the other many items that go to make up any major airline's operations. Finding qualified people in these various countries only months after the end of the most devastating war in history was anything but easy. Consequently, it took TWA a number of months to reach the point where it considered itself ready to begin overseas operations. When it did, it did so by serving only a portion of the total number of overseas terminals awarded to it. Operations were gradually increased as personnel became more proficient and as more aircraft were delivered.

In the meantime, starting in November 1945, TWA crews began to train at Kansas City on the first few L–049s delivered plus one or two C–69s borrowed from Lockheed with ATC's blessings. But this time the training was not under the overall supervision of the military or, as had been the case with ICD's crews, with TWA itself deciding how to carry out the training. This time the CAA was on hand to make sure that this new, "hot" aircraft was properly understood by all who were to fly it.

Captain John (Jack) I. Schnaubelt of TWA, now retired, was among the first of TWA's pilots to transition into the brand new L–049s in November and December 1945. Schnaubelt was a check pilot for TWA, and all such supervisory personnel were in the initial transition classes. Schnaubelt had already been flying DC–3s, the Boeing B–307 Stratoliners, and the Douglas C–54 (DC–4), the latter for ICD.

Schnaubelt's memories of this transition period provide a revealing insight as to the reaction of airline pilots first coming into contact with the Constellation. At this time, pilots transitioning into the L–049 found themselves flying an airplane that was much heavier, faster, and more sophisticated. However, these factors were mitigated by the extremely honest flying characteristics of the Constellation, the assistance rendered by the hydraulic control boost system, and the fact that many of the aircraft systems were controlled only by the flight engineer stationed at a separate and distinct panel. For these reasons, two items stood out in this training program. First, the ground school was more complicated than any to date as far as aircraft systems were concerned. Second, pilots were able to transition into the L–049 in a surprisingly few hours. Despite the lack of simulators in those days, Schnaubelt remembers flying fewer than 10 hours prior to taking his rating flight with a CAA inspector.

One of the oddities that occurred during this period related to this very item, the CAA rating flight. The CAA was initially quite concerned about the reliability of the hydraulic control boost system, this despite the dual system that provided complete redundancy. This concern was actually not particularly surprising considering that this was the first commercial aircraft with all control surfaces power boosted. Combined with the fact that the L–049 was also the largest and fastest commercial airplane flown up to that time, the CAA's excessive caution can be more easily appreciated. At any rate, the CAA wanted reassurance that the L–049 could be flown and landed safely with the power control boost system completely inoperative. Thus, all pilots had to make an approach and landing without benefit of the boost system.

Schnaubelt remembers how these approaches and landings contributed some exciting moments to TWA pilots' rating rides. This was especially true because the L–049, with the boost system off, was expected to be flown by both pilots simultaneously. But during the rating ride, only one pilot actually had his hands and feet on the flight controls. For one person to operate the flight controls without boost required just about all the muscular strength an individual could muster, and, as a result, maneuvering was anything but highly accurate.

The result was some strange flying and much colorful language used above the Missouri plains during those fall days. Pilots would try to line themselves up with the runway a good distance away, because the Constellations became relatively unmaneuverable without the boost system. But even then they had problems, especially if they had to contend with a cross-wind at touchdown, and a number of hard landings resulted.

After a few weeks of this, the CAA realized that it really was an unnecessary procedure, not to mention potentially dangerous! So, with great sighs of relief, transitioning pilots were able to fly at all times with the control boost system in operation. In an interesting footnote, readers should know that no Constellation accident was ever attributed to a malfunction of the control boost system. This not only proved the basic reliability of the dual system but also the fact that the Constellation could indeed be flown with complete safety without the control boost system if such a measure became necessary.

INITIAL POSTWAR PERIOD: 1946-47

TWA's initial Constellation deliveries from Lockheed were grouped together in a period of only four months as befitted its position as initial customer and major motivator of the original project. There were 3 airplanes delivered in November 1945, 7 in December, 3 in January 1946, and a final 5 in February, for a total of 18. Two of these were converted C–69s, but all the rest were new L–049s. There were to be no more deliveries for seven whole months. However, it appears that at least two additional C–69s were loaned to TWA by the Air Force during this period to assist in the training program.

With this considerable fleet, TWA could now institute a large-scale training program followed in February 1946 by actual Connie service. On February 5, a weekly transatlantic service was inaugurated between New York and Paris with stops at Gander and Shannon. Ten days later, on February 14, a New York–Los Angeles transcontinental service was begun. This was a daily service with an optional fuel stop en route included in the schedule. The flight time was a full five hours shorter than the existing best schedule with Boeing Stratoliners.

Then, in April, with more crews and aircraft on hand, TWA felt ready to further expand their schedules. The New York–Paris flight became a daily affair. Two daily New York–Chicago flights were added. In the following months, this service was continued until July 1946 when the crash of a TWA Constellation training flight at Reading, Pennsylvania triggered a CAA grounding of all Constellations (see Chapter 15). After modifications, the L–049 fleet was gradually returned to service beginning in mid-September. Simultaneously, Lockheed delivered three more L–049s that same month, as well as two L–49s and one converted C–69 in October. At this time also, the short-term loan of some unused C–69s from the Air Force was negotiated. These were used solely for training.

The Constellation grounding in mid-1946 naturally disrupted the entire program, and it took some time for things to get back to normal. Nevertheless, by this time, one flight to Paris each week continued on to Geneva.

The year was, to be sure, one of excitement for the airlines in general and TWA in particular. Certainly the Constellation contributed to a large part of this. After all, it was the first modern postwar transport flying. But overall, its impact on TWA's operations was minimal. Between the fact that relatively few were in service and the fact that all Constellations were grounded for a period, not many of TWA's passenger-miles were flown by the big, triple-tailed aircraft. Internationally, out of 22 transatlantic trips per week, only 4 were operated by L–049s.

Nevertheless, 1946 was the year that TWA reached the big time in a way that only a few years earlier no one could have foreseen. The Constellations played a crucial part in TWA's growth to that level of prominence.

In spring 1947, international service was up to five trips per week to Paris. Two of these continued to Geneva, then on to Rome, Athens, and Cairo. There was also one flight per week to Lisbon, Madrid, Rome, and Cairo. In June, TWA began seven flights across the ocean each week, including six to Paris, with one each originating in Washington, Philadelphia, and Chicago. Geneva and Rome were now served three times weekly, Cairo four times, Athens twice, and Jerusalem, a new stop, once. In 1947, TWA had 34 transatlantic flights per week, as compared with 22 in 1946.

In the United States there were 10 Constellation schedules daily. Five were between New York and the West Coast with two intermediate stops, one with no stops, plus three from the Midwest to the West Coast and one New York–Chicago. At this point, it is worth digressing to mention an interesting sidelight to these schedules.

Readers may remember that TWA had begun a nonstop transcontinental flight with an optional stop. But a few months later we see that five out of six of these flights made two scheduled stops, thus adding considerable overall flight time. One can theorize that all this was merely to ensure greater passenger loads. But the fact was that TWA's marketing people had come up with a curious reaction to the service. They felt that the nonstop flight was too long for passengers to go without stretching their legs. So, the longer nonstop services were generally frowned on. In retrospect, it is doubtful this was actually the case. In fact, putting in the extra stops diluted the tremendous speed advantage that the Connie had over contemporary aircraft of the 1946–47 era. Thus the negative effect of the marketing people can be seen. In later years, all the airlines were to put reciprocating transports on much longer nonstop schedules with excellent results.

During 1947, TWA, in spite of numerous financial setbacks, ordered 12 L–749s from Lockheed. In the meantime, they had also acquired an additional 4 L–049s for a fleet total of 28 Constellations. The fact that TWA was able to obtain quick delivery on the last four L–049s fabricated may indicate that these were originally started as aircraft for another airline that later canceled its order.

During this entire period of time, Jack Frye was the president of TWA. He had been appointed back in December 1934, and he remained in that position until he resigned in March 1947. His 13-year tenure was the longest of any TWA president during the period 1930–70. Frye, as a former line captain, certainly was attuned to the operational side of TWA's activities and was a big booster of the Constellation. He had been a major part of TWA's fast postwar growth. But by then, he and Hughes no longer saw eye to eye, and thus 1947 saw Frye's leave-taking. He was replaced shortly thereafter by Lamont T. Cohn, who together with two others had established the Northrop Aircraft Company years before. Thus, Cohn was certainly experienced in aviation management.

The 1946–47 period was one of trailblazing and innovation for TWA. It saw the introduction of a new, complex airplane; the initiation of overseas service; and, in general, the transformation of TWA into a major international airline. As part of this overall growth, domestic schedules grew considerably, making TWA more of a factor as an east–west trunk carrier.

A word of explanation is probably in order at this point regarding the relative importance of Constellations used domestically versus internationally. In terms of scheduled flights and number of passengers, domestic operations were about twelve times bigger than international services. But it should be remembered that international flights operated over far longer distances. Therefore, in terms of passenger-miles, domestic services were only about five times as large. Looked at in that light, international flights assumed a far greater importance. It should also be remembered that TWA always made a strenuous effort to have their international passengers travel to and from their U.S. gateways via domestic TWA flights.

GROWTH AND CONSOLIDATION: 1948-49

The new L-749s ordered in 1947 began arriving in March 1948, and all 12 were received by July. With these airplanes on hand, TWA could now expand their horizons a bit further. Not only did they constitute an expansion of their total Connie fleet, but they had additional capabilities over the L-049s. In short, with a L-749, an operator could either stretch the range while carrying the same payload or increase the payload while maintaining the same range as the L-049. The new L-749s were all assigned to transatlantic operations, which permitted eight L-049s to be switched to domestic operations to augment the Connies already assigned there.

With this fleet, TWA now began flying 24 transatlantic Connie flights weekly out of 44 total during July. Paris was served eight times per week, Rome five times, and Cairo four.

By October, the weekly total flown by Connies had risen again to 30, one of which was an all-sleeper, luxury flight to Paris that skipped the Shannon fuel stop in both directions. This latter must have been in direct response to the similar flight operated by Air France since 1947.

In summer 1948, there were 16 domestic Connie flights, but this increased to 18 in October. Constellation service was inaugurated to such cities as Washington, Dayton, Philadelphia, Pittsburgh, and Albuquerque. It should also be noted that TWA had picked up a used converted C-69 returned by the Air Force in October and another in November. Both of these had been originally delivered to the Air Force just prior to the end of hostilities in Europe, and thus were probably very low-time airplanes.

The reader may have noticed that there were actually more domestic Connie flights in 1947 than in 1948. This may well have been because TWA elected to shift more Connies to the International Division during early 1948 due to an expected increase in revenue traffic. Furthermore, by 1948, transatlantic competition had quickened with more operators, some of which were offering Constellation or Douglas DC-6 schedules.

At this time, it should be explained that TWA's fleet of Connies was by no means the only equipment on the transatlantic or transcontinental flights. TWA had a large fleet of DC-4 Skymasters as well as five prewar Boeing Stratoliners. The latter were used in the United States exclusively, while the DC-4s flew both domestically and abroad. It is interesting to note that up to this time (October 1948) TWA had limited the Connies to operating as far east as Cairo and Jerusalem. The route to India used only DC-4s. This certainly was not because of any operating limitations of the Connies. Rather, the writer believes that TWA used the payload capabilities and over-the-weather comfort of the Connies where the demand was much greater, namely, across the Atlantic and within Europe.

Unfortunately, 1948 was a very poor year for TWA. In June, Cohn resigned after only some 13 months in office. His departure may have been hastened by the fact that TWA lost $5 million in the second quarter, which in turn may have precipitated a clash between Cohn and Hughes. A four-man group temporarily replaced Cohn and, by the end of the year, higher traffic and revenue totals combined with reduced costs improved the picture for the company.

The serious financial losses of 1948 may be explained partly by the lack of growth in the industry as a whole. TWA was obviously gearing up for some real expansion as shown by the delivery of 12 L–749s during the year. This is indicated by the increase of transatlantic Connie service as compared with 1947. But the statistics on passenger-miles show that in 1948 traffic as a whole was almost identical to 1947. The long-awaited boom did not materialize; as a result, TWA suffered.

In January 1949, Ralph S. Damon was elected president of TWA. Damon had a solid aviation background and had been president of American Airlines for the previous six years. The following month TWA began their first Sky Coach flights, a move that was to prove highly successful. The Constellation fleet flew approximately the same frequency in 1949 as in 1948. However, the three weekly flights to India used Constellations for the first time.

The year saw both competition and traffic grow, so much so that 20 Model L–749A Constellations were ordered. It also saw the company post a healthy profit at year-end.

This period, 1948–49, also saw a subtle but encouraging change in passenger attitudes. Flying was becoming more routine, especially among tourists, and the domestic Sky Coach fares made the decision to fly easier. Flying commercially was not something people did automatically, but its acceptance was visibly growing.

TRAFFIC JUMPS: 1950-52

TWA began the new decade with a real need for additional equipment. In fact, the summer traffic forecast was such that the order for L–749As was increased by 5 to 25 aircraft. Of this number, 18 were received during 1950, with the balance coming in 1951. Six of these L–749As were received in time to augment the fleet during that summer.

In May 1950, the weekly frequency across the Atlantic increased to 32 Connie flights and 6 DC–4 flights. By November, when additional L–749As were available, this had grown again to 44 flights per week. For the first time all transatlantic flights were with Constellations.

In July 1950, the CAB approved the purchase of a major transatlantic competitor, American Overseas Airlines, by Pan Am. However, as part of the transaction, TWA was awarded London and Frankfurt as new destinations. Service to these cities, along with Milan, Italy, was initiated during the year and was another step in TWA's growing overseas market.

By the end of the year, TWA boasted a fleet of 55 Constellations, the largest fleet of one model of aircraft in the world. But it wasn't enough. Accordingly, at the end of the year, TWA ordered 10 L–1049 Super Constellations.

During the year, TWA also introduced Constellations on transcontinental Sky Coach service, replacing older equipment. In addition, all Constellations were restyled with standardized interiors.

An important year for TWA was 1951. With the last 7 of its L–749A order having arrived by June, the Constellation fleet now numbered 66 aircraft, a truly impressive total. This fleet expansion was clearly reflected in its scheduling. During the busy summer months, there were 58 weekly flights across the Atlantic and 26 daily flights across the United States.

The L–749A's longer range permitted TWA to initiate a nonstop berth/sleeper service New York–Paris and New York–London with two round-trips to each city each week. This service was again no doubt partly a direct response to the similar operation started by Air France.

Domestically, TWA began a low-fare Sky Coach service New York–Los Angeles with two daily flights via Chicago and two via St. Louis. The transcontinental fare was only $99 one-way, and the service was received very favorably by the traveling public.

The year 1951 was one of prosperity for TWA with a year-end net income of $8 million. This was in spite of a disastrous flood of its major overhaul base in Fairfax, Missouri, in July, which resulted in a $6 million loss.

In 1952, TWA found that it needed to use its fleet of 66 Constellations to the utmost to compete successfully. Overseas the airline scheduled 64 flights a week, a new high, and domestically there were 32 transcontinental flights each day. This, of course, kept the fleet more than a little busy.

Over the Atlantic, new, low-fare, Sky Tourist flights were introduced with 28 flights per week. This constituted 44 percent of the total TWA transatlantic service. Domestically, there were 10 Sky Coach transcontinental flights or 31 percent of the total company service. Low-cost, no-frills flights were quickly becoming very popular and highly profitable.

One of the factors that TWA had to contend with was the introduction of the Douglas DC–6B. First flown in passenger service in April 1951, by 1952 a number of both domestic and foreign airlines were operating this aircraft. The DC–6B's cruising speed was somewhat higher than the L–749/749A models, and thus the aircraft enjoyed a certain amount of competitive advantage, which TWA had to work hard to overcome. One answer that was forthcoming in 1952 was the introduction of 10 L–1049s, all of which were delivered between May and September. In September, they were placed on one-stop service, New York–Los Angeles and in November, one-stop service, New York–San Francisco. None of the L–1049s operated across the Atlantic at this time, probably because their range was such as to make their use not operationally desirable.

A STEADY EXPANSION: 1953-54

For 1953, TWA had their entire complement of L–1049s on hand. These were used exclusively on U.S. coast-to-coast services protecting two daily New York–Los Angeles round-trips and one daily New York–San Francisco round-trip all with one stop. However, in October, one of the Los Angeles–New York round-trips was scheduled nonstop.

When TWA acquired their 10 L–1049s, they were a trifle premature. The L–1049 was the initial model of the Super Constellation and, as described in an earlier chapter (Chapter 7), constituted only the first of two steps leading to the true Super Constellation design. The L–1049 had a maximum gross weight of 120,000 pounds, a considerable improvement over the 107,000 pounds of the L–749A model. But, if TWA could have waited 13 months to receive delivery, it could have had L–1049C models, with a gross weight of 133,000 pounds, higher cruising speed, and 5,500 pounds more fuel capacity than the L–1049. It might almost have paid off for TWA if, in 1950, instead of ordering the 10 L–1049s they had ordered instead 5 or 6 L–749As. These could have been delivered rather quickly; there would have been more capacity available sooner, and TWA could then have ordered L–1049Cs for 1954 delivery. The latter aircraft would have prevented TWA from experiencing a competitive disadvantage as other airlines put Douglas DC–7 and 7B models as well as Lockheed L–1049C, D, and E models in service.

At any rate, in October TWA placed an order for 12 Super G Constellations. This was in addition to a previous order of 8, thus making a total of 20. The ever-increasing competition caused TWA to once more add service. In the summer of 1953 transatlantic service was up to 76 flights per week, with some days having 6 flights each way. Over half the flights, 42, were Sky Tourist coach service.

Another 16 were sleeper flights, 6 of which were scheduled eastbound nonstop to either Paris or London. Domestically, there were 42 daily transcontinental flights with 22 of these being Sky Coach.

The year 1954 could be said to be simply more of the same, except that in the case of TWA this was obviously more success. Passenger increases, in general, were substantial although not spectacular. With competing airlines continuing to add flights, the company felt it had little choice but to do the same. This in spite of the fact that its Constellation fleet did not grow during the year.

Accordingly, for the busy summer months, TWA scheduled a new high of 84 weekly flights over the North Atlantic. Of these, 60 were Sky Coach, 18 were sleeper flights, and a mere 6 were all first-class flights.

Domestically, there were 46 daily coast-to-coast flights. Of these, 26 were Sky Coach and 8 were L–1049 Super Constellation flights. One westbound New York–Los Angeles flight and one each eastbound Los Angeles–New York and San Francisco–New York were operated nonstop with L–1049 equipment.

These increased frequencies were achieved with the same size fleet by greater utilization. One reason this became possible can probably be attributed to the increase in the TBO (time between overhauls) of the aircraft engines. On the L–049s, the TBO was running around 600 hours initially. But operating and maintenance experience gradually increased the interval on all the Constellations until it eventually was well over 1,000 hours.

The year was a very profitable one for TWA, with a net income of over $10 million, more than double the figure for 1953. It was also the 17th consecutive year in which traffic and revenues increased over the previous year.

THE SUPER G CONSTELLATION AND MORE GROWTH: 1955–56

The year 1955 was important for TWA in general and its marketing department in particular. This was the year of the Super G Constellation. Ordered almost a year and half previously, in March they began arriving from Burbank. The first 19 Super G's were all delivered by June, and all were initially used on domestic routes. It was not until late in the year that the Super G's began crossing the Atlantic. Specific information explaining why the delay in using the Super G's on the overseas routes was not available, but two reasons do come to mind. With the Super G's, TWA was using, for the first time Turbo-Compound engines. It may well have been that they felt somewhat more secure in flying the Super G's over land and generally near emergency airfields until a certain amount of operating and maintenance experience had been accumulated. In addition, there is the irrefutable fact that 1955 overseas passengers on TWA constituted only 6 percent of all passengers carried, and thus the Super G's were first used where the greatest potential lay.

In that year, TWA scheduled 42 daily domestic coast-to-coast flights using Constellations. There were only three round-trip nonstops using the Super G and another six transcontinental flights using Super G equipment too. Twenty-nine of the 42 daily flights were Sky Tourist, attesting to the increasing popularity of the economy service.

Over the Atlantic service was also increased once again with the L–749s and L–749As providing 94 flights per week, of which 64 were Sky Tourist.

The year showed a 13 percent increase in passengers and a 65.2 percent load factor. Traffic projections were such that TWA ordered 25 L–1649A Super Constellations for delivery in 1957. However, this was also the year when eight Boeing 707s were ordered, clearly denoting the beginning of the end for propeller aircraft.

The year 1956 was the time of the Super G Constellation, as delivery of all 28 was completed. TWA cranked up its marketing and publicity staffs to be able to sell the additional seating capacity represented by the Super G fleet. The scheduled seat-miles were increased by a substantial 16 percent for 1956, but the passenger-miles went up by only 10 percent.

In that summer, TWA scheduled 56 coast-to-coast flights daily, of which one westbound and two eastbound were nonstop. These three, plus nine others, were all Super G flights. Overseas there were now 100 flights per week with 28 or 4 per day being Super G flights. Because overseas operations carried only about 6 percent of all passengers carried on the system, it was only natural that the majority of the new Super G's were being employed domestically. Not only did TWA need the seating capacity there, but the glamour represented by the Super G's served to compete with the DC–7's and DC–7B's of other airlines.

The year showed another healthy increase in both passengers carried and passenger-miles, but the load factor sank about 3 percent, which was probably a reflection of the appreciable increase in seat-miles resulting from the addition of the Super G fleet.

There was one other significant event that year. In January, Ralph Damen, president of TWA, died after having been at the helm of TWA for seven important years. His stay in office was the longest to date except for that of Jack Frye. He shepherded TWA through a growing and demanding period, and he managed to do this and still get along with Howard Hughes, no mean achievement. The position remained vacant for almost 12 months thereafter.

TWA 985 ROME TO NEW YORK

Before this historical narrative is continued, let us take a break to relive a flight the author took on TWA in summer 1956.

In August, TWA's summer international schedule carried a westbound flight identified as Flight 985. Operating between Rome and New York, TWA 985 followed a circuitous routing that included six stops en route. This flight was the only such flight between Italy and the United States that followed such a southerly routing and made so many stops. The routing resulted in better flying weather than was generally found farther north in Europe. The equipment assigned to this flight was a reliable L–749A Connie.

TWA 985 is scheduled to make en route stops at Tunis, Tunisia; Algiers, Algeria; Madrid, Spain; Lisbon, Portugal; Santa Maria, Azores; and Gander, Newfoundland. Because the flight is to leave Rome's Ciampino Airport at 7:30 A.M., we must leave the hotel very early. At the appointed hour we taxi from the ramp. Ciampino Airport is quiet at that time, and very shortly we lift off. The flight turns to a southwesterly heading, and as we climb out, flies near the famous beach at Anzio, which was the scene of a mighty battle in World War II.

The weather is sunny and clear, and visibility over the Mediterranean is phenomenal. About 30 minutes out of Rome, passengers can see two land masses, one on either side of the plane. On our right is the island of Sardinia, and on our left is Sicily. Although each is about 75 miles away, they are dimly visible from our altitude.

Some 90 minutes after take-off we begin our let-down, and soon we cross the Tunisian coast. We are very close to the coastal city of Bizerte, which in World War II was the scene of bitter fighting as Hitler's Afrika Corps was decimated. Large amounts of war matériel are still strewn over large areas of North Africa, but we cannot see any from the aircraft.

In a few minutes the city of Tunis becomes visible in front of us, buildings brilliantly white in the sun. We line up with the runway, and then the Connie touches down with a hard jolt. The gentleman sitting next to me turns, and with a strangely embarrassed expression offers the opinion that "turbulence" must have caused the rough landing. More likely the first officer was flying the aircraft and slightly misjudged the sink rate. Later I am amused to learn that our seat companion (who disembarked at Tunis), is TWA's Tunis station manager returning to his duty station. No wonder he appeared embarrassed!

Through passengers are permitted to disembark, and as we step through the aircraft's doorway, a wave of dry heat hits me. As I walk toward the terminal, I notice a large number of veiled Arab women standing behind the boundary fence.

Suddenly the air is filled with a weird, keening sound. It comes from these women, and it is so strange that my skin prickles. Later I discover that the singing is a form of Arab greeting for a Tunisian gentleman who arrived on this flight.

After 35 minutes on the ground, we depart Tunis; our next stop is Algiers, almost directly due west. Under a clear sky, TWA 985 climbs to 10,500 feet over the North African coast. At this altitude the ground is clearly visible, and our path over the Atlas Mountains reveals a darkly forbidding landscape. The terrain is not merely mountainous but appears broken up and strewn with boulders, certainly at variance with the picture one visualizes watching and hearing the operetta *The Desert Song*!

The Tunis–Algiers leg is scheduled for slightly less than two hours, and right on schedule we begin to let down. As we approach our destination, we glance out the window and are startled to see that we have picked up a French Air Force fighter escort. In 1956 the Algerian uprising is at its peak, and evidently the French are taking no chances. The only question in our minds is: Do they think we might be a terrorist aircraft, or are they protecting us? Either way, it is an uncomfortable feeling!

The feeling of concern becomes even more acute after we land at Algiers's Maison Blanche Airport. The aprons are surrounded by barbed wire, armed sentries are visible everywhere, and the transient passengers are unceremoniously hustled into a small lounge and told rather pointedly not to wander! Somehow we find it difficult to believe any of them would want to. Our stay is mercifully short, and soon we are once more aboard our Connie.

After take-off we cross the Algerian coast almost immediately, and once more we are flying over the Mediterranean, this time in a northwesterly direction. About 1 hour, 45 minutes after take-off we reach the Spanish coast, crossing it near the famous old city of Valencia. Below us Spain looks brown and dry. Soon we are approaching Madrid at a lower altitude. The entire city looks brown, hot, and very still. Under the wing I catch a glimpse of a huge circular sports arena, no doubt used for the bullfights. Then we are down, and as we walk to the terminal, Madrid's midsummer heat really makes itself felt.

The terminal also is very hot, and we all mill about restlessly, waiting to reboard and sit in air-conditioned comfort. But after some 20 minutes an impersonal voice informs us over the PA system that TWA 985 will be delayed some 45 minutes. Later I learn that the delay is caused by a cylinder on number 2 engine developing only partial power.

Eventually, we all file back aboard and depart hot, stifling Madrid. The flight to Lisbon takes about an hour and a half, much of it over more dry, barren terrain.

But as we reach the vicinity of Lisbon, everything turns green and verdant. Our landing approach takes us over the city, and I can see large amounts of vegetation and wide boulevards filled with traffic. As we bank over the coast, and line up to land at Portela Airport, I reflect that nearby, in the Tagus River, Pan American used to land their Clippers in 1939. In those days, crossing the Atlantic as a passenger was a real adventure; now, some 17 years later, we take it all for granted.

It's almost six in the evening in Lisbon; the air is surprisingly cool and carries with it the salty tang of the Atlantic Ocean. Certainly quite a change from Madrid. I learn that a crew change takes place here, and I am able to strike up a conversation with one of the new crew members. He is a flight engineer, one of the two that will be carried from here to New York. He tells me that number 2 engine is still not functioning properly and an additional hour's delay will be required while further repairs are attempted.

He also mentions that the captain has been considering calling up the spare Connie that TWA keeps in Paris. However, the captain finally decides to carry on to the Azores, a flight of some 900 miles and almost four hours flying time, all of it over water. So, as the sun begins to set, we once again thunder down the runway.

Almost due west we climb out over the Atlantic, the weather still clear and perfect. The flight to Santa Maria in the Azores is smooth and uneventful, and late in the evening we touch down on that lonely, volcanic island. The night is cool and quiet, and we are beginning to feel the accumulated fatigue of some 17 hours since leaving Rome. Unfortunately, here I discover that our old friend number 2 engine is still not right in the head. Once again I seek out my new acquaintance, the flight engineer. He somewhat gleefully informs me that the captain has decided that until and unless number 2 performs properly, he is not about to take off and attempt the long, lonely transatlantic crossing. So for some two and a half hours our rather forlorn group wanders disconsolately around the tiny terminal at Santa Maria.

Outside, the maintenance crew, working under floodlights, changes the spark plugs and ignition harness on number 2 in a further attempt to bring the engine to full power. As the work is finally completed, the flight engineer goes aboard to test our recalcitrant Curtiss-Wright. The rest of the crew gather nearby to witness the test. Noticing what is happening, some of us passengers drift outside and stand around in the night air watching. There is very little formality at Santa Maria, and we are the only flight on the ramp.

We are rewarded with the thundering roar and flaming exhaust of a full-power run-up at night, a sight not generally witnessed by passengers at close range. Evidently the results are reassuring to our captain, because in short order we are rounded up and hustled aboard. Now operating some 3.5 hours late, the crew fires up the four big Curtiss-Wrights. As we taxi away from the terminal, the landing lights come on. Sitting just over the wing, I am treated to the sight of a night take-off performed by a smooth, professional, and highly skilled crew. The fully laden Connie rumbles down the taxi strip and onto the run-up pad. Quickly all the checks are performed, and then the Connie is slowly taxied onto the runway and lined up. There is a moment of hesitation, then as the aircraft is held in place with brakes, the throttles are advanced. The power comes on, and we can clearly see long exhaust flames coming from the engines. As some two-thirds of maximum power is reached, the brakes are released and the Connie starts down the runway. Quickly and smoothly more power is applied, and within a very few seconds we are accelerating at maximum take-off power, the Curtiss-Wright 3350s each putting out a full 2,500 horsepower. Faster and faster we roll, the noise of the engines dominating everything. The exhausts are clearly visible, their long bluish-red flames the only visible proof of the power being generated. Some 40 seconds after brake release, we lift off the runway.

Almost immediately, the rumble of the landing gear being raised can be heard. Then the landing lights are turned off, and engine noise lowers as the first power reduction is made. The long overwater leg to Gander has begun.

Seventeen hundred miles over the North Atlantic, which tonight will take seven hours, seven minutes to cover. The weather is still good, and we all try to make ourselves comfortable and sleep the night away. The extra flight engineer sits quietly in a window seat over the left wing. For the next seven hours, or at least until sunrise, he periodically checks the color of the exhaust from number 2 engine. Evidently, the captain is taking no chances.

When I wake up the next morning, it is already light. Below us there is a solid, flat undercast that stretches endlessly to the west. I can tell we are beginning our let-down into Gander, and as we skim lower we suddenly enter the clouds. The crew makes an ILS approach to Gander, and as we break out of the overcast at a low altitude, I can see that we are low over dark green forests. Then, shortly, we touch down at Gander.

As I disembark to wait for the aircraft to be refueled, I see that three other transports are on the ground. We all walk into the terminal feeling generally grubby and tired. But only a few minutes pass, and we are called to reboard our flight. It becomes rather obvious that the crew is endeavoring to expedite the departure. As soon as we are aboard the engines are started and we quickly taxi out to the runway. We can see in front of us the other three aircraft taxiing also. Then, in what appears to be very short intervals, all four take off and quickly disappear into the rapidly lowering overcast.

Later I learn from the crew the reason these four commercial transports departed Gander in a manner vaguely reminiscent of a military fighter scramble. Gander Airport has been predicted to close down to commercial traffic for a considerably long period of time because of the approaching low ceiling. As a result, many aircraft had diverted to other Canadian airports, the majority to a Royal Canadian Air Force base at Moncton. Unfortunately, Moncton does not have adequate refueling facilities to handle a number of large, thirsty aircraft. As a result, aircraft stopping there are being subjected to long delays. Our captain decided to gamble on going into Gander and departing again before the weather closed the field down. TWA 985 is actually the last aircraft in and out of Gander the rest of the day.

As we climb out from Gander through the woolly, clammy cloud, the Connie quivers and sways, but turbulence is surprisingly light. At our cruising altitude we are clear of the undercast and fly in clear air. As we fly southwest the undercast gradually breaks up. It's almost 1,150 miles to New York, just about a five-hour flight.

Our routing takes us over Nova Scotia, which we can see quite clearly, despite some haze. Then again over water to a landfall not far from Cape Cod. I receive an invitation to visit the cockpit, which I gratefully accept. Standing in the rather crowded cockpit, with a radio headset on, I hear another TWA flight, also New York-bound, making a position report. The captain turns to me and suggest I look through one of the left side windows straight up. I manage to comply, and there some 4,000 feet above us, I see another Connie. The Captain tells me we're looking at the flight that just reported in. Togetherness at 20,000 feet over the Atlantic!

TWA 985 crosses the coastline and begins a gradual descent over Rhode Island and Connecticut. Although the sky is clear of clouds, the air is very hazy, and summer thermals bounce us around. Some of the passengers become ill from the uninterrupted turbulence. Luckily, I seem to be immune to it! Soon we are flying over Long Island at a low altitude. I watch the flaps come down and can feel the landing gear being lowered.

Slowly the aircraft turns over Long Island Sound in the approach pattern to New York International (later known as John F. Kennedy Airport). The flaps are extended still further, and the engine noise increases as the propellers are put into low pitch. We turn onto our final approach, and the flaps come out fully. Engine noise now dies down. The Connie pitches and sways over the end of the runway, bounces once gently in the hot updrafts, and settles to the runway. The props go into reverse, the engines roar briefly, and we are trundling along and turning off onto the taxiway.

TWA Flight 985 has completed its journey of some 5,270 miles. The trip, originally scheduled to be completed in some 28.5 hours, actually took 32 hours. It's been tiring and long. Despite what the marketing people would have you believe, an economy seat is not designed for sitting in for over 30 consecutive hours!.

We have just flown over parts of three continents, one ocean, a large sea, and a few bays for good measure. We've seen seven countries and a large number of islands. It's been a memorable trip, made more so by having flown it in the truly beautiful, graceful bird they call Connie!

This, then, is what it was like flying on TWA over a large chunk of Earth. Mention has been made previously of the overall reliability of all the Constellation models. One example of Connie reliability was TWA's Far East route from New York to Colombo, Ceylon. Operated during the late 1950s with Model L–749A Connies, this was one of the longer routes in existence serviced by a single through aircraft. The route originated in New York and made en route stops at Paris, Geneva, Rome, Cairo, Basra (Iraq). and Colombo. A total of seven intermediate stops and 8,760 statute miles!

Of the seven stops, only one lasted 1 hour and the remainder were 30–45 minutes long. The schedule called for a total trip time, including stops, of 44-1/4 hours. Almost two days of virtually nonstop flying! The aircraft had a turn-around layover of 17 hours, which permitted considerable maintenance to be performed if necessary. The aircraft then retraced its steps, but with added stops at Athens, Milan, and usually Gander. The return schedule called for a total time of 52 hours; the approximately 8 hours of additional time was required by a combination of the three added stops and the prevailing westerly winds.

BUSINESS FAILURES AND OPERATIONAL TRIUMPHS: 1957-58

At the beginning of 1957, Carter L. Burgess became the new TWA president. The year was to be a busy one for TWA. In 1957, the long-awaited L–1649A began to enter service. Called the Jetstream by TWA, the aircraft was almost a year behind its competitor, the Douglas DC–7C. This, coupled with the imminent advent of commercial turbojets in late 1958, cut the useful life of the L–1649As to a fraction of what might have been expected. But they were operated as first-line aircraft, and they performed nobly.

During the year, TWA once again increased their flight frequencies. Domestically, the total available seat-miles went up by some 15 percent with a number of L–749/749As displaced from the International Division, augmenting the domestic fleet. There were also four nonstop daily flights coast-to-coast using the new Jetstreams. Overseas, the weekly flight total went up slightly to 110. The big change was in having 52 of those flights operated with L–1649As with another 26 having Super G equipment.

The year saw the inauguration of the polar route from the West Coast to London with many of the flights making the trip nonstop. All in all, TWA had reason to feel satisfied with what it achieved during 1957, but at the end of the year, Burgess suddenly resigned, and it was a widely held opinion that once again Hughes and his ways were responsible.

In 1958, TWA was to experience a number of significant trends. For one thing, this was the last year in which their entire fleet was made up of propeller aircraft. For another, business leveled off that year for the first time since 1946. This was no doubt due in part to the U.S. economy, but may also have been a reflection of the constantly increasing competition, both domestically and abroad. Regardless of the reason for the slump, TWA forecasted it correctly (at least domestically), and reduced their available seat-miles slightly while the passenger-miles climbed slightly.

Unfortunately, the same did not hold true overseas. The seat-miles were increased by a whopping 23 percent, whereas the passenger-miles rose only 7 percent. In 1958, the overseas seat-miles made up 19 percent of the system total, and thus the International Division did not do too well. However, readers should keep in mind that much of the additional overseas capacity was generated by replacing all the L–749/749As with Super Constellations, which had a greater capacity. Thus the operating costs did not, in fact, increase anywhere near as much as the 23 percent additional seat-miles might lead one to believe.

In 1958, the overseas flights went from 110 to 128, with 72 operated by the new L–1649As and 20 by Super G's. The remaining 36 flights were operated with L–1049s, the first time these aircraft were ever used overseas. The L–1049s had the least range of any Super Constellation, and all their schedules (New York–Paris, New York–London) had at least one fuel stop. But in their all-economy configuration, they were impressive money-makers.

In the continental United States, no L–1049s were used. The Jetstreams and Super G's replaced them. Now there were 12 nonstop coast-to-coast flights, a new high.

In this same year, TWA acquired or leased a total of eight Super H Constellations. The first was actually leased in December 1957, with two more leased in January 1958 and one in February. Four Super H's were received from Lockheed in April/May.

This fleet was to be used primarily for all-cargo services, but because they were quickly convertible to an all-passenger configuration, TWA was also able to use the big Super H's for charter operations. This they did for typical charters as well as for military contracts. In 1959, a once-a-week transatlantic cargo flight was operated with Super Hs between New York and Rome, with en route stops. This flight replaced one formerly flown with Douglas C–54s.

Finally, in July 1958, Charles S. Thomas was elected president of TWA after a seven-month period in which TWA had no CEO.

THE LAST VICTORY: 1959-60

The year 1959 was significant for both TWA and the Constellation. During the year, turbojets were introduced on both domestic and international routes. It spelled the beginning of the end for the reciprocating transport.

Overseas, the jets did not begin operating until late in the year, and the very busy summer months over the Atlantic saw a schedule of 90 flights per week, all operated with L–1649As. Included in this number were two round-trips between the West Coast and Europe via the polar route, two nonstop roundtrips each New York–Madrid and New York–Lisbon, and two eastbound nonstop flights New York–Rome. In addition, of course, all other flights were nonstop between the United States and London/Paris/ Frankfurt. The number of flights overseas was down from the 1958 peak, and the available seat-miles reflected this by dropping some 18 percent, the first time this happened since 1946. However, because the passenger/miles dropped only 10 percent, the net effect was to increase the overseas load factor from the 54.2 percent in 1958 to 59.2 percent.

In the United States, the glamour of nonstop coast-to-coast flights was all taken over by jets. But the Constellations were still the backbone of the fleet. For the year, the load factor rose to an impressive 70.5 percent, the highest since 1953. The result of all this was that for 1959, TWA had a net earnings of $9.4 million, the second-best year in their history.

Late in the year, the first L–049s were sold off, a true indication of things to come.

THE CONNIES ARE DOWNGRADED: 1960-61

The year 1960 began not only a new decade but also a new era for TWA. During the year, jets began making real inroads in the schedules formerly handled by the Constellations. As more jets entered service, the Constellations were either downgraded or grounded. Thus schedules formerly operated with Martin 404s were taken over by L–049 or L–749 equipment, with L–1049 and L–1049G aircraft taking over schedules formerly using the standard Constellations. The net result was that of larger aircraft being used on schedules having numerous stops and relatively short legs. It also had the effect of making more seats available for small and medium-sized cities as larger equipment filtered downward to multi-stop schedules.

The speed with which TWA converted from an all-propeller to an all-jet fleet is possibly best dramatized by noting that early in 1960, the company had 28 jet transports on hand, whereas by 1964, the number had quadrupled to 104. Thus 1960 was the last year that Constellations flew the North Atlantic. Out of 88 overseas flights, only 20 (23 percent) were propeller aircraft, all operating with L–1649As. In addition, the overseas cargo service was expanded to six weekly flights, all using the Super Hs.

Domestically, all of the long-haul, nonstop flights used jet equipment. One result of this was that the 10 L–1049s, the first Super Constellations, were grounded and within months many had been sold or leased. It was the beginning of the end for the Constellations. Further contributing to the demise of the Constellations was the fact that for 1960 the revenue passenger-miles were down, so there was no real need to use any available surplus Constellations.

With the L–1649A fleet no longer being fully utilized, six of the aircraft were converted to freighter configuration during the year. In the first few months of 1961, an additional batch of six was also converted to all-cargo interiors.

By 1961, the Constellation fleet had been downgraded further. No Constellations were operated overseas, except for the L–1649As converted to freighters. In the United States the Martin 404s were all retired and replaced by L–749s and Super G's. The few L–1649A Jetstreams still in service were used on the Miami–Kansas City run with three intermediate stops! Truly a sad ending for the finest, longest-range reciprocating transport ever built. Other converted Jetstreams operated four daily cargo flights between New York and the West Coast. Overseas, this was the last year that Constellations carried passengers. A Jetstream made the last passenger flight on October 28.

During the year, the lease on the three remaining Super H Constellations was terminated, the fourth aircraft having crashed in late 1959. The four owned Super H's were sold or leased during 1961–62. They were replaced by the previously converted L–1649As.

THE END OF THE CONSTELLATIONS: 1962–67

In 1962, TWA sold off the last 25 of the L–049 fleet. This was also the last year the L–1649As were used domestically on passenger flights. The

Constellation schedules shrank still further, although there were now 12 weekly cargo flights between New York and Rome with intermediate stops.

In 1963, the last Jetstream flew a cargo run over the Atlantic. The next year, 1964, saw the Super G's beginning to be disposed of, leaving only the L–749/749As in passenger service. The last Super G's were gone by the winter of 1966–67.

Even during this period of final decline and eclipse, the fast-shrinking Constellation fleet was nevertheless paying its way. For example, in the summer of 1966, there were still some 58 daily Constellation flights scheduled. They were generally short-length trips, such as New York–Louisville, Detroit–St. Louis, Boston–Kansas City (with eight intermediate stops), and Philadelphia–Kansas City.

But the end was rapidly approaching. The extreme costs incurred in maintaining power plants and airframes for which spare parts were no longer available must have been an important factor.

The last few cargo L–1649As left the inventory in early 1967. The very last Constellation passenger flight took place on April 6, 1967, when a L–749A flew New York–St. Louis with en route stops at Philadelphia, Pittsburgh, Columbus, and Louisville. It was an emotional, sentimental journey with a number of VIPs aboard. A few weeks later, on May 11, a cargo L–1649A made the last Constellation flight for TWA.

An era lasting some 21 years had come to an end. The familiar and somehow reassuring triple-tailed, dolphin-shaped, Roman-nosed planes would no longer be seen at airports on the TWA system stretching halfway around the world.

To make an overall judgment as to specifically what influence the Constellation had on TWA's fortunes during this period is far from easy. There obviously were a number of factors affecting the airline at any specific moment. Among these were:

1. The current state of the economy.
2. The level of competition by other airlines, as well as other forms of transportation, that is, passenger ships.
3. How the public perceived commercial flying, especially in terms of safety.
4. The quality of TWA's management.
5. The kinds of decisions made by Howard Hughes.
6. The state of the world in terms of international strains and local wars.

In retrospect, it appears that the Constellation influenced the fortunes of TWA in two major ways. Initially, when the Connies were a brand-new experience to the public, they constituted a dramatic symbol of advanced technology and an improved means of transportation. Newspaper accounts of the various record-setting flights of Constellations provided more free publicity to TWA than their marketing department could have ever hoped to achieve. This in spite of the fact that in the early years, 1946–48, the total seat-miles provided by the Constellation fleet constituted only a fraction of TWA's total operation. But during this period, the Constellation services served to spread the word about their comfort and speed and to some extent whetted the appetite of the American traveling public.

Beginning in 1949, the combination of the expanded Constellation fleet and the increased ridership resulted in these aircraft becoming ever more important to TWA. By 1950, all the international services were operated with Constellations, and the Douglas DC–4s were used only sparingly on domestic routes. By 1953, the last of 70 Douglas DC–3s had been replaced with 40 Martin 404s plus some 12 previously leased Martin 202s. This meant that for the decade of the 1950s, the majority of TWA's revenue passenger-miles were generated by the constantly growing Constellation fleet, which nearly tripled from 55 aircraft in 1950 to 146 in 1959.

The Constellation, in the various TWA versions, can be said to have brought certain characteristics to the airline's operations. These would have to include:

1. A highly distinctive appearance.
2. An excellent safety record.
3. Operating costs as low or lower than competing transports.
4. A good maintenance record.
5. The ability to handle turbulent weather better than any other comparable aircraft.
6. Excellent short-field take-off and landing characteristics.
7. Adequate cruising speeds similar to competing transports.

With these characteristics to rely on, TWA was able to, at the very least, hold its own against competition, which grew continuously in the period 1946–61. During this period TWA's domestic ridership quintupled and the revenue passenger-miles grew almost sixfold. Internationally, the number of riders mushroomed by 1,100 percent and revenue passenger-miles kept pace by increasing 831 percent. There can be little doubt that the Constellation played a significant part in this period of phenomenal growth. TWA also had another advantage. By standardizing on the distinctive Constellation, it set up a connection in the public's mind that resulted in TWA and the Constellation often being thought of simultaneously and interchangeably. This particular factor was likely helpful in TWA's marketing efforts.

However, the writer believes there were two serious mistakes made by TWA in its acquisition program of the Constellation. The first took place at the end of 1950 when an order for 10 L–1049s was placed. TWA correctly judged they would need additional capacity within a short time. But in ordering the L–1049 they erred in two ways. First this aircraft was not available for some 18 months. If additional L–749As had been ordered instead, it is likely they could have been delivered much more quickly, particularly since Lockheed was delivering a batch of 25 to TWA in 1950–51. Thus the additional aircraft would have been available sooner and at a lower price. Second, the L–1049 was not a design particularly suited to TWA's routes because it did not have the range to either fly nonstop coast-to-coast or one-stop across the Atlantic.

By ordering more L–749As as an interim measure, TWA would then have been in a position to order L–1049Cs for mid-1953 delivery. They would have had long-range Super Constellations some 24 months earlier than when their Super G's were to eventually arrive. This two-year advance would have given TWA a tremendous advantage against domestic competitors awaiting deliveries of Douglas DC–7s and foreign competitors who received both Douglas and Lockheed transports.

The second mistake, which actually may have been partly induced by the first, relates to the delay in ordering the L–1649As. These were not ordered until 1955, at the same time as TWA ordered Boeing 707s. By that year, it was already obvious that the jet revolution was fast approaching. But it is reasonable to suppose that a large order for L–1649As by TWA a year earlier might well have decided Lockheed to go ahead with the project sooner. If these aircraft had been flying a full year earlier, TWA would have been in a much better competitive position, especially across the North Atlantic. The Jetstreams, instead of flying passengers for only some three years, could have flown effectively for four or five years. As it was, their productive life was phenomenally short.

CONCLUSION

Looking back over the period 1946–60, this author concluded that the Constellations and Super Constellations did indeed influence TWA's fortunes for the better. In that period, the airline grew almost without pause, with the international services growing almost twice as fast as the domestic. The Connie became synonymous with TWA and vice versa, and the Connie's shape and TWA logo developed into familiar sights to people all over the United States, Europe, North Africa, and the Middle East.

The Connie did the job it was meant to and in the process brought a measure of fame and fortune to TWA. But its full potential appears to have been missed. One might quickly point a finger at company management, but the real power and all the financial control rested with that shadowy figure, Howard Hughes. It is ironic that the one person who was the catalyst for the creation of the Constellation was not able to fully exploit its potential through the operation of its major customer, TWA.

13-1 A TWA L–049 Connie takes off! Landing gear is just coming up! (Lockheed Martin)

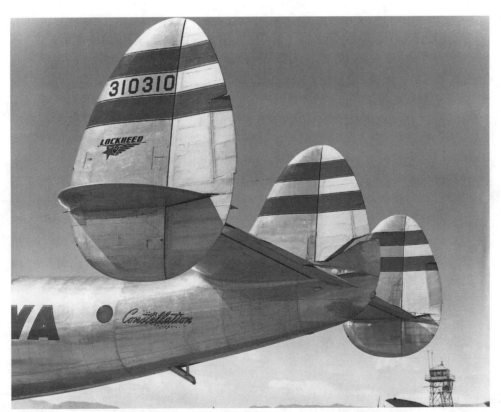
13-2 A view of the tail of a TWA L–049. Note that part of the rudder surfaces are covered with fabric rather than aluminum. (Lockheed Martin)

13-3 An internal view of a TWA Connie. (Lockheed Martin)

13-4 A TWA Connie SPEEDPAK being loaded with luggage. (Lockheed Martin)

13-5 A TWA Super Constellation, probably one of the early L–1049 models they purchased. (Lockheed Martin)

13-6 A close-up of the weather radar on a TWA Super G Connie. (Lockheed Martin)

13-7 A TWA L–1649A "Jetstream" flying in loose formation with a USN WV–2 AEW radar picket aircraft. (Lockheed Martin)

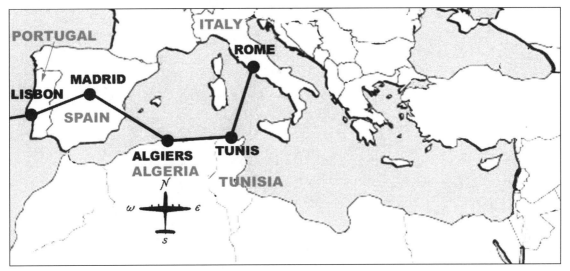

13-8 Chart showing the route of TWA 985, Rome to Lisbon, in the summer of 1956. (Luisada)

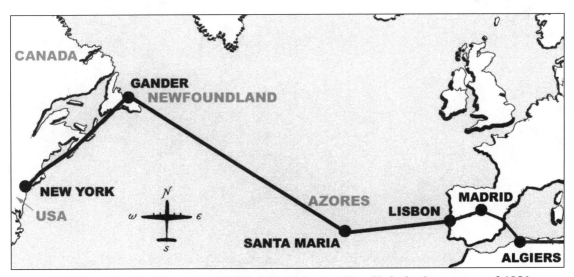

13-9 Chart showing the route of TWA 985, Lisbon to New York, in the summer of 1956. (Luisada)

13-10 "Instruments and Automatic Flight Control" (Lockheed Martin)

Chapter 14

FADING GLORY

Commercial airplanes have over the years often been sold to successive owners. This secondhand market has enabled some airlines to dispose of equipment at a good price while permitting others to meet expanded fleet requirements. This practice was in effect with the venerable Douglas DC–3 and has continued right up to this day.

Many of the Constellations and Super Constellations also changed hands during their useful lifetimes. However, unlike other aircraft, some of these Connies changed hands early in their career and continued to be used as first-line aircraft. On the other hand, one group of aircraft, which we shall talk about shortly, was given a new lease on life late in their life span.

First of all, it should be recognized that many airlines kept their Connies for many years until they were either grounded (and usually broken up) or sold to an aircraft broker or finance company. Among the airlines who kept their Connies to the end of their useful lives were TWA, Eastern, Air France, and Lufthansa. Interestingly enough, the first three mentioned were the three largest commercial customers of Constellations.

Other Constellations and Super Constellations were sold to leasing companies who in turn leased them to various small supplemental air carriers or other commercial interests. For example, in the 1970s, a few L–749s were operated by a small firm as firefighting aircraft, a form of utilization not likely to have ever been forecast by the design engineers at Lockheed!

As previously discussed, the Constellation first saw regular service in 1946. At that time, the basic design was already some seven years old. By the early 1960s, this aircraft, in spite of its many years of continuous improvements, was reaching what appeared to be the end of its useful career. To be sure, it was expected that some Constellations would be flying for some time yet. But in the commercial field, the turbojet transport was the new leader, and everybody was either flying jets or planning to shortly. It remained for one of the biggest customers of Constellations to veritably pull a rabbit out of its corporate hat and fashion a second career for the now-venerable Constellation.

THE EASTERN "SHUTTLE"

The company was Eastern Air Lines, which by 1957 owned and operated no fewer than 56 Constellations and Super Constellations, plus a few more they leased from TWA. By 1960, EAL was replacing these aircraft as first-line equipment with Lockheed Electra turboprops and Douglas DC–8 turbojets and had begun selling some Constellations as secondhand equipment. At this point, EAL was grappling with the problems associated with the short-haul market on the Boston–New York–Washington route. Competition was keen, costs were high for such short route segments, and the route as a whole was simply not very attractive to EAL. Yet it had been obvious all along that there was a huge market of riders among these three cities. How to exploit it successfully and profitably was the issue.

EAL's marketing and operating departments put their heads together and, by going back to transportation basics, came up with a plan that paid handsome dividends and, in the process, wrote a new and different chapter in the history of the Constellation.

The need was to move fairly large numbers of people short distances, quickly, and at fares competitive with the private car and with rail services, all with a minimum of fuss for the traveler. The answer that came forth was brilliant in its simplicity. It was known simply as the "Shuttle." It consisted of a fleet of airplanes dedicated wholly to these New York–Boston, New York–Washington, and Boston–Washington flights. It provided passengers with fast, low-cost, convenient, and simple transportation. The fleet initially consisted of 16 L–1049 and L–1049C Super Constellations. These aircraft, with their large passenger capacity and low landing speeds, were ideally suited to the market, as well as the relatively short runways at Washington National and New York LaGuardia Airports. This fleet grew over a period of time until it reached 33 Super Constellations and 6 Martin 404 backup aircraft.

The Shuttle was inaugurated on April 30, 1961. At that time, it operated 8 flights per day each way between Boston and New York and Washington and New

York for a total of 32 flights per day. There were also some Boston–Washington flights. All aircraft were configured to have 95 seats. For each scheduled flight, there was an aircraft that sat at the gate, and a backup aircraft with a crew on board waiting nearby.

Tickets for the Shuttle were sold by machine. No reservations were accepted, although tickets could be purchased in advance. Each passenger presented his ticket at the special Shuttle counter and received a numbered boarding pass. When 95 passes were issued, the flight was full.

The lead airplane at the gate, known as the first section, normally would leave on the scheduled time. If, however, it filled up prior to departure time, it left as soon as the 95th passenger was aboard. In such cases, that could occur as much as 20 minutes before the scheduled departure time.

If the first section left early, the second section aircraft was immediately brought to the gate. This aircraft would then leave at the scheduled time, even if there was only one passenger aboard. Bringing up the second section also meant that an additional aircraft had to be moved into the backup position.

During especially busy times, such as holidays, it was not uncommon for a third section to be immediately moved to the gate to receive the overflow. This third section would then leave about 20 minutes after the scheduled departure time. Thus during busy periods, the Shuttle could accept up to 285 passengers per scheduled departure by using three sections. This system of sections was actually a copy of what railroads used to do during very busy holiday periods.

In spite of both their age and basic function as long-range transports, these Super Constellations proved to be well suited for the Shuttle assignment. Their long fuselages permitted them to be configured in a high-density arrangement, seating 95 passengers, a scheme that was eminently workable due to the short flights (normally 60 minutes or shorter) and the lack of any serving amenities. Their low landing speeds were particularly well suited to using the short runways at LaGuardia and Washington National Airports. The low altitudes (13,000 feet or less) were economical with low-blower operations (which reduced engine wear) and fit right in with the short trip lengths. Finally, the small fuel loads required permitted operation at weights well below maximum gross weights with resultant savings in wear and tear and thus maintenance.

The Shuttle chalked up a truly impressive record right from its inception. It carried 400,000 passengers in the first 7 months, and 600,000 passengers in the second 7 months. In the four-year period 1961–65, a total of 10 million passengers were boarded. During one holiday period, 160 extra sections were operated in a 24-hour period, and the Shuttle carried 21,000 passengers, a truly phenomenal performance!

By 1964, all the remaining Super Constellations (L–1049, L–1049C, and L–1049G), 33 in all, were being used on the Shuttle, and additional aircraft were also participating to keep up with the growing demand. In 1965, Eastern had excess Lockheed Electras, which were being replaced by jet equipment. These Electras began taking over from the Super Constellations, which began to be retired in early 1967. During the period 1965–67, the Connies were relegated to backup status. By the spring of 1968, all of them were gone from the Shuttle. But, for a continuous period of over six years, these proud birds chalked up a tremendous record on the three segments of the Shuttle and earned a handsome profit for Eastern long after anyone would have considered them candidates for top moneymaker.

OTHER SECOND-HAND APPLICATIONS

There were, of course, other instances of used Constellations finding a new lease on life, sometimes at a second home.

Air India, which had a fleet of nine Super Constellations (two L–1049Cs, three L–1049Es, and four L–1049Gs) turned them all over to the Indian Air Force (IAF) in 1961–62. IAF operated them successfully for a number of years, well into the 1970s.

Flying Tiger Airlines, a big cargo line, was the largest operator of L–1049Hs with a fleet of 15 aircraft at one time. The carrier was plagued with a poor safety record, losing one L–1049H in 1958, four in 1962, one in 1964, and one in 1965 for a total of seven. To make up for these losses, they picked up a used L–1049H in 1959 and four more in 1966. Slick Airways, another cargo line, leased a number of L–1049Hs during the early 1960s. Both Slick and Flying Tiger found themselves looking for additional capacity because they were flying more and more U.S. military charters to South East Asia.

One other airline to utilize used Constellations was Pacific Northern Airlines (PNA). This carrier started out by obtaining three L–649As from Delta in March 1955, first by leasing, then purchase. Two L–749s were bought from BOAC in April 1957 and November 1958. One of these had been owned by Air India and Qantas prior to BOAC, and the other by KLM and Capital before going to BOAC. A L–749A was leased from TWA in August 1960 and purchased in 1963. A second L–749A was sold to PNA by TWA in June 1966. So here was a carrier with a fleet of seven Connies, all used and high-time aircraft. The fleet became part of Western Air Lines when that carrier acquired PNA in June 1967. Western finally divested itself of the Connies in April 1969.

As far as can be determined, the Connies operated by Western until 1969 were the last in scheduled service anywhere in the world. A few commercial Connies were still flying in the 1970s, but these were for such diverse uses as forest firefighting, smuggling, and an occasional travel club.

Basically, the end for the commercial Constellations and Super Constellations came during the mid-1960s, hastened by the rapid introduction of jets and the extreme cost of upkeep of reciprocating-engine airplanes. By 1965, everyone felt it was only a matter of time before the last proud Connie was grounded. Little did anyone know that the military was about to add another couple of chapters to the already illustrious history of these aircraft.

OTHER CONSTELLATION APPLICATIONS

In the 1970s some of the by now rather old Connies and Super Connies found a few additional applications. At least one Super Connie was used to airlift supplies secretly to guerrillas in African Biafra. Other Super Connies were flying for small companies hauling cargo, especially in South America.

One Super Connie, which crashed on take-off at Columbus, Indiana, was rumored to have been carrying illegal drugs. Sadly, the pilots killed in the crash were the former Lockheed test pilot "Fish" Salmon and his son, who was believed to have actually been flying the airplane. The aircraft was flying with avgas that had less than the normal octane rating, and the resulting drop in engine performance made it impossible for it to reach flying speed on that given runway.

Later on, in the 1980s and '90s a few Constellations were brought back to life and flown each summer at air shows. One such is the L–1049H acquired by the Save-A-Connie Group, composed mainly of TWA employees or former employees.

Another such case is the 1948 L–749 acquired originally by the Air Force as one of a lot of 10. This aircraft, S/N 2601, was known in the Air Force as a C–121A. It was bought in 1987 by a former Microsoft executive, Vern Raburn. Raburn and his wife, Dottie, created a Connie Club, had the aircraft put in flying condition, and have had it operated at air shows ever since. (Raburn, incidentally, is now the CEO of Eclipse Aviation, an Albuquerque-based start-up manufacturer, which is currently tooling up to build a six-place low-cost business jet.)

So, to this day, some Connies are still flying, 60 years after their initial flight!

14-1 Eastern Airlines Super G Constellation which was taken from first-line service and used on the highly successful "Shuttle" connecting Boston-New York-Washington. (Lockheed Martin)

14-2 Flying Tiger Super H Constellation used for high-priority cargo operations. (Lockheed Martin)

14-3 Slick Airlines, another mostly cargo airline, also employed Super H Constellations. (Lockheed Martin)

14-4 A view of a Western Airlines L–749 departing on the last scheduled Connie flight from Alaska, November 26, 1968. (Lockheed Martin)

14-5 The "Crash Landing Nightclub" in New Orleans with a Connie as a rather dramatic artifact sitting in front. (Chester H. Liebs, *Historic Preservation Magazine*)

14-6 A former Air France L–749 transferred to the French Air Force and used for Search and Rescue missions. (Col. J. C. LeBrun, French Air Force)

14-7 A French Air Force Search and Rescue (SAR) L–749 dropping rescue containers. (Col. J. C. LeBrun, French Air Force)

14-8 "Electrical and Electronic Systems" (Lockheed Martin)

14-9 "Ground Handling" (Lockheed Martin)

Chapter 15

ACCIDENTS, INCIDENTS, AND THE LEGEND GROWS

The history of any airplane includes such events as accidents. This is unavoidable, and, in keeping with virtually all new aircraft designs, the Constellation family had its share of accidents, incidents, and mechanical problems during the 36 years these aircraft were actively flown. The great majority of the accidents were directly attributable to human error, either by flight crews or maintenance personnel. But some of these events related directly to design flaws, and some were notable because, as a direct consequence, meaningful changes in some aspect of aviation resulted.

EARLY DAYS

In the earliest days of the Constellation, 1943–44, a number of problems arose, all of a mechanical nature. Although these are always disconcerting, they were by no means unexpected, as virtually all new aircraft designs experience a certain number of these, and the Constellations were not merely new but of a design that incorporated previously untried advances. There was the hydraulically boosted control system, for one, which many thought would turn out to be a constant source of trouble. The opposite turned out to be the case, in large part no doubt because Kelly Johnson insisted on taking as much time as he considered necessary to refine the system. The full-size operating model of this system was an excellent example of the care and thoroughness of both Johnson and the entire Lockheed design and development team.

Then there were those new, powerful, but cranky Curtiss-Wright Cyclone engines that initially gave so much trouble and also slowed the entire test flight program of the prototype. However, in spite of engine fires, feathered propellers, and abrupt terminations of test flights, those problems had been largely resolved by 1944.

Actually, some of the initial problems were from unexpected sources. The wheel brakes were unreliable and required improvement. The landing gear struts, with their great length, showed a disturbing potential for failure, until the design of one component was altered, and that problem disappeared.

Then, on September 9, 1945, the 12th C–69 delivered to the Air Force encountered serious trouble while in the air. A fire began in the number 1 engine nacelle, and fire extinguishers could not put it out. The fire eventually melted the engine mounting struts, and the engine fell off. The crew flew the C–69 some 100 miles to a safe landing at Topeka, Kansas. Subsequent investigation, which took place only after a second similar incident occurred in June 1946, revealed that the fire was caused by overheating of the supercharger drive shaft bearing. No injuries were sustained in this case.

During 1946 a number of L–049 accidents occurred as the total number of these aircraft in operation grew to 62. Altogether, there were eight accidents, with six of these having no injuries or fatalities. Of the eight accidents, five were attributed to pilot error, a sixth partially to pilot error, two to equipment failure, and one partially to equipment failure.

On June 18, 1946, a Pan Am L–049 was flying over Connecticut when an uncontrollable fire developed in the number 4 engine. The engine fell off completely, and the crew made a safe emergency landing at Willimantic, Connecticut. This incident seemed to be an absolute duplicate of the one over Kansas experienced by a Air Force C–69. Subsequent investigation showed the supercharger drive shaft bearing to have once again been the culprit. The problem was resolved and never arose again.

FIRE OVER READING, PENNSYLVANIA

On July 11, 1946, a far more serious situation arose. A TWA L–049 was on a crew training flight near Reading, Pennsylvania, with six crew members on board. A fire started in the forward baggage compartment. It produced smoke of such density that the crew, unable to see either outside or their instruments, crashed the airplane about half a mile short of the airport while attempting an emergency approach. Five of the crew members died, with the instructor pilot the only survivor. The aircraft was destroyed by the combination of the crash and fire.

As a result of this crash, the CAA almost immediately grounded all Constellations for a minimum of 30 days and began an intensive investigation. This investigation turned up defects in three areas and actually covered not only the direct cause of this accident but also touched on the accidents at Topeka and Willimantic. Lockheed assisted in the investigation and were eager to uncover the cause(s) and get the Constellations flying again.

The inquiry uncovered three separate and distinct contributing causes of the accident. The first was the arcing of through-studs located in the left wing root. Through-studs are specially designed bolts that provide relatively airtight electrical conductors through the skin of the pressurized fuselage. It was determined that at least two out of three through-studs located on the left side burned so badly from arcing that they could have caused the fire.

The second cause centered on the forward baggage compartment, which was the location of the burned through-studs and the fire. Here it was determined that the high temperatures caused by the electrical arcing could have easily ignited the soundproofing lining of the compartment. It was further shown that due to high-pressure hydraulic lines running inside the fuselage walls, any leakage of hydraulic fluid, a common occurrence, would result in a serious fire. The hydraulic fluids used were highly flammable.

The third and direct cause of the crash was the total lack of cockpit visibility due to the intense smoke. Tests showed that the crew, in opening the crew hatch to alleviate the situation, had actually drawn smoke forward into the cockpit and thus made matters worse.

The investigation also looked into the overall electrical system of the L–049 and fire prevention and extinguishing equipment. This portion of the investigation revealed defects in the cabin supercharger drive shafts and in the engine nacelles, which were pinpointed as having been the cause of the early accidents at Topeka and Willimantic.

Out of all this investigative work came a number of important modifications and design changes. These were:

1. The electrical system was modified to prevent wire chafing. The now infamous through-studs were replaced with units of new design.
2. Fire extinguishing systems in the engine nacelles were changed and improved.

3. Hydraulic lines running inside the fuselage walls were in some cases relocated to reduce fire hazard.
4. A procedure for venting smoke from the fuselage was established, which ensured such smoke would not infiltrate the cockpit.
5. The cabin supercharger drive shafts were redesigned to prevent failure.

The grounding, investigation, and modification were expensive and unpleasant for Lockheed and for the air carriers that had already received the L–049s. Throughout this painful period, Lockheed worked hand-in-hand with the CAA and the airlines, assisting in the investigation and then carrying out the modifications. Out of this episode there resulted not only a safer Constellation but, because of the new regulations issued by the CAA, improved safety in all other commercial transports.

ACCIDENTS DURING THE 1940S AND EARLY '50S

As Connie operations increased greatly in the late 1940s and throughout the 1950s, it was to be expected that the number of accidents would also rise. Many of these accidents, though attributed directly to pilot error, were undoubtedly caused in part by such factors as poor or nonexistent landing aids at airports all over the world.

LANDING ACCIDENT AT PRESTWICK

Once such accident involved a KLM L–049 that crashed on December 27, 1948, while on a Ground-Controlled Approach (GCA) at Prestwick, Scotland. There was an 800-foot ceiling, and as the aircraft broke out of the overcast, the pilot realized there was a 20-knot cross-wind. He elected to make a go-around. As he pulled up, the aircraft hit a high-tension wire, which apparently ruptured a fuel tank and started a fire. The severed wire caused the runway lights to go out. On fire and unable to see the field, the L–049 crashed 2 miles away, killing 39 of the 40 on board.

Ironically, the pilot of the aircraft was Captain K. D. Parmentier, KLM's chief pilot and a legendary aviation pioneer of the 1920s and '30s. Also killed in the crash were KLM's vice president and Lockheed's European sales representative.

This accident came to mind some 30 years later when, in the worst aviation disaster of all time, two Boeing 747s, one with Pan Am and the other KLM, collided in dense fog on a runway in Tenerife, Canary Islands. The accident, which claimed over 500 lives, was charged to the KLM captain, who took off without proper clearance. Ironically, this captain had been a leading figure in aviation circles in promoting safety. Lest readers be misled, it should be mentioned here that KLM is not only one of the world's oldest and largest airlines but also one of the safest.

MIDAIR OVER LONG ISLAND

On October 3, 1949, the structural integrity of the Constellation was put to a severe test. A Pan Am L–049 was climbing out over Long Island, New York, bound for London, having just taken off from LaGuardia.

At an altitude of 4,000 feet, the Connie was struck by a two-seat Cessna, which penetrated the top of the fuselage just behind the flight deck. The pilot landed the damaged aircraft safely at Mitchel AFB in New York. No injuries were suffered on the L–049, but both men in the Cessna died. Parts of the nose and engine of the Cessna were embedded in the top of the Constellation fuselage, but the big plane was flown to its emergency landing with no apparent difficulties.

ENGINE FIRE NEAR CAIRO

On August 31, 1950, TWA's *Star of Maryland* crashed and burned 48 miles from Cairo. The aircraft, an L–749A, had been in service only some four months. Fifty-five died in the crash. The investigation pinpointed the cause of the crash to be the failure of the rear row master rod bearing on the number 3 engine during the climb-out from Cairo. The failure caused an uncontrollable fire in the nacelle, and the engine fell off the wing. Out of this accident came a better means of lubricating the engine's moving parts. No such type of accident ever happened again to any Constellation that had received proper maintenance.

FIRE OVER THE ATLANTIC

On June 20, 1956, late in the evening, an LAV L–1049E departed New York for Caracas. While flying over the Atlantic, some 250 miles east of Norfolk, Virginia, the flight experienced trouble with the number 2 propeller. It began to overspeed, and the pilot, unable to feather it, turned back to New York. The flight was picked up and escorted by a Coast Guard Search and Rescue Albatross Amphibian.

Approaching the New York area, the pilot began dumping excess fuel over water off the coast of New Jersey. The Coast Guard crew flying nearby suddenly saw a flicker of flame on the right wing near the number 3 engine. Before the horrified gaze of the Coast Guard crew, the flames quickly spread. Then the aircraft began to descend, and, completely on fire, crashed into the ocean, carrying a total of 74 persons to their death.

The crash prompted Lockheed to conduct a number of fuel-dumping tests using an L–1049G that had the same wing cowls and flaps as the ill-fated aircraft. The tests were purely voluntary and not government requested. The results all showed that at various air speeds and flap settings, and with landing gear either down or up, there was no way the fuel being dumped could ignite.

No specific cause for the fire and the ensuing crash was ever determined. However, it is interesting to note that no other such accident has ever befallen a Constellation, leading this writer to speculate that there may have been some other mechanical malfunction of the LAV aircraft that, together with the fuel dumping, caused the fatal fire.

RENDEZVOUS OVER THE GRAND CANYON

Only 10 days after the above-described crash, an even greater tragedy occurred. On June 30, 1956, a TWA L–1049 and a United DC–7 collided in broad daylight in the vicinity of the Grand Canyon. Both planes crashed with total casualties of 128. The midair collision occurred in clear skies when one aircraft, which was in a slow climb, collided with the other, which was overtaking it.

This accident, the worst crash to that date in aviation, caused much furor, both public and in government circles. The CAB spent months investigating the tragedy, and in so doing, unraveled an ironic set of events that showed the true culprit to be the FAA regulations under which the aircrafts had been operating.

The two flights left Los Angeles three minutes apart, both eastbound, but to different destinations and via different routes. However, the routes crossed near the Grand Canyon. The weather was generally clear, although there were some build-ups of cumulus over the mountains. The flights were both initially operating IFR. However, by the time both flights were in proximity of each other near the Grand Canyon, they were in effect VFR and operating in uncontrolled airspace.

UAL 718 was cruising at its assigned altitude of 21,000 feet. TWA 2 had climbed to its initially assigned altitude of 19,000 feet but, as it approached the Grand Canyon area, began encountering cumulus build-ups over the mountains. Not wanting to shake up the passengers unnecessarily, the captain requested a clearance to climb to and maintain 21,000 feet, but ATC denied the request, noting that UAL 718 was at 21,000 feet and on a converging course. TWA 2 then requested to climb to and maintain "1,000 feet on top," which was actually a form of VFR clearance. ATC approved TWA's request.

TWA promptly climbed to 1,000 feet above the clouds, which turned out to be 21,000 feet. At this point, both flights were on intersecting airways at the same altitude. Both were estimating a reporting point known as Painted Desert at the same exact time. ATC was aware that this indicated a potential collision but made no special effort to divert either flight.

Neither flight radioed in over Painted Desert, but at 1031 hours ATC monitored a garbled transmission, which was later clarified. The chilling words were: "Salt Lake City, United 718 . . . ah . . . we're going in."

United 718 and TWA 2 were already pieces of metal and flesh scattered over a wide area of mountainous terrain. The United DC–7, traveling at a slightly faster speed than the TWA flight, had overtaken and collided with the Super Constellation.

Out of this tragedy there came a number of realizations, the most significant being that commercial flights should be operated under positive ATC direction at all times. The VFR rules of "see and be seen" was shown to be highly inadequate, especially because tests of the cockpits of the two airliners involved clearly demonstrated that crew visibility was restricted.

A considerable uproar ensued from this collision, not only among the public and the various aviation interests but also in Congress and the administration. From this there resulted the closing of a number of the loopholes in the FAA regulations and a sizable increase in the facilities and personnel allocated to the FAA for the purpose of air traffic control, especially the en route portion. But another midair collision only four and a half years later served unmistakable notice that serious ATC problems still existed.

STATEN ISLAND, CHRISTMAS

December 16, 1960, was a rather typical wintry day in New York City, with temperatures hovering around the freezing mark and a light snow falling from the gray clouds pressing down from overhead. Thoughts of Christmas passed through the minds of many of those hurrying through the blustery weather.

Overhead the skies were filled with many aircraft arriving and departing from the area's three major airports. Many of these were the new jet transports, which less than two years prior had arrived on the scene in this country. But not all of the transports were jets, and one arriving aircraft was TWA 266, an L–1049 Super Constellation inbound to LaGuardia Airport.

The TWA flight was down to 5,000 feet and 140 knots and approaching Linden Intersection over Staten Island. Seconds later, at 1034 hours, the Super Constellation and a United Douglas DC–8 bound for Kennedy Airport collided. The TWA aircraft went down out of control and crashed on Staten Island on an old abandoned Army airfield, and only 100 feet from a public school full of children.

The United DC–8, Flight 826, with one engine ripped off and under only partial control, hit the top of an apartment building and crashed on a street in Brooklyn, also just missing not one but two schools. A total of 134 persons were dead, 8 of them pedestrians.

The collision and ensuing crashes were the worst since the 1956 Grand Canyon accident. Ironically, the same two airlines were involved, and in addition, the collision took place at almost the same time of the morning as the one over the Grand Canyon.

The intensive investigation which followed revealed a number of contributing causes:

1. The UAL DC–8 had one of its two omni-receivers not operating, which made it more difficult for the crew to pinpoint its position. However, ATC had not been advised of this fact.
2. The DC–8 was traveling at a speed estimated to be over 300 knots, versus the then-generally accepted speed within terminal areas of 180–200 knots.
3. The DC–8 overshot its assigned holding fix (Preston) by some 11 miles.
4. The FAA en route radar had discontinued surveillance of the UAL flight some 90 seconds before the collision.

The CAB placed all the blame on the United flight, but the findings of the investigation rather clearly indicated that the FAA's own procedures were a contributing cause. As a result of the investigation and its findings, the FAA initiated a number of far-reaching moves.

Specifically, the FAA instituted the following:

1. Reduced the maximum permissible speed for all aircraft within terminal areas.
2. Increased the level of radar surveillance of all aircraft in terminal areas.
3. Improved the way in which flights are handed off between en route centers and approach control facilities.
4. Required that all jets have two operating navigation aids at all times.
5. Directed all air carriers to equip their transports with transponders, which greatly facilitates the identifying of a flight on a radar scope.
6. Ordered all air carriers to begin equipping their fleets with distance-measuring equipment, which provides more exact navigational positions to flight crews.

The lesson learned from this accident was indeed an expensive one in terms of human lives, but in retrospect there is no doubt that the improvements and changes that resulted from this tragedy were instrumental in saving the lives of many who flew after this date. It was unfortunate however, that, as with the Grand Canyon collision, the necessary changes required this kind of tragic catalyst.

THE CONNIE'S ABILITY TO SURVIVE

Early in the history of the Constellation, pilots first became aware and then enthusiastic over the extreme stability of the aircraft. Coupled with this were the excellent flying qualities even when the plane was handicapped by malfunctioning systems, or even severe damage. These characteristics proved vital over the years in saving many lives in a variety of circumstances.

Below are two actual examples which clearly demonstrate these qualities. Readers should note that in both cases these qualities so evident in the Constellation prevented loss of life.

CRISIS OVER THE PACIFIC

In January 1959, an Air Force RC–121D of the 551st AEW&C Wing was returning from a routine mission over the Pacific Ocean. This particular RC–121D, tail number 530555, had been on station over the Pacific and was based at Hickam AFB, Hawaii. The aircraft, which incidentally was nicknamed "Triple Nickel," was to have a famous career, and we shall meet Triple Nickel again in this book. Triple Nickel was commanded by Major Earl W. Bierer, with Major Mervin G. Getty in the right-hand seat.

At 0600 hours, while cruising at 6,000 feet VFR in clear weather some 200 miles SSW of Honolulu, a sudden moderately severe vibration was felt, which lasted only 2 or 3 seconds. Sensing that the vibration came from the port side, Bierer looked off to his left. A quick glimpse of number 1 propeller made him think something was wrong. Then he saw pieces of the propeller flying into space, and he promptly ordered the number 1 engine shut down. Immediately afterward, the flight engineer reported that number 2 engine was completely missing! Bierer reacted by calling for 60 percent flaps, METO (maximum except take-off) power on number 3 and 4 engines, and fuel dumping operations to be started.

By this time, both pilots, working together, had jammed on hard right rudder to prevent extreme yaw caused by having power on the right side only. As soon as full right rudder trim was rolled in, some of the pressure on the right pedal was relieved, but it still took the combined efforts of both pilots to keep the RC–121D from yawing excessively to the left.

The aircraft had been vibrating badly ever since the number 1 propeller began disintegrating and the number 2 engine had fallen off, but with 60 percent flaps the buffeting decreased considerably. With the number 3 and 4 engines at METO power, Triple Nickel was slowly descending, and when leveled off, air speed was only 150 knots and the buffeting that precedes a stall began to develop. Bierer called for maximum power on numbers 3 and 4, and then tried the flaps at 40 percent to reduce drag. But buffeting started up again, so the flaps were lowered once again to 60 percent.

By now, some 10,000 pounds of fuel had been dumped, but even with that much weight gone the RC–121D continued to gradually descend. The combination of the immense drag from the number 2 nacelle firewall, power from only two engines, plus the additional drag from the 60-degree flap setting, was such that the aircraft continued to descend down to 1,500 feet.

By this time a serious concern had developed as to the ability of the two remaining engines to continue to function at such high power settings. The engines had been operating at maximum power for some 30 to 45 minutes, and it was a tribute to Curtiss-Wright and the mechanics of the 551st Wing that they were still functioning at all. Normally, maximum power is permitted for only 5 minutes. A little experimentation showed that a power setting between maximum and METO power, in this case 2,700 rpm/50-inch MP/240 BMEP, resulted in reasonably stable flight at 130–135 knots. The RC–121D continued to wallow along at 1,300–1,400 feet.

The Air Force's Air Rescue Service had received word of the emergency shortly after it began, and an SC–54 intercepted the stricken aircraft and escorted it toward Hickam Field in Oahu. The firewall where the number 2 engine had been located caused the portion of the wing behind it to lose most of its lift. This, combined with the low air speed that could barely be maintained, meant that any further reduction of power would put the Warning Star into the water. Not wanting to take any chances, Bierer had already ordered the crew into their life jackets and had them standing by at their ditching stations.

One other problem facing Bierer and his crew was the loss of the primary hydraulic system, which occurred when the number 2 engine fell off and the number 1 engine was shut down. The back-up system operated by the number 4 engine with cross-over was used, thus maintaining the all-important flight control boost system in operation. In any event, Oahu was finally sighted, and then Hickam Field. The crippled Warning Star was brought in on a standard approach, except that the base leg was flown higher than normal. When the aircraft was turned onto final, the gear was lowered with no problems. The touch-down and rollout were normal.

A postmortem of the incident came to the conclusion that a safe return was accomplished because the vital early steps, such as shutting down the number 1 engine, retrimming the aircraft, dumping fuel, and being willing to attempt to fly with 60 percent flaps, were all carried out expeditiously.

But in addition to the highly professional job by Majors Bierer and Getty, there seems to be little doubt but that the structure of the Super Connie, its broad wing and triple tail, and the reliable power plants may well have made the basic difference between a mid-ocean ditching and a safe return.

ILLUSION OVER CONNECTICUT

In the late afternoon of December 4, 1965, an EAL L–1049 flying the Shuttle between Boston and Newark was cruising at 10,000 feet thru thin, scattered clouds over south-central Connecticut. Suddenly the co-pilot yelled a warning as he spotted an oncoming jet. Captain Charles J. White, together with co-pilot Roger Holt, hauled back on their yokes in an attempt to climb over the jet. But the jet, a TWA Boeing 707, did the same thing, and the two aircraft collided. The 707's left wing hit the Connie's tail, cleanly removing a third of that vital structure; in the process the jet lost the outboard portion of its wing. At this moment, a total of 112 people's lives were in mortal danger.

The TWA flight crew discovered they still had adequate control in spite of the missing section of wing, and the plane was safely landed at New York's Kennedy Airport a few minutes later.

The Eastern flight was not so fortunate. When a portion of its tail was cut off, a number of hydraulic lines were severed, and the hydraulic boost system for the tail assembly was made totally inoperable. The mechanical linkages for the tail had also been cut, and the crew now had no elevator or rudder control.

The big Connie nosed up, stalled, and went into a dive. By means of skillful manipulation of the throttles, the captain managed to keep the aircraft under some sort of control, but he could not keep it from steadily losing altitude. By varying the power settings on the four engines, the captain also managed to acquire a small amount of directional control.

By this time dusk had settled, and with time and options running out, the crew picked out a pasture on the side of a hill as the best place for an emergency landing. Captain White managed to make a smooth belly landing, and it appeared that a small miracle had been achieved. But as the plane slid along, a small tree suddenly appeared out of the dusk. The left wing was sheared off. The fuselage and right wing continued their uncontrolled slide, with the right wing catching fire, and the fuselage splitting open. This turned out to be a godsend, as passengers rapidly escaped through these openings.

Captain White never left the airplane. He was found next to a dead soldier who failed to leave the aircraft. Two others died later of their injuries, for a total of 4 out of 54 on board. The extraordinary stability of the fatally damaged Super Constellation, combined with the skill and courage of Captain White and his crew kept the death toll to a fraction of what it might have been.

The National Transportation Safety Board investigation of this collision revealed a totally unexpected cause of the accident. In spite of what both crews believed their eyes were telling them, the two aircraft were not on a collision course, but were, as they should have been, separated by 1,000 feet of altitude. Both planes were flying just above a solid bank of clouds which, unknown to them, was sloping and thus presented a false horizon. This optical illusion caused both crews to believe they were on a collision course. One more possible cause of danger to flight had been identified, but at the cost of four lives.

CONCLUSION

In retrospect, the entire Constellation family of airplanes, both commercial and military, accumulated an enviable safety record. Except for its initial problems during the period 1943–46, when very few Constellations were flying, the airplane had almost no accidents over the next 33 years that could be attributed to design faults. Moreover, when problems did arise, whether because of mechanical or human failure, its design provided an excellent margin of safety. This was partly due to its fail-safe design, partly to its system redundancy, and partly to its extremely honest flying characteristics.

Many of the kind of problems that plagued other large aircraft, both reciprocating and turbine, were simply nonexistent in the Constellation. One cannot give too much credit to the basic design and detail execution as carried out by Kelly Johnson and his team of design and development engineers and technicians. Nor can too much be said about the quality manufacturing for which Lockheed's thousands of production workers had already been deservedly renowned. Countless numbers of safe flying hours and satisfied crew members and passengers must be attributed to this. And let's not forget Robert Gross's credo that Lockheed had to stand behind their products 100 percent, which is something they have always done.

15-1 An overhead view of the Super Constellation family, sitting on the Burbank Airport ramp. From the top, clockwise, the VC–121 "Columbine," a USAF C–121 transport, a L–1049H cargo version, a USAF RC–121D Warning Star, a USN WV–2 Warning Star, an Avianca Colombian Airlines L–1049E, and a Seaboard and Western cargo L–1049H. (Lockheed Martin)

15-2 "Operating Instructions" (Lockheed Martin)

Chapter 16

SECOND STRING STAR-SEA

Readers may remember that in Chapter 8 it was pointed out that the role of the Warning Star AEW&C fleets was being gradually phased out in the early 1960s. In fact, many of the big birds with the strange humps were already sitting on the ground at Davis-Montham AFB, Arizona, which is the storage depot for mothballed aircraft of all the military services. But a new national emergency was waiting in the wings ready to step center stage. When it did, the now elderly and somewhat worn-out Warning Stars would be called forth in what was to become their finest hour. Indeed, it would be that for all of their flight and ground crews as well.

South East Asia (SEA) is a latter-day term for the region that includes Thailand, Malaysia, Singapore, and that area formerly identified as French Indo-China. The latter had been a French colony and the center of guerrilla fighting since shortly after the end of World War II. By the early 1960s it was made up of four separate and distinct countries: Laos, Cambodia, North Vietnam and South Vietnam. North Vietnam had for years been infiltrating its southern neighbor. The United States had a military assistance treaty with South Vietnam, and in 1964 President Lyndon B. Johnson decided that U.S. military intervention was needed if the total collapse of South Vietnam was to be averted. A fictitious naval incident was created in which U.S. naval vessels in the Gulf of Tonkin were "attacked" by N. Vietnamese gunboats. On the basis of this supposed attack, plus some other incidents affecting U.S. forces, President Johnson was able to justify the sending of a half million man army to this jungle area some 8,000 miles from the continental United States.

The pros and cons of the Vietnam War are not in any way a part of this story. Suffice it to say that this was a major military effort by the United States, and air power played a large part in the bloody fighting, which dragged on through the 1960s and into the early 1970s. Against the always confusing backdrop of Vietnam, a new chapter in the history of the Warning Stars was about to be written.

As the U.S. military force in SEA mushroomed, air strikes of all types against both North Vietnam and the Viet Cong insurgents in South Vietnam became the order of the day. All this rather frenetic air activity led to the early realization that some kind of airborne radar control was badly needed. Thus it was quite early in this war that the Pentagon made the decision that AEW&C aircraft could be a valuable and even necessary asset in the fighting to come.

Although other aircraft equipped with search radar existed, the Warning Star boasted certain features not found in any other aircraft. For one thing, the WV–2/RC–121Ds featured excellent on station loiter capabilities. For another, their 17.5-foot search antenna would, at sufficient altitude, result in an excellent search range. Then, too, the big fuselage permitted a relatively large number of controller positions, which in turn meant that one aircraft could comfortably deal with larger masses of data than smaller radar aircraft.

So it was that the radar picket aircraft of the 1950s was called to the center stage as the tactical control aircraft of the 1960s. The new role of this plane differed in various aspects from that for which it had originally been designed. However, readers may remember that the role originally envisioned by the Navy in formulating the WV–2 concept included control and direction of air strikes.

Actually, the Warning Stars now available differed in some important ways from the original aircraft delivered by Lockheed. In the early 1960s the aircraft were updated with new electronics. New radar consoles were installed. Data links were introduced, which enabled distant commanders on the ground to view real-time radar displays relayed to them and based on which changes in orders could be formulated. Communications gear was also upgraded, with more bands and frequencies added so that a greater number of simultaneous transmissions could be handled.

The converted aircraft were now identified as EC–121s, with various suffixes used to indicate differences in their electronic configuration. In fact, as part of the conversions, the Warning Stars lost their upper radar domes, with that antenna being integrated with the belly-mounted search radar. Upgrading of the Warning

Stars was carried out on both the Air Force and Navy versions. But in any event, it was to be the Air Force and not the Navy that furnished and operated the aircraft on this new mission in SEA.

Accordingly, in April 1965 the 552nd AEW&C Wing at McClellan AFB, California, was directed to deploy a task force of their EC–121Ds to Southeast Asia. The task force was initially identified as Big Eye Task Force but was later renamed College Eye Task Force. The aircraft and crews of this task force were considered part of the newly created Detachment 1 of the 552nd Wing. These aircraft and crews were still officially based at McClellan and would continue to be, but a certain number of them were periodically rotated to SEA. However, while this Asian mission was going on, the Air Force offshore radar picket flights continued unabated for some time.

The deployment of Air Force EC–121D aircraft (plus H and T models) to SEA between 1965 and 1974 was a notable effort for a number of reasons. To begin with, the actual aircraft all had been flying continuously for 8–10 years. In fact, some of the planes that flew in SEA were former Navy WV–2s that had been retired to Davis-Montham, and then were brought out of retirement, updated as to their electronics, and then assigned to the Air Force. Because of the type of missions that these aircraft all had flown, operating 12–16 hours per mission, even the low-time planes had accumulated substantial total flying hours. Furthermore, operating continually from coastal fields and over the ocean at low to intermediate altitudes, they were exposed to large amounts of salt corrosion action, which tended to weaken the various structural members. The reciprocating engines had been out of production since 1957 and, with no replacements available had to be maintained through overhaul and rebuilding. To top all this off, some of the major airplane overhauls normally scheduled for all airplanes had been either skipped or delayed indefinitely because the Pentagon believed that the useful life of these fleets of aircraft was limited and shortly to come to an end. Little did anyone realize how much flying was still ahead for the Warning Stars.

Colonel James H. West, USAF, was a member of the original cadre that was set up by the 552nd Wing 30 days in advance of the alert to deploy to SEA in March 1965. He remembers flying in with the six aircraft assigned initially. These planes were flown to Taiwan (Formosa), which was used as the main operating base. The forward operating base was Tan Son Nhut AB, Saigon, South Vietnam.

Sergeant Edward E. Simpson, USAF (Ret.) was also a member of the 552nd Wing in 1965 and went to SEA with the original deployment. Simpson was a radar operator and went overseas with the rest of the radar crews and maintenance personnel via a MAC flight. Only the flight crews flew with the 121s to Taiwan. He relates how a complete crew would depart Taiwan, fly to Saigon, and prepare for the next day's mission. The crew would then fly 6 missions back to back, with each one lasting up to 12 hours. On the sixth day, having flown the last mission, the crew would return to Saigon, pick up another 121, and immediately fly back to Taiwan with no rest. After six days of rest, the cycle would begin again. Crews were supposed to be on 90-day tours of duty to SEA, but this usually was extended to 120 days before the crews would be rotated back Stateside. It was a hard, demanding routine, with both planes and crews taking a beating.

There were different types of missions flown from the very beginning. The primary one was to monitor morning and afternoon strike formations, which were attacking various targets in North Vietnam. This was done from a station located over the Gulf of Tonkin just north of the demilitarized zone. This station was flown at extremely low altitudes, 100–150 feet off the ocean surface, which meant flight crews could not relax at any time. The low altitudes flown permitted the search radar beam to be bounced off the ocean surface, and any enemy fighters taking off from airfields in the vicinity of Hanoi (the capital of North Vietnam) could be painted on the radar screens very shortly after departure.

Thus the U.S. attacking forces and any escorting fighters would receive the maximum possible warning of attacks by the Communist defense forces. There were other important duties to perform as well. Once the strike forces were well on their way back south, the EC–121 on station would vector air refueling tankers to rendezvous with any aircraft running short on fuel, a not uncommon situation with military jets. This alone helped materially in bringing many airplanes and airmen back home safely. Another mission was search and rescue. When the EC–121 had an indication of an aircraft going down, it would pinpoint the exact location and then vector a rescue force precisely to that location. These rescue missions plucked air crews out of the jungle not only in South Vietnam but also in North Vietnam and later Laos and Cambodia, sometimes right out of the clutches of enemy forces moving in to capture these crews. Many airmen alive today owe their lives in part to the role played by the EC–121s during these missions.

Still another mission related to making sure that the Chinese were not in any way aroused to offensive action by U.S. aircraft crossing into their airspace. This entailed controlling U.S. aircraft so that none inadvertently entered Chinese airspace, whether that was by crossing the North Vietnam border into China, flying over the Chinese island of Hainan just east of the Gulf of Tonkin, or crossing into China from the Gulf itself.

Later in the war, EC–121s helped vector SAC B–52s into position for their carpet-bombing raids, as well as ensuring that air-to-air refueling took place when required. They vectored materiel air drops into position, as well.

The mission station used by the 121s over the Gulf of Tonkin was only a few minutes jet flying time from the North Vietnam fighter bases. Thus there was always the potential for enemy air attacks on these highly vulnerable planes. Air Force F–4's Phantom jet fighters would orbit at altitude to provide a top cover for the EC–121 on station. On more than one occasion enemies planes were painted headed in the direction of the EC–121, and the crew would turn south and go to maximum power, something that did the already-worn power plants no good at all. However, there is no recorded case that this writer could find of an actual enemy plane attack ever being made on an EC–121.

As the war progressed, the Tonkin station was abandoned in favor of one that was over Laos and was sometimes referred to as Charlie Route. The missions here were the same. But as the years passed, additional uses were found for the EC–121's electronic equipment and the highly skilled controllers that manned it. On air strikes, aircraft were actually counted going in and out of the strike area. In this manner, any missing aircraft were identified very quickly.

Then another mission developed, partly as a result of a modification made on the EC–121s called the CO–62. The CO–62 involved installing certain equipment that permitted the radar displays to be relayed in real time to a base many miles away. If the distance involved required, the display was relayed via an airborne Boeing C–135 Command aircraft. Back at the base, the battle staff could then view an air battle as it developed, and could, in effect, direct their task force(s) even though they were hundreds of miles from the scene of the action. In fact, these officers obtained a better overall picture than if they had been in the cockpits of the attacking force. Thus, with the CO–62 modification, an entirely new dimension in air battles was introduced. This particular modification actually was a direct result of the Vietnam conflict. It was installed on the EC–121s in the late 1960s and early 1970s by LTV in Greenville, Texas, and aircraft with this added feature changed from the D model designation to the T model.

As more experience and confidence was gained in the utilization of the EC–121s in the SEA environment, air strikes were no longer merely monitored but actually vectored to their targets, thus diminishing in some cases the danger of either ground anti-aircraft fire, missiles, or defending enemy fighters by rerouting the task force's approaches to the targets.

The ability to achieve very accurate vectoring of airborne aircraft led to the EC–121s working hand-in-hand with Air Force fighter pilots and assisting them in attacking enemy fighters. One of the earliest such efforts took place with Captain

Ritchie, USAF, the first jet ace of the Vietnam conflict. Ritchie quickly realized the significance of this type of cooperation between himself and the "big birds with the ugly humps." He spent considerable time familiarizing himself with the routine of the EC–121s. As a result, he was later to publicly give credit for at least two of his five enemy aircraft kills to the excellent warning and control provided by the AEW&C weapons controllers aboard the EC–121s. It is interesting to note, however, that this type of vectoring was by no means a true innovation. In 1940, during the famous Battle of Britain, Royal Air Force fighters were routinely and successfully vectored against German formations from the ground by controllers using the earliest rudimentary radar sets. Even then, with that early type of equipment, the system worked well and was credited with having materially helped in stopping the Nazi aerial onslaught.

In 1970–71, with the EC–121s now flying from Thailand and operating on a station roughly over Laos, Captain Bart C. Cusick III, USAF, was flying first as an intercept officer and then as senior controller. Cusick was with the 552nd and accumulated over 850 hours in the EC–121s. He remembers clearly the type of missions that would come up. In a personal interview, Cusick described it thus:

> What you really did out there in SEA, while I was there, you directed ground strikes. The ground commander would call in for help, saying he was being overrun at such and such a location. You'd check the charts to see where they were. You'd already have determined what aircraft were in the area and what armament they carried. This was a tactical mission. You would coordinate this with a Colonel that was a representative of some headquarters. You would then contact the bases that were flying the support, you'd recommend what weapons you thought were necessary, what type of strikes you thought were needed, and they would tell you what tactical airplanes they had ready to go and when they could reach the target area. If possible, you'd call up a 0-2 observation aircraft with a Forward Air Controller [FAC] on board. If there was a U.S. representative along with whoever was hollering for help, he would also give you his estimate of what was going on. You could get very distorted stories at times! If somebody shot at you from behind a rock, I'd guess you'd holler for help too!
>
> In turn, the FAC would pick up the fighter-bombers coming out of their home base. When a FAC was on hand, he would do all the directing, coordinating, checking on their fuel, navigate for them, etc. If a FAC was there, all you had to do was bring them into the area, search around, and

pass words back and forth until the strike leader found the targets and attacked. At the same time, you'd be watching out for all other air traffic. You'd be watching out for enemy air traffic if that was where you were working at the time. If they were out of range you would still get unknowns, and you'd try to contact them and keep them from running into each other.

This was the simple thing, having one mission. At the same time, you might also have air-to-air refueling going on in one area, search and rescue somewhere else, and you could have 70-odd other airplanes flying in different directions all around you.

This is what it was like for the controllers, and all this traffic was being directed and monitored by the crew of one airplane, a single EC–121! Over-land missions were usually flown at around 10,000 feet, seldom higher. In SEA at this altitude, flying through turbulent, nasty, possibly dangerous weather was a routine occurrence, rather than something that might cause special comment. The weather was merely one factor the crews had to contend with. As Cusick pointed out, they would be flying at 10,000 feet for 6 to 8 hours, in extreme heat, with no pressurization or oxygen. The heat was not only what existed all over SEA but also that generated by the tons of electronic equipment inside the cabin. In fact, sufficient air conditioning in the Warning Stars was a problem that was never adequately resolved.

The missions were tough on the airplanes as well as the crews. On the Gulf of Tonkin station, extreme salt corrosion was present at the wavetop altitudes flown. Because the flights were fairly long, take-offs were just about always at max gross weights for the temperature and runways being used. The heat tended to cook the electronics, and the all-enveloping tropical humidity got into all parts of the airplane. Always there was the possibility of engine failure, which was far from rare, given the combination of over-age power plants and high power demands. Thus it was common for an aircraft to return on three engines, with some getting back to an emergency base on only two. There is even the story, not verified, of the EC–121 that successfully made a total dead stick landing when the last engine still operating had to be quickly shut down shortly before reaching an emergency base. To say the least, it was not fun and games!

A secondary mission of the Warning Stars was to keep track of shipping in the Gulf of Tonkin. Although painting such surface targets was not something the search radars did well, it was one more mission successfully carried out.

The EC–121 force in SEA would in time grow to nine aircraft at any given time. These aircraft and crews were all periodically rotated back to the United States, with others replacing them. In addition, at various times, Navy EC–121s were also in the area, although their missions seem to have been more limited and not continuous. This author believes that their role was primarily that of assisting the strike forces flying from the decks of carriers stationed in the northern portion of the Gulf of Tonkin.

The EC–121s did not only fly out of various forward bases in both South Vietnam and Thailand. At times, when temporary U.S. peace efforts were under way, they would be pulled back, sometimes all the way to South Korea. However, even then the big birds still came south and flew on station, day and night, no matter what.

THE "BATCATS"

There was another EC–121 unit in SEA, and the activities of this one were shrouded in even more secrecy than those of Det. 1, 552nd Wing. This unit was the 553rd Reconnaissance Squadron, known informally as the Batcats. As the reader will shortly see, the name was most appropriate.

The 553rd was actually a detachment of the 551st AEW&C wing at Otis AFB, Massachusetts. The unit was formally organized at Otis in January 1967, although it actually existed before then for some months in an unofficial capacity. The Batcats had a unique mission, and to fully understand it, one must go back to the beginning of the conflict in SEA.

The North Vietnamese supplied and replenished their units in the very heart of South Vietnam by means of an ingenious supply system that used a complex of trails and roads known collectively as the Ho Chi Minh Trail. This is not by any means a single trail, but rather a network of secondary roads and trails that starts in central North Vietnam, runs south to near the North–South Vietnamese border, then curves west into Laos, and hence follows the Laos– South Vietnam border for a considerable distance. At various points, branches of the trail curve into South Vietnam. Laos was a neutral country, and therefore the location of the Ho Chi Minh Trail, together with the fact that the vehicles and personnel moved only at night, made detection very difficult. The problem was compounded by the existence of multiple parallel trails, and their location through thick jungle, which provided a perfect umbrella of thick vegetation.

In 1966 the Rand Corporation, a well-known think tank, studied the problem of interdiction of the Ho Chi Minh Trail and came up with a concept designed to reduce its effectiveness. The plan involved laying down by parachute, or "seeding," vast areas of the trail with self-powered sensors. These could be triggered by either noise or vibration, at which time the sensor would broadcast on a discrete VHF frequency whatever it was sensing. Airborne aircraft would receive the broadcasts, pinpoint the sensor location, and call down an air strike. A second step to this plan, never carried out, would have involved erecting an electronic fence along the entire South Vietnamese border, which would then trigger signals if anyone crossed the border.

Then Secretary of Defense Robert MacNamara accepted this plan and in 1967 began implementing the first part of it. This first portion involved seeding various portions of the Ho Chi Minh Trail in Laos and southwest North Vietnam with the sensors. Old U.S. Navy sonobuoys, originally designed to be dropped into the ocean to monitor the passage of submarines, were converted for this use. These sensors each had a particular VHF frequency on which they relayed whatever they heard. The sensors came in two types and were battery-powered. Their battery life was supposed to be up to four months of intermittent use, but many actually operated up to eight months. Whenever the sound or vibration ceased, the sensor turned its transmitter off. They were dropped in place by the Navy using specially adapted Lockheed P2V Neptunes.

The Air Force had the responsibility of monitoring these broadcasts at night, the only time there was much activity on the Ho Chi Minh Trail. It was for this mission that the 553rd Recon Wing was created. The Wing was equipped with specially converted EC-121Rs, which came out of storage at Davis-Montham AFB, and had originally been Navy WV-2s. These aircraft had no search or altitude finding radar, and hence no radomes. They did have special VHF radio receivers, a digital data processor, and a data link. They also had a nose-mounted weather radar, which doubled as terrain mapping radar and thus was useful in determining one's position.

The 553rd had some 25 aircraft assigned to it at Otis AFB, of which 20–21 were in SEA at any one time, operating from Korat Royal Thai Air Force Base, Thailand. Their missions involved flying over the general area of the Ho Chi Minh Trail at altitudes of up to 20,000 feet. The altitudes were dictated by the need to receive VHF line-of-sight transmissions from the sensors on the ground even from considerable distances.

Jerry L. Henderson, Major, USAF (Retired), flew with the 553rd as a navigator during 1967–68 and remembers those missions well. He explained how there would be up to eight monitoring positions in each aircraft, manned by combat information monitors (CIM). There was also a combat information control officer (CICO). The various CIMs would each monitor certain specific frequencies assigned to them. If signals were picked up that sounded promising, the CIM would tell the CICO on the intercom. The CICO, who could monitor all the frequencies on his console, would listen in. He would then try to evaluate the signal and attempt to decide if it meant something worth reporting to intelligence officers back on the ground. To help him in this task, the CICO had large-scale maps that accurately showed the exact locations of all the sensors. If the CICO decided to relay the information back to base, he would do so via data link, thus permitting the intelligence officers on the ground to evaluate the information in its original state. However, the next part of the plan, to call down air strikes, never developed, primarily because the EC–121 air crews themselves were not qualified to make good judgments as to the advisability of doing so. Furthermore, these crews did not have the same intelligence that the bases had. It is possible that some strikes were actually made based on the information broadcast by the sensors. But the Batcats were never involved at that point.

The 553rd reached the point where it had five different stations to cover, four over Laos, and one just south of the DMZ. Later, a sixth station was added over the Gulf of Tonkin. Each station would have an EC–121R on it for eight hours at a stretch. Allowing for some 2 hours flying to the station and 2 more returning to home base, each crew flew missions of close to 12 hours. Three aircraft were needed per station every 24 hours. The stations were 200–300 miles from each other.

Apparently due to reasons of safety, the EC–121Rs patrolled their individual stations at different altitudes, especially if two stations were adjacent. Thus, at one station the aircraft assigned would begin the mission at 16,000 feet, and halfway through go to 18,000 feet. At the next station, the starting altitude might be 17,000 feet, with 19,000 feet as the final altitude. If an aircraft had to abort its mission, and its time on station was past the midpoint, then one of the adjacent aircraft would move to a point where it could cover both areas. In such a case, this airplane would climb to 20,000 feet. Naturally, if an aircraft had to abort early in the mission, a backup plane would be launched in relief.

Crews were scheduled to fly approximately nine times each month. This meant a crew would fly some 100 hours per month, or 1,200 hours per year, which is a lot of flying. Sometimes they flew even more. Each crew would be scheduled to fly a 12-hour mission on Day 1, rest for 24 hours, then be on a 5-hour alert as the backup aircraft. The next day, or Day 4, they would begin the whole thing over again. Of course, if the backup crew was launched as the replacement aircraft, this meant they were flying with only one day off, rather than two.

Major Henderson remembers the problems the unit experienced with these aircraft. By 1967 these were high-time airplanes, and pretty well worn out. After a few months in SEA things could only get worse, in spite of the very best efforts of the ground crews, who struggled to maintain the aircraft as best they could. But spare parts were at times not available and had to be made from scratch. The power plants, oh those poor power plants! There were no new ones available. So it was a matter of fixing and fixing again, and, if possible, rebuilding.

The altitudes to which these aircraft had to climb caused one of the more serious problems that plagued the unit for a long time. In the early days of the 553rd, during training, it was discovered that the long, slow climbs to the operating altitudes was causing serious overheating in the power recovery turbines (PRTs) of the R–3350 engines. This in turn resulted in the lubricating oil "cooking" off, after which there would occur severe wearing of the bearings. This in turn caused fires in the PRTs, an event that was most disconcerting to any crew, the more so if it happened over water or enemy territory. The immediate action often taken was to dive the aircraft in an emergency descent! The airstream thus created would usually blow the fire out. But a means had to be found to prevent these fires. The preventive measure arrived at involved step-climbing to the desired altitude, which permitted the entire power plant to cool down periodically. A second means was to climb at a slightly reduced angle and a correspondingly higher air speed. The increased airflow also prevented overheating. In this manner, the PRT fires were reduced in number, as were engine shut-downs. At any rate, while the PRT fires lasted, there were some rather exciting and uncomfortable moments aboard the EC–121s.

Throughout their stay in SEA, the EC–121s had engine problems, caused in part by the combination of hard usage and old age. It was common to lose one engine, in which case the aircraft would usually continue its mission. If two engines expired, then a backup would be called into action, or an adjacent aircraft, after which the stricken EC–121 would limp back to base, or to some other field that was closer. In some cases, three engines were lost, at which time loud and violent curses would compete with fervent prayers aboard the airplane. As previously mentioned, there is the unconfirmed story that more than once a EC–121 actually touched down after the last operating engine had joined its sick companions and had to be shut down. Although not confirmed, this scenario is certainly not beyond credibility. Readers should realize that if one or two engines were shut down, the remaining power plants had to be operated at much higher power settings, which in turn made the chances of further problems even more likely.

The EC–121Rs of the 553rd were operated in SEA for approximately two years, until sometime in 1969, after which they were replaced by C–130 Hercules. During their stay in SEA, the EC–121Rs did not have any other actual types of missions except this one. They were, however, used to fly familiarization flights for ECM operators being trained to help suppress missiles launched by the Communists.

It could, no doubt, be argued that the mission of the Batcats was not accomplished. This may or may not be the case. The answer to that is probably shrouded in secrecy. But there is no doubt as to the continuing effort of its crews in completing their missions, nor of the fact that once more the old, worn-out, but gallant EC–121s were still up there completing their assigned missions in spite of age, lack of spare parts, and all the rest. It was one more interesting and revealing chapter, and it added another segment to the growing legend of the Constellation.

To try to put the contribution of the EC–121s in SEA into proper perspective is far from easy. At first glance one would have to conclude that compared to many other types of aircraft that flew during that fracas, the Warning Stars actually played a very minor and unimportant role. Their numbers were never very large. What's nine aircraft (not counting the Batcats) after all, compared to air strikes by B–52s numbering in the dozens or fighter-bombers in even larger numbers?

The planes were few, they were old, and even the total number of crew and ground personnel on hand at any one time was relatively small, especially in a war where the ground troops from the United States alone numbered more than a half a million. To top it all off, this was not even an actual complete unit, but a detachment from a wing based thousands of miles away.

But one must look a little closer. One must realize that for a period of approximately nine years there was *always* an EC–121 somewhere in the air over SEA keeping track of all airborne traffic of an area of some 150,000 square miles. That's right. Nine long years, day and night, in good weather and bad, with fresh personnel, but mostly weary men hanging in and doing a job that demanded razor-sharp judgment and the ability to keep large amounts of information straight.

As Colonel West put it, "Here was an aircraft that had outlived its usefulness as a segment of the air defense system. But it was found to be very useful in SEA." That's probably an understatement, because *no other aircraft then flying could have done the job*.

For those nine years, from 1965 to 1974, the crews of the Warning Stars were, in effect, the people who monitored and/or controlled everything that was a great deal of metal flying around through that congested chunk of air space. This aging plane with the funny shape and the far-from-new engines and the aging electronics did such a fantastic job that new uses for it were being discovered almost up to the time it was finally retired back to the United States. Readers mustn't forget that by 1974 we are talking about airplanes that were at least 15 years old, and based on designs that went back fully 30 years!

If the various strategic and tactical aircraft deployed to SEA were the ones that actually brought the war to the enemy, then it must be said that the EC–121s of the 552nd Wing constituted the means by which this entire air war was made more feasible and more likely to succeed. The EC–121s and their crews had finally won their hard-earned spurs in a for-real war environment.

Statistics taken from the historical records compiled by the 552nd AEW&C Wing, for the period April 1965 through May 1974 summarize the story neatly.

- Over 13,931 combat sorties flown, with a 98 percent sortie success rate.
- More than 2,761 days flown in a 12-year period.
- Flew 98,777 combat hours.
- Issued 3,297 MIG (enemy aircraft) warnings.
- Controlled more than 20,000 aircraft over enemy territory.
- Detected over 400 unknowns.
- Achieved 187 consecutive on-time take-offs.
- Credited with 80 recovery assists of downed U.S. airmen.
- Assisted in 25 MIG kills.

The personnel were awarded 2 Legion of Merits, 63 Distinguished Flying Crosses, 3,351 Air Medals, 59 Bronze Stars, 22 Air Force Commendation Medals, 231 Purple Hearts, and 4 Airmen's Medals.

In 1974, the last EC–121 departed SEA, and everyone felt that these planes had finally come to the end of the road. It wouldn't be long before the last one would be retired. Little did anyone then realize that the proud old birds would have one more chapter to write.

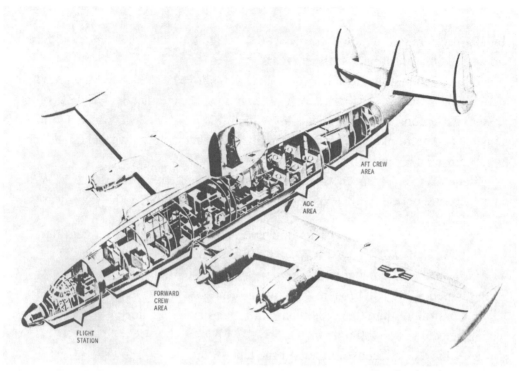

16-1 General arrangement of the interior of a EC–121D Warning Star. The Airborne Operations Center housed the various radar and communications consoles. (USAF)

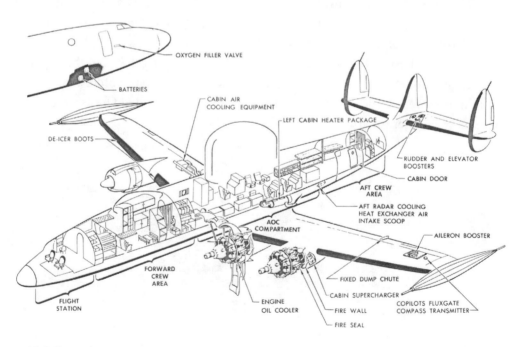

16-2 General arrangement of the interior of a EC–121H Warning Star. (U.S. Air Force)

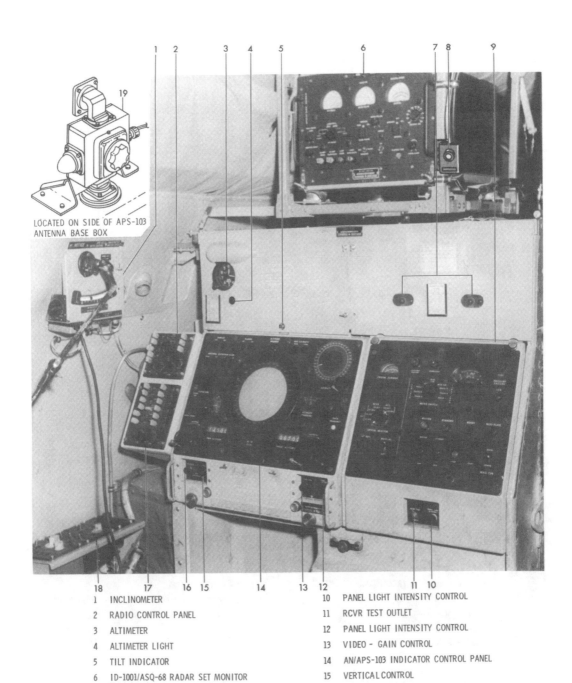

16-3 Detail of the Height Finder's Station, EC–121H and Q. (U.S. Air Force)

1. INCLINOMETER
2. RADIO CONTROL PANEL
3. ALTIMETER
4. ALTIMETER LIGHT
5. TILT INDICATOR
6. ID-1001/ASQ-68 RADAR SET MONITOR
7. POWER SUPPLY INDICATING LIGHT
8. APS-103 DUMMY LOAD TEMPERATURE WARNING LIGHT
9. AN/APS-103 CONTROL PANEL
10. PANEL LIGHT INTENSITY CONTROL
11. RCVR TEST OUTLET
12. PANEL LIGHT INTENSITY CONTROL
13. VIDEO - GAIN CONTROL
14. AN/APS-103 INDICATOR CONTROL PANEL
15. VERTICAL CONTROL
16. HORIZONTAL COUNTER
17. ICS CONTROL PANEL
18. AN/ARC-85 NO. 3 CONTROL PANEL
19. DUMMY LOAD WAVE GUIDE SWITCH

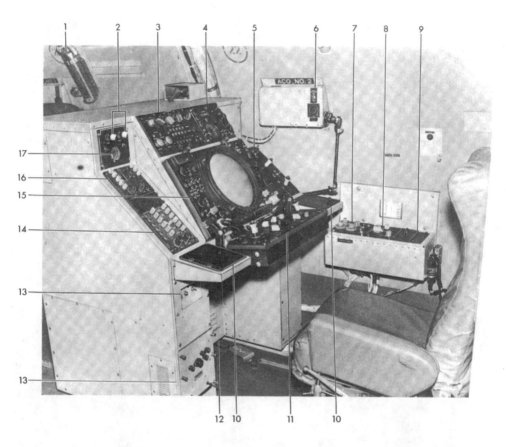

1 HAND FIRE EXTINGUISHER
2 C-4817/APA-159 DESK AND PANEL DIMMER RHEOSTATS
3 RHI (RANGE HEIGHT INDICATOR) ASSIGNMENT PANEL
4 C-4815/APA-159 INDICATOR CONTROL PANEL
5 CP-738/APA-159 TARGET-INTERCEPT COMPUTER PANEL
6 UHF ANTENNA SELECTOR SWITCH
7 C-2187/APX-49 DECODER CONTROL (MODE 2/3)
8 AN/ARC-85 UHF TRANSCEIVER CONTROL PANEL
9 PANEL LIGHTS RHEOSTAT
10 WRITING SURFACES (2)
11 C-4814/APA-159 COMPUTER CONTROL PANEL
12 PP-4037/APS-95 POWER SUPPLY
13 PP-3830/APA-159 POWER SUPPLY PANEL
14 ICS CONTROL PANEL
15 IP-719/APA-159 AZIMUTH-RANGE INDICATOR PANEL
16 C-628/ARC-27 UHF RADIO CONTROL PANEL
17 CLOCK (24 HOUR)

16-4 Detail of the Search Radar Operators Station, EC–121D. (U.S. Air Force)

16-5 One of the many versions of the EC–121 that flew in SEA. Notice that this aircraft carries fuselage camouflage. (Lockheed Martin)

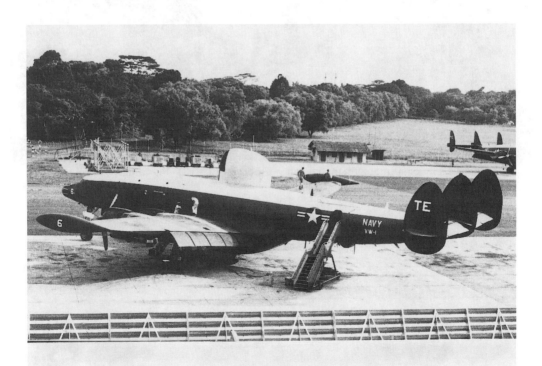

16-6 A USN WV–2 shown at Changi, Thailand, August 1964. (Flt. Lt. Tony Fairbairn, Royal Air Force)

16-7 Radar Technician/Intercept Technician position on EC–121. Photo taken during Project College Eye, 1970. (B. C. Cusick)

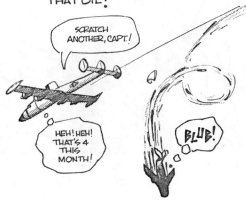

16-8 Cartoons illustrative of Warning Star operations in SEA. (*Air Force Magazine*)

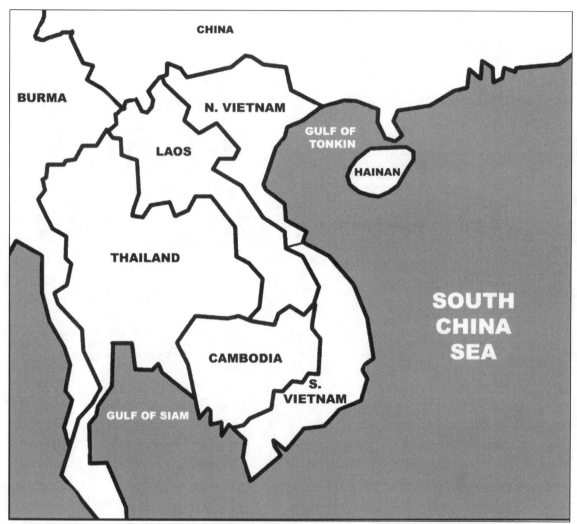

16-9 Map of Southeast Asia theatre of operations, over which the EC–121s flew with distinction during the period between 1965 and 1974. (Luisada)

Chapter 17

SO CONNIES DON'T FLY ANYMORE, HUH? THE 915TH AEW&C GROUP

Come, take a little trip with me. It's spring 1977, and the Southeast smells nice. Those warm breezes are sure great after the winter up north. You want to know where we're going? All in good time, my friend. For the moment, just sit back and enjoy the scenery. We've landed at Miami International Airport in one of those oversized blowtorches they call a jet. Now, having finally left the immensity of that airfield behind, we drive south along Florida Route 1.

Some 25 miles south of the center of Miami lies the town of Homestead. Some people think this is just one more suburb of Miami, but don't say that too loud in front of these folks. Its a fairly small town, and after checking in at the motel we head east on an arrow-straight two-lane road. The town ends almost immediately, and for some four miles there is little to see except small cultivated fields and long drainage canals. Nothing breaks the horizon except the overpass of the Sunshine Toll Road. A little way beyond we come to a sentry hut in the middle of the road staffed by two armed Air Police, one of which is a woman. Above the sentry house is a sign: WELCOME TO HOMESTEAD AIR FORCE BASE.

Once inside we follow directions, and after a mile or so, we come to a neat, two-story building that could be taken for quarters of some kind. But the sign in front of the semi-circular driveway sets us straight immediately: 915TH AIRBORNE EARLY WARNING AND CONTROL GROUP (AFRES).

Inside we are greeted by a tall, slim captain, Claude H. Stewart, who hastens to tell us he goes by the name of Holly. We are here to visit one of the two Air Force Reserve units that, as of 1977, still fly Constellation equipment of one type or another. The Navy has at least one such unit at Pt. Mugu, California. Of the two Air Force units, one is at Spaatz AFB, Harrisburg, Pennsylvania, and flies both EC–121s and C–121s. The 915th here at Homestead flies EC–121T airplanes only.

We've wangled an invitation from the Pentagon to visit the 915th and find out precisely what they do and also to fly a training mission in one of their graceful birds. Captain Holly Stewart is the group Information Officer (IO) and also a EC–121 navigator. He gives us some of the unit's background, and then takes me to meet some of the people who run this outfit. Among the officers I meet are Colonel Evan E. Clements, Air Force Reserve, the commander; Colonel James H. West, Air Force, the vice-commander; LTC Joseph I. Whitmore Jr., Air Force, deputy commander for operations; Major David Harper, Air Force, deputy commander for maintenance; Major Dennis Weber, Air Force, primary weapons control and flight examiner; and others.

The events that led up to the creation of the 915th go back to 1968. Iceland, which is a member country of NATO and has a U.S. base at Keflavik, had two ground-based radars on the south side of the island that could not be used to paint low-flying aircraft approaching from the north. There used to be a radar platform on the north side of the island, but it was blown down in heavy seas, was rebuilt, got blown down again, and then was not rebuilt. At that time, three EC–121s from the 551st Wing at Otis AFB were sent to Iceland on TDY. Since then, EC–121s have been on duty there constantly for a period of 10 years!

Actually, there was another reason why the EC–121s were sent there. In that part of the world there is a gap in the continuity of radar coverage which is known as the GIUK Gap. This is an acronym for Greenland, Iceland, United Kingdom. Although there is a certain amount of radar coverage, it had been realized many years previously that an AEW type of coverage would greatly increase the overall level of vigilance possible. In fact, since August 1, 1961, the Navy's Atlantic Barrier Headquarters had been located at Keflavik. This operation was shut down in 1965, concurrently with the removal of the Navy's Pacific Barrier, partly as an economy measure.

In 1968 the Pentagon considered it important to reestablish an AEW operation in that part of the world. In this the Pentagon was heavily supported by the NATO countries, and interestingly, by the government of Iceland, which had originally indicated its relief at having the EC–121s removed from Iceland in 1965. So it was that the 551st Wing's EC–121s came to be stationed at Keflavik.

By 1973, with the SEA conflict ended, a number of reorganizations took place. The 551st at Otis had been deactivated. The 552nd Wing's Detachment 2 had been moved from McCoy AFB, Florida, to Homestead. Then, in November 1974 the Pentagon announced that the 552nd would be deactivated during summer 1976.

In December 1975 the 552nd Group, which was all that remained of the 552nd Wing, was deactivated after 22 years of continuous service with the EC–121s. Simultaneously, a Detachment 1, 20th Air Defense Squadron, was activated at Homestead AFB using men and aircraft of the defunct 552nd. This Detachment 1 was to work together with the 79th AEW&C Squadron. Actually, the 20th AD Squadron was based at Ft. Lee, Virginia. Precisely one year later, in December 1976, the 915th AEW&C Group was created as the sole manager of the remains of the entire EC–121 program.

This, then, is the unit we've come to visit. Its mission and structure are unique in Air Force history. The basic mission is to provide airborne radar surveillance, command, and tactical control as directed by the Aerospace Defense Command (ADC) and the Joint Chiefs of Staff (JCS). Specifically, it is responsible for the Iceland mission, and for this mission reports directly to the JCS. It has a secondary training mission that, by pure coincidence is carried out over the Florida Straits. This mission conveniently enables the 915th to maintain a watchful radar eye on the activities over Cuba.

The way all this came about is that at the time the 552nd Wing and all the EC–121T's were being phased out, the JCS went to the Air Force and asked what plans they had for maintaining the Iceland mission. In retrospect, it appears that back in 1975 the Air Force had not planned to continue this particular mission. The Air Force then found itself with two options. One would have been to try and reactivate the 552nd, which would have been a very expensive proposition. The other option was to create a new Reserve unit, which it did.

The Air Force at that point could have done one of two things to ensure that the unit be able to carry out what amounted to a year-round, full-time mission, which moreover had the main base (Homestead) separated from the advance, operational base (Keflavik) by thousands of miles of ocean.

The first was to hire a considerable number of Air Force technicians, who are all actually civilian employees of the Air Force, to work on a day-to-day basis. The second was to augment the Reserve unit with regular duty personnel. Although the two may seem identical to the reader, there is actually quite a difference in terms of organization.

After much discussion it was finally decided that the best possible way, under the circumstances, would be to have a Reserve unit augmented by sufficient numbers of regular active-duty officers and men to ensure adequate manning at all times. As part of this, the 79th AEW&C Squadron (Reserve) would have its quota of EC–121s increased from 6 to 10. This was later increased again to 12 aircraft.

As part of this overall mixing of regular and Reserve personnel, it was also decided that because the reservists were by far the larger group, the entire unit would be a Reserve unit with an active-duty officer as commander. This type of setup was expressly forbidden by Air Force regulation, which specifically states that a regular cannot command a Reserve unit, and inversely a reservist cannot command a regular unit. A one-time waiver was granted for the 915th and its subordinate units.

The result was a combined group with some 800 Air Force reservists and 280 active-duty personnel. The commander, Colonel Clements, is a Reservist; the vice-commander, Colonel West, is active duty, and the deputy for operations, LTC Whitmore, is also active duty. So it goes down the line, with both categories intermixed. From the foregoing, readers can see how the 915th is indeed a unique unit, first because of its rather strange mixture of personnel, and second, because of the fact it is the only Reserve unit with a full-time mission for which it reports directly to the JCS.

The 915th AEW&C Group consists of three of its own units and provides training for three Military Airlift Command units. Additionally, two active-duty units are indirectly involved with the operations of the 915th. The units are:

- The 79th AEW&C Squadron is the group's tactical unit. It is responsible for the training of aircrews and the actual flying of mission.
- The 915th Consolidated Aircraft Maintenance Squadron is responsible for maintenance on the aircraft and associated weapons systems. Its various branches include Aircraft Maintenance, Field Maintenance, Avionics Maintenance, and so on.
- The 915th Combat Support Squadron works much like a combat support unit at base level. Its personnel are mainly involved with the administrative problems of keeping the group running.
- Detachment 1, 20th Air Defense Squadron, is an active-duty organization. It handles all administrative matters involving the active duty personnel assigned to augment the 915th AEW&C Group.
- Operating Location M, Detachment 1, 20th ADS, is responsible for the NATO mission in Iceland. It is located at Keflavik Naval Air Station there and reports not only to the Aerospace Defense Command but to the Air

Force Iceland commander as well. This branch is staffed with approximately 56 active-duty personnel.
- The 915th Civil Engineering Flight and the 70th and 90th Mobile Aerial Port Squadrons, located at Homestead, are all military airlift gained units. They are assigned to the 915th for training purposes and administrative functions only.

The 915th AEW&C Wing was officially activated on December 1, 1976. Its total life span was a little less than two years, with the last aircraft leaving Homestead for the bone yard on October 12, 1978. Actually, of course, the EC–121s flew out of Homestead from 1971 on, but under the direction of other organizational units. The short life of the 915th was a function of the time is took to introduce the new Boeing E–3A Airborne Warning and Control System (AWACS) aircraft as an operational system that would replace the EC–121s. Setting up a special unit such as the 915th for such a relatively short span of time speaks volumes for the importance attached to the overall mission by the Pentagon and the JCS.

Let us for a moment examine the missions of the 915th in some detail. At Homestead the mission is basically one of training. To accomplish this, the unit periodically mans a number of patrol stations off the coast of Florida. During these missions the crews maintain surveillance of normal traffic, and, if available, works with air defense fighters directing them on intercept runs. In addition, their flights may include vectoring aircraft for air refueling operations, air searches, border warnings, and missile launch radar tracking. Unofficially, the unit is in an excellent position to monitor air traffic in and out of Cuba as well as shipping traffic to the island, and can also easily maintain communications with the U.S. naval base at Guantanamo Bay, Cuba. On the ground, the maintenance personnel have the back-breaking job of keeping these old, complex aircraft in the best possible operational shape (more on that later).

At the Keflavik NAS, Iceland, known as Operation Location Alpha Alpha (OLAA), the 915th stands 24-hour alert tours that augment NATO and the Iceland Defense Force, flies random radar missions, provides early warning and control against any airborne intruders penetrating the Iceland ADIZ, and routinely detects and directs interceptors against Soviet aircraft. They are also available to fly search missions, maintain surveillance on shipping, and basically can extend airborne radar surveillance hundreds of miles to the east. In 10 years in Iceland, the EC–121s have made over 600 detections and directed over 200 intercepts.

A look at the map on page 365 clearly shows that airborne radar aircraft based in Iceland can command a radar view of the approaches not only to Iceland itself but also air traffic flying north and west of there toward Greenland and North America, as well as air traffic over Scandinavia and the northern approaches to the British Isles. Because the Icelandic mission worked very closely with NATO, it is believed that a certain amount of their information would be passed on to Danish and Norwegian defense personnel. All of this is classified information, but the mere fact that the Iceland mission was picked up by the new AWACS, which replaced the EC–121s when they were finally retired, gives a clue to the importance of the entire project. There are very few AWACS aircraft in service, and assigning one to Iceland on a continuing basis says volumes for the priority given to that part of the world.

The Iceland mission required that the 915th position three EC–121s with full crews at Keflavik every two weeks. This means that crews, regardless of whether they are regular or Reserve, are gone for two full weeks at a time. While there, each crew and aircraft pull a 24-hour alert from 1000 hours one day to 1000 hours the next day. During this period they are on a 1-hour scramble alert, although in reality they are normally airborne in 40–50 minutes. They are permitted that long a period of time because the crews, enlisted men and officers, are billeted in separate facilities on the base. Also, an EC–121 is not a one-man F–102 or F–106 specifically designed for quick scrambles.

The command that directs the scramble is forewarned, by some classified means, that the Soviets are airborne somewhere in that general part of the world and are heading in that general direction. The scramble order is delayed until the intruder aircraft is estimated to be about one hour away from reaching the maximum radar range from Keflavik. The actual intercept, if there is one, may be a visual one by the EC–121 or, more likely, the EC–121 vectors F–4 Phantoms, scrambled out of Keflavik, against the intruder. Fighters of the Royal Air Force can also be scrambled from northern Scotland.

Meanwhile, a second crew is on a two-hour alert status. If the primary alert crew is scrambled, the secondary, or back-up crew, automatically moves up to the primary alert slot. If the second crew, in their role as the primary crew, is also scrambled, the third crew goes on one-hour alert status. Normally, the second crew is available to fly a training mission, or any other mission that may be assigned to it, usually not exceeding an eight-hour duration. The day after being on scramble alert, a crew would normally be off, or on what is called its spare day. However, the spare crew may get pulled back to two-hour alert status, or even scrambled, on its spare day. Thus, the two weeks at Keflavik are anything but a vacation, especially with the kind of weather prevalent in that part of the world!

Now that we know a bit more about this unit that operated the EC–121s, it's time to take a day and go fly a training mission. Air Force units all have more or less rigorous training schedules year-round. A Reserve unit would normally consider its training to be a major part of its total activity. In the case of the 915th that's not strictly speaking true, because despite its Reserve status, it also flies a great many hours operationally. Keep in mind that every two weeks the 915th dispatches three aircraft to Iceland. During their two-week period there, the aircraft may do little flying and be simply on an alert basis ready for a quick scramble, or they may be required to fly almost continuously. Circumstances at the time vary greatly, and thus so do their total flying time out of Keflavik NAS.

FLYING AN EC–121 MISSION

It's April 23, 1977, and time to go fly a Connie! Today we have the blessings of the Secretary of the Air Force to ride on one of the 915th training flights—a most uncommon kind of training flight.

I struggle out of bed at 5:30 A.M., shave, get into my old Civil Air Patrol flying suit and my black flying boots, and go have breakfast in the motel's dining room. By 6:45 I am slowly driving through the base looking for Building 596, the home of the 79th AEW&C Squadron. As I park, a big Lockheed C–141 Starlifter whistles in for a landing, its landing lights glowing in the early morning twilight.

Inside I go to the Flight Operations Room. A young lieutenant is filling out the typical Air Force forms necessary to get a plane off the ground. I ask if Captain Merrill Tank, Air Force Reserve, has arrived. The Lieutenant says no, but that he will be the co-pilot. Introductions made, I learn that he is Steve Steinbring. Shortly, Captain Tank arrives, also young and sporting a healthy red mustache. He suggest I tag along with him and Steinbring during the various steps prior to going out to the airplane.

At 7:15 I go to the Briefing Room, together with the other 21 personnel manifested on this flight. Tank begins his briefing, which is mercifully brief. All manifested personnel are called by name to be sure each is present at the briefing. When my turn comes, I am presented as Colonel Luisada of the Civil Air Patrol, a writer. I am somewhat embarrassed at the use of my rank, which means little or nothing on a military installation. The aircraft today is SN 50122, known in the unit merely as 122, a 1955 vintage EC–121. Our mission will take us to Station 50 Alpha. Tank goes on to say that he wants everyone aboard and the aircraft ready to go by 0830 hours, with take-off scheduled for 0900. The mission is to run a total of six hours.

Then comes the bad news of the morning. The box lunches have not arrived.

Rather than delay the flight, someone has been sent to buy TV dinners. This piece of information is met with jeers and derisive comments by all. Evidently the flight kitchen at Homestead enjoys a well-earned reputation for screwing up, especially for the weekend Reserve activities.

The briefing over, I follow the two pilots to Base Operations. There weather is rechecked and confirmed. Today it looks good, with the usual small buildups starting at around 4,000 feet. These are daily occurrences during spring in this area. The flight is filed with the dispatcher, who in turn passes it on to ATC. I learn our tactical call sign today will be Unity 78.

Then its out to the waiting aircraft, sitting quietly, but with a highly vocal APU whining near the left main landing gear. Steinbring asks if I'd like to accompany him on the walk-around inspection, and I quickly agree.

Starting under the tail cone and moving clockwise, Steinbring explains what he is looking for. Signs of fuel, oil, or hydraulic fuel leaks, unsecured hatches, indications that elevators, ailerons or flaps are not secured properly, landing gear linkages, and a series of other potential trouble spots. When he reaches the number 3 engine he quickly spots an unsecured latch on the lower cowling. With vigorous arm motions he waves a ground crewman over. Quickly the loose latch is put to rights, and the walk-around continues back to its stating point.

Then its time to go aboard, climbing up the tall metal stairway. As I enter through the rear door, the heat inside the aircraft is already noticeable. Somewhat gingerly I follow Steinbring forward, threading my way between radar consoles, electric equipment, flight bags, crew seats, and various crew members busy fitting parachute harnesses. Although the EC–121 is most assuredly a long-range aircraft, chest chutes are carried in the unlikely event of their need.

After I'm shown my seat, fitted for a chute, and told I may stand in the cockpit during take-offs and landings, I go forward and observe all the goings on. The three-man crew is making itself comfortable, and I recognize the flight engineer as a man I met yesterday in the EC–121 flight simulator located at Homestead.

Shortly we are ready to get things under way. Tank turns to me and mentions that the engines are started in a 3, 4, 2, 1 sequence. Finished with the Before Start Engines Check List, the crew now begins to bring life to the big Curtiss-Wrights on the wings.

I hear a voice belonging to a ground area member over the cockpit speaker. These 121s have an interesting feature. Rather than using the intercom, the ground crew hears the pilots through a speaker mounted on the nose gear. When the ground crew replies, their voices are heard on both intercom and the cockpit speaker.

The co-pilot punches the starter button and the number 3 starts turning. I hear the voice over the speaker saying: "Two blades, four blades, six blades." It is then that the ignition is turned on by the flight engineer while the pilot eases the number 3 throttle forward. Through the still-open forward door right next to the cockpit, I hear the unmistakable sound of an R–3350 with power recovery turbines (PRTs) starting. There is a growl as of a giant clearing his throat, some backfiring, and the propeller turns slowly. Then, as all the cylinders begin to fire, a large gray-white gob of smoke is released, and the propeller gradually picks up speed. Unlike other reciprocating engines without the PRTs, these R–3350s start much more gradually, almost like a turboprop power plant.

The process is repeated for the other engines, and Unity 78 is alive and throbbing with power. The doors are closed and sealed, and taxi clearance is obtained from Homestead Ground Control. With only a very small increase in power, the big EC–121 rolls off the blocks at 0842.

I had previously been alerted to the fact that when a Super Connie begins to taxi, the main gear performs in a very strange fashion. Namely, it waddles from side to side, with first one main gear moving forward a short distance, and then the other. This is caused by the relatively large amount of play in the main gear struts, which in turn is a result of the uncommonly long length of the main gear. Sure enough, as we taxi out I feel the waddling shaking me as I stand on the flight deck just behind the two pilots.

Take-offs this morning are from Runway 05. Homestead used to be a SAC base, and in keeping with many such, has only one runway, in this case 05/23, 11,600 feet of concrete. As we taxi out, the pilot makes a quick check of the propeller reversal system. As we approach the runway, I notice what appears to be a general aviation flight line off in a corner of the field, and I make a mental note to ask about this. I was not then aware that Homestead was one of those dual-purpose fields, military and commercial, which were becoming more frequent at the time. I was extremely surprised at the explanation of that row of small aircraft!

Holding short of the runway on the run-up pad, the crew now goes through the lengthy Before Take-Off Check List. The flight engineer, in particular, spends a number of minutes carefully checking the operation of those big R–3350s. While checking the magnetos, I notice that he firmly taps the RPM gauge repeatedly to make absolutely certain that a drop in revolutions does not go unnoticed because of a sticking needle. Then, after the mag check is completed to his satisfaction, he runs each engine up to 2350 RPM, and examines the jagged green traces showing up on the engine analyzer. Somehow, all this trained, professional behavior is highly comforting to me. With 22 people on board and a gross weight of 126,000 pounds, I feel that it would be most desirable if those four big power plants function with no trouble whatsoever!

The checks are completed at last. Tank quickly reviews the take-off data with the other two crew members, not failing to include his intensions in case of engine failure during either the take-off or immediately after. Then Steinbring contacts the tower for ATC and take-off clearance. After a short delay, back comes the word.

"Unity 78, you are cleared for a right turn out to a heading of 180°, climb and maintain 4,000 feet, cleared to station 50 Alpha. Contact Departure Control after take-off." The clearance is checked and confirmed, and then Steinbring changes to the tower frequency. Unity 78 is told it can taxi into position and hold, Runway 05.

Tank gets on the cabin speaker system and alerts everyone to the impending take-off. Then he releases the parking brake, and slowly we taxi onto the runway and turn to face down its two miles of length. Now Tank moves more quickly. Holding the aircraft with the toe brakes, he calls for the Line-Up Check List. Quickly disposed of, Tank then calls out "35 inches." The flight engineer advances the throttles until the engines are roaring at 35 inches of manifold pressure. During all this I am standing behind the A/C's seat, hanging on with one hand and holding a small cassette tape recorder with the other.

The A/C comes off the brakes, and, as the EC–121 starts forward with a jerk, calls, "Rolling." Immediately thereafter he calls, "Maximum power!" and the flight engineer rapidly advances the throttles to the stops. The engines bellow with the noise characteristic only of R–3350s. The EC–121 accelerates very rapidly, so much so that I almost lose my grip on the seat back, in which case I would go staggering back into the main cabin! As the A/C steers with his left hand and keeps his right on the control wheel, the co-pilot has his left hand holding the throttles full forward. His eyes are on the air speed indicator. In seconds his voice calls out firmly, "Seventy knots'" This is the point at which acceleration is checked. Another thousand feet of runway goes by, during which I hold on tightly to the back of the flight engineer's seat, and then the co-pilot calls out, "V–1!" Tank puts both hands firmly on the control wheel, and pulls back slightly, easing the nose gear off the runway. Then comes the call, "V–2!" Tank now pulls back more firmly, and the EC–121 roars off the runway.

Tank's right hand flashes out, his thumb up, as he calls for gear retraction. Steinbring duplicates the movement with his left hand, echoes the call, and then reaches down and moves the gear lever to the up position. As we roar up from the runway I check my watch. It is 0859. Not bad for a scheduled 0900 hours take-off! As soon as Tank sees positive confirmation on the center panel that the gear is up and locked, he turns his head slightly and calls over his shoulder "METO power!" Immediately the flight engineer pulls back the throttles and reduces the manifold pressure shown.

Now, as a standard climb is established, Tank gently banks the EC–121 to the right until it is heading due south and continues the climb. Flaps are slowly retracted, and the bird is cleaned up. Soon we are over the Florida Keys and approaching 4,000 feet. Leveling off, Tank puts the aircraft on autopilot and slides his seat back, as the flight engineer sets cruise power. It becomes much quieter on the flight deck. Everyone visibly relaxes. Below me the shallow waters off the Keys are a beautiful, light blue-green, with darker areas where the puffy air mass clouds cast their shadows. Its approximately a 28-minute run to Station 50 Alpha, and we cruise serenely along at 185 knots indicated air speed.

At 0927 Unity 78 reaches Station 50 Alpha. This is a racetrack-shaped course some 50 miles long, running roughly east–west, and located south of the Florida Keys. As the map on page 366 shows, the station is not far from the boundary with the Cuban area of jurisdiction.

Still maintaining 4,000 feet, Tank turns Unity 78 on a westerly heading on the initial leg of the station. The aircraft is trimmed slightly nose up, with a deck angle of 4°, which permits the search radar to obtain better resolution. In this slightly begging attitude, the air speed is reduced, and we drone through the clear sky at 174 knots. Then, at 0938 we are cleared to climb to 6,000 feet. The reason for the increase in altitude is that a layer of scattered to broken cumulus is developing at our altitude, and the flight is becoming increasingly bumpy and uncomfortable.

Engine noise increases appreciably, and the big Connie assumes a steeper angle of attack. In a few minutes we are at our new altitude, the big R–3350s are again throttled back, and once more we drone comfortably through the sky. As the end of Station 50 Alpha is reached, the autopilot is set up to bring the EC–121 around in a smooth, gradual 180° turn. Then back we fly toward the opposite end of the station.

Back in the cluttered main cabin area the radar equipment is being turned on and warmed up. The Reserve radar controllers are preparing for their stint at the scopes, which, after all, is the purpose of this training exercise.

Suddenly, at 1030 hours, a fuse blows and puts the gyrocompasses out of commission. As I watch, Sergeants Looney and Shultz quickly open a hatch in the floor of the forward portion of the cabin. One of them goes down head first into the hold underneath. The two work together for over 10 minutes, then go into the cockpit to talk to Tank. Shortly, I hear Tank's voice on the P.A. system informing us the mission is being aborted and we are returning to base.

I go forward to talk to Tank. He explains that an inverter has failed and put both gyrocompasses out of action. With the clouds outside building up in intensity, a common daily occurrence in this area, precise navigation could become dicey. Moreover, the weather forecast for the next few hours is predicting frontal action. As Tank points out, we are over water, not far from Cuban air space, and it wouldn't do to stray too far. Inasmuch as operational regulations for this type of mission clearly specify that the A/C has the option of aborting a training mission if both gyrocompasses fail and the weather is deteriorating, Tank feels there is no percentage in taking unnecessary risks. This is particularly true today when he has aboard a number of nonflying Reservists on orientation plus one nosy civilian writer.

So at 1047 we turn back to a northerly heading. Its back to the barn for us. Our return leg to Homestead will take just under 30 minutes. Tank now turns the controls over to Steinbring, who will land the big EC–121 from the right seat. It seems that in almost no time we are ready to begin our letdown from 6,000 feet for our approach to Homestead. Steinbring calls for 2,400 RPM, and the flight engineer eases the throttles back. There is a corresponding reduction in the engine noise and the nose dips. With the aircraft trimmed for descent, we slide down at some 1,000 feet per minute rate of descent.

Everyone in the airplane is now strapped in, except, once again, yours truly, who is standing behind and between the pilots' seats and hanging on tightly!

Our air speed is slowly decreasing. Steinbring calls for 60 percent flaps, and Tank quickly complies. I lean over and look backward out the side window but cannot see the big Fowler flaps extending. But I can feel them as the aircraft rapidly slows down. At 170 knots we come down. As we approach 4,000 feet we penetrate the condensation layer and encounter light to moderate turbulence; then more turbulence as we cross the coastline, now at below 3,000 feet.

The field is now in sight, and as we approach pattern altitude 1,200 feet above the ground, Steinbring levels off and the speed comes down to 150 knots. This will be a visual approach. Steinbring now calls for 2,600 RPM, and the flight engineer puts the propellers in low pitch and increases the RPM. The typical unsynchronized thrumming noise of a large-propeller aircraft approaching for a landing can now be both heard and felt. As we turn onto base leg to the runway, Steinbring calls for gear down, and Tank moves the gear extension lever. I can hear the gear extending and feel us slowing down some more. Speed goes down to 140 knots, and Steinbring calls for 80 percent flaps. Turning final, with landing clearance already given by the tower, we are down to 125 knots.

The Connie flies slowly, with the characteristic stable feeling that has endeared it to countless flight crews. Steinbring eases her down on the final approach, speed gradually decreasing to 100 knots. As he flares out just short of the runway, a slight cross-wind causes the plane to drift right. Tank laughingly calls out to Steinbring that he's going to land in the grass! Not a chance! Skillfully he eases the EC–121 back to the center line, pulls back the throttles, floats over the runway numbers, and at 1116 touches down just beyond them. No reverse power is applied in deference to the old and weary engines, and with gentle use of the toe brakes, the EC–121 slows down and is turned off the runway.

In short order we taxi back to the ramp and, guided by a signal man, roll to our parking position. The engines are shut down, and stillness surrounds the aircraft. Our 6.5-hour mission was reduced to a little more than 2 hours but nevertheless was certainly interesting. As we disembark I have the opportunity to ask again about the long row of private aircraft parked on a remote area of the field. I come to find out that they are all airplanes caught smuggling drugs and impounded by federal agencies. Having noticed some mighty expensive turboprops and business jets, it clearly demonstrates the level of activity that this sordid business has reached.

Later that day, while I'm back at my motel, heavy thunderstorms blanket the area, and I am generally relieved that Tank had decided to abort the mission. I really hadn't packed any clothes for an extended visit to Cuba, nor would I have particularly enjoyed coming eyeball to eyeball with a Cuban MIG if we had flown inadvertently across the U.S./Cuba airspace boundary!

MAINTAINING THE EC–121TS

Now that I've flown in the EC–121, I'm very curious to find out more about the maintenance problems that must be plaguing the 915th. For this kind of information I go to talk to Major David Harper, the deputy commander for maintenance of the 915th. Harper has been in the maintenance business a long time, despite his deceptively youthful looks, and has been involved with such diverse aircraft as F–105s and F–106s and also C–47s, C–7s, C–9s, and C–141s. The comparisons he draws for me are truly illuminating in a number of ways.

The EC–121s have been on the verge of being completely retired from the inventory for a very long time. In the mid-1960s some were already being mothballed. Then the Vietnam War came along, and many (but not all) of the aircraft were taken out of retirement and flew again, either in SEA or on the Barrier patrols. By the early 1970s they were again being retired, and then once again were put back on active duty, as it were, to fly the Iceland mission for one thing. A few others were still flying for the Navy. During at least the previous 10 years of this on-again off-again operations, the funding for the EC–121s was on a yearly basis. Thus, no long-range, systematic maintenance programs could be carried out. The net results were nothing short of catastrophic in terms of aircraft reliability and sometimes safety.

For example, the Air Force EC–121s had their last major corrosion facility contract in 1967, and the last depot maintenance in 1972. Both are essential to this particular aircraft. All aircraft normally go through isochronal inspections. These are inspections based on a fixed time interval regardless of the amount of flying hours during that interval. In 1977 the 915th was putting the EC–121s through a minor isochronal inspection every 90 days and a major one every 180 days. But even these could in no way make up for the total lack of proper maintenance during the previous decade.

Major Harper and his maintenance people found themselves in a position where they never knew either what they might find that required repair or replacement or what might fail next in flight. Engines, of course, were always a problem. However, the type of maintenance carried out by the 915th resulted in the R–3350s often lasting up to 1,500 hours TBO. Considering the age and history of these particular power plants, this is nothing short of phenomenal. Consider that in the late 1950s commercial airlines had R–3350s with only 700-800 hours TBO.

Control cables would fail and have to be replaced. Ditto for landing gear components, electronic gear, or for practically any part of the airplane, moving or fixed.

Readers must keep two things in mind while reading about this battle to keep the EC–121s in the air. First, really comprehensive inspections and repairs have historically been carried out at depots, where the work is done indoors with special equipment and tools. Second, for each aircraft type in the inventory, there is normally an entire back-up system to supply replacement parts, components, and even entire portions of the airplane. For the EC–121s, there is no back-up whatsoever. Parts are either cannibalized from mothballed EC–121s or else fabricated on the spot. In the 1970s, the 915th could count on having no basic technical training on the EC–121, no engine overhauls, no depot-level maintenance, and no contracts for the subsystems. What they did have was a superb, dedicated group of men led by Harper and staffed in large part by men who had previously been with the EC–121s at McClellan AFB with the 552nd Wing! They were probably the only organization that still retained the active knowledge and experience on this aircraft.

Given all of that, keeping these worn-out, highly complex weapons systems operating meant performing something akin to a miracle that had to be repeated periodically. The more so because, unlike a typical Reserve unit, with a pure training mission, the 915th *had* to put those three birds into Keflavik every two weeks, and they'd damned well better be in good flying and operating condition!

One of the truly fun problems encountered by Harper and his maintenance crews was corrosion. This is something that can and does occur in virtually all airplanes in varying degrees. But the EC–121s always had more of it—in fact probably as much as any airplane flying, with the possible exception of carrier-based aircraft. Some of this was caused simply by age. Some was due to the type of alloys used, which today are somewhat more resistant to corrosion. But much of this corrosion is caused by the contact of metal to salt-impregnated air. The EC–121s of both services lived practically all their lives in highly corrosive environments: McClellan, Otis, Hawaii, Alaska, Newfoundland, Homestead, Keflavik, even SEA. On many of their missions they flew low over the ocean, picking up even more salt from the air and adding to the corrosion. Combined with the total lack of any major corrosion facility contract for the previous 10 years, the results were truly horrendous.

One aircraft was being inspected while I was at Homestead. It was found to have major corrosion damage behind the number 1 and 4 engine spar caps as well as the horizontal stabilizer leading edge spar. It would take an estimated 1,400 man-hours to rectify all this damage. On another aircraft they started cleaning an area on the left outer wing. As Harper put it in an interview with the author, "We started cleaning a particular area, trying to go in to clean it and went right into the fuel cell! It just kept exfoliating until there was just nothing left and we went all the way through! So we had to change the whole outer wing and replace it. We got another wing section from a bird at Davis-Montham and it wasn't a helluva lot better!"

On another aircraft, a regular isochronal inspection revealed an 18-inch crack in one of the main wing spars! The aircraft was considered a total loss. To get the aircraft out of there, the Group had to get a special FAA order authorizing ferrying the aircraft back to Davis-Montham. It was a one-time-only permit, VFR. They stripped the aircraft of all nonessential weight and flew it back with a fuel stop en route to reduce the load. When I asked how it was done, the somewhat sardonic reply was, "Very carefully, without ginger!"

One way the 915th tried to keep ahead of the insidious corrosion was by washing all the aircraft's lower surfaces after each flight. This means all the undersides of wings, fuselage, engine nacelles, and tail surfaces. But this is still only a portion of the overall problem in maintenance. Harper told of changing an electronic tube, which new cost $5,000! That gives some insight why the Air Force was not willing to authorize the funding for proper maintenance. Harper also mentions how aileron control cables suddenly began failing completely. It was discovered that due to inadequate major maintenance, cables that would have been automatically replaced years before were left in place. Eventually they frayed and snapped. But the 915th didn't have the aircraft maintenance historical records available to them, and thus had no way of knowing that these flight control cables were way beyond the point at which they would normally have been changed. Luckily, rudder and elevator cables are 100 percent redundant; aileron cables are not. This situation led to a potentially dangerous incident, of which more later.

Harper, interestingly enough, saw this job as the biggest challenge he ever had to face in maintenance. As he put it, "But it's fun because it's not routine maintenance headaches. They're nonroutine. I thought I had a pretty good handle on what maintenance was all about, but I've learned more in the last six months than I had in the last six years. We're constantly improvising." Harper feels strongly that the regulars in maintenance with their background with the 552nd Wing at McClellan plus the Reserve maintenance people, most of whom have worked on nothing but the EC–121 and the C–124 (another reciprocating aircraft) before that, made a mighty contribution to the success of this entire program.

Harper was also very impressed with the design philosophy he discovered prevails in the EC–121s, and actually, all Constellations. Harper again: "You know what I think is interesting, though? The fact that the original designer on the bird must have had some of these things in mind. I doubt if a lot of other weapons systems could sustain what this airplane has without that attention over the last 5–10 years. This aircraft is built like a tank, much more so than current aircraft."

Comments like this are obviously high praise for the basic thinking that Kelly Johnson and his designers put into the Constellations and Super Constellations. It shows an ability to forecast the kind of situation that an airplane can encounter in terms of being neglected. It also shows real concern for the safety of the people who would eventually have to trust their lives to the aircraft.

Harper rather neatly puts the entire program in perspective when he says,

> It's a new ball game every day. It really is. You've got two forces right now, in the dying days of the EC–121 program, that are pulling against one another. On the one hand is the very important, very critical JCS mission that this aircraft just has to carry out. On the other hand is the money situation, the age of the airplane, the spares program, all the things that are holding it back. And we're trying to keep those two forces held together. We're the glue in the middle. We're the rubber band.

There is no doubt that the valiant efforts of these maintenance people, combined with the careful handling on the part of the flight crews was what managed to keep these tired, old worn-out airplanes still flying. Yet in spite of their condition, they still represented a very live, potent weapons system; in fact, in 1977, they were still the only one in the U.S. Air Force inventory. The brand-new AWACS would take over from the Warning Stars, but until it reached the operational stage, the EC–121s had to be kept flying.

Somehow, the Department of Defense is very quietly spending a lot of money on this unit. The real costs are buried. So there must be people at the top who feel that this mission is really important. The effect of the lack of consistent maintenance over many years was clearly demonstrated in an incident that occurred a short time before this writer visited the 915th.

The incident involved an EC–121 on final approach to Homestead. I later interviewed the aircraft commander of the flight.

Captain Robert K. Andre, Air Force Reserve, talks about matters in an understated kind of way. But the fact remains that what happened at the time could well have had an entirely different ending. Andre was flying right seat as instructor pilot and the student was in the left seat as the operating aircraft commander. As part of an accepted training procedure, the EC–121 was making a practice boost-out approach with the aileron hydraulic boost off. In such cases, aileron control is replaced by using rudder, asymmetrical power on the outboard engines, and aileron trim, which still operates normally.

The student was making a straight-in approach to Homestead at dusk, with the aileron boost off. The aircraft was at about 200 feet altitude, and the student was just correcting a slight drift to the right from a left cross-wind. Suddenly a loud snap was heard, the control yoke deflected sharply to the right, and the left wing started to drop. Andre immediately got on the controls with the student to feel things out. The student and Andre looked at each other, and Andre told the student he was taking over. He then immediately called for maximum power, held the EC–121 in a level attitude, and, with the student helping, held the yoke over to counteract the drop of the left wing.

At this point, Captain Andre knew he had a control problem, but wasn't really sure of the extent. Asymmetrical power was used to assist in keeping the left wing up. The 121 was doing 128–130 knots when trouble began. Under max power with the aircraft level, a little more altitude was lost, but speed came back up, and Andre climbed back out, reducing power to METO as they went through 500 feet at 140 knots. Back in the pattern, and well clear of the field, Andre took time to analyze his problem.

Visual inspection revealed the left aileron stuck in an up position. The right aileron was also in a slightly up position. Andre decided to reengage the control boost, and, having done so, found he had right aileron control, but the left aileron remained stuck in the up position. Postflight inspection later revealed that a cable had snapped, and a tension regulator between the two ailerons, compensating for the sudden slack, forced the left aileron up.

With the right aileron up also, the EC–121 was flying around with, in effect, two speed brakes. With a little experimentation, the crew determined that the aircraft had adequate control by using mostly rudder and asymmetric power, with the flaps still down at 60 percent.

By this time it was getting dark, and with emergency equipment standing by, Andre brought the aircraft in on a long final approach assisted by precision approach radar. The landing proved to be uneventful.

I asked Andre whether, at the time of the cable failure, he thought he could have continued the original approach and landed safely. Andre said he considered that pretty chancy, and that he felt if he had continued the approach with the air speed bleeding off and the boost off, the aircraft would probably have rolled uncontrollably to the left and dug a wingtip into the ground. What Andre didn't say was that if the cable had snapped 15–30 seconds later as the aircraft was almost over the runway threshold, there is an excellent chance the plane could have rolled up in a fiery ball and killed everyone aboard!

As a consequence of this incident, aileron cables on all the 915th's aircraft were pulled and inspected over a period of time. A number were found to be frayed and were replaced. In addition, training procedures were altered so that boost-out approaches were no longer required. The incident simply reinforced the argument that good maintenance can never be ignored. It also showed once again that the basic Constellation design was truly remarkable, and that even when things started going all to hell, the airplane would bring you back safely, given the chance.

Shortly before the EC–121s left Iceland for the last time, a serious and sad accident occurred. Aircraft Tail No. 0021 was taxiing out at Keflavik for a mission take-off. Suddenly the left side landing gear strut failed, allowing the airplane to settle on the left side. The left engines and propellers struck concrete and were destroyed. Simultaneously, the left wingtip fuel tank also struck the concrete, and the highly volatile avgas flowed out and ignited. All of the crew escaped unscathed, but the aircraft was totally consumed in the ensuing fire. Number 121 deserved a better final fate than that!

THE END OF THE EC-121S

October 1, 1978, was to be the end of the EC–121 mission to Iceland and, consequently, the end of the last military unit to operate Constellations. Within two weeks, the last EC–121 would leave Homestead for the boneyard at Davis-Montham. Obsolescence had finally caught up with the EC–121, and the new Boeing E-3A AWACS would take over the Iceland mission. But during these last few days a number of events took place that would be long remembered by those involved.

Toward the end of September, there were a number of small parties at both Homestead and Keflavik, a "wake" at Homestead, and a formal dinner at Keflavik. In Iceland there were people who attended from other than Detachment 1. Some were from other U.S. military units on the base. Others were Icelandic citizens. To the Icelandic people, who had seen these big, ungainly planes for so many years, it was a powerful and somber leave-taking. So they found it difficult to accept the realization that no more would the Warning Stars be going out to protect them with their radar. Of course, they all knew AWACS would take over the vigil without any interruption. But somehow, the EC–121s and their crews had become family. How does one say good-bye to family?

So, during those last few days there was a spontaneous outburst of emotion on the part of many people, both those directly associated with the EC–121s and those who were essentially lookers-on. There was a feeling that it wasn't really happening, that it shouldn't happen, mustn't be allowed to happen. This, of course, was rather illogical considering the worn-out condition of many of the aircraft and the fact that the decision had been made at the top levels of the Air Force long before as to precisely when the 915th would be deactivated and AWACS take over. But this very lack of logic is what made the whole thing so sincere and real.

The changing-of-command ceremony took place the evening of September 30–October 1, 1978. Some 75 people had been expected at the ceremony, which was sponsored by the Commander, Air Force Iceland. But before it started, military buses began mysteriously shuttling back and forth to the various billets, and the party swelled to 300 participants. Colonel West of the 915th was there, as was LTC Clifton Touranger, chief of Detachment 1. Touranger had been in Iceland for the past 10 years in one capacity or another.

The actual ceremony consisted of passing the walkie-talkie, which Touranger always had to carry with him, to LTC Edward Zompa, commander, Detachment 2, 552nd Airborne Warning and Control Wing (AWACS). This ceremony is known as "passing the buck," the "buck" of course being the walkie-talkie. West and

Touranger passed the buck to Zompa at one minute past midnight, October 1, 1978, and the last full-time Air Force mission for a Constellation was over.

The next-to-last EC–121 left Iceland on October 2 to return to Homestead. Shortly after take-off it monitored the AWACS E-3A being scrambled on its first mission. The E-3A had encountered a problem while still on the ground and was late becoming airborne. The EC–121 crew, hearing this, were about to divert and take over the intercept of two Russian TU–95 Bear bombers, when they heard the E-3A finally take off. For a moment it seemed the old, faithful EC–121 would have to come to the rescue.

On that same day another strange event occurred. Members of various U.S. military units based at Keflavik each approached the crew of the lone remaining EC–121 and asked permission to paint their individual unit insignia on the fuselage as a sign of their respect. To top this off, some employees from Loftleider Icelandic Airways did the same. After all this, the aircraft, tail number 122, had a rather strange appearance! This, incidentally, is the same aircraft the author flew on a few months earlier.

The next day, October 4, a clear, cold day, the last EC–121 left Keflavik. Many of the Air Force and Navy personnel assigned to the base were on hand to see number 122 taxi out. Some Icelandic citizens were there, too.

With literally hundreds on hand watching, EC–121 S/N 50-122 took off, then swung around and made a final pass over the field. At this point a little surprise had been arranged by the 57th Flight Interceptor Squadron based at Keflavik, whose F–4 Phantoms had often been vectored by their big cousins, the Warning Stars. Two F–4s formed up on the big Connie, one on each wingtip. A third F–4 flew nearby and took pictures. It must have indeed been a moving moment for all, as the two F–4s escorted the EC–121 out over the ocean until it was out of sight. On the way back to Homestead, 50-122 diverted slightly and made a low pass over Otis AFB where 24 years earlier the entire AEW&C program had started.

Then on October 12, the last two EC–121s left Homestead and flew to their final resting place at the boneyard, Davis-Montham AFB.

It was the end of an era; actually, one of which all too many people are totally unaware. There are no doubt many ways in which to portray in words what the Warning Stars meant to a lot of people. I have chosen to use someone else's words. They are those of JOC Mike Murphy, Navy, writing in the September 29, 1978, issue of the *White Falcon*, a newspaper published for military personnel based at Keflavik, Iceland:

You've made history and the time has come for you to glory in it. As your personnel disperse throughout the globe, they will carry with them part of you. For none who have served will let dust gather on your fame. Your last flight is but a new beginning.

There will be no requiem, for your feats will live on long after the queen of the skyways disappears over the horizon. Memories will be stirred and tales of your past will be listened to. The hearts and minds of the men and women who have served with you, who sweated for you and labored for you, who loved you, will swell with pride at the mention of your name. You gave your best and brought honor to them.

The Navy thanks you for a job "Well Done." The Air Force thanks you for making tradition. I thank you, for you leave me the friendship of your crews. And now as you retire, I bid you "Fair winds and following seas." Bless.

IS IT REALLY THE END?

The 915th is no more. The Warning Stars are no more. Only words, pictures, and memories are left. But the memories die hard. This author, in conversation with a former navigator of the 915th now flying on AWACS, stumbled across some curious and interesting facts and ideas, which may be said to form a postscript to the story of the 915th in particular and the Warning Star program and airplanes in general.

A single E-3A AWACS cost taxpayers the staggering amount of $130 million in 1977 currency. Currently there are just 22 of the aircraft in the inventory, and the Air Force deploys them all over the world. The E3-A sports a 30.5-foot Rotodome, bigger than that on the EC–121's but smaller than the famous 37.5-foot Rotodomes of the WV–2E. The radar equipment provides a better resolution than did the radar gear on the EC–121s. But a direct comparison is really not fair. Aside from 25 years' difference in electronic sophistication, the entire approach is different. The EC–121's radar gave a return on the scopes of whatever it was reflected from. But on the E-3A a number of radar hits, probably five at a time, are fed consecutively into a super-efficient computer. This in turn processes the returns, screens out all extraneous portions of each return, such as ground clutter, and then feeds a cleaned-up computer image to the radar scopes.

There are obviously other major differences. The E3-A cruises at almost twice the altitude, and thus avoids much of the weather and reaches a greater distance with its radar antenna. However, its time on station is about half that of the EC–121. It is a brand-new airplane, and its airframe systems and engines, basically those of the proven commercial Boeing 707, are more reliable and need less maintenance. Whether that's also true of the many electronic systems is not known. On the one hand, black boxes are more reliable, but on the other hand, the complexity is far greater.

The navigator I spoke to made a very revealing remark. He said there is not much challenge to flying in the AWACS, and that if the old EC–121s were to be taken out of mothballs for whatever reason, he would volunteer to fly them again! He also indicated that others previously associated with the EC–121 program also felt that way.

Possibly such affection is misplaced in the harsh world of global politics and conflicts. Nevertheless, it does reveal, in a very direct and believable manner, the confidence, respect, and even affection that the Constellations generated.

If I may be allowed to hypothesize for a moment, one wonders if the days of the EC–121 are really over and finished. During the turbulent early days of 1980, it seems not at all inconceivable that a situation might have developed in which the AWACS fleet is not of sufficient size. The Pentagon, desperately needing more long-range airborne radar platforms, takes some EC–121s out of mothballs. Once again the bellow of those R–3350s rings out like a bugle, and the humpbacked yet graceful shapes of the Warning Stars slide into the air and rise to once again take up duties as sentinels of the sky.

Fanciful you say? Possibly so. But who could have foreseen that these aircraft would have been taken out of mothballs and sent to an active battlefield (SEA) in the 1960s? Who could have foreseen that they would have been brought back to life in the 1970s? Will they, can they, come back again? Only time will tell. But, if they do, can anyone doubt that they will rise to the occasion and one more time perform their vital mission?

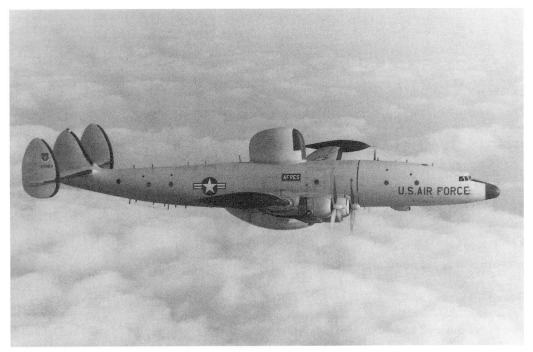

17-1 EC–121 of the 915th AEW&C Group, (AFRES). Note the Reserve designation on the fuselage. This aircraft still carried the separate height-finding radar antenna. (Luisada)

17-2 Two EC–121s of the 915th AEW&C Group en-route to Iceland. (U.S. Air Force)

17-3 A Soviet Tupolev TU–95 turbo-prop bomber being escorted by USAF McDonnell Douglas F4 Phantom fighters in the general GIUP area. These are some of the Soviet aircraft the EC–121s were deployed to Iceland to locate and identify. (U.S. Air Force)

17-4 The 3-man cockpit of a EC–121. (Lockheed Martin)

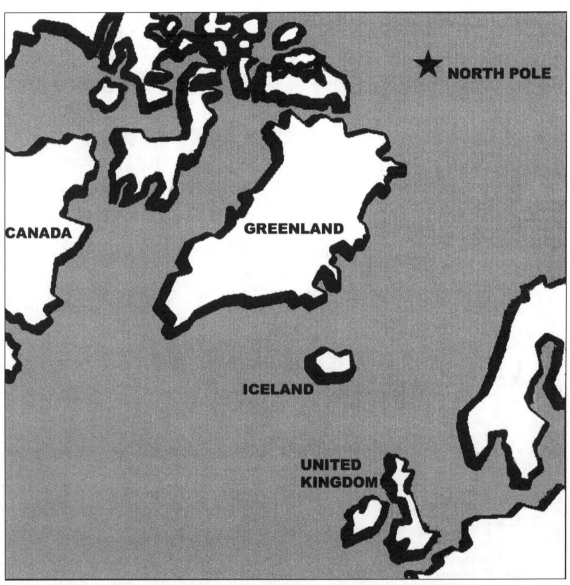

17-5 Map showing the area protected by the EC–121s operating from Iceland. This general area encompassed what became known as the GIUK Gap, which stood for Greenland, Iceland, United Kingdom. (Luisada)

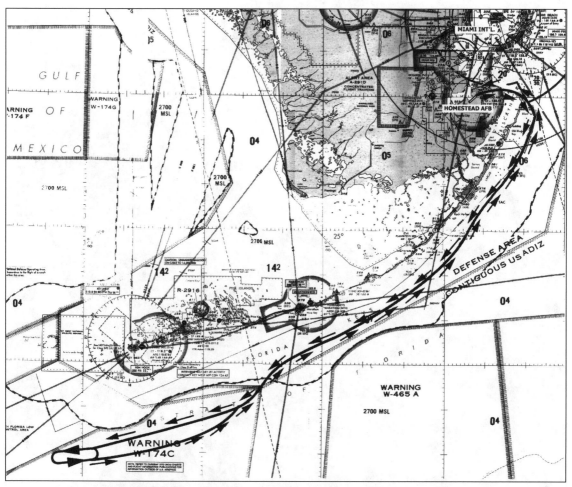

17-6 Map of southern Florida, Cuba, and the Florida Straits over which the author flew on a EC–121T training mission. (Luisada)

Epilogue

HOW DID SHE REALLY STACK UP?

The year 1983 marked 40 years since the first Constellation took to the air. During that period, Constellations were operated by the scheduled airlines for about 20 years (1946–66). In a military capacity, the Constellation flew for some 33 years (1945–78). During these years other highly successful aircraft of competitive design also flew, chief among them the DC–4/-6/-7 of Douglas Aircraft. Together, the commercial aircraft fleets of many nations established a network of routes and services that covered the entire globe and forever changed the lives of many people.

The Constellation played a large part during this period of growth and change. From 1946 to 1949 an impressive array of new routes were either established or restored all over the world. Because in this period the Constellation was the only transport in its class flying, it fell to these graceful aircraft to initially operate a major portion of these trail-blazing routes.

Lest readers be misled, it should be pointed out that in the 1930s airlines (such as Air France, Empire Airways, KLM Royal Dutch Airlines, Pan American, and Panagra) had indeed already begun scheduled services to distant points all over the world. But these services took many days and were infrequent and often not dependable. In the late 1940s those same services and more became routine, dependable, and year-round, thanks in large part to the Constellation. It was the beginning of the Constellation heritage.

WHAT MIGHT HAVE BEEN

In a historical account like this there is sometimes an almost irresistible urge to indulge in the age-old game of "what if." In the case of the Constellation the author is going to play such a game, even if only briefly, because there were indeed a few major turning points in the history of this airplane. Specifically, there were five of these turning points.

1. *The Delay of the Prototype.* As described in Chapter 3, the uncertain posture of the federal government concerning the development of the prototype Constellation resulted in a delay of at least a year. If such a delay had not occurred, the early history of the Constellation could have been considerably different. For one thing, the recurring problems of the Curtiss-Wright Cyclone engine, which were simultaneously plaguing the new Boeing B–29 Superfortress, would have come to light much sooner and thus have been resolved more quickly.

2. *World War II Production.* As described in Chapter 4, the sum total of Constellation production in World War II turned out to be insignificant. There were a number of factors that contributed to this occurrence. The developmental delay was one, and the head start that Douglas had with their C–54 Skymaster was another, although that aircraft was not in the class of the Constellation. But it is possible that the one most significant factor may have been Lockheed itself. The company's design team, headed by Kelly Johnson, and its greatly expanded production facilities resulted in a number of very large contracts for such aircraft as the P–38 Lightning, the PV–1 and PV–2 Ventura patrol bombers, as well as a major subcontract for Boeing B–17 Flying Fortresses.

   Thus, Lockheed's ability to produce in quantity may well have been a key factor in convincing the Pentagon that C–69 production had to take a back seat. If the original contract for 260 C–69s had been well under way at the end of the war, then the early postwar period might have developed in an entirely different manner. With more C–69s on hand, the Air Force would probably have mothballed a large number and then put them back into service when the Cold War began to take shape a couple of years later. By the same token, with too many large transports on hand in 1945, the Air Force would have tried to sell more of their C–69s to the airlines, thus preventing Douglas from flooding the market with their C–54/DC–4 aircraft to the extent they did.

3. *Super Connie Development.* In Chapters 7 and 10 the growth of the Constellation into the Super Constellation was detailed. It took almost two full years for Lockheed to go from the L–1049 model with 2,700-hp engines to the vastly superior L–1049C with the 3250-hp Turbo-Compound power plants. A portion of this period was absolutely necessary to effect the required troubleshooting of the Turbo-Compounds, which initially were quite bothersome. However, this work was going on anyway under considerable pressure from the Pentagon, which was quite anxious to begin taking deliveries on both the L–1049A AEW&C version and the L–1049B cargo model. In retrospect it appears that the military services had cornered the market on the entire early production of the Turbo-Compounds, thus delaying introduction of the true Super Constellation into commercial service by close to a full year. The author believes that this delay lost considerable orders for Lockheed, orders that went to Douglas for their DC–7 series transports. However, it must be admitted that in time the military orders proved to be of such size as to possibly make up for any commercial losses caused by them.

4. *Acceptance of the Advanced Warning Star.* In spring 1957 Lockheed had proposed to the Pentagon that they procure a new version of the Warning Star known as the CL–257. This aircraft would have used the 150-foot span wing of the L–1649A, the Allison T 56 turboprop engines of the Lockheed C–130 Hercules, the 37.5 foot Rotodome antenna, and the APS–70 radar. Lack of funds caused the project to be canceled a few months later.

If the CL–257 project had, in fact, gone ahead, then some very interesting things would in all likelihood have happened. Assuming deliveries to have started in 1959–60, the aircraft would have been involved in the SEA theater of operations. The Boeing AWACS might well have been delayed. And with an AEW&C fleet already in operation (RC–121/WV–2) the Pentagon might have opted for a long-term production run with only 6–12 aircraft being delivered per year. Lockheed has been famous for this type of stretched-out production, as witness the PV–2 Neptune (20 years), the C–130 Hercules (60 years and still in production in 2004), the P–3 Orion (over 60 years and still in production in 2004)!

Furthermore, a CL–257 built in the early 1960s and equipped with new electronics and turboprop engines would not have run into the spare parts problems of the RC–121/WV–2 fleet. Such an aircraft flying in the early 1970s would very possibly have caused the cancellation of the Boeing AWACS program.

5. *The L–1649A Super Constellation.* At the time the L–1649A began flying in regular service in mid-1957, commercial jets were only 18 months away from making their debut. Thus the last of the Constellation models faced an insurmountable double barrier—namely, the approaching commercial jet age on the one hand and the almost one-year head start of the Douglas DC–7C on the other. The question that arises is: Could Lockheed be reasonably expected to have done anything different so as to ensure the success of the L–1649A?

A number of factors were at work during this period. The Lockheed Constellation assembly line was operating at close to full capacity producing both commercial Super Constellations and military Warning Stars. The development effort for the advanced versions of the Super Constellations appears to have been slow during 1954–55, possibly because the company was busy with a number of other major projects. The company's marketing philosophy seems to have undergone a subtle change as Lockheed grew ever larger and became quite conservative. Finally, Burbank's engineering people appear to have had serious questions about virtually all the turboprop engines available at the time.

Nevertheless, there was an approach that could have been tried and, if successful, might have paid handsome dividends. By 1955 Lockheed was using Allison T56 turboprops in their Air Force C–130 Hercules attack transports with a high degree of confidence. It seems reasonable to suppose that Allison could have been persuaded to produce a version of this engine adequate to the needs of a model L–1649A. Such an aircraft, if available in 1956, would have been able to enjoy at least 4–5 years of first-line service on the North Atlantic, and another 3–4 years as a first-rate back-up to the jets. At the time it was rumored that Lockheed was reluctant to introduce a T56-powered Super Constellation on the grounds it might compete with the similarly powered Model L–188 Electra, which they brought out in 1958. In any event the Electra had only moderate success and was always meant for an entirely different market. Furthermore, the Electra was designed to serve only the short and middle distance markets, while the L–1649A served the very long distance market.

SOME NOTABLE ACHIEVEMENTS

When one sits down to put into historical perspective the impact and success of an aircraft that flew for four decades, certain obstacles become quickly apparent. For one thing, it is necessary to rely on memories and reactions that have now become dim with time. For another, the commercial jet age has changed our view of aviation. Thus one must attempt to analyze memories and written records of the time, as well as evaluate past events, which are not only partly forgotten but also distorted by the hindsight that the passage of time inevitably brings. Nevertheless, as one reviews the four decades of the Constellation, a number of significant points help show the part that the Connie played in history.

1. *The First of Its Kind.* In terms of other large aircraft flying at the time, the Constellation was undoubtedly the first of its kind. It was pressurized, it was considerably faster, it had longer range, and it had the first boosted controls. True, there were a lot of problems with the engines. But this was generally true for all large reciprocating engines of new design. Essentially, the Constellation was 4–6 years ahead of the competition, which is a big lead indeed. Some of the design philosophies incorporated in it were better than anything the competition developed until the advent of the jet transport.
2. *Prototype Performance.* From the very inception of its flight testing through the early period of its commercial service, the Constellation racked up an impressive record. In 1943, its first year, it showed that it had a speed close to that of contemporary single-engine fighters. Its altitude capability was also shown to be as good as many military aircraft then flying. In 1944 came the celebrated record coast-to-coast flight with Hughes and Frye as pilots. Later that year and in 1945 the long-range speeds at relatively low power settings were proven on numerous flights over the North Atlantic, including a number of record-breaking ones. This period in the history of the Constellation clearly demonstrated its advanced design and overall superiority over contemporary aircraft.
3. *Showing the Way Around the World.* During its first 24 months of commercial service, the Constellation established a string of commercial speed, altitude, and range records then unmatched in aviation history. Not until the introduction of the Boeing 707 turbojet was such a record-setting performance to be matched. Almost single-handedly, the Constellation established a network of routes all over the world. But when one reads the news stories of the day, the accomplishments of this one aircraft seem to be taken almost for granted.

As always, it is difficult to be sure why this was so. But two theories appear plausible. One is that in the postwar period of 1946–48 there was so much turbulence, both domestically and internationally, that news such as this was overshadowed. The other is that after all the superlative adjectives used in World War II for everything, including matters relating to aviation, the news media simply did not view aviation matters as being all that newsworthy.

The fact remains that during those rather confused 2 years, the Constellation established a solid base for future airline services, both in terms of airline operations and passenger acceptance. Beyond that the distinctive shape became familiar to people all over the world as they watched Constellations at low altitudes during climb-outs and let-downs, It was one more way in which the Connie sold flying to the general public.

4. *Super Connie Luxury.* One of the factors that contributed to the success of the Constellations as a commercial airplane was the degree of comfort afforded passengers. During the early years of the Constellation era, the L–749 and L–749A provided comfort and a cabin noise level that was remarkably low. On long flights this relative degree of quiet was, naturally, much appreciated by the passengers.

When the Super Constellations came along, the degree of comfort was improved further, with better seats and a more effective system of cabin air circulation, cooling, pressurizing, and humidifying. The greater noise level generated by the bigger engines was largely nullified by more insulation. The Super Constellation also had another virtue. The structural design of the fuselage was such that in turbulence there was little or no bending or "nodding." By contrast, the Douglas DC–7 series airplanes were said to exhibit a considerable amount of nodding. The Super Constellations were generally employed on the longer routes. The level of comfort they offered was an important asset in attracting passengers to such routes.

5. *The Warning Star.* The Airborne Early Warning and Control (AEW&C) program simultaneously started by the U.S. Navy and Air Force turned out to be a real boon to Lockheed. The Burbank plant eventually produced a grand total of 232 of AEW&C versions of the Super Constellation, which constituted 27 percent of the total Constellation production. But the real value of this Air Force/Navy fleet was not to Lockheed but to the people of the United States.

During its first decade of service, this fleet was deployed to maintain the world's first airborne radar warning net along both coasts of the United States. This was a difficult, demanding, boring assignment that was carried out at a high level of professionalism. The impact on the Kremlin of this particular defensive strategy may never be known, but it is this author's opinion that it was one factor that weighed heavily on Soviet planning during that period.

In the second decade of service, the Warning Stars were switched from a defensive to an offensive role. The fleet of aircraft, by now greatly reduced in size, moved from the continental United States to Southeast Asia, and there proceeded to more than justify their existence by carrying out a variety of missions simultaneously and doing so continuously for over six years.

But these weary planes were still not finished with their work. Called on yet once again they took on an AEW&C role which encompassed both southeast U.S. and the northern approaches to Europe, and once again they performed admirably.

Aside from the actual missions they carried out so faithfully for so many years, the Warning Stars also gave rise to a general appreciation on the part of the military for the overall value of AEW&C-type aircraft. So although initially the mission dictated the design and utilization of the Warning Stars, in the end their splendid capabilities resulted in the wholesale modification and growth of that very mission.

6. *The L–1649A: Too Much, Too Late.* The L–1649A was essentially a special plane for a special application. It was undoubtedly the finest long-range reciprocating transport to ever fly. But the cards were already stacked against it from the start. It was a year behind the competition (only a year and a half before jets), had limited seating, and used the wrong power plants. Circumstances no doubt helped force the outcome, but for Lockheed it was a financial setback.

However, in its own way the L–1649A was a fitting climax to a long line of Constellation models. It constituted a bridge between the reciprocating aircraft of post–World War II and the jet age. But the level of technological achievements it represented was appreciated by only a few. The flying public as a whole never really comprehended what this airplane represented. The various circumstances listed above guaranteed that its life would be short.

7. *She Died with Her Boots On.* The waning years of the Constellation era in passenger transport, 1961–67, were notable in that this airplane continued to be a viable machine right to the end. TWA and Eastern used their Constellation equipment after most others had grounded theirs. TWA assigned their Connies to multistop schedules, mainly east of the Mississippi. Eastern manned their enormously successful Shuttle with theirs. Although these applications were admittedly limited, the fact

remains that this elderly equipment, in some cases over 20 years old, brought in substantial revenue on all of these schedules.

Various factors, primarily economic, hastened the end of the Connies in passenger service. But it is noteworthy that these airplanes performed their assigned duties routinely until finally grounded permanently.

THE PRODUCTION PICTURE

Invariably, when an aircraft is being evaluated historically, its production totals are taken into account, especially as they compare to competing designs. So it is appropriate in this concluding chapter to do the same for the Constellation.

There were a grand total of 856 Constellations produced over a span of some 17 years. This figure makes the Constellation the second most popular aircraft of its size built during the 1940s and 1950s, second only to the Douglas DC–6/7 series.

If one analyses, the order breakdown of Constellations by customer, certain interesting facts become very obvious. The top 10 customers of these aircraft and their total orders were:

Airline	No. of Aircraft	% Commercial Orders	% of Total Orders
1. TWA	146	29	17
2. Eastern	61	12	7
3. Air France	57	11	7
4. KLM	44	9	5
5. Pan Am	26	5	3
6. Qantas	24	5	3
7. Air India	16	3	2
8. Flying Tiger	15	3	2
9. Trans-Canada	14	3	2
10. Lufthansa	12	2	1
Total	415	82	49

From this table it can be seen that only 5 airlines ordered a whopping 66 percent of all commercial Constellations produced, and the top 10 airlines ordered 82 percent of all such orders.

Furthermore, what the table does not show is that in the late 1940s and early '50s, sales were considerably slower than in the mid- and late 1950s. A number of reasons caused this to happen, including the slower rise of ridership worldwide in the immediate postwar period, the economic slump of the late 1940s, the inability of many companies to expand their air services until the mid-1950s, and the inability of companies and nations to generate the necessary capital.

There is no doubt that if Lockheed could have convinced even one or two additional U.S. airlines to buy Constellations, overall sales might have been much better. But a number of circumstances mitigated this. For one thing, in 1945 some carriers like American and United opted to go with converted Douglas C–54s (DC–4s) to obtain quick delivery. Once they were flying four-engined Douglas transports, they elected to remain with the same manufacturer. A second problem that faced Lockheed (and Douglas also, no doubt) is that aircraft of this size cannot be built on speculation. Lockheed would order materials and manufacture their transports in lots of 20, and a lot was not started unless the majority of that lot was already sold. Thus there were numerous instances when Lockheed could not promise quick delivery, especially if a lot under production was already sold out. Nevertheless, the total number of Constellations produced for commercial buyers (509) was still a most respectable number.

Readers may ask why, in comparing Connie sales to those of its main competitor, Douglas, the DC–4 was not included along with the DC–6/7. There are two reasons. First, the Connie was a whole generation ahead of the DC–4, what with a 60 mph speed advantage, longer range, and a pressurized cabin that enabled it to fly 10,000 feet higher. Second, the DC–4's production was in the period 1941–44, before the Connie went into production. Thus the DC–4 is really an aircraft of a previous era.

Readers should not attempt to make direct comparisons of quantities of Constellations built versus quantities of certain models of jet transports. Any conclusion drawn from such comparisons would be invalid because circumstances in the 1960s and 1970s were completely different than in the 1940s and 1950s when the Constellations were being built.

On the one hand, in the '60s and '70s passenger traffic became far heavier plus a great many more airlines began flying. Thus, in 1980 one saw production totals of 1,800 for Boeing 727s, 950 for Boeing 737s, and so on. On the other hand, military expenditures in 1980 were generally lower, and relatively few aircraft are being built in any sizable quantities. Thus the success (or lack thereof) of Constellation sales has to be measured in terms of events of that time only.

One last index can be examined that rather clearly points up two important aspects of the Constellation history; namely, the growth of commercial aviation during the 1940s and 1950s as compared with the enormous expansion of aviation during the jet age.

Over the North Atlantic the world's airlines carried 311,000 passengers in 1950, whereas in 1958, the last year before the jets, they carried 1,193,000, or 3.84 times as much. But by 1960 this number had increased to 1,761,000, and in 1973 had mushroomed to 10 million passengers! The much larger carrying capacity of jets along with lower fares, among other factors, made this possible. Still, the growth achieved by the propeller transports in a much tougher economic climate was something that in retrospect was quite phenomenal.

Along these same lines, the reciprocating-engined planes carried 7,533 tons of cargo in 1951, but tripled that to 23,886 by 1958. In 1974 the jets carried a mind-boggling 591,049 tons! So although the numbers of the Connie era were much smaller, the sustained growth in spite of high fares and a society often afraid of flying was and still is not only a record to be admired but also a base on which the jets could build.

From a strictly numerical point of view, there were indeed fewer Constellations produced than its chief competitor. But in terms of what those Constellations achieved as compared to the Douglas transports, this author has to say that the record favors the Connies.

HOW DID SHE REALLY STACK UP?

Now that you have wended your way along the memory path of the Lockheed Constellation, the author wishes to close this bit of aviation history by briefly attempting to answer the question above.

How did she really stack up? I believe that the material presented herein substantiates the contention stated in the Prologue: namely, that although there were fewer Constellations built and flown than their chief competitor, Douglas, these proud birds had, in retrospect, a considerably greater impact on aviation in particular and society in general.

To recap, let us remember the following Constellation firsts:

- The first fully pressurized transport
- The first to have boosted controls
- The fastest and longest-range transport of its day
- The first to fly many long over-water routes
- The Super Constellation was the most comfortable and luxurious of its time
- The Constellation, in all its versions, showed the ability to perform well as a transport in roles never foreseen for it
- The first production AEW&C aircraft ever conceived

This, then, was part of the legacy of the Constellation. So, too, are the memories of multitudes of travelers, many flying for the first time, who experienced the wonder of flight. Then there are the countless airline crews who actually spent the equivalent of years aboard Constellations shuttling back and forth around the globe and who finally bid sad good-byes, knowing full well that their lives had been in part protected by the reliability designed by Kelly Johnson and built by Lockheed.

The military crews also should not be forgotten. First they flew Connies under the worst possible weather conditions imaginable, again and again, and always returned safely. Later on they flew worn-out Connies, which probably should have been grounded, and still kept coming back safely.

Finally, there was the man, woman, or wide-eyed child on the ground. There were lots of these people all over the world who came to look on the graceful Connies with affection and fond recognition, as for an old friend.

No more do those graceful wings cut through the sky. No more can one hear the roar of the mighty Curtiss-Wrights. But although the Connies are no more, one should not think that it's as though they had never been.

The end of the Constellations also marked the end of an era—that of large reciprocating-engine propeller transports. History may decide to treat this rather short period, 1935–1965, as not very important compared to the jet transport age that followed. But that would be a serious mistake in this author's judgment. For just as a child must first crawl so as to walk and then run, so did aviation technology need to go through the development phase represented by the Constellation and its contemporaries. It was a period of trial and development, mistakes and victories, and a discipline, a society, and a world growing in part through the efforts and achievements of large transports.

No aircraft did more than the Constellation. With grace and beauty, strength and safety, speed and range, and always with elegance and class, the Constellation moved the frontiers of aviation forward. It left a subtle but indelible mark on aviation and on all who came in contact with her.

Yes, the Constellation is no more. But can any student of aviation seriously believe that it will ever be forgotten?

18-1 A Lockheed L–049 Constellation, which formerly flew as TWA "Star of Switzerland," shown after restoration. It is part of the Pima Air Museum in Tucson, Arizona. At extreme right hand corner are former TWA Captain John Miller, who flew the plane originally, and his wife, Jane Bomar Miller, dressed in the TWA hostess uniform she once wore. The men in white are 9 TWA volunteer workers who worked on restoring the aircraft. (Lockheed Martin)

18-2 On the tenth anniversary of the first flight of the Constellation prototype, Dick Stanton, Clarence "Kelly" Johnson, and Rudy Thoren are pictured. (Lockheed Martin)

Appendix A

BREAKDOWN OF CONSTELLATIONS MANUFACTURED

Model	Customer	Quantity	Delivery Dates	Subtotal
L-49/C-69	U.S. Air Force	22	7/43 thru 9/45	
				22
L-049	TWA	25	11/45 thru 5/47	
	Pan Am	22	1/46 thru 5/46	
	American Overseas	7	7/46 thru 6/47	
	KLM	6	5/46 thru 5/47	
	Air France	4	6/46	
	LAV	2	10/46	
				66
L-649	Eastern	14	5/47 thru 10/47	
				14
L-649A	Chicago & Southern	6	8/50 thru 5/51	
				6

Model	Customer	Quantity	Delivery Dates	Subtotal
L-749	Aerovias Guest	1	6/47	
	Air India	3	1/48 thru 2/48	
	Air France	9	4/47 thru 9/47	
	Pan Am	4	6/47	
	KLM	13	8/47 thru 11/48	
	Aerlinte Irish	5	8/47 thru 10/47	
	LAV	2	9/47 thru 10/47	
	Qantas	4	10/47	
	TWA	12	3/48 thru 7/48	
	Eastern	13	2/49 thru 12/49	
				66
L-749A	Air India	4	10/49 thru 3/51	
	KLM	7	8/49 thru 2/51	
	South African	4	4/50 thru 7/50	
	Air France	10	1/50 thru 8/51	
	TWA	25	3/50 thru 6/51	
	Hughes	1	6/51	
	U.S. Navy (PO-1W)	2	12/49 thru 8/50	
	U.S. Air Force (C-121A)	10	11/48 thru 3/49	
				63
L-1049	TWA	10	5/52 thru 9/52	
	Eastern	14	11/51 thru 4/52	
				24
L-1049A	U.S. Air Force (RC-121D)	72	6/54 thru ?	
	U.S. Navy (WV-2)	142	10/53 thru 12/57	
	U.S. Navy (WV-3)	8	3/55 thru 6/55	
				222
L-1049B	U.S. Navy (R7V-1)	18	1/52 thru 12/54	
	U.S. Air Force (C-121C)	33	11/52 thru 12/54	
	U.S. Air Force (VC-121C)	1	N/A	
	U.S. Air Force (RC-121C)	10	10/53 thru ? 62	

BREAKDOWN OF CONSTELLATIONS MANUFACTURED

Model	Customer	Quantity	Delivery Dates	Subtotal
L-1049C	KLM	9	6/53 thru 12/53	
	Eastern	16	11/53 thru 2/54	
	Qantas	4	3/54 thru 6/54	
	Trans-Canada	5	2/54 thru 5/54	
	Air France	10	6/53 thru 11/53	
	Air India	2	4/54 thru 6/54	
	Pakistan Int.	3	2/54 thru 4/54	
				49
L-1049D	Seaboard & Western	4	8/54 thru 9/54	
				4
L-1049E	Trans-Canada	3	6/54 thru 8/54	
	KLM	4	5/54 thru 10/54	
	Air India	3	1/55 thru 2/55	
	Avianca	4	8/54 thru 10/54	
	Iberia	3	6/54 thru 7/54	
	LAV	2	10/54 thru 11/54	
	Qantas	6	1/55 thru 3/55	
				25
L-1049F	U.S. Air Force (C-121G)	32		
				32
L-1049G	Northwest Orient	4	1/55 thru 4/55	
	TWA	28	3/55 thru 9/56	
	Trans-Canada	4	4/56 thru 12/57	
	KLM	6	12/55 thru 7/56	
	Air France	14	7/55 thru 2/57	
	Iberia	2	7/57 thru 8/57	
	Avianca	1	10/55	
	Cubana	3	2/56 thru 7/57	
	Eastern	10	9/56 thru 11/56	
	Air India	3	6/56 thru 12/56	
	Qantas	6	10/55 thru 11/57	
	TAP	3	7/55 thru 9/55	
	Varig	6	5/55 thru 1/58	

Model	Customer	Quantity	Delivery Dates	Subtotal
L-1049G *(cont.)*	Lufthansa	8	3/55 thru 8/56	
	Capitol	1	1/60	
	LAV	2	2/56 thru 8/57	
	Thai	3	7/57 thru 9/57	
				104
L-1049H	Qantas	2	10/56 thru 11/56	
	Seaboard & Western	5	12/56 thru 2/57	
	Slick Airways	3	8/59 thru 9/59	
	Resort Airlines	2	5/57 thru 6/57	
	Transcontinental S.A.	2	7/58	
	Real Aerovias	4	2/58 thru 3/58	
	National	4	9/57 thru 10/57	
	KLM	3	4/58 thru 5/58	
	Pakistan Int.	2	2/58 thru 3/58	
	Air Finance Corp.	3	5/57 thru 7/57	
	Flying Tiger	14	2/57 thru 10/58	
	TWA	4	4/58 thru 5/58	
	Trans-Canada	2	12/58 thru 1/59	
	California Eastern	3	4/57 thru 7/57	
				53
L-1249A	U.S. Air Force (YC-121F)	2		
	U.S. Navy (R7V-2)	2		
				4
L-1649A	Lockheed	1	10/56	
	TWA	29	9/57 thru 3/58	
	Air France	10	6/57 thru 2/58	
	Lufthansa	4	9/57 thru 1/58	
				44

Total Production: 856

Note: The detailed breakdown adds up to 860 aircraft. The discrepancy may be due to leased aircraft later sold.

Appendix B

MODEL SPECIFICATIONS

Model Changes	Gross Weight	First Delivery	Model
L-49/C-69	75,000	5/29/46	Basic conversion of C-69
L-049	96,000	11/14/45	Inner wing reinforced and landing gear strengthened
L-649	94,000	5/13/47	Fuselage and inner wing reinforced
L-649A	98,000	8/1/50	Additional fuselage and inner wing reinforcing, new brakes
L-749	102,000	4/18/47	Additional wing and fuselage reinforcing, outer wing fuel tanks
L-749A	107,000	10/20/49	New brakes, tires, and main landing gear
L-1049	120,000	11/26/51	Lengthened fuselage
L-1049A	152,000	10/15/53	Redesigned fuselage, integrally stiffened outer wing, fuselage fuel tank, upper and lower radomes, wing tip tanks.
L-1049B	145,000	11/15/52	Fuselage and inner wing reinforced, new main landing gear, floor reinforced, cargo doors, oil transfer system
L-1049C	133,000	6/10/53	Wing reinforced, new main landing gear
L-1049D	133,000	8/19/54	Center section fuel tank

Model Changes	Gross Weight	First Delivery	Model
L-1049E	133,000	6/26/54	Fuselage and wing reinforced
L-1049F	145,000	8/15/54	Fuselage and wing reinforced
L-1049G	137,500	1/22/55	New engines, stronger main landing gear
L-1049H	137,500	10/13/56	Increased zero fuel weight
L-1249	169,800	9/15/54	Reinforced fuselage and wings, turbo-prop engines, stronger main landing gear
L-1649A	156,000	5/4/57	New wing, solid props, increased zero fuel weight

Appendix C

AIRCRAFT DELIVERIES: TEN LARGEST CUSTOMERS

Customer	Total Quantity Delivered
1. U.S. Air Force	182
2. U.S. Navy	172
3. TWA	133
4. Eastern	61
5. Air France	57
6. KLM	48
7. Pan Am	26
8. Qantas	20
9. Trans-Canada	14
10. Lufthansa	8
Total:	**722**

(84% of all Constellations manufactured)

Note: The largest customer, the U.S. Air Force, initially known as the U.S. Army Air Force, was both the first and last (in 1978) organization to operate the Connie. This does not include small cargo operators or individually-owned Connies.

BIBLIOGRAPHY

The Lockheed Constellation, by Holmes G. Anderson. Profile Publications, 1966.
The Lockheed Constellation, by Terry Morgan. Arco, 1967.
Time Magazine, January 18, 1943l April 24, 1944.
The Lockheed Constellation, by M. J. Hardy. Arco, 1973.
L–1011 TriStar and the Lockheed Story, by Douglas J. Ingalls. Aero, 1973.
The Modern Airliner, by Peter W. Brooks. Putnam, 1961.
Loud and Clear, by Robert J. Serling, Doubleday, 1969.
The Search for Air Safety, by Stephen Barlay. William Morrow, 1970.
Sea Wings: The Romance of the Flying Boats, by Edward Jablonski. Doubleday, 1972.
Howard—The Amazing Mr. Hughes, by Noah Dietrich & Bod Thomas. Fawcett, 1972.
The Sky's the Limit, by Arch Whitehouse. Macmillan, 1971.
Aviation Week and *Space Technology* Magazine, various dates.
New York Times, various dates.
Legacy of Leadership—A Pictorial History of Trans World Airlines. TWA Flight Operations Dept., Walsworth, 1971.
The United States in Vietnam, by George McTurnan Kahin & John Wilson Lewis. Dial Press, 1967.
Above and Beyond—The Encyclopedia of Aviation and Space Flight. New Horizons, 1968.
From the Captain to the Colonel, by Robert J. Serling. Dial Press, 1980.
Lockheed Aircraft Corp., by J. K. Butters & J. V. Lintner. Harvard University, Division of Research, 1944.
Revolution in the Sky, by R. S. Allen, Stephen Greene, 1964.
Super Constellation Pocket Handbook, by Lockheed Aircraft Corp.
Airliners—Lockheed Constellation—Airliners No. 8, by Peter J. Marson. Airline Publications & Sales, Air Transport, 1944

ACKNOWLEDGMENTS

Note: The names listed below show titles and military ranks which are accurate as of the period 1974-82.

Lockheed Aircraft Corp., Burbank Calif., News Bureau
James W. Ragsdale, Manager
Robert Ferguson, Photographer
Rudy Perez, Public Affairs
Dick Martin, Public Relations Representative
Greg Waskul, Public Relations Representative

Lockheed Aircraft Corp., Burbank, Calif.
Hall Hibbard, Vice President of Engineering
Clarence "Kelly" L. Johnson, Chief Design Engineer
Carl Haddon
Bob Kananen, Engineering Dept. & Product Support
Robert E. Reidy, Manager of Sales Marketing
James H. Wood, Field Service Representative
Robert F. Turner, Field Service Representative
Dale Wright, Constellation Sales Program
Henry Rempt, Electronics Engineer

Northwest Orient Airlines
Roy K. Ericson, Public Relations

U.S. Air Force Museum, Wright-Patterson AFB, Ohio
Richard L. Uppstrom, Col., Air Force, Director
Nelson, N. Hal, Aircraft Restoration Div.
Charles W. Gebhart, Chief, Aircraft Restoration Div.
Ruth Hurt, Research Div.
Robert G. Raw, Information Office

Albert F. Simpson Historical Research Center, Maxwell AFB, Alabama
Judy Endicott, Chief, Circulation Section
Wayne Robinson, MPA, Archivist
Presley Bickerstaff, Archives Technician
Kathy Nichols, Secretary

915th AEW&C Group (AFRES), Homestead AFB, Florida
Col. Evan E. Clements, Air Force Reserve, Commander
Capt. Claude H. (Holly) Stewart, Air Force, Navigator, Chief of Information
Major Dennis F. Weber, Air Force Reserve, Primary Weapons Controller, Flight Examiner
M/Sgt. Robert J. Doucette, Air Force, Primary Radar Technician, Flight Examiner
CMSgt. Victor M. Taggart, Air Force, Flight Engineer Superintendent
Capt. Roger D. Bell, Air Force, Maintenance Administration Officer
Maj. David J. Harper, Air Force Reserve (Technician), Deputy Commander for Maintenance
Capt. Robert Andre, Air Force Reserve (Technician), Flying Safety Officer
2/Lt. William M. Lower, Air Force, Weapons Controller

Captain Jack Schnaubelt, TWA
Lt. Col. Eugene Halbach, USAF
Manley B. Holt, Ferry Command, U.S. Army Air Corps and Pan Am
Tech Sgt. Edward E. Simpson, USAF
1/Lt. Michael J. Kasiuba, USAF
Louis Barr, Flight Engineer, TWA
W. L. Donovan, Maintenance Instructor, TWA
Lt. Col. William H. Trammell, USAF (Ret.)
Charles F. Thomas, Manager, Western Region, Raytheon Co.
Lucien Leclere, Flying Tiger Lines
Herbert W. Shiver, USAF, Early Warning Radar Technician
Col. William F. Ramsey, USAF (Ret.)
Flt. Lt. Tony Fairbairn, RAF
Rear Admiral George A. Whiteside, USN (Ret.)
Col. J. C. LeBrun, French Air Force
Major Jerry L. Henderson, USAF (Ret.)
Captain Charles A. Barton, USN (Ret.)
Gail Dow
Jack Real, Hughes Helicopters
Rear Admiral J. W. Byng, USN (Ret.), Commander, AEW Wing, Atlantic, 06/55-12/56
G. Guillot, Manager, Product Support, Curtiss-Wright Corp.
David C. Frailey, Vice president for Public Relations, American Airlines

INDEX

Note: page numbers in **bold** refer to photographs.

A

accidents and incidents, 307–18
   C-69, Topeka, Kans. (1945), 52, 64, 308, 309
   EC-121s, Iceland and Florida (1970s), 357–58
   L-049, over Long Island (1949), 311
   L-049, Prestwick, Scotland (1948), 310
   L-049, Reading, Pa. (1946), 73–75, 81, 203, 270, 308–10
   L-049, Willimantic, Conn. (1946), 308, 309
   L-749, Cairo (1950), 311
   L-1049, on Staten Island (1960), 313–15
   L-1049, over Connecticut (1965), 317–18
   L-1049, over Grand Canyon (1956), 312–13, 314
   L-1049A,/RC-121D, over Pacific (1959), 315–17
   L-1049E, over Atlantic (1956), 311–12
Aerlinte Irish
   L-749, 88, 204, 205–6, **216**, 380
Aeromedical Evacuation Squadrons, 158, **164**
Aerovias Guest, 380
AEW&C (Airborne Early Warning and Control). *See* Airborne Early Warning and Control (AEW&C);
L-1049A (WV-2/RC121) for AEW&C; 915th AEW&C (AFRES)
Airborne Early Warning and Control (AEW&C), 115–45, **146–51, 319**
   early development of system, 115–23
   radar development, 125–27, 130, 138, 144–45
   radar picket system, 120–25, 134–37, 143–45, **147, 148–49** (maps), 372–73
   use of EC-121s in Vietnam War, 321–33, **334–40,** 373
   See also L-1049A (AEW&C)
551st AEW&C Group, 342–43
552nd AEW&C Group, 323–33, **334–40,** 343
915th AEW&C Group, 341–62, **363–66**
   EC-121T repairs, maintenance, and incidents, 353–58
   history, 341–43, 345
   structure and missions, 343–47
   training flight (memoir), 347–53
   See also EC-121s
Air Express (Vega), Lockheed, 3–4
Air Finance Corp., L-1049H, 382
Air France
   early transatlantic service, 367
   total quantity of aircraft delivered, 385
   resale, reuse, and disposal of aircraft, 297

L-049, 73, 200, 203, **217,** 379
L-749A, 88, 89, **92,** 204–5, 207, 208, **304,** 380
L-1049C, 168, 210–11, 381
L-1049G, 171, 214, 381
L-1649A, 230, 231, 232, **258,** 382
Air India
    resale, reuse, and disposal of aircraft, 300
    L-749A, 88, 89, **92,** 206, 208, 380
    L-1049C, 212, **218,** 381
    L-1049E, 212, 381
    L-1049G, 171, 381
Air Safety Board, 15
airspeed functions, 63–64
Alitalia, L-1649, 231
Allen, Eddie, 33, **40,** 50
aluminum alloy skin, 108, **113**
American Export Airlines, 62
American Overseas Airlines (AOA)
    purchase by Pan Am, 274
    transatlantic service, 6–8, 62, 68, 200, 203
    L-049, 67, 73, **77,** 197, 379
Andre, Robert K., 357–58
Avianca
    L-749, 208
    L-1049E, 212, **319,** 381
    L-1049G, 381
aviation, history of
    to late 1930s, 1–9, 13–15, 21–22, 62, 86–87, 367
    in World War II, 19, 45–48, 53–56, 61–62, 65, 87, 118–19, 200–201, 368
    in World War II: chronology (1940–1946), 48–53
    from 1945 to 1947, 66–71, 75, 193–204, 371
    from 1947 to 1950, 81–82, 85–87, 155, 193–95, 204–9, 371–72, 374
    from 1950 to 1955, 87, 95–97, 102–4, 109, 158–59, 193–95, 207–13, 372, 375
    from 1955 to 1960, 193–95, 213–15, 285, 372–73
    from 1960 to 1965, 141–42, 193–95, 285–86, 373–76
    from 1965 to 1974 (Vietnam War), 321–33, 375–76
    aircraft resale, reuse, and disposal, 297–301, 373–74
    Constellation production, summary, 374–77, 379–82
    factors affecting airline industry, 265–66, 287–90
    transatlantic service (1930s to 1950), 62, 64–72, 75, 86–87, 95–97, 198–203, 371
    See also Airborne Early Warning and Control (AEW&C); Boeing Aircraft; Constellation (before L-1049); Douglas Aircraft, aircraft production; Lockheed Aircraft Corporation, history; record flights; Super Constellation (L-1049 and later); turbojets and turboprops; TWA, history, *and specific models*
Aviation Week
    advertisements for Constellation, 62
    first mention of Constellation, 33
Avro Jetliner, 98

B

B-17 Flying Fortresses, 55, 67
Bailey, William, 233–35, 243, 244, 247
Barker, Charles, 66
Batcats (EC-121s)
    use in Vietnam War, 328–33, **334–40**
Berlin Airlift (C-121A), 154
Bierer, Earl W., 315–17

Boeing Aircraft
   B-15 bomber, 21
   B-17 Flying Fortresses, 55, 67, 105, 120, 368
   B-29 bomber, 48, 53, 55, 62, 90, 118–19, 126
   B-47, 137
   B-52, 137
   B-247, 5
   B-307 Stratoliner, 9, 16–17, 30, 69, 197, 266
   B-314 Clipper Flying Boat, 16, 21, 62, 68
   B-377 Stratocruiser, 35, 168
   C-97, 65
   C-135, 158
   E-3A AWACs aircraft, 140, 151, 345, 359, 361–62
   XB-29 prototype, 50
   707 turbojet, 231, 371
booster systems
   on L-49 prototype, 27–30, **37**
Bristol Brittania
   first long-range turbo-prop aircraft, 213
British Overseas Airline Company (BOAC)
   resale, reuse, and disposal of aircraft, 300
   transatlantic service, 62, 68, 86, 200, 203
   use of second-hand L-749s, 206
Burcham, Milo, 33, **40**
Burgess, Carter L., 283, 284
Busch, Frank, 233, 235, 245, 247, 248
Bying, Wes, 132

C

C-119 Flying boxcar, 107
CAA. *See* Civil Aeronautics Authority (CAA)
California Eastern, L-1049H, 382

Capital Airways
   resale, reuse, and disposal of aircraft, 300
   L-1049G, 382
Chapnellet, Cyril, 66
Charles Report on air defense (1951), 121
Chicago & Southern
   L-649A, 208, 379
Civil Aeronautics Act (1938), 15
Civil Aeronautics Authority (CAA)
   certifications by, 68, 196, 197, 268–69
   founding of, 15
   L-049 grounding after accident (1946), 73–75, 81, 270, 309–10
   L-49 prototype, requirements, 34–35
Civil Aeronautics Board (CAB), 62
CL-257, 369
Clements, Evan E., 342, 344
CO-62 (EC-121s), 325
Cohn, Lamont T., 271, 273
Cold War
   impact on L-1049A, 118–23
Columbine I/II/III, 154, 156, 158–59, **163, 166, 180, 319**
Connecticut, L-1049, midair illusion (1965), 317–18
Connie Club, 301
Consolidated Aircraft Corporation
   B-24 bomber, 21–22
   B-36 bomber, 122–23
Constellation (before L-1049)
   airspeeds, 63–64
   first Constellation, 13–19, 21–22 (*See also* L-49 prototype)
   cockpit design, 69–70
   commercial aircraft production, summary, 374–76, 379–82
   design changes during WWII, 63–64
   firsts, 371–72, 376–77
   ground speeds, 64

last scheduled service, 300–301, **303**
overview and evaluation, 367–77
resale, reuse, and disposal of aircraft, 297–301, **302–5**
service ceiling, 64
specifications summary, 383
WWII military aviation contributions to development of, 69
See also Super Constellation (L-1049 and later), *and specific models*
control systems
L-49 prototype (1943), 27–30, **38, 39**
Cotton, Sidney, 6
Crash Landing Nightclub, New Orleans, **304**
crashes. *See* accidents and incidents
Cuba, 343, 344
See also 915th Airborne Early Warning and Control Group
Cuban Missile Crisis, 141–42, 144
Cubana, L-1049G, 381
Curtiss, Glenn, L.
Curtiss-Wright engines. *See* Wright Aeronautical Corporation (Curtiss-Wright)
Cusick, Bart C., 326–27

D

Damon, Ralph S., 273, 277
Davis-Montham AFB (aircraft graveyard), 145, 321, 323, 329, 355, 359, 360
De Havilland, 98, 102, 225
Delta, 300
disposal of aircraft, 297–301, **302–5,** 321
See also Davis-Montham AFB
Distant Early Warning (DEW) Line, 122
Doolittle, Jimmy, 4
Douglas Aircraft, aircraft production
B-19 bomber, 22, 24
C-54, 368
DC-1, 5
DC-2, 9
DC-3, 9, 17, 32, 204, 288
DC-4 Skymaster, 35, 65, 73–74, 85, 202, 204, 272, 288, 368, 375
DC-4E, 16, 22, 24
DC-6/DC-7, 65, 70, 85, 89, 107, 120, 155, 168, 206, 207, 213, 224, 226, 275, 277, 375
DC-7, 312–13, 370
DC-7C comparison with 1049H & 1649A, 229–31, 372
DC-8, 298, 313–15
DC-54A Skymaster, 54, 62, 266
L-49 prototype development, 32
Dreyfuss, Henry, 170, 179

E

Eastern Air Lines
accidents, L-1049 (1965), 317–18
history, 1947 to 1950, 82, **91,** 266
resale, reuse, and disposal of aircraft, 297–301, 373–74
total quantity of aircraft delivered, 385
L-649, 67, 73, 82, 83, 88, 200, 204, 379
L-749, 88, 206, 208, 380
L-1049, 101, 209–10, 298–300, 317–18, 380
L-1049C, 168, 210–11, 298–300, 381
L-1049G, 171, 214, 300, **302,** 381
EC-121s, 322–62, **334–40, 363–66**
Batcats in Vietnam War, 328–33, **334–40**
comparison with E-3A AWACS, 361–62
conversion of L-1049As for SEA service, 322–33, **334–40**
maintenance and repair, 353–58
retirement of EC-121s, 359–61
training flight (memoir), 347–53

use by 915th AEW&C group, 342–47
Eclipse Aviation, 301
Edgerton, Brian, 233–51
Eisenhower, Dwight D.
    use of *Columbine I/II/III,* 154, 156, 158–59, **163, 166, 180, 319**
El Al, 200
Electra. *See* L-10 Electra
Ellinger, Ralph, 31
Empire Airways, 367
engines. *See* Wright Aeronautical Corporation (Curtiss-Wright)

F

F-80 Shooting Star jet fighter, 103
F-94 Starfire, 103
F-104 Starfighter, 90, 126
Fairchild, C-119 Flying boxcar, 107
Fairfax, Missouri, overhaul base, 274
Federal Aviation Administration (FAA), 312–15
Ferguson, Ken, 102
Flying Tiger
    L-1049H, 214, 300, **302,** 382
France, Air Force, reuse of L-749, **305**
Frye, Jack
    history of TWA, 16–17, 19, 63, 72, **77,** 199, 271, 277
    Hughes/Frye transcontinental flight of C-69 (1944), 63, **76,** 371
    L-49 prototype development, 31, 32

G

General Electric, radar, 138
Getty, Mervin, G., 315–17
Gibson, Kenneth, 132
Grand Canyon midair collision, L-1049 (1956), 312–14
Gross, Courtland S., 66
Gross, Robert
    Lockheed career, 4, 17, 31, 34, 65–66, 74, **77,** 209, 318
Ground Speed (GS), 64
Gulf of Tonkin station, Vietnam War, 327–28
Guy, John E., 31–33

H

Halbach, Eugene, 136
Harper, David, 342, 353–56
Henderson, Jerry L., 329–31
Hibbard, Hall
    career at Lockheed, 4, 17, 19, 66
    L-49 prototype development, 25, 31, 32
    L-1049 prototype development, 102
    P-38 fighter design, 8–9
Ho Chi Minh Trail
    surveillance by Batcats (EC-121s), 328–33, **334–40**
Holt, Manley, 55–56
Holt, Roger, 317–18
Homestead Air Force Base, 341, 345, 349, 359
Hudson bomber (L-14), 8, **12,** 45, 47, 67
Hughes, Howard
    around-the-world speed record (1938), 7–8
    history of TWA, 16–19, 63, 68–69, 101, 197, 199, 209, 265, 273, 277, 284, 290
    Hughes/Frye transcontinental flight of C-69 (1944), 63, **76,** 371
    L-14 uses, 7–8
    L-49 prototype development, 22, 31, 32–33, 45–46
    L-049 prototype (Old 1961), 99–100
    L-1049 prototype development, 99–100, **110, 112**
Hughes Tool Co., 18
Hungarian refugee project, 157–58

I

Iberia
  L-1049E, 169, 212, 381
  L-1049G, 381

J

Jarrell, Howard R., 118
Johnson, Clarence L. "Kelly," **146, 378**
  career at Lockheed, 17, 19, 21–22, 66, 318, 356, 368
  F-80 Shooting Star jet fighter, 103
  L-10 design and development, 5–6
  L-49 prototype development, 25–26, 28–29, 31, 34, 307
  L-649 design and development, 84, 86
  L-1049 design and development, 98–100, 104, 108
  L-1049A design and development, 116, 130
  L-1049C design and development, 168
  L-1649 design and development, 228
  P-38 design and development, 8–9, 56
  T-33A jet trainer, 103
  WV-2E design and development, 138

K

Keeler, Fred S., 3
Keflavik Naval Air Station, Iceland
  retirement of EC-121s, 359–61
  915th AEW&C missions, 342–43, 344–47, **365**
Kenney, George C., 122–23
Klawinski, Casimir, 233–42, 248–52
KLM Royal Dutch Airline
  accident, L-049 (Dec. 1948), Prestwick, Scotland, 310–11
  early transatlantic service, 65, 367
  resale, reuse, and disposal of aircraft, 300
  total quantity of aircraft delivered, 385
  L-14, **11**
  L-049, 46–47, 73, 198, 200, 203, 310–11, 379
  L-749A, 88, 89, 204, 205, 207, 208, 380
  L-1049C, 168, **218,** 381
  L-1049E, 210–12, 381
  L-1049G, 171, 214, 381
  L-1049H, 214

L

L-10 Electra, 5–7, 9, **10,** 15, 103
L-12, 6, **10,** 103
L-14, 6–9, 8, **11, 12,** 15, 17, 26, 27, 45, 47, 67, 103
L-18 Lodestar, 9, 15, 17, 21
L-18 Ventura, 30, **37,** 47, 67
L-27, 15
L-44 Excalibur, 15–19, **20,** 31
L-49 prototype (1943), **xiv,** 21–35, **40–44,** 368
  booster system, 27–30, **37**
  control systems (ailerons, rudder, elevators), 27–30, **38, 39,** 307–8
  first flight, 33–35, **40, 41,** 49
  fuselage, 24–25, **42, 44**
  nose and tail, 25–27, **36**
  orders for, 33
  power plants (Wright 3350), 22–24, 30, 33, **36,** 308, 368
  specifications, initial, 22–30
L-49/C-69, **57–59**
  orders from commercial airlines, 62, 197, 266, 272
  orders from military, 48–55, 61, 153, 368, 379
  record flights, 63–65, **76**
  safety after 1944 crash, 73–75
  safety issues re engine, 50, 52, 53, 308

specification changes during WWII,
63–64
specifications, 54, 383
training, 51, 55–56, 269–70
L-149, 48, 50, 65, 73
L-349, 48–50
L-049, **43, 78, 217, 291, 378**
accident, Reading, Pa. (1946),
73–75, 81, 203, 270, 308–10
accidents, other, 308–9, 311
design and specifications, 69–70,
73–75, **77,** 83, 196–97,
309–10, 383
orders and production, 55, 66,
68–71, 73, 81, 196–200,
269–72, 285, 379
training, 69, 196–98, 267–69
use in commercial aviation, 195–204,
267–72, 285–86
L-649/649A (Gold Plate), **91**
design and development, 65, 66
design and specifications, 65, 82–88,
204, 207, 383
orders and production, 73, 85,
204–9, 379, 383
use in commercial aviation, 204–9
L-749/749A/C-121A, **91–93, 146, 163,
216**
accidents and mechanical failures,
311
Columbine I/II (C-121), 154, 158,
163
design and specifications, 87–90, 97,
101, 104, 120, 204, 207, 210,
383
flight, Rome to New York (memoir),
278–83, **295**
last scheduled service in world, 301,
303
military model (C-121A), 153–54
orders and production, 88–90, 104,
204–9, 272–75, 283, 380
resale, reuse, and disposal of aircraft,
297, 301, **304, 305**

use in commercial aviation, 204–9,
272–75, 277, 285–87, 372
L-849/949, 98
L-1049 (1950), 95–109, **110–14, 293**
accidents, 312–18
design and specifications, 97–109,
210, 275–76, 383
orders and production, 101, 209–10,
274–76, 289, 369, 380
prototype development, 95, 97–103
Turbo-Compound engine, 104–8,
111, 133–34, 143, 144, 167
use in commercial aviation, 209–10,
275–76, 285–86, 289,
298–300
L-1049A (WV-2/RC121) for AEW&C,
115–45, **146–51, 319, 334–40**
accidents, 315–17
Cold War impact on development,
117–23
crisis over Pacific for Triple Nickel,
315–17
Cuban Missile crisis use, 141–42,
144
design and specifications, 100,
104–9, 116–18, 130–31, 136,
141, 155–56, 383
first WV-2E/RC-121L (1953),
137–40
nicknames, 125, 130
orders and production, 107, 109,
117, 120–21, 123–30, 132,
369, 372–73, 380
prototype (PO-1W/WV-2), 89–90,
117, 120, 125–27, **146**
prototype (RC-121C), 125–27
safety and reliability, 133–34, 137,
143–44
training and implementation, 131–36
weather problems, 129, 131–36
weather reconnaissance (WV-3s),
140–41
See also EC-121s
L-1049B (C-121/R7V-1), **163–66, 181**

Columbine III (Eisenhower's), 156, 158–59, **166, 180, 319**
   design and specifications, 104–9, 131, 155–59, 383
   orders and production, 107, 109, 117, 155–59, 209, 369, 380
L-1049C, **180, 218**
   design and specifications, 104–9, 168–70, 210–13, 383
   orders and production, 109, 167, 210–13, 275, 289, 369, 381
   similarities of C/E/G/H, 169, 179
   use in commercial aviation, 210–13, 289, 298–300
L-1049D, **180, 217**
   design and specifications, 104–9, 210–13, 383
   orders and production, 109, 210–13, 275, 381
   use in commercial aviation, 210–13
L-1049E, **180–91, 319**
   accidents and mechanical failures, 311–12
   design and specifications, 104–9, 169–70, 179, 210–13, 384
   orders and production, 109, 169, 210–13, 275, 381
   similarities of C/E/G/H, 169, 179
   use in commercial aviation, 210–13, 300
L-1049F (C-121)
   design and specifications, 104–9, 156–57, 384
   orders and production, 109, 156–57, 381
L-1049G (Super G), 167–79, **180–91, 219, 220, 293, 302**
   design and specifications, 104–9, 169–79, 213–15, 228–30, 276–77, 384
   orders and production, 109, 170–71, 213–15, 285–86, 289, 381–82
   similarities of C/E/G/H, 169, 179, 312
   use in commercial aviation, 213–15, 275–77, 284–90, 300
L-1049H, **180–91, 220, 302, 303, 319**
   design and specifications, 169, 179, 213–15, 228–30, 384
   orders and production, 169, 213–15, 284–85, 382
   resale, reuse, and disposal of aircraft, 301
   similarities of C/E/G/H, 169, 179
   use in commercial aviation, 213–15, 284–86
L-1149, 160
L-1249, **166**
   design and specifications, 160–61, 230, 384
   orders and production, 160–61, 223–24, 382
L-1349, 224
L-1449/1549, 22, 224–26, 230
L-1649A, **xiv,** 223–52, **253–63, 294**
   design and specifications, 226–30, 384
   fictional flight, Los Angeles to London (1958), xi–xiii, 232–52
   orders and production, 229–32, 289, 369, 370, 373, 382
   use in commercial aviation, 283–90
Loftleider Icelandic Airways, 360
Looney, Sergeant, 351
Luisada, Claude G.
   EC-121 flight (1977) memoir, 347–53
   L-749A flight (1956) memoir, 278–83
   L-1649A flight (1958) fiction, 232–52
Land, Ed, 127
LAV (Linea Aeropostal Venezolana)
   accident, L-1049E, flight to Caracas (1956), 311–12
L-049, 73, 200, 203, 379
L-749, 88, 89, 204, 206, 380

L-1049E, 212, 381
L-1049G, 382
Lehman Brothers Banking Firm, 16
LeVier, Tony, 84
Lindbergh, Charles, 4
Lipschulz, Jason, 233, 235, 245, 248–51
Lockheed Aircraft Corporation, history to late 1930s, 1–9
   first Constellation, 13–19, 21–22
   World War II and, 45–48, 53–56, 61–62, 65
   World War II chronology (1940–1946), 48–53
   after World War II (1945 to 1947), 66–69
   after World War II (1947 to 1950), 81–82, 85–87, 95–104, 108
   resale, reuse, and disposal of aircraft, 297–301, **302–5**
   See also specific models
Lockheed, aircraft production (other than Constellations or Super Constellations)
   B-17 Flying Fortresses, 55, 67
   C-130 Hercules, 158, 225, 369, 370
   Electra turboprops, 298, 300, 370
   F-80 Shooting Star jet fighter, 103
   F-94 Starfire, 103
   F-104 Starfighter, 90, 126
   Hudson bomber (L-14), 8, **12,** 45, 47, 67
   L-188 Electra, 225
   P-3 Orion, 369
   P-38 Lightning fighter, 8–9, 26–27, 45, 47, 48, 51, 56, 67, 368
   P-80, 55
   PV search planes, 55
   PV-2 Neptune patrol bombers, 82, 104, 105, 106, 126, 131, 329, 368
   T-33A jet trainer, 103
   U-2 photo reconnaissance, 142
   Ventura (L-18/P-2V), 67

   See also specific models
Lockheed, Allan (Loughead), 1, 3
Lockheed, Malcolm (Loughead), 1
Long Island, L-049 accident (Oct. 1949), 311
Lufthansa
   resale, reuse, and disposal of aircraft, 297–301
   total quantity of aircraft delivered, 385
   L-1049G, 171, 214, 382
   L-1649A, 230, 231, 232, **259,** 382

M

MacArthur, Douglas, **163**
Martin, Glen, L.
mechanical problems. *See* accidents and incidents *and specific models*
medical evacuation missions (R7V-1), 158, **164**
Mickish, William J., 119
Mid-Canada Line radar sites, 122
Miller, John and Jane Bomar, **378**
Moss, Sanford A., 7
Murphy, Mike, 360–61

N

National Airlines
   L-1049G, **219**
   L-1049H, 382
National Transportation Safety Board, 318
New York Times aviation reports, 72, **79**
Northrop, Jack, 2–3
Northwest Airlines
   L-1049G, 170, 214, **220**
Northwest Orient
   L-1049G, 171, 381

O

O'Malley, Tom, 233, 235, 239–44

Operation Safe Haven, 157–58
Orion, Lockheed, 4
overhaul base, Fairfax, Missouri, 274

P

P-38 Lightning fighter, 8–9, 26–27, 45, 47, 48, 51, 56, 67
P-80, 55
Pacific Northern Airlines, 300
Pakistan Int., L-1049H, 382
Palmer, Donald, 31
Pan American Airways (Pan Am)
  first round-the-world scheduled service, 205
  first scheduled transatlantic flight, 71–73
  midair accident, Long Island (Oct. 1949), 311
  total quantity of aircraft delivered, 385
  transatlantic service, 27, 62, 65, 68, 71–73, 75, 86, 195–204, 367
  L-44, 16
  L-49/C-69, 62–63, 266–67
  L-49 prototype development, 45
  L-049 and L-149, 46, 49, 67, 70, 72, **78,** 197, 308, 311, 379
  L-749, 88, 89, 204–5, 208, 380
Panair do Brasil (PAB), 202
Parmentier, K.D., 310
PBW-17 radar picket, 120
Pima Air Museum, Tucson, Arizona, **378**
Pinetree Line radar sites, 122
PO-1W radar picket aircraft, 89–90, 117, 120, 125–27, **146**
polar flight of L-1649A (fictional), Los Angeles to London (1958), xi–xiii, 232–52
Polaroid, 127
Pratt and Whitney
  L-49 prototype engines, 33
  R-2800 engines, 53
Prestwick, Scotland, L-049 accident (1948), 310
Price, Weston H., 118–19
Pt. Mugu, California, 342
PV-2, 30, **37,** 50, 67
P2V Neptune, 82, 104, 105, 106, 126, 131, 329

Q

Qantas Airlines
  resale, reuse, and disposal of aircraft, 300
  total purchased, 385
  L-749, 88, 89, 204, 205, 380
  L-1049C, 168, 211–12, 381
  L-1049E, 212
  L-1049G, 214, 381
  L-1049H, 215, 382

R

Raburn, Vern and Dottie, 301
radar. *See* Airborne Early Warning and Control (AEW&C)
Reading Pa., L-049 accident (1946), 73–75, 81, 203, 270, 308–10
Real Aerovias
  L-1049H, 382
record flights (1947 and earlier)
  Burbank to Miami (1947), 84, **91**
  Hughes around-the-world speed (1938), 7
  Hughes/Frye transcontinental flight of C-69 (1944), 63, **76,** 371
  New York to England by Pan Am (1946), 72
  New York to England (1946), 200
  New York to Paris (1944), 64
  P-38 coast-to-coast (1938), 8
  Seattle to Washington (1945), 65
  Washington to Paris by TWA (1946), 72–73

Rempt, Henry (Hank Radar), 125–27, 129, 138–39
resale, reuse, and disposal of aircraft, 297–301, **302–5,** 321, 373–74
See also Davis-Montham AFB (aircraft graveyard)
Resort Airlines, L-1049H, 382
Richter, Paul, 16, 31–32
Rickenbacker, Eddie, 82, 83, 88, **91**
Ritchie, Steve, 325–26
Rotodome radome, 138–40, **151**
Royal Air Force
   L-14 (Hudson bomber), 8, **12,** 45, 47, 67
   L-18, 9

S

Salmon, Herman "Fish," 90, 301
Save-A-Connie Group, 301
Scandinavian Airways System, 232
Schnaubelt, John I. (Jack), 64, 196–97, 268
Seaboard & Western
   L-1049D, 212–13, 381
   L-1049H, **319,** 382
Shultz, Sergeant, 351
Shuttle (L-1049C), Eastern Air Lines, 298–300
Simpson, Edward E., 323–24
Sirius, Lockheed, 4
skin, aluminum alloy, 108, **113**
Slick Airways
   L-1049H, **303,** 382
   resale, reuse, and disposal of aircraft, 300
Smith, C.E., 84
South African Airways, L-749A, 89, **93,** 380
South East Asia, Vietnam War (1965 to 1974), 321–33, **334–40**
Soviet Union
   Cold War impact on L-1049A, 118–23

   Cuban Missile Crisis, 141–42, 144
   TU bombers, development of, 118–19, 121–22, 143–44
Spaatz AFB, Harrisburg, Pennsylvania, 342
Squier, Carl, 66
Stanton, Dick, 34, **146, 378**
Staten Island, L-1049 collision (1960), 313–15
Stearman, Lloyd, 4
Steinbring, Steve, 347–53
Stewart, Claude H., 342
Stockdale, John, 84
Super Constellation (L-1049 and later), 153–92, **180–91**
   air conditioning, 176–77
   aviation clubs, 301
   cockpit, 177–78, **182–91**
   commercial aircraft production, summary, 374–76, 379–82
   dimensions, 130
   engine (Turbo-Compound), 104–8, **111,** 133–34, 143, 144, 167, 174–75, 210, 227, 228
   fictional flight, Los Angeles to London (1958), xi–xiii, 232–52
   first true passenger transport (L-1049C), 168
   firsts, 376–77
   fuselage and main cabin, 108, 171–72, 179, 229
   hydraulic and electrical systems, 175–76
   L-1049 prototype, 95, 97–103
   L-1049B improvements, 131
   L-1049C/E/G/H similarities, 169, 179
   L-1249 turboprop prototype, 159–62, **166,** 223–24
   last scheduled service, 300–301, **303**
   overview and evaluation, 367–77
   specifications summary, 383–84
   stability of, 315–17

tail and landing gear, 174
resale, reuse, and disposal of aircraft, 297–301, **302–5**
wings, 173, 227–28
wingtip tanks, 108–9, 130, 131, 134, **151,** 173, 227–28
See also Constellation (before L-1049), *and specific models*

T

T-33A jet trainer, 103
Tank, Merrill, 347–53
TAP, L-1049G, 381
Thai Airlines, L-1049G, 382
Thomas, Charles S., 102, 285
Thoren, Rudy, 34, 84, **146, 378**
Tomlinson, Tommy, 31
Topeka, Kansas, C-69 accident (Sept. 1945), 52, 64, 308, 309
Touranger, Clifton, 359–60
Trans-Canada
  total quantity of aircraft delivered, 385
  L-1049C, 168, 381
  L-1049G, 215, 381
  L-1049H, 215, 382
Transcontinental S.A., L-1049H, 382
Transcontinental Western Airlines. *See* TWA, history
Tripani, Ed, 31
Trippe, Juan, 45
True Air Speed (TAS), 63–64
TU bombers (Soviet), 118–19, 121–22, 143–44, 360
turbo-charger, invention of, 6–7, **12**
Turbo-Compound engines. *See* Wright Aeronautical Corporation
turbojets and turboprops
  in commercial aviation, 98, 102, 107–8, 116, 224–26, 285–90, 373, 376
  first long-range turgo-prop, 213
  L-1249 turboprop prototype, 159–62,

166, 223–24
Soviet TU models, 118–19, 121–22, 143–44
TWA, history, 265–90, **291–95**
  from late 1930s, 16–19
  from 1940 to 1950, 62, 69, 71–73, 75, 197, 198–202, 265–73, 287–88
  from 1950 to 1955, 95–97, 101, 109, 265–66, 273–76, 287–88
  from 1955 to 1967, 276–77, 283–90
  accidents, 311–15
  factors affecting airline industry, 265–66, 287–90
  resale, reuse, and disposal of aircraft, 297–301, 373–74
  total quantity of Constellations delivered, 265, 385
  L-49/C-69, 62–63, 69, **76,** 266
  L-049, 49, 67, 69, 72, 73, 81, 196, 200, 267–72, **291, 378,** 379
  L-649, 81, 83–84
  L-749A, 88, 89, **93,** 208, 272–75, 278–83, **295,** 380
  L-1049, 101, **114,** 209, 274–76, **293,** 380
  L-1049G, 171, 214, 275–77, **293,** 381
  L-1049H, 382
  L-1649A, 226, 230, 231, 232, **260–63, 294,** 382

U

U-2 photo reconnaissance, 142
United Airlines, accidents, 312–15
U.S. Air Force
  Strategic Air Command, 133, 137, 324–25
  total quantity of aircraft delivered, 385
  WWII indecisiveness, impact on aviation, 53–54

L-49/C-69, 66, **76,** 368, 379
L-749A (C-121A), 89–90, 153–54, **163,** 207, 300, 380
L-1049A (RC-121C/D) Warning Star, 128, 372–73, 380
L-1049A,/RC-121D, incident over Pacific (Jan. 1959), 315–17
L-1049A (RC-121D) conversion to EC-121s for Vietnam War use, 322–23, **334–40**
L-1049B (C-121C), 155, 380
L-1049B (RC-121C), 155, 380
L-1049B (VC-121C), 156, 380
L-1049F (C-121-G), 156–57, 381
L-1249A (YC-121F), 160–61, **166,** 223–24, 382
See also Airborne Early Warning and Control (AEW&C)

U.S. Army Air Corps
C-69 (L-49 prototype), 30–31
L-12A, 6
P-38 Lightning fighter, 8–9, 67
XC-35, 6

U.S. Navy
Polaris program, 133
total quantity of aircraft delivered, 385
L-18, 9
L-749A (PO-1W), 89–90, 380
L-1049A (WV-2) Warning Star, 128, 140–41, **294,** 372–73, 380
L-1049A (WV-2) conversion to EC-121s, 322–23, **334–40**
L-1049A (WV-3), 128, 380
L-1049B (R7V-1), 155–58, **164–65, 181,** 209, 380
L-1249A (R7V-2), 160, 223–24, 382
See also Airborne Early Warning and Control (AEW&C)

U.S. Office of Production Management (WWII), 48

V

Varig Airlines (Brazil), L-1049G, 171, **191,** 214, 231, 381
Varney, Walter T., 4
VC-121E. See Columbine
Vega (Lockheed), 3–4
"Ven-tellation," 30, **37,** 50
Ventura (L-18/P-2V), 30, **37,** 47, 67
Vietnam War (1965 to 1974), 321–33, **334–40**
Vogeley, C.G., 120

W

The War Lover (movie), 120
Warning Star. See Airborne Early Warning and Control (AEW&C); L-1049A (WV-2/RC121) for AEW&C; 915th AEW&C Group (AFRES)
Weber, Dennis, 342
West, James H., 323, 332, 342, 344, 359
Western Air Lines, 300–301, **303**
White, Charles J., 317–18
Whitmore, Joseph I., Jr., 342, 344
Willimantic, Conn., L-049 accident (June 1946), 308, 309
wingtip tank designs, 108–9, 130, 131, 134, **151,** 213–14, 227–28
World War I, 2
World War II, aviation history, 45–56, **57–60**
  chronology (1940–1946), 48–53
  impact on aviation, 32, 45–48, 53–56, 61–62, 65, 67–69, 87, 118–19, 200–201, 368
Wright Aeronautical Corporation (Curtiss-Wright)
  BD-1 engine, 82, 88
  GR2600 engine (L-49), 46
  Power Recovery Turbines, 106–7, 331

R3350 L-49 prototype engine, 23–24, 30, 33, **36,** 37
R3350 L-49/C-69 engine, 47, 48, **58**
R3350 L-649 engine, 65, 82, 85
R3350 safety issues, 50, 52, 53
R3350-26W engine, 97–98, 100–101
R3350-30W EC-121 Turbo-Compound engine, 354
R3350-30W L-1049 Turbo-Compound engine, 104–8, **111**
R3350-30W L-1049A/B Turbo-Compound engine, 133–34, 143, 144, 167
R3350-30W L-1049C/D/E Turbo-Compound engine, 210
R3350-30W L-1049G Turbo-Compound engine, 170
R3350-30W L-1649 Turbo-Compound engine, 227, 228
R3350-30W 972TC18-DA-1, EA-3, EA-6 Turbo-Compound engine, 174–75

X

XC-35, 6–7, **12,** 30

Z

Zenith Plastics, 130, 138
Zompa, Edward, 359–60